The War Beat, Pacific

The War Beat, Pacific

The American Media at War Against Japan

STEVEN CASEY

OXFORD

UNIVERSITY PRESS

OXFORD
UNIVERSITY PRESS

Oxford University Press is a department of the University of Oxford. It furthers
the University's objective of excellence in research, scholarship, and education
by publishing worldwide. Oxford is a registered trade mark of Oxford University
Press in the UK and certain other countries.

Published in the United States of America by Oxford University Press
198 Madison Avenue, New York, NY 10016, United States of America.

© Oxford University Press 2021

Library of Congress Cataloging-in-Publication Data
Names: Casey, Steven, author.
Title: The war beat, Pacific : the American media at war against Japan / Steven Casey.
Other titles: American media at war against Japan
Description: New York, NY : Oxford University Press, [2021] |
Includes bibliographical references and index.
Identifiers: LCCN 2020030386 (print) | LCCN 2020030387 (ebook) |
ISBN 9780190053635 (hardback) | ISBN 9780190053659 (epub) | ISBN 9780190053666
Subjects: LCSH: World War, 1939–1945—Press coverage—United States. |
World War, 1939–1945—Public opinion. |
Mass media—Political aspects—United States—History—20th century. |
War correspondents—United States—History—20th century. |
War correspondents—Japan—History—20th century. |
War correspondents—Pacific Area—History—20th century. |
Censorship—United States—History—20th century. |
Civil-military relations—United States—History—20th century. |
World War, 1939–1945—Campaigns—Pacific Area. |
Public opinion—United States—History—20th century.
Classification: LCC D799.U6 C385 2021 (print) | LCC D799.U6 (ebook) |
DDC 070.4/4999405426—dc23
LC record available at https://lccn.loc.gov/2020030386
LC ebook record available at https://lccn.loc.gov/2020030387

DOI: 10.1093/oso/9780190053635.001.0001

1 3 5 7 9 8 6 4 2

Printed by Sheridan Books, Inc., United States of America

For Lauren

Contents

Acknowledgments

This book is an outgrowth of two earlier projects—one on casualties, the other on war reporting in the European theater—on which I have been working since 2008. In that time, I have accumulated numerous debts. I want to begin by thanking the organizations that helped to fund this project, especially the British Academy, which awarded me one of its Small Grants in 2010, and the International History Department at the London School of Economics, which has repeatedly provided me money from its Research Infrastructure and Investment Funds.

I owe a large debt to all the staff members at many archives, especially Valerie Comor and Francesca Pitaro at the AP Archives, James Zobel at the MacArthur Library, Janis Jorgensen at the US Naval Institute, Tal Nadan at the New York Public Library, Hannah Soukup at the University of Montana, Sheridan Bishoff at Syracuse University, Liza Talbot at the Lyndon Johnson Library, Art Miller at Lake Forest College, and Eric Gillespie at the McCormick Archives.

A number of colleagues have read earlier versions of the manuscript. I would particularly like to thank Kevin Bemel, MacGregor Knox, Philip Woods, and the four anonymous peer reviewers. I have been fortunate to work for a fifth time with Susan Ferber at Oxford University Press, and I am extremely grateful for her continued support, advice, and editing expertise. I would also like to thank Mary Becker for her excellent copyediting and Jeremy Toynbee, who skillfully shepherded the book through the various production stages.

My final and most important thanks go to my family: my parents, Terry and Margaret, and above all my daughter, Lauren. This book was completed during the C-19 crisis of 2020, and Lauren, who always lightens up by life, kept me laughing throughout the lockdown. This book is dedicated to her.

The War Beat, Pacific

Introduction

When Ernie Pyle arrived in Honolulu in early 1945, he immediately realized the enormity of his new challenge. Pyle had spent almost two years slogging through North Africa, Sicily, Italy, and France with the infantrymen he so memorably dubbed "the-mud-rain-frost-and-wind-boys," but nothing had prepared him for covering the Pacific War.[1] "Things over here are so different," Pyle wrote to his wife in February, "—the distances, and the climate and the whole psychological approach—that I still haven't got the feel for it yet. Also censorship is much different, due to a different type of security necessity, and I'm afraid I may be frustrated quite a bit in trying to give the average guy's picture of the war."[2]

These differences were manifold. The sheer scope of the Pacific theater—which stretched south from China and Burma through the Philippines and New Guinea, and east to the numerous islands dotted across the central Pacific—had no parallel in the war America was fighting in Europe. Simply getting to one of the Allied military headquarters required a much longer journey than a trip across the Atlantic.[3] And once Pyle and his colleagues arrived at a command center, their problems quickly multiplied. In a business where speed often meant the difference between success and failure, Brisbane, Chungking, and even Honolulu initially had nothing approaching the state-of-the-art communications network that the big news organizations enjoyed in London, America's longtime news hub.[4]

As Pyle could testify, wartime London had its obvious disadvantages, from strict rationing to dank winters, but he and most of his colleagues found conditions in the Pacific much more taxing. After reaching one of the Allied headquarters, the correspondents still faced another long journey if they wanted to report directly from the battlefield. A sea voyage entailed long periods of boredom on an alcohol-free ship, punctuated by short bursts of terror whenever someone spotted an enemy plane or submarine. An air trip could be infinitely worse. Some of the planes the military used to transport men back and forth were unreliable. Correspondents who boarded them knew they were taking their lives into their own hands, even if their aircraft managed to avoid the terrible tropical turbulence that, as one noted, made the sky "as rough and solid seeming as an angry sea."[5] Once they were safely on the ground, the climate presented another challenge, from the vicious heat and humidity of summertime to the torrential downpours of the rainy season, while jungle life had many unsavory aspects: "spiders as big as saucers . . .," noted one correspondent in New Guinea, "butterflies as big as birds, lightning bugs like flashlights." Mosquitoes posed the biggest menace of all, since they spread malaria; but other nasty diseases also took their toll, including dysentery, dengue fever, and "jungle rot."[6]

The hardened reporters who managed to survive all of these travails encountered a military machine that was very different from the one waging war against Nazi Germany. War correspondents in the Pacific found Douglas MacArthur and the US Navy much tougher to deal with than Dwight Eisenhower, who managed to forge a relatively constructive relationship with the press. Thrown on the defensive after Pearl Harbor, MacArthur and Chester W. Nimitz not only needed to manage public expectations about the catastrophic defeats in the Philippines and Hawaii, but also had to deny a rampant enemy valuable strategic and operational information. Both pressures pushed them toward extremely strict censorship. Faced with an Allied strategy that prioritized defeating Germany, MacArthur and the navy had to lobby hard for resources to stem, and hopefully reverse, the Japanese offensive—and here, their media strategies differed. MacArthur, based thousands of miles from Washington, frequently used war correspondents to take his case for reinforcements to the American public. The navy, under the leadership of Ernest J. King, rarely saw any need to ease censorship during the first phase of the war. For one thing, the Washington-based King could use his position on the Joint Chiefs of Staff to push for more resources behind closed doors. For another, King's navy was fighting on a vast ocean in which American ships rarely saw the Japanese fleet. Since neither side had a clear sense of the damage it was inflicting on the other, King was determined not to volunteer any information that might give the enemy an edge.[7]

For war correspondents, dealing with both organizations posed a major test. MacArthur found ways of rewarding those who toed his line, while punishing anyone who strayed. The navy often seemed to take perverse pleasure in alienating any reporter unfortunate enough to be accredited to it for any length of time. Between this and the dangers of getting to and from the battlefield, many correspondents quickly became disillusioned with covering the Pacific War.

In contrast to Europe, where a relatively small band of big hitters joined the invasion of North Africa in 1942 and then followed Eisenhower's army all the way to the heart of Germany, the Pacific saw a much greater turnover. Indeed, most of the star names who had arrived in Australia or Hawaii in the months after Pearl Harbor—including Bob Casey of the *Chicago Daily News*, H. R. Knickerbocker of the *Chicago Sun*, and Stanley Johnston and E. R. Noderer of the *Chicago Tribune*—had left by early 1943. Some simply wanted to return to a domestic beat, "aching," as one joked, "for a good murder story." Others headed straight to the European war, which offered the dual advantages of relative safety and a more open censorship regime. Those who stayed faced a much higher chance of becoming casualties.[8]

Pyle himself lasted only four months in 1945 before a Japanese sniper struck him down as he toured Ie Shima, a small island just off Okinawa. Many others shared the same tragic fate. When the War Department compiled a list in 1948 of the fifty-four reporters who had died "while serving with United States forces during World War II," it revealed that twenty-three had been victims of the Pacific fighting, compared with sixteen killed in the Mediterranean and Western European campaigns.[9]

Those who did survive would not have been surprised by the disparity. "It was a common observation among Western war correspondents," observes historian John Dower, "that the fighting in the Pacific was more savage than in the European theater. Kill or be killed. No quarter, no surrender. Take no prisoners. Fight to the bitter end."[10] This deadly ferocity had two main causes: Pearl Harbor and race. After the sneak Japanese attack, few Americans doubted the need to wage war until Japan had been compelled to surrender, whatever the cost. Yet Pearl Harbor also had a paradoxical impact on how the Pacific War was reported. Although the Japanese attack united the nation, it also became the original reason for the navy's super-strict censorship. No admiral wanted the enemy to know precisely how much damage it had inflicted on the ships that had been lined up so neatly on battleship row. Nor did any of them relish the prospect of being tied publicly to such a major catastrophe.

Racial attitudes toward Japan only compounded the bitterness unleashed by the strike on Pearl Harbor, but race also played a less significant role in war reporting than has previously been argued, especially during the first phase of the war.

* * *

Crude racial imagery pervaded the public discourse inside America. Members of the US government, from President Franklin D. Roosevelt down, depicted "the Japanese as a faceless mass of subhuman enemies worthy of extinction." Media voices from across the political and geographic spectrum vociferously agreed, dubbing the Asian enemy "Japs, beasts, yellow monkeys, nips, or slant-eyed rats."[11] After Pearl Harbor, the public found it easy to view the enemy this way, with most of those polled agreeing that "the Japs aren't like us" and that they were a people who "will always want war."[12]

The American correspondents sent to report on the fighting in the Pacific shared this overwhelming consensus about the Japanese enemy. Some had covered the brutal war Japan had been waging in China since 1937, and long before Pearl Harbor, they had come to loathe the many excesses they had seen: the "citywide looting, summary executions, enslavement of able-bodied men, rapes, and other crimes." Others heard the oft-repeated stories circulated by American soldiers and sailors that the Japanese were "extraordinarily cunning, atrocious, and fanatic." And none of them forgot why they were spending so many months so far from home in such trying conditions: the Japanese attack on Pearl Harbor, which had to be avenged.[13]

Yet these racially charged views rarely made their way into the published dispatches from the battlefield, especially during the first years of the war. The correspondents who never made it beyond the command centers had to deal with public relations officers (PROs) whose main goal was not to drum up hatred of the enemy but to inform the home front about the overall military situation. The briefings and communiqués these reporters received therefore focused on dry, factual material—the wins and losses, sinkings and casualties, what units were advancing and how far, who held the whip hand, and how the next phase of the fighting was likely to develop. Similarly, the war correspondents who did get to the front did not see their job as principally one of reinforcing racial stereotypes. Although they knew their readers were highly responsive to racial imagery, these reporters were also aware that their audience really craved stories about "the 'heroes and goats' of the war"—those average American soldiers, sailors, and Marines who had been torn away from their homes and were trying to cope with a desperately alien environment.[14]

Crucially, the audience's main demand chimed perfectly with the reporters' daily experience. In any war, correspondents have to forge a close relationship with their own military in order to acquire transport, food, shelter, and communications. But in this particular war, correspondents depended even more heavily on their own army and navy. Covering the sea campaign meant enduring weeks cooped up on a battleship with only American sailors for company. On the day of battle, the closest most reporters came to catching sight of the enemy was briefly witnessing a Japanese plane drop bombs on a US ship;

they had no firsthand knowledge of what was happening to the distant enemy fleet. "Watching a modern sea battle from an aircraft carrier," observed Richard Tregaskis of the International News Service (INS) shortly after the Battle of Midway in June 1942, "is like witnessing a football game from a locker room. It consists of seeing the boys dash out of the door, then waiting nervously, endlessly for them to come back, and finally putting together a picture of what has happened from the stories they pant out as they sink into welcome relaxation."[15]

The ground war placed war correspondents closer to the Japanese, but here too the enemy was still an elusive presence. "It is probable," wrote George Weller of the *Chicago Daily News* in May 1944, "that in the Pacific campaign not more than one percent of the troops have ever seen living, non-captured Japanese."[16] To both the GI and the war correspondent, the Japanese soldier was invariably on the other side of the jungle, entrenched in a formidable position or waiting to launch a surprise ambush. Reporters could hear the shouts of "banzai" or the sniper and artillery fire, but they rarely got more than a fleeting glimpse of enemy soldiers until after the fighting was over. Then, they could eye the prisoners herded into makeshift compounds or count up the bloated corpses that littered the battlefield, although for much of the war the censors kept details about both of these subjects strictly off-limits.[17]

Because their field of vision was so narrow, the war correspondents spent much more time writing about American virtues than Japanese viciousness. This was unsurprising. For most reporters, ordinary US soldiers and sailors were not only their fellow sufferers before, during, and after the battle; crucially, they also provided the best copy. Each day at the front, the correspondents took reams of notes recounting the experiences of these men, their trials and tribulations, their hopes and fears, their successes and failures, their bravery and their deaths. Small wonder that Pyle was not the only reporter to concentrate on the "average guy." Most of his colleagues also focused on stories of US heroes rather than the evil enemy. It was what they knew best.[18]

* * *

Since the correspondents' experience cast a long shadow over what they reported, the pages that follow start by uncovering what they did in and around the battlefield. Yet, unlike other works on this subject, which focus almost exclusively on "how foreign correspondents risked capture, torture, and death to cover World War II," this book goes beyond simply telling their exciting backstories.[19] The focus, instead, is on uncovering the main contours of what actually made it into print. Here, there was often a massive disconnect between the peculiarly savage combat the reporters observed and the relatively anodyne stories that their editors published—a disconnect that was crucial because it shaped how the home front perceived so much of the fighting in this distant war.

Shifting the focus from the backstory to the published story requires recognizing that war correspondents, although invariably portrayed as "exceptional individuals in exceptional circumstances," are never free agents.[20] In the Pacific War, not only did they face major military obstacles when trying to report the story, from super-strict censorship to the challenge of getting to and from the front, but they also encountered a surprising lack of interest from the senior management in their own media organizations.

Newspaper editors had long viewed events in Asia as far less newsworthy than what happened in either America or Europe. Before Pearl Harbor, a poll of the most interesting news stories had placed the Sino-Japanese War in ninth place, and even the attack on Hawaii did not decisively change this dynamic.[21] During the ensuing months, the desperate battle between Hitler's Wehrmacht and Stalin's Red Army frequently received as much space as America's fights in the Philippines and the central Pacific. After November 1942, when US forces entered the European war in earnest, most editors bumped the Pacific War even further down the pecking order, much to the annoyance of the correspondents who risked their lives to report it. The bloody battle at Buna provides a good example. The *New York Times* gave more than four times as many front-page column inches to the North African invasion, and almost double the space to the fighting around Stalingrad, as it did to MacArthur's first major victory in New Guinea. Saipan offers another illustration. Despite more than fourteen thousand American casualties, this battle, as one correspondent complained, was given the "brush off" by most editors, who placed it a "very bad fourth," way behind the Normandy invasion and the Republican National Convention.[22]

This sense of neglect was a surprisingly common refrain throughout much of the war. On one occasion in late 1942, Hanson Baldwin of *New York Times* became so frustrated that he claimed that the Pacific War had become "the 'unknown war.'"[23] This was an exaggeration. Even at times when military censorship was overly stringent or when editors were preoccupied with events elsewhere, the home front usually received some basic information on the fight against Japan.

As the war progressed, the situation also began to improve. During 1943 and 1944, both the army and the navy made a conscious effort to lift the veil that had descended over the Pacific War. In fact, the two services engaged in a dynamic rivalry, as first one and then the other tried to grab the biggest share of the headlines. MacArthur invariably took the lead, prodding his PROs to devise new methods to speed the flow of stories about his numerous invasions in New Guinea and then the Philippines in 1943 and 1944. The culmination came during the liberation of Luzon in January 1945, when MacArthur's officers established a "floating press headquarters on three small ships . . . whereby correspondents, PROs, censors, and a transmission set-up were able to move in just behind the assault waves and begin functioning immediately."[24] The navy retaliated in kind, so that during the battle for Iwo Jima in February 1945 it had the capability of sending both dispatches and photographs to America in time for publication on the same day—an innovation the press praised as ranking "among the miracles of modern transmission."[25]

By this stage, with the fighting in Europe coming to an end, a growing number of big-name correspondents were arriving in the Pacific. No one by 1945 could accuse the media of treating this as a forgotten war. Nor, for that matter, could anyone claim that the war correspondents were ignoring the nature of the enemy—not when "fear and anger" were the dominant moods at the front, where the fight became, as historians Waldo Heinrichs and Marc Gallicchio have shown, "a battle for survival, a struggle without sanctuary."[26] There had already been a few stories about Japanese "treachery" during the more savage battles in New Guinea.[27] There had also been a firestorm of anger when the government had belatedly publicized details about the Bataan death march in early 1944. Then, when MacArthur liberated Manila, the correspondents finally acquired horrific firsthand evidence of the terrible treatment meted out to American prisoners. During the protracted battles for Iwo Jima and Okinawa, reporters became so struck by the fanaticism of Japanese resistance that they started to focus more frequently on what it would take to compel the enemy's unconditional surrender.

By 1945, then, the reports from the battlefield were finally providing a fuller depiction of the Pacific War. Yet this was a remarkably late development. For the first three years, it was striking just how little battlefield information Americans received about some of the biggest, most controversial events, from Pearl Harbor and the Bataan death march to the Marines' heroics on Guadalcanal. During this period, the war news that made it into print did nothing to undercut the racial hatred that Americans felt toward the Japanese enemy, but the relative absence of eye-catching trigger stories did little to exacerbate this emotion either.[28]

We therefore need to revise our image of how the Pacific War battles were reported at the time. In the dispatches that appeared in the nation's newspapers, the Pacific War was less a race war than a shrouded war, particularly during the months immediately after Pearl Harbor.

PART I
THE SHROUDED WAR

1

The Paradox of Pearl Harbor

Infamy

Sunday morning, December 7, 1941, dawned crisp and sunny in Washington. The small band of reporters heading to the Washington bureau of the Associated Press (AP) anticipated a busier shift than usual. Someone, they knew, would have to monitor the steady stream of football scores that would come clattering over the wires. Someone else would have to get a cab to the Soviet Embassy, since the new Soviet ambassador had just arrived in town; although no one expected him to say very much—not with German troops approaching the outskirts of Moscow—perhaps his wife might provide some fascinating insights into how a communist woman anticipated life in the American capital. And then there were the ongoing talks between US officials and the Japanese Embassy. The two sides had been meeting for weeks already. Little progress had been made, and over the past few days the American government had made no secret of its pessimism about the outcome, but someone would still have to go over to the State Department to check on the latest developments.

William T. Peacock, the slow-moving, methodical editor in charge, decided that no one would have time for a leisurely lunch at a nearby restaurant that day. Instead, he sent out one of his junior staffers to grab some takeout food, which would have to be eaten amid the din and clutter of the frenetic newsroom, with its constant calls, desks piled high with copy, and cigarette smoke wafting from overflowing ashtrays.

At 2:20, Peacock put down his half-eaten sandwich to take a phone message from the White House. He was told to expect something big. "Break the wire," Peacock ordered, and a rare silence descended upon the newsroom. Within seconds the phone rang again. Stephen Early, the White House press secretary, came on the line and began to speak in a "strangely high-pitched" voice. "I have a statement from the president," Early began. "The Japanese have attacked Pearl Harbor and the island of Oahu from the air." Peacock was so stunned he could barely speak. Reaching for a piece of paper, he scrawled out the news and handed it to an equally shocked teletype operator: "WHITE HOUSE SAYS JAPS ATTACK PEARL HARBOR."

Within minutes the AP flashed the news across the country, and then the frenzy began. More than thirty AP reporters hurried to the office, all desperate to do their bit. Peacock had to decide where to deploy them, while also trying to find the time to write some sort of story. Information was at a premium. Peacock even had to ask one of his colleagues to check the spelling of Oahu. Precisely how the Japanese had attacked that island, or the amount of damage they had inflicted, remained a total mystery.[1]

Almost five thousand miles to the west, where it was still early morning, the reporters who watched the attack unfold found it equally difficult to comprehend what was happening. The AP had just two correspondents in Hawaii that Sunday, and one of these was a reservist who reported for duty soon after the Japanese bombs began to fall. By pure chance, Tom Yarbrough, an experienced reporter who had covered the London blitz a year earlier, was approaching the island on a ship destined for the East Indies. As he sat down for breakfast, Yarbrough heard explosions go off in the distance. He figured the US military "was blasting for new fortifications," but like a good pro he stopped eating and headed off to take a closer look. "I popped out on deck," he recalled years later, "—and there, in the stabbing sunshine, was all the contrast of the times. In the bluest of blue skies we saw planes moving about, but, and this was the first disturbing note, we saw anti-aircraft guns on the beach in rapid actions. We could see guns belching with fire as shells were pushed into them by sailors in white."

As soon as his ship docked, Yarbrough dashed to the AP office to offer his services. The Japanese attack had started at 7:55 a.m. local time (1:55 p.m. in Washington), but by midmorning Yarbrough had been unable to find much usable information. Officers were either too preoccupied with fighting the enemy or too discombobulated to reveal anything concrete. Dashing to a drugstore, Yarbrough asked to use the phone. He managed to get a line to San Francisco, but all he could reveal was what he had seen with his own eyes: the appearance of a small number of bombers, the death of at least five people, and the injuries of many more. He also relayed the words of a local bystander, whom he had heard say, "I bet the mainland newspapers are going to exaggerate this." Then the phone line went dead. The US Navy had decided to cut all commercial communications as the first step in a total clampdown of information from Hawaii.[2]

By now, the news had reached many American homes. At 2:26, the Mutual Broadcasting Company interrupted its Sunday afternoon program—a commentary on the Dodger-Giants football game from the Polo Grounds in New York City—to reveal the White House announcement. CBS and NBC followed four minutes later. All the radio networks recognized the costs of breaking into their scheduled programming with sudden news flashes, especially the complaints of advertisers, whose commercials were shelved and who demanded a rebate. But this was one occasion when the scale of the news justified the expense. In the patriotic fervor of the moment, David Sarnoff, the NBC chairman, even sent a telegram to President Roosevelt. "All our facilities and personnel are ready and at your instant service," Sarnoff pledged. "We await your commands."[3]

The president's first public action came the next day. In a speech before Congress, Roosevelt described December 7 as a "date which will live in infamy," called on legislators to formally declare war on Japan, and pledged that "no matter how long it may take us to overcome this premeditated invasion, the American people in their righteous might will win through to absolute victory."[4]

The response both on Capitol Hill and across the nation was overwhelming. For more than two years, a great debate had raged over whether the United States should become directly involved in the wars that were ravaging Europe and Asia. Although most Americans clearly sympathized with the nations battling Axis aggression, a large majority had opposed sending US troops overseas. Only a few weeks earlier, Roosevelt had complained that "his perpetual problem was to steer a course between the two factors represented by: (1) The wish of 70 percent of Americans to keep out of [the] war; (2) The wish of 70 percent of Americans to do everything to break Hitler, even if it means war."[5]

Now, the mood shifted abruptly. On the afternoon of December 7, mayors placed their cities on a war footing, the FBI rounded up Japanese Americans, and tearful families gathered at train and bus depots as soldiers and sailors, their leaves canceled, headed off to fight.[6] In Congress the next day, every legislator, bar one, voted for the declaration of war, while the Republican leadership pledged to support the war effort and offered to adjourn politics "for the duration." One opinion survey found Americans "deeply resentful of the treachery." Another concluded that "commentators of all political hues are in agreement that the first Japanese bomb dropped upon Hawaii wrought suddenly the miracle which no amount of logic or persuasion had previously been able to achieve," making isolationism "the initial casualty of the war."[7]

Paradox

Isolationism might have been killed stone dead, but the president still faced a major home-front conundrum. Roosevelt had long ago concluded that Nazi Germany posed the gravest threat to American security. He believed that Adolf Hitler wanted world, not regional, domination. He also thought that Hitler possessed a military machine impressive enough to menace the Western Hemisphere, especially if Britain or the USSR were to collapse. In Roosevelt's thinking, Japanese aggression had to be contained where possible, but the overriding priority must be to use America's resources to defeat Germany first. When Winston Churchill arrived in Washington toward the end of December, he discovered to his delight that Pearl Harbor had not changed the president's strategic thinking. Roosevelt's focus remained firmly fixed on Europe, not Asia.[8]

Many Americans saw the situation quite differently, however. Horrified and outraged by the Japanese attack, newspapers across the political spectrum—from the stately *New York Times* to the isolationist *Chicago Tribune*—argued that "for the present, at least, our single war aim must be the crushing of the Japanese, . . . the principal and proximate enemy."[9] The public agreed. When pollsters asked which enemy the United States should concentrate on fighting, the result could not have been clearer: 62 percent thought Japan, while only 21 percent wanted to direct men and materiel against Germany first.[10]

From Roosevelt's perspective, then, Japan's day of infamy solved one public opinion problem, only to create another. This was the first paradox of Pearl Harbor, but it was largely resolved by a second one: while the very fact of the Japanese attack made the nation desperate for as much information as possible, its nature and outcome pushed officials toward their first major act of concealment.

It began automatically, as an instinctive reflex, the minute the government began trying to absorb the blow. On the afternoon of December 7, the Navy Department sent out a terse instruction to all officers: "Place naval censorship in effect."[11] As a result of this order, Yarbrough was not the only reporter on Hawaii suddenly severed from his home office. His United Press (UP) rival had a news alert cut off halfway through transmission. For the next four days, no civilian was allowed to communicate with the mainland, much to the intense frustration of an increasingly fretful and restive home front, which was desperate for information from the first American battlefield of the war.[12]

In Washington, senior officials did little to fill this public void. The Navy Building on Constitution Avenue, usually so quiet, became a frenzy of activity—"an ant hill with the top kicked off," according to one observer—as, behind closed doors, officers tried to piece together the full scale of the catastrophe.[13] In crucial respects, some concluded, the outcome could have been worse. Not only had three American aircraft carriers escaped unscathed, but the Japanese planes had also failed to destroy the large fuel dumps, which meant that the surviving ships and planes would have the oil to start operations of their own at some stage in the future.[14]

Yet, despite these slight shards of silver lining, most officials could not help concentrating on the darkest of dark clouds: 18 US vessels sunk or damaged, 180 aircraft destroyed, and 2,403 men killed, with another 1,178 wounded. In one sudden assault, American power in the Pacific had been gravely weakened. Whether the navy retained the strength to support the American garrisons in the Philippines, Wake Island, and Midway, let alone launch a sustained counteroffensive, remained highly questionable. Even Hawaii was not safe. Thrown dangerously back on the defensive, senior naval officers quickly decided that their initial instinct had been correct. Although many reporters had managed to piece together the scale of American losses, such details had to remain censored. It was vital to the war effort, they decided, to keep the Japanese guessing.[15]

Frank Knox initially agreed, although his own fraught experiences during these tumultuous days would soon make him partially reconsider. The navy secretary had been the Republican vice presidential candidate in 1936 and he remained a controversial figure. The president had appointed him in the summer of 1940 in an effort to give his administration a bipartisan complexion. This ploy might have worked had it not been for the fact that Knox had owned the Chicago Daily News since 1931 and had decided to retain possession on entering government. Other newspaper bosses naturally queried Knox's conflict of interest, no one more vociferously than Colonel Robert McCormick, the isolationist owner of the Chicago Tribune. For years, McCormick had loathed Roosevelt for his politics and Knox for his newspaper. As soon as the two men joined forces, his hatred knew no bounds, especially since Knox's job was to further Roosevelt's interventionist agenda.[16]

Over the past eighteen months, Knox had set about this task with great gusto, his efforts culminating in a major publicity blitz in the week before Pearl Harbor. As peace talks with the Japanese government threatened to break down, Knox had decided that the time had come to boast about his achievements. "The Navy Is Ready," thundered the headline that accompanied a story about Knox in *Collier's* magazine. "The biggest, toughest, hardest-hitting, straightest-shooting navy in the world is primed and ready to write 'finis' to aggressors," ran an advertisement accompanying Knox's interview with the *American* magazine. "Let 'em come—from both sides, if they want to—'WE CAN WIN ON TWO OCEANS!' says Secretary of Navy Frank Knox."[17]

Such spectacularly ill-timed remarks placed Knox in a particularly vulnerable position now that a significant portion of this navy lay at the bottom of Pearl Harbor. Many politicians, while mouthing platitudes about the necessity of rallying around the flag, were frantically searching for a scapegoat for this disaster, and Knox fitted the bill perfectly. With barely concealed glee, the *Chicago Tribune* amplified the attacks of former isolationists like Senator Burton K. Wheeler (D-MT). "Support of the war," Wheeler declared ominously, "does not mean there must be no criticism of our domestic policy or the conduct of the war. There are some people in Washington," Wheeler added,

> who seem to believe the American people are not to be trusted with the facts concerning their own efforts. This has been particularly true of Secretary Knox. He has sought to impose undue censorship on the press while at the same time writing for magazines and ballyhooing from one end of the country to the other that our navy was ready to fight all over the world.[18]

Republicans joined the attack, openly wondering whether the navy's censorship policy was less about denying Japan crucial information than about protecting senior officials whose mistakes had contributed to the disaster. On the floor of the Senate, Charles W. Tobey (R-NH) even demanded "an immediate congressional hearing, the prompt dismissal of Secretary Knox, and an undelayed and detailed statement of damage."[19]

Desperate to protect his position and reputation, Knox made up his mind "in a flash" to fly to Pearl Harbor in an effort to preempt Congress by launching his own investigation.[20] He returned in mid-December with a report that served two purposes. On the one hand, Knox revealed for the first time the number of Americans killed, explaining candidly that the disaster had occurred because neither the army nor the navy had been on alert. On the other hand, he provided the press with its first accounts of the US fighting man's "magnificent courage and resourcefulness." "To a recruit seaman aboard a battleship," Knox told reporters, "probably goes the honor of striking the first blow in the fleet's defense. Even before general quarter sounded, this youngster single handedly manned a machine gun and blasted the attacking torpedo plane as it levelled against his ship."[21]

Most newspapers gratefully accepted the information that Knox doled out. "The losses which he documented," according to one media survey, "were less than had been feared. And, while there was some tendency to wonder about the damage undisclosed by the Knox catalogue, the emphasis in news stories and in editorial comment was placed mainly on the heroism of American sailors and officers."[22]

Many media voices also welcomed Knox's efforts to streamline the navy's censorship operations.[23] In the immediate shock after Pearl Harbor, reporters had bombarded various navy bureaus and offices with demands for information. With no clear guidelines on what should and should not be released, each bureau chief had erred on the side of caution, refusing to release anything at all. When Knox returned from Pearl Harbor, his second order of business was to revamp this system. He asked Paul C. Smith, the editor and general manager of the *San Francisco Chronicle*, to draw up simple guidelines as to what could be made public and what should be withheld.[24]

Over the coming months, these guidelines would become one facet of a complex censorship structure. Stories written inside the United States would be subject to a voluntary code overseen by the Office of Censorship. Headed by Byron Price, the executive news editor of the AP, this bureau, as Michael Sweeney points out, "asked the nation's journalists to censor themselves and provided guidelines to help them. Civilian censors could cajole, suggest, argue, and threaten but had no authority to punish beyond publicizing the names of the violators." The correspondents heading to the war zone faced a much more onerous regime overseen by whatever service they were stationed with. In order to get accredited, these reporters had to sign an agreement pledging to submit any story they wrote to the military authorities, who would check to ensure it did not disclose any information that, among other things, "would be disastrous to us if known to the enemy," would "injure the morale of our forces," or would embarrass the United States, its allies or neutral countries." In return, war correspondents were granted eating, traveling, and accommodation facilities at the rank of a commissioned officer, although they were also "subject to military law," meaning they could lose their credentials if they violated their signed agreements; in "extreme cases," they could even be "placed in arrest to await deportation or trial by court martial."[25]

It would take weeks to erect this elaborate edifice. In the meantime, the naval authorities used other methods to ensure that the correspondents in Hawaii remained unable to report any details about the biggest story they were ever likely to cover. Most obviously, these officers did not allow the reporters to visit Pearl Harbor until December 20, and even then, their trip was carefully chaperoned. The navy permitted them to speak to a couple of officers who had been in the thick of the action, but as one of the reporters noted, "the interviews were arranged inside a building from which nothing of the harbor was visible." At least the correspondents departed with a positive impression. "There was a steady calm attitude everywhere we went inside the yard and on the part of all the naval personnel," recorded Joseph Harsch of the *Christian Science Monitor*. "The trip," he concluded, "while offering limited opportunities to witness the scene of action and the aftermath leaves one with [the] conviction that the damage was far less than original estimates, and that regardless of how unalert was the condition at the moment of the original attack the Japanese lost the power to ever catch the fleet off-guard again."[26]

Thus, a comforting blanket was starting to descend over the Pacific War, although the more astute officials were already notching up the obvious dangers that came with imposing a complete clampdown. Political opponents, they realized, tended to fill the resulting information vacuum. So did the enemy, as newspapers, anxious for some hard news, rushed to publish Japanese claims that its "magnificent early gains" had given it "naval mastery over the United States in the Pacific."[27] Wild rumors were rife as well, including a savage "whispering campaign . . . to the effect that 1,500 bodies had arrived [in New York City] without coffins from Hawaii."[28] Then there was the final paradox of Pearl Harbor: the growing fear of some officials that the news out of Hawaii had been so comforting that it was starting to spark a serious bout of unwarranted optimism about how easily the Japanese could be defeated.[29]

As yet no one in the navy thought that either the rumormongering or the overoptimism outweighed the basic need for operational security. Nor, crucially, was naval censorship the only reason for the lack of information coming out of the Pacific. As Japanese forces swept southward across Asia, media bosses across the nation were caught as unprepared as the government, with many of their resources in the wrong place. The stunning surprise at Pearl Harbor was one reason. Another was the simple fact that Asia had for many years invariably been allocated fewer column inches than Europe by America's news editors, who in turn were reflecting what they took to be the priorities of their audience.

Chaos

When Americans had thought about Asia before Pearl Harbor, their sympathies had been clear: a large majority supported the Chinese cause, while almost two-thirds favored an embargo against the Japanese aggressor.[30] The trouble was that Americans had not thought about Asia very often. Even in 1938, while war raged in China but Europe remained precariously at peace, popular attention had been fixed on the Czech crisis and the Nazi persecution of the Jews. In a survey of the most interesting news stories of that year, these two European events had clearly come out on top, with the struggle between China and Japan relegated to ninth place, behind the World Series and a New England hurricane.[31] Two years later, not much had changed. One poll conducted during December 1940 had found that 45 percent of respondents had no idea where Singapore was, while 41 percent had no opinion when asked the simple factual question of whether Japanese seizure of the Dutch East Indies would greatly improve its oil supply position.[32]

With the nation's attention concentrated on Europe, the big news organizations had naturally funneled their resources in this direction. The *New York Times* had long viewed London, with its extensive imperial communications network, as "the principal 'post office,' or relay point of THE TIMES abroad." The string of startling events in 1940 and 1941, from the fall of France to the London blitz, had only sharpened the *Times'* inclination to send the vast majority of reinforcements to Britain—and it was by no means alone. The AP, which most newspapers relied on for spot news, had a typically imbalanced deployment, with no less than forty-one reporters in Europe by December 1941, compared with only nine in Asia, including two in Honolulu and three in the Philippines.[33]

Nor did the big news organizations necessarily have the right reporters in the right places. In the fall of 1941, with tensions mounting between

Washington and Tokyo, editors had started to reshuffle their big names around, but many of these moves were totally disrupted by the surprise Japanese attack. Indeed, Tom Yarbrough was not the only reporter who suddenly found himself stranded—stuck, in his case, in Hawaii when he was meant to be traveling to Cairo via the Dutch East Indies.[34] Many more ended up in Burma, Malaya, or Singapore, where they became caught up in the military debacles that were about to overcome the British Empire. Leland Stowe of the *Chicago Daily News* was one. Exasperated by the excessive censorship in China, Stowe hoped to go to the Soviet Union via Hong Kong, but ended up in Rangoon, where he stayed three months to report on the British retreat out of Burma.[35] Tillman Durdin of the *New York Times* was another. Having been stationed in China for a decade, where he had made his name with an exclusive on the infamous Nanking massacre, Durdin spent the first months of the war covering the twin catastrophes in Malaya and Singapore.[36] E. R. Noderer was a third. The *Chicago Tribune* correspondent was in New Zealand on December 7 when he received a cable from his office instructing him to "FLY MANILA IMMEDIATELY." With no flights to the Philippines operating, he headed to Singapore instead and quickly found himself stuck there for the next six weeks.[37]

More by luck than judgment, then, some of America's star reporters were positioned to cover the British, rather than the American, war in December 1941. The capital of the Philippines, by contrast, was where many US news organizations had long housed their Far Eastern "news centers."[38] In Manila's bars and restaurants, the recent chatter had inevitably revolved around a single topic: if and when America would fight Japan. Even so, few correspondents were ready for what was about to unfold.

Mel Jacoby was a case in point. Jacoby had been traveling around Asia since 1936, but had arrived in Manila only in September, to be installed as the Far East bureau chief for *Time* and *Life*. This new job was a big step up for the twenty-five-year-old, whose previous media experience had been confined to his work as a publicist for the Chinese nationalist government and a stringer for various American news organizations. Adjusting to his new role, Jacoby spent most of his time during October and November either in the social whirl of forging new contacts or in anxious anticipation of the arrival of his fiancée, Annalee Whitmore, from China, on November 24.[39]

The AP's Manila operation was in a particularly chaotic condition. It consisted of just two staffers in mid-November, Russell Brines and Ray Cronin. Although both were Asia veterans, they were, as Brines later conceded, "unprepared for the war," being "still geared to the routine distribution of incoming news on the same old basis." To compound the situation, Brines was scheduled to leave the Philippines altogether, with orders to take up a new position in Bangkok on December 11. His replacement would be Clark Lee, who landed in Manila in late November on his way home, having spent the past six and a half years in China. Two days before his ship was scheduled to depart for California, Lee received a message from his New York bosses instructing him to "remain Manila until further orders." Despite his deep disappointment at missing out on a long-awaited stateside leave, he tried to be philosophical. It was simply part of the job to be moved around the globe at the whim of distant bosses. It was also part of the job to learn the ropes fast in unfamiliar surroundings. Lee had never been in the Philippines before, but as Brines admiringly observed, he immediately brought a new "force and vigor" to a bureau that remained mired in a peacetime rut.[40]

Whatever their level of readiness, the reporters in Manila still held obvious advantages over their colleagues in other Asian cities. Communications back to the United States were better, the product of decades of imperial rule and the absence of formal censorship. "Manila," concluded one private assessment for *Time*'s editors, "is the only place in the Far East where absolutely free and unhampered news transmission is possible."[41] Recently, Douglas MacArthur, who commanded a combined US and Philippine force, had also pledged "that coverage of this war would be more complete from a newspaper and photographic standpoint than any other war in the past."[42] Compared with those caught in Hawaii, the reporters in the Philippines were even given a short grace period to prepare for the onslaught.

The Pearl Harbor attack had come out of the blue on Sunday morning. The stunning news had filtered through to Manila, on the other side of the international dateline, at about 3:00 a.m. on December 8. The ensuing hours were a tense time in the Philippine capital as the media and the military braced themselves for war. Phones rang incessantly. Rumors swirled around offices. People looked anxiously up at the sky. Across the city, it was as if there were a collective pause while everyone waited to see what the Japanese would do next. The answer was not long in coming.

2

Fiasco in the Philippines

"Too Grim for Public Dissemination"

Shortly after 4:00 p.m. on December 8, members of the Manila press corps assembled at MacArthur's headquarters for their first official briefing of the war. Most had come by car, entering the old walled city through an ornate archway. At the western edge of what used to be a fort, they had turned down "a fifty-yard passageway flanked by the plaster wall of buildings." At the end was a garage containing MacArthur's gleaming black Cadillac, adorned with the three stars of a lieutenant general. To the right of the garage lay a small room, unfurnished except for "a hat stand of Philippine mahogany and a large stag head and antlers." It was here that Major LeGrande A. Diller, MacArthur's boyish-looking spokesman, would brief them on the events of this historic day.

In the moments before Diller began to speak, the reporters had a chance to review their own reactions to what had happened so far: first the shock and outrage at events in Hawaii, and then a sense of alarm, followed by a growing self-confidence about developments closer to home. The Japanese, the more bullish proclaimed, would be no match for the Americans. "Our boys would knock them out," ran the typical prediction, "and it would be pretty to watch." After that, Washington would supply MacArthur with plentiful reinforcements and the perfidious Japanese would be sent packing all the way back to their home islands.

When Diller entered the room, the reporters got a chance to see his expression, and their mood swung again. The major looked serious even before he began to speak. "At about one this afternoon," he announced, "Clark Field was badly bombed. Many planes were destroyed and it appears that casualties were heavy." This was perhaps the most shocking news yet. The reporters knew that Clark Field was home to thirty-five Flying Fortresses that Washington had recently sent to the Philippines. They also knew that these planes were meant to be the capstone of the islands' defense. Had the Japanese really eradicated these crucial weapons in their first strike of the war? The reporters immediately pressed Diller for more details, only to be stonewalled. "I don't have any," the major replied. "There is only one telephone line to Clark Field and that has been cut." The more experienced scribes eyed the officer skeptically. Surely, they muttered to themselves, someone could drive the fifty miles to the airfield to assess the situation. Then almost immediately the sharper among them grasped that Diller's curtness stemmed from much more than ignorance. He "knew the truth," realized Clark Lee, "but it was too grim for public dissemination at that time."

In the coming days, as the reporters began to investigate what had happened, they recognized just how grim the truth really was. One evening, Lee encountered a group of New Mexico guardsmen manning an anti-aircraft gun, and they told him that the stricken airbase had suffered more than 350 casualties, adding, "There's not much left of our Air Force"—a fact fully confirmed by the reality that Japanese planes were bombing Manila at will.[1]

If the reporters found it relatively easy to piece together what had happened, they struggled to understand the cause of this fiasco, and their minds raced with disturbing questions. Why had the military command, from MacArthur down, been caught so unawares in the hours after the Pearl Harbor attack? Why, in particular, had the precious Flying Fortresses been lined up so neatly on the runway, making them a perfect target for the Japanese raid? Naturally, MacArthur's command did not relish such questions being aired in public, for they might easily provoke a full investigation followed by disciplinary action against the leading culprits.[2] Nor did senior officers want to divulge to the Japanese the extent of their initial success. Instead, they instructed the censors to place super-tight control over any story that mentioned Clark Field, despite increasingly "vituperative" protests from the press.[3]

* * *

Beyond the room where Diller met with reporters, MacArthur's headquarters buzzed with hyperactivity, much of it focused on a single goal. Hating to be on the defensive, MacArthur wanted to strike back hard. Brimming with a fiery faith undimmed by the destruction at Clark Field, he favored a major air strike on the Japanese home islands—and that was only for starters. MacArthur also called for a total rethinking of American grand strategy, shifting the focus from Europe to Asia, on the basis that Japan was isolated from its allies and "completely susceptible to concentrated action."[4]

While awaiting Washington's response to these grandiose proposals, MacArthur began to ponder what message he wanted to send to the world. He had long considered himself the military's preeminent press-relations expert, having been the army's very first PRO, back in 1917 when the United States had been preparing to enter World War I. During his ensuing career as army chief of staff and military adviser in the Philippines, he had become, as his main biographer states, "more aware than ever of the significance of role-taking, image-projecting, and commanding men's minds through commanding the right words."[5] In the wake of the Japanese attack, the press became, as one of his aides recalled, "MacArthur's domain." Although he preferred not to meet personally with reporters—deploying Diller as "an intermediary who could absorb and deflect some of the heat that inevitable friction would produce"—he often wrote and always scrutinized the press releases and communiqués his PRO issued.[6]

Desperate for reinforcements, MacArthur decided that these documents had to strike an upbeat tone. His efforts to reframe them culminated on December 12, when he issued what one correspondent called the "most encouraging communiqué" to date. A small number of Japanese troops had just landed in the far north of Luzon, but MacArthur stressed that the situation "was completely in hand." These first Japanese attacks, the resulting dispatches loyally explained, "were being disposed of and . . . mopping up operations were continuing."[7]

In and around Manila, the correspondents could see the reality of the intensifying air campaign for themselves, and they swiftly reached a far less reassuring conclusion. When Japanese planes dropped their loads in a major raid on December 10, the reporters watched in horrified awe as the fire and smoke billowed high into the sky. The big naval base at Cavite, nine miles from the city center, was the obvious target, but from afar the reporters had little idea of precisely how much damage it had sustained. So a small group of them sped off in their cars for a firsthand look. Along the way, they saw burning wooden shacks, dead civilians, and indescribable damage to vital military installations. But when it came time to write up their stories, they willingly followed MacArthur's lead and focused on the US response rather than the Japanese attacks.[8]

Russell Brines's reporting was a case in point. The AP correspondent watched the raid on Cavite from his beach house, surrounded by frightened civilians who crouched behind a sea wall to shelter from the bombs, but he still accentuated the positive. "The attack," Brines wrote in his dispatch, "stirred alive a gigantic hornet's nest as American interceptors which had droned over the air base thruout [sic] the morning went into action."[9] In reality, there were only a pitifully small number of these obsolescent interceptors, but Diller's briefings concentrated on the damage they had wrought on the raiders. Eleven enemy planes had been shot down on December 12, the press dutifully reported, and another four on December 14.[10]

* * *

By the second week of the war, the reporters in Manila had settled into a new, albeit perilous routine. The more gregarious would enjoy long lunches on a terrace near the waterfront, watching bombs explode less than a mile away. Their diligent colleagues would make three daily journeys to attend Diller's press conferences, despite the hazards of traveling around a city where drivers had to run a gauntlet of inexperienced volunteer guards and overexcited armed gangs. "Our chauffeured car," recalled Brines, "was endangered by nervous sentries on the bridges and from brigands who often hijacked cars," forcing him and his AP colleagues to duck down in "the backseat, to avoid stray bullets, clasping a long knife, to beat off hijackers."[11]

The briefing on December 22 proved almost as nasty as the car journey. Over the previous fortnight, Diller had exuded a cheery patience, but that day, as he entered the small, crowded room where the communiqués were handed out, he found it impossible mask his anxiety.[12] "I have a bulletin here for you," he began. "I shall pass it out. There is no additional information and no comment." The room immediately went quiet as everyone anxiously scoured the short document. At least eighty enemy transport ships had been spotted off the Lingayen Gulf, just one hundred miles northwest of Manila. "Undoubtedly," the communiqué proclaimed, "this is a major expeditionary drive against the Philippines."[13]

This stunning bulletin sparked Clark Lee into action. Within an hour, he had taped a large cardboard "Press" sign onto the AP's car and was speeding north through the flat plain lined with recently harvested rice fields. What he encountered during the next few days proved to be deeply alarming: carloads of refugees clogging the roads heading south to Manila; jittery Filipino troops who ran away the minute they saw the enemy; and the intentional demolition of key bridges, which forced Lee to abandon his car and scurry back to the capital by foot and then train.[14]

Lee's arrival at the Manila Hotel on Christmas evening caused a sensation. He looked like "a mass of mud," noted Brines, and "even his four-day

Fig. 2.1. AP reporters in the Philippines: Clark Lee (*center*), Russell Brines (*left*), and Dean Schedler (*right*).
© AP/Shutterstock.

growth of beard was matted." Settling down to a surprisingly good Christmas dinner of turkey and champagne, Lee discussed with other reporters their dangerous position. MacArthur, hoping to stave off further destruction, had declared Manila "an open city." No one around the table thought either it or the Philippines would hold out for long. After the remnants of the meal had been cleared, Lee spread his map out on the dinner table and discussed with his colleagues possible evacuation routes south through the Philippine archipelago and then on to the Dutch East Indies.[15]

When it came time to write up his story, however, Lee struck a very different note. Despite the scenes of abject chaos and the real possibility of a catastrophic defeat, he continued peddling an optimistic line in the hope of convincing Washington to send vital reinforcements. "The Japanese army rushing toward Manila from the Lingayen Gulf," Lee began, is an ill-uniformed, untrained mass of young boys between 15 and 18 years old, equipped with small-caliber guns and driven forward by desperate determination to advance or die. Hundreds of them already have died under the fire of American and Filipino artillery, machine guns, and rifles, but they keep coming, and up until tonight had been only partly checked. The United States Armed Forces in the Far East, holding the Lingayen area, have rallied and are putting up a determined defense in many sections.[16]

Over the next few days, this conscious effort to drum up domestic support for more aid was greatly helped by the continued Japanese air raids, which, with Manila declared an "open city," appeared increasingly savage and vindictive. On December 28, the authorities even ended the nighttime blackout in order "to conform with its declared status of an . . . undefended, civilian center."[17] But still the Japanese bombs continued to fall, often on houses, offices, and schools. The United Press—the AP's great rival—suffered particularly badly.

* * *

At first glance, the antiquated radio transmitter sitting in the corner of the UP's Manila office seemed to typify everything about this "underdog news agency," for it was low on power and had an antenna held together by little more than bamboo poles. Yet this was a case in which surface looks truly were deceptive.

Although the UP had a hard-earned reputation "for being miserly," it had recently assembled an impressive bureau in the city. Its acting head was Frank Hewlett, a tough thirty-two-year-old from Idaho, who had spent the past five years roaming the Pacific "looking for headline material and adventure." The Manila posting appealed to him, because it promised the chance to settle down with his wife, Virginia, who immediately volunteered to work as a stenographer on the high commissioner's staff. But the job came at a cost. Hewlett had never worked as a wire-service reporter before, and he initially struggled with the immense pressure of always trying to get to the latest breaking story before the AP.

Resourceful as well as brave, Hewlett started to flourish only after the war started. With communications in other parts of Manila under strain, he even managed to get the venerable radio transmitter working, establishing a reliable link to New York via Chile, which enabled him to regularly beat his company's wealthier rival.[18]

Then the Japanese planes appeared. One evening, Hewlett was compiling a story on the damage done to the walled city when bombs struck the building where the UP had sixth-floor living quarters. According to one survivor, "Flying shrapnel shattered windows and ripped through walls," but luckily no one was killed, unlike the situation in many other parts of the blazing city.[19]

As Hewlett took to the streets to survey the damage, his anger boiled over. "Rescue crews searched for dead and wounded in the charred wreckage of Manila's ancient walled city today," he reported on December 28, "as the angry populace roared a demand for the United States Army to return for a 'last man stand' after [the] murderous Japanese air bombardment of this officially declared open capital." The walled city, Hewlett added, was more than a mile and a half from the port area, where the main military targets lay, but the Japanese had attacked it with impunity. "The destruction was terrific," he recorded. "The area, a congested region normally populated by about 100,000 persons—many Spanish and Chinese—had been considered safe from Japanese bombs under the 'open city' proclamation."[20]

If such wanton destruction promised to boost American sympathy, the absence of US resistance threatened to confirm that the Philippines were doomed. On December 29, Clark Lee decided to take another firsthand look at the battle. Just before leaving, he bumped into Diller, who told him—off the record—to head for Bataan. "Bataan?" Lee replied. "We thought headquarters were at the Lingayen front. And where the hell is Bataan?"[21]

Lee found out soon enough. As he toured the countryside just north of Manila, he discovered that MacArthur was conducting a staged withdrawal from Lingayen, with the aim of buying time for US and Philippine forces to retreat to the Bataan peninsula. He also received another important lesson on the limited utility of trying to report this fighting retreat from the frontlines.

At the Twenty-Sixth Division's headquarters (HQ), Lee encountered Franz Weissblatt, a forty-two-year-old UP reporter. Weissblatt was no stranger to war, having covered countless battles in the Sino-Japanese conflict since joining the UP as a Far Eastern correspondent in 1931. He was also in the process of becoming the only American to continuously cover the ground fighting since the start of the Lingayen campaign—and it showed. Weissblatt was so grimy as to be almost unrecognizable. He had also managed just one dispatch back to the States, and this had done little more than bolster the military's optimistic message. "We have tanks here," Weissblatt had reported on December 23, "and tough, seasoned Army forces, both American and Filipino. Their morale is high and they are meeting the enemy eagerly."[22]

When Lee returned to Manila, he was staggered to find MacArthur's command still pushing the same rosy line. "Our forces," the December 30 communiqué insisted, "are holding firmly on all fronts." In reality, Manila was caught in the jaws of a vise, with Japanese troops pressing from both north and south—and by now there was scarcely any front at all in the south. Only later did Lee come to realize why there remained such a disjunction between public statements and the military reality. "It had to be done," a PRO explained to him a few weeks later. "We were trying to deceive the enemy and conceal the fact that we were withdrawing to Bataan."[23]

For a brief period, this military misinformation campaign also threatened to deceive the reporters into thinking they could escape to the south. Not until early on the morning of December 31, when Lee visited Diller's press office, did he discover the bleakness of the situation at that part of the front. MacArthur had left the city a week earlier, taking most of his top aides to the island of Corregidor in Manila Bay.[24] His old HQ building was almost deserted, with walls stripped of maps, papers packed into boxes, and full suitcases strewn everywhere. Lee encountered an officer and asked him whether he could take a look at the situation in the south. "If you do," the man replied, "it will be the last thing you will see." Japanese troops were so close that the US military would be dynamiting all of Manila's wireless stations in the next few hours to prevent them from falling into enemy hands.

Suddenly faced with the prospect of losing contact with New York, Lee dashed back to his office and began tapping out a raft of urgent messages, hoping that at least one would get past the censor. After a number of failures, he realized that to alert his editors without contradicting the army's relentless optimism would require bending the facts. "Just returned from southern front stop," Lee wired, "departed 630 by automobile returned 730 stop stories coming shortly if time." As Lee conceded later, this cable was simply untrue— he had been expressly told not to go south—but AP staffers in New York got the message. If the front was so close that a reporter could drive there and back in an hour, Manila must be doomed.[25]

Just before noon on the last day of 1941, the veil over the US war in the Philippines, which MacArthur had briefly lifted in order to convince Washington that this battle could be won, slipped firmly back in place. MacArthur's men blew up the wireless stations, and the line went dead. For the next three weeks, Americans on the home front would receive only a single 150-word story from the Philippines. In that time, they would have to make do with reading about the searing British retreats in Malaya, Singapore, and Burma, wondering all the while what had become of their boys in the Philippines.

Corregidor and Bataan

Throughout New Year's Eve, as explosions rocked the city, the thirty-two reporters still in Manila convened for "frenzied" discussions in the Bay View Hotel, at least one of them thinking, "Maybe we will be dead tomorrow; oh, God, how do we get out?"[26]

Mel Jacoby and his new wife, Annalee, acted as hosts. Along with Clark Lee, the Jacobys wanted to leave the city as soon as possible. All three had recently arrived from China, and they knew how brutally the Japanese treated captives. To make matters much worse, all three had either written stories critical of Japan or had worked for the Chinese Nationalist government, and they suspected that their names were on a blacklist, meaning almost certain execution if they surrendered. Desperate to escape, Mel Jacoby spent part of the day dashing around the docks looking for any boat that might get them out of town. In his hotel room, the other reporters debated whether to go along. Many had families, and they did not relish the prospect of a risky cruise through the heavily mined waters of Manila Bay. Nor did the idea of retreating to Bataan hold much appeal. No one knew how many American troops had escaped to the peninsula or how long they would hold. Most correspondents decided against a risky escape that would only delay the day of inevitable capture.[27]

After dark, Lee and the two Jacobys said their goodbyes to the remaining reporters, packed a few clothes and their typewriters, and headed to the docks. American demolition squads had just blown up the city's main gas dump, and flames licked high into the sky. The three Americans boarded a small freighter just before midnight and arrived on Corregidor at dawn. As soon as they landed, an air-raid siren began to wail. Following everyone else, they dashed along a track that led into a long tunnel carved into the middle of a hillside.[28]

Few people forgot their first reaction on entering the Malinta Tunnel. "The stench of sweat and dirty clothes," recalled one PRO, "the coppery smell of blood and disinfectant, . . . and overall, the heavy stink of creosote, hanging like a blanket in the air that moved sluggishly when it moved at all." The main compensation, as Lee and the Jacobys immediately recognized, was that Malinta was "not only the safest place during air-raids but the nerve center of the defenses on Bataan and Corregidor." Twenty-five lateral branches ran on either side of the central tunnel. Some contained different sections of MacArthur's headquarters, from quartermaster to signal corps. Others served as ordnance shops, storage centers, and a hospital.[29]

At first, the correspondents' fortune in stumbling into MacArthur's new headquarters was overshadowed by the appearance of the military police, who asked them what they were doing in such a sensitive spot. Unable to locate the sea captain who had transported them from Manila and still dazed by their recent adventures, the reporters failed to provide a plausible answer. The policemen therefore hauled them to a guardhouse. Fortunately, Diller soon appeared. He was "astonished to see us," Lee recalled later, "but friendly." No plans had been made for the press on Corregidor, Diller explained, and so the reporters might have to be shipped to Bataan. Lee and Jacoby both feared that, once on Bataan, they "would be completely out of touch with everything, with no possibility of getting any stories out." But if they wanted to stay on Corregidor, they needed permission from the very top. After an anxious few days, Diller finally confirmed that MacArthur had "regularized" their status, which meant that they would be provided with uniforms and access to the officers' mess. There was only one snag. For the time being, they would not be allowed to report anything at all.[30]

This complete news blackout, the reporters soon discovered, was partly due to the administrative chaos surrounding the evacuation. On top of a complete absence of press planning, the army's communication network was so overstretched that there was simply no capacity to send the reporters' dispatches back to the United States.[31] Even more important, with straggling US and Filipino forces still trying to dash through the last roads that remained open to Bataan, MacArthur wanted to avoid at all costs handing the enemy any information of value.[32]

For the hard-driving Lee, the situation could not have been more frustrating. He and Jacoby had already written stirring accounts of their dramatic escape from Manila, which they were desperate to send to their editors. Once they were freed from the guardhouse, a friendly official with the US High Commission provided them with cots on a porch next to MacArthur's house. Each morning, as the general paced his large lawn, they would fall into step and pepper him with questions. After gaining such priceless information,

Lee and the Jacobys faced many harrowing hours sheltering from the incessant bombing raids. All of this made such great copy that they soon began to
feel professional guilt about not doing their job properly—a guilt only wors-
ened by the realization that they were eating a precious share of the army's
dwindling food supply.

Then one day Lee got chatting with a naval officer. "Since we haven't
too many ships," the man explained, "our wireless is not too busy. We can
transmit some stories for you." Lee still needed to convince the censor, but
once that obstacle was overcome he returned to the navy tunnel with his dispatch. It was only 150 words, just long enough to reassure the outside world
that he was alive. But it would soon have ramifications out of all proportion
to its length.[33]

* * *

After Lee's first story made it back to the States, MacArthur began to reconsider the blanket ban. By the last week of January, his forces on Bataan
had withdrawn to much more defensible positions and were repulsing everything the Japanese could throw at them. MacArthur therefore had every
incentive to publicize their newfound success, although his mood was not
entirely upbeat. He grudgingly began to come to terms with the prospect that
decisive help from the outside was unlikely and that his troops were effectively doomed, but that did not mean he was prepared to let them go down in
silence. The "fame and glory" of the men on Bataan, he cabled Washington
on January 23, had to be "recorded by their countrymen."[34]

MacArthur's decision to relax censorship came just as an intense new rivalry was starting to flare between the remaining American wire-service
correspondents in the Philippines. Lee's 150-word cable provided the spark.
When the UP bosses in New York learned that an AP correspondent had
managed to get a dispatch out of Corregidor, they immediately contacted
senior officials in Washington. Why, they asked, had there been a story from
Lee but nothing from Hewlett and Weissblatt? Was it because their own
men were dead or missing? In reply Diller confirmed that Hewlett was alive,
while Weissblatt was "probably in hands of enemy." But this response only
provoked another question from the top people at the UP. Why, they wired
Hewlett, had Lee beaten him to the first story from the Philippines since
Manila's fall?[35]

Such a missive is the bane of any reporter's life, but this one made Hewlett
particularly livid, for he had hardly been skiving for the past three weeks.

On New Year's Eve, he had originally planned to surrender to the Japanese with his wife, Virginia. But at the last minute they had decided that his job was at the front, while hers was to remain with US officials. After a hurried goodbye, Hewlett had jumped into his car after dark, passing over the bridges that led to Bataan just minutes before the army detonated them. The next day at noon, he met up with Weissblatt and Nat Floyd of the *New York Times*, who had also escaped to Bataan by road.

The three reporters joined forces over the next few weeks, spending their days bumping around on dusty roads and their nights sleeping on the slopes of a wooded mountainside. Bataan, they soon discovered, had a way of turning even the most competitive individuals into a tight-knit band. "Friendliness and courtesy," observed Floyd, "were the marks of the men on Bataan. More than that, they forgot selfishness. When a man had cigarettes, special food, razor blades or any of the scarce goods he shared them." There was only one downside to this camaraderie: dealing with the sudden loss of cherished new friends. By mid-January, Hewlett found himself agonizingly alone, after Weissblatt, suffering a hip wound, surrendered to a Japanese patrol, and Floyd, struck down with a bad case of dysentery, was confined to bed in a Filipino house.[36]

Then came the UP cable. Hewlett was so affronted by its content that he immediately jumped on a boat to Corregidor. Once there, he sent his bosses an arch response. "Associated Press," Hewlett wired New York in retaliation, "unrepresented in Bataan."[37]

This bald claim, Hewlett knew, touched the rawest of nerves. On the one hand, it suggested that Lee was little more than an HQ stooge whose success in getting his stories out stemmed from the cozy relationships he had forged with senior officers in the relative safety of the rear. On the other hand, it implied that Hewlett was the real combat veteran, while the AP man was avoiding the rigors of frontline life.

Until that point, Clark Lee had reveled in his reputation as a reporter who was "as brave as any man jack." He also had the wounds to prove that Corregidor was no soft option—not just a broken hand from diving into a foxhole to escape strafing Japanese planes, but also deafness in one ear after a stick of bombs had exploded fifty yards away. Yet, with the real battle taking place in Bataan, Lee knew that Hewlett's cable meant he had to get off Corregidor as quickly as possible in order to safeguard his courageous image.[38]

Mel Jacoby described with detached amusement what happened next. "There is the keenest rivalry amongst the press," Jacoby noted in early February, "particularly between the association representatives, who don't trust each other, both swearing they didn't have a dispatch through for weeks." Before long, Hewlett and Lee even stooped to seeking out the other's frontline itinerary in order to win the race to file first.[39]

* * *

Had either man paused to reflect, he might have realized that, in many respects, he was wasting his energy. Filing first matters most when there are breaking stories to report. On Corregidor, however, the security-obsessed censors still prohibited any Bataan-datelined dispatch that revealed operational facts. The reporters therefore had little choice but to focus on "feature color, background, personal experiences stories," none of which were time-sensitive. Nor could they be prolific. Even the winner of the daily race was permitted to file a maximum of only five hundred words.[40]

As a result, from January 23, when the first Bataan stories came through, until April 12, when news of the surrender on Bataan hit American newsstands, the home front received only a highly selective version of this gruesome battle. Some stories stressed how well the fighting men were adapting. "Camouflage," reported Lee in late January, "is the Americans' only defense against detection and they have become masters of it." Many more dispatches emphasized the valor of what Hewlett dubbed "MacArthur's scrappy jungle fighters," from Major General Jonathan M. Wainwright, who could often be seen at the frontlines, to the troops engaged in all manner of tasks.[41] Men like Edward DeLong from Springfield, South Dakota, who went on "a perilous mission behind the Japanese lines" and survived only after sailing a fragile craft back to US positions.[42] Or Father John E. Duffy, who carried on "heroically amid greater handicaps" than any spiritual guide had encountered in previous wars. Or Clinton A. Pierce, who, as commander of the southern section of Bataan, was showing himself to be "one of the fightingest men in the United States army" and telling anyone who would listen that the Japanese were "rotten rifle shots."[43]

War correspondents behaved with great bravery as well. Hewlett turned his first Bataan dispatch into a tribute to Weissblatt. "What a guy he was!" Hewlett recorded one officer as saying. Before he was captured, the man explained, Weissblatt had refused to buy any Christmas presents so he that had the funds to purchase cigarettes and candy "for the soldiers who spent the yuletide fighting the Japs."[44]

Lee, meanwhile, had struck up a close friendship with Nat Floyd. One day, he spotted the *New York Times* reporter "leaning against a fence post," wearing "Waikiki sandals and an immense straw sombrero." That morning, Lee reported, Floyd was waiting outside a hospital, having just taken a wounded captain there for treatment. A few days later, he and Floyd became so worried about Japanese snipers that they each promised "to write the other's obituary if we are hit."[45]

In reality, malnutrition and malaria increasingly posed the greatest menace to the men on Bataan, but the reporters, following the censors' lead, carefully concealed both of these dangers from the folks back home. Instead, Lee claimed that the "worst hardship" facing anyone moving around the peninsula came from "dust in great choking waves," while Hewlett produced an account of hospital life that carefully avoided mentioning the specific ailments afflicting so many of the troops on Bataan.[46]

Other aspects of the battle remained hidden, too. In the privacy of his diary, Lee recorded that many Americans distrusted their allies, claiming that "the Filipinos should have been able and prepared to defend their country without our help, since they were asking for independence."[47] Yet Lee also knew that senior officials wanted to counteract Japanese attempts to win over the population. His reports therefore echoed the military's call to stress "the glorification of Filipino loyalty and heroism."[48] "These Filipino boys are toughening into real soldiers," Lee reported. "Grimy and blood stained Americans," he explained, "fight and die day by day beside their Filipino comrades, and the closest comradeship prevails on the battlefield and in quarters."[49]

As the siege ground on, few soldiers on Bataan pretended to feel any sort of comradeship with MacArthur and his clerks on Corregidor. Hewlett, who spent the vast bulk of his time on the peninsula, penned a short poem on "the battling Bastards of Bataan," which captured the mood of the average fighting man, especially his sense of isolation from, even abandonment by, the military hierarchy. Hewlett also knew of an even more explosive ditty that was doing the rounds, based on the fact that MacArthur, who made only one trip from Corregidor to take a look at the front, was widely known among the men as "dugout Doug." Set to the tune of the *Battle Hymn of the Republic*, it began:

> Dugout Doug lies a'shaking on the Rock
> Safe from all the bombers and from any sudden shock
> Dugout Doug is eating the best food on Bataan
> And his troops go starving on.[50]

Of course, Hewlett never thought for one minute that MacArthur would countenance the publication of a story containing such a slur. Like all the other correspondents, he knew that the general was engaged in a major operation to protect and promote his own image.

Each day on Corregidor, MacArthur would wake early, don his freshly pressed uniform, and stride purposefully to his damp, dimly lit office in the Malinta Tunnel. After meeting with aides and perusing incoming cables, he would devote a large chunk of time to the command's press releases. Indeed, he would personally compose "practically" all of these documents—which, as more than one reporter acerbically noted, not only "accounted for the dramatic wording of those communiqués," but also revealed the central role that MacArthur played in each of them.[51] According to one content analysis, more than three-quarters of his command's communiqués "mentioned only one individual, MacArthur."[52]

Whatever they thought of this egocentricity, both Hewlett and Lee loyally datelined their stories "With Gen. MacArthur's Army." They also name-checked the general as often as possible. "It's high time for those rip-roaring, death-defying seldom-sleeping engineers of Gen. Douglas MacArthur's army," began a characteristic Hewlett story, "heroes every one, to take a bow."[53]

* * *

By February, as the prospect of a major reinforcement dwindled, the reporters' private thoughts turned increasingly to a major reverse earlier in the war. The British at Dunkirk in June 1940 had suffered a significant defeat that had some obvious parallels with developments in Bataan. It had come at the start of Britain's war, and after this turning point British fortunes had revived. Above all, it had proved a boon to British propagandists, who had transformed it into a heroic retreat in which three hundred thousand men had been saved from capture to fight another day. Eighteen months later, the reporters on Bataan were working hard to write a story of individual heroism in the midst of a tragic reverse, but they lacked one obvious hook that could turn the Philippines into a similar story of ultimate triumph. With Japan in control of the skies and the sea, no one thought they had much chance of escaping the enemy. On Corregidor and Bataan, observed Annalee Jacoby, "there could be no Dunkirk."[54]

Or perhaps there could be, at least for a chosen few. On February 23, MacArthur summoned Lee and Mel Jacoby to a conference in his tunnel office. "Do you want to go now?" he asked the two reporters, before telling them of his plan. Although MacArthur no longer expected major reinforcements, he knew that Washington was trying to get relief supplies to him through the Japanese blockade. One of these blockade runners had just arrived, and it could take them south, to the island of Cebu, which was still in American hands. From there, they could hitch a ride to Australia, where, MacArthur explained, they should write that he needed only a handful of planes in order to hold out for a few more months. "Start public opinion, get the press working on it," he instructed, "and maybe . . . they will realize how important it is, more than Washington does." The general cautioned that the voyage would be so dangerous that they would need to carry firearms for protection, but he was confident they could make it. Accepting a stiff drink from Diller, Jacoby and Lee headed off to find Annalee. Then they packed their small bags and prepared to join the boat scheduled to leave that night.[55]

With Lee's departure, Hewlett no longer had to fret about his biggest wire-service rival, but as the days dragged by, he found his job ever more arduous. The temperature averaged more than 95°F, and even the jungle shade provided little respite from the sapping heat. With supplies dwindling, malnutrition and disease became rampant. By early March, five hundred men a day were being admitted to the hospitals for malaria alone, putting unsustainable pressure on the remaining stocks of quinine. Then there was the "fatigue resulting from constant nervous tension," which, one frontline surgeon observed, was increasingly common in men who had had no opportunity to rest from the battle.[56]

Hewlett still made regular trips around the front, but in the fifty-one days he remained in the Philippines after Lee's departure, he managed to get only thirteen stories back home. This relative paucity stemmed partly from the lack of new things to report. During the last week of February and most of March, a lull descended over the battlefield as the Japanese focused on bringing in reinforcements for one final push. Enemy activity did start to revive in late March, with more aggressive patrolling and sustained air attacks, but Hewlett found these aspects of the battle difficult to cover. He still had the car that had carried him out of Manila on New Year's Eve, but he no longer had enough gas to keep it running. Like everyone else, he spent much of his time sheltering from bombs and shells. The only saving grace was that at least his bosses recognized his contribution. "Believe Hewlett has done excellent job," they cabled on March 7, "under circumstances which [were] probably even more extreme than we realize."[57]

Four days later, MacArthur left Corregidor in a move that only added to the sense of gloom on Bataan. Roosevelt had ordered him out on February 22, the day before Lee and the Jacobys had made their escape bid. MacArthur had reluctantly agreed, asking only if he could choose the "right psychological time" to depart. That moment came on the night of March 11. Under rainy clouds that hampered enemy observation, MacArthur and his top aides, including Diller, boarded four PT boats heading for the island of Mindanao, where they would catch a plane to Australia.[58]

Hewlett left Bataan for good a short while later, just before the Japanese launched their final offensive. He watched the battle's last rites from Corregidor before interviewing the men and women who had managed to scramble across the bay in every ship the navy could muster. These heroes, Hewlett reported on April 9, had survived all the blows the Japanese had hurled at them for ninety-eight days. "Then fever, hunger, and fatigue cut down their strength. But even in the final showdown," he concluded, "the remnants of that gallant army swam and rode across the four-mile watergap to bring nurses and the wounded to Corregidor Island." "The last two days have been a nightmare," Hewlett reported one of the nurses saying. "The Japs bombed us twice. I thought the end had come when bombs exploded in the ward next to me, but I am okay and I'm ready for duty."[59]

Then it was Hewlett's time to escape. With a quick glance at the place he had called home since the start of the year, he took one of the last "crude air taxi" hops off Corregidor to a southern Filipino island before boarding a big bomber for the long flight to Australia.[60]

Dashing Escapes and Bitter Truths

From his perch in the War Plans Division of the General Staff in Washington, Brigadier General Dwight D. Eisenhower read the newspaper accounts of these depressing events with a grim fascination. Then on March 19, he made a note in his diary. "MacArthur is out of the Philippine Islands," he wrote. "The newspapers acclaim the move—the public has built itself a hero out of its own imagination."[61] Eisenhower was only half right. Americans had certainly found a hero, their first of the Pacific War, but they had not constructed him out of their own imagination. Rather, MacArthur's image had been consciously constructed over the past four months by the general's own press operation—and that operation did not remain idle once he arrived in Australia.

Indeed, it was symbolic that when MacArthur's train finally reached Melbourne on March 21, the first person to step off was Diller, his press officer. MacArthur followed closely behind, and as one reporter noted, "he was not in uniform; he was in costume—Douglas MacArthur starring as Douglas MacArthur."[62]

Over the hours that followed, senior US officers directed the next episode of the unfolding MacArthur show with much care and great aplomb. They had arranged for a welcoming party, a guard of honor, and a car appropriately adorned with a four-star flag. When MacArthur appeared on this stage, he uttered his lines beautifully. A few days earlier, he had explained to a small group of reporters how he had been ordered to "break through Japanese lines . . . for the purpose of organizing an American offensive against Japan, a primary objective of which is the relief of the Philippines. I came through," he declared, "and I shall return."[63]

Not for the last time, MacArthur repeated the final three words when he stepped off the train in Melbourne, in a transparent effort to pressure Washington to support a drive to Tokyo via Manila. During the next few weeks, however, MacArthur's press officers would concentrate far more effort on embellishing the story behind the first half of this famous soundbite: the dramatic dash through Japanese lines. In Diller's official version, the starting point was MacArthur's extreme reluctance to leave his men behind. Only after repeated orders from the president, Diller emphasized, did MacArthur finally decide to depart, and even then, he assumed he would return in weeks, not years. Nor, Diller's press team stressed, did MacArthur slink away in disgraced defeat. Along with his wife and four-year-old son, he "roared out" of Corregidor in a PT boat.[64]

Of all of MacArthur's Philippine exploits, his dashing escape proved the most salable. The New York Times apparently offered "Mrs. MacArthur $20,000 for her personal story," while the general himself remembered being "deluged" by offers from newspapers and magazines to purchase an exclusive account of the events, including "one proposition [that] reached the dazzling figure of five hundred thousand dollars."[65] Even the correspondents unable

to match such inflated sums had little difficulty conjuring up a dispatch destined for the front page. "Seven days of death-defying travel," began a typical
one, "through Japanese dominated sky and sea—first by speedboat to out-
strip enemy subs and then by lightning fast planes—brought Gen. Douglas
MacArthur, with his wife, child, and staff, to his new command here as chief
of all United Nations forces in the southwest Pacific."[66]

Not long after, Lee and the two Jacobys became the first in a steady flow of
correspondents to arrive in Australia from the Philippines. Each had their
own stirring escape stories to tell. Freed at last from constant danger and enervating hunger, they also had the time and space to write more vivid and
insightful accounts of the doomed Bataan campaign.[67]

Mel Jacoby created a particularly large splash, partly because he wrote for
Time and *Life*, whose press runs approached one million and four million a
week, which meant they had readerships of roughly six million and twenty-
three million, respectively.[68] During his time in the Philippines, Jacoby had
cabled home stories about the successful resistance of American troops he
had dubbed "MacArthur's men."[69] "It's hard to say who has the most colorful
personality in Corregidor and Bataan," Jacoby had written in a March article.

> Maybe it's the big thick-skulled Texas A. A. battery breech operator who is
> untalkative and illiterate and learned to work his gun "by ear." When a shell
> jammed in his gun with the fuse already cut, he hauled off and punched the
> shell home with his bare fist. Maybe it's men like Captain Horace Greeley,
> former Air Attaché in Chungking who, like the majority of other airmen,
> grows a beard and tramps through the jungles fighting the Japanese on the
> ground or sits in his foxhole at the frontline wishing for an airplane to fly.

Upon his arrival in Australia, Jacoby sent his editors the photographs he
had taken over recent months. Lavishing thirteen pages on what it called the
"Philippine Epic," *Life* featured them to reveal the shocking destruction in
Manila after the Japanese air raids; the inside of Corregidor's tunnel complex,
including wounded soldiers in the American hospital; and the jungle terrain
of the Bataan peninsula.[70]

In the pages of the *New York Times* Nat Floyd added yet more detail.
Floyd had felt shackled in Bataan, managing to write just seven stories in almost four months, as a combination of illness, censorship, and overloaded
communications had hampered his ability to report. Along with Frank
Hewlett, he had been one of the last reporters to escape from Corregidor to

Fig. 2.2. Mel Jacoby at work in Australia on a Bataan story.
© Getty Images.

Australia; on arrival in Melbourne he suddenly felt liberated.[71] Only days later, Floyd completed a long account of his experience in the Philippines, which contained vivid details of hunger and disease that had, until now, been largely absent from newspaper accounts. "During the last weeks," he wrote in an article that appeared on April 22, "the health of the men of Bataan gradually declined. . . . Just before the fall as high as 80 percent of a typical regiment had malaria, 30 percent had amoebic dysentery and some had hookworm.

This is indicative of the condition of the men when the Japanese started their last big drive, reinforced by men, planes, and tanks."[72]

* * *

As the battle came to its grim conclusion, one final hero emerged. "The story of 'Wainwright's Rock'—Corregidor," ran one account, "—is the story of men who held on and fought until their endurance was stretched beyond human limits." "You should be leaving," a correspondent recalled saying to Wainwright before boarding one of the last planes out of the Philippines. "I have been one of the 'battling bastards of Bataan,'" the general replied, "and I'll play the same role on the Rock as long as it is humanly possible."[73]

Wainwright's surrender in May, one survey revealed, occasioned "a keener, more personal feeling of loss" for many Americans than any other Japanese victory.[74] Even so, the public's anger proved surprisingly fleeting. Part of the reason, as Floyd's editors realized when they received his summation of the Bataan campaign, stemmed from how much of the war's grim reality had been concealed so far. "The American people," the *New York Times* editorialized on April 23, "probably suffered from illusions" about the situation in the Philippines.

> What was officially given out, and what was permitted to appear in print, was altogether too optimistic. The reader at home might easily have thought that in spite of the constant danger the men on Bataan were leading an excitingly interesting, and at times jolly, life. In memory of the dead and in honor of the living, most of them now prisoners, it is well to have some of the bitter truths which are set forth yesterday in a dispatch to this newspaper sent by Nat Floyd after his escape to Melbourne.[75]

As to why so much of this harsh reality had been concealed, there was plenty of blame to go around. Many Americans singled out their government for engaging in yet another cover-up. Indeed, with almost 60 percent convinced "that some important portion of the story about Pearl Harbor [was] still being held back," it did not take much of a mental leap to believe that the same process had been at work in the Philippines.[76] In April, one survey found that "about half the people in the country feel dissatisfied with the quantity of the news they are receiving about the progress of the war." The media, concluded another report, laid the responsibility squarely on the administration, which, it charged, was deliberately withholding bad news, with the army and navy seen as the biggest offenders, since they tended to be particularly "inflexible in releasing information of strategic value."[77]

The government, for its part, thought that journalists, editors, and headline writers had to shoulder some of the blame. Yes, correspondents like Floyd had recently revealed a darker side of the war, but such reports remained the exception rather than the rule. One study of newspaper and radio coverage revealed "a marked tendency on the part of both media to emphasize good news in preference to bad news in the early stages of the war. Dramatic treatment," it concluded, "was generally given to every minor American success; and individual acts of heroism on the part of our armed forces were accorded a prominence out of all proportion to their real strategic significance." The headline writers seemed particularly culpable. One analysis of the biggest stories in the nation's metropolitan press found that during the week of April 15–21, when the press might have been expected to be picking over the carcass of the surrender on Bataan, almost 60 percent of headlines had emphasized "good news." A week later, while the *New York Times* was bemoaning the paucity of realistic stories on the Bataan battle, this figure shot up to 75 percent.[78]

As Nat Floyd began to readjust to life outside the war zone, he reached exactly the same conclusion. The thirty-eight-year-old Texan arrived back in the States in May, "getting madder and madder," according to one observer, every time he read another overoptimistic story below an even rosier headline. The problem, he believed, only partly stemmed from the military's attempt to sugarcoat the news. His own profession, he was convinced, had a dangerous addiction to "phony headlines." Floyd felt so strongly about the perils of such reporting that he used $275 of his personal savings to take out an advertisement in the trade journal *Editor & Publisher*. "If 3,000 Chinese catch 300 Japs in a cane field and slaughter them," Floyd warned the nation's media bosses, "we leave out the numbers and hail Victory. I've seen more dead Japs than that on Bataan, in one bunch, and it didn't change anything. . . . How would it be to start playing war stories on their merit?"[79]

Whether the media would heed this heartfelt plea remained unlikely, especially as many editors considered hopeful headlines the best way of boosting circulation. The more cynical observers also doubted MacArthur's willingness to provide information that did not burnish his own image, and they did not have to wait long to have their suspicions confirmed. On May 8, Diller began releasing a string of communiqués revealing a great sea battle in the Southwest Pacific, in which enemy losses far outstripped those suffered by the Allies. The navy reacted with rage, convinced not only that MacArthur was aiming to take the credit for victory but also that his "premature" release placed the fleet in real danger. As imperious as ever, MacArthur brushed aside the navy's allegations. Diller's press releases, he insisted, had disclosed nothing of value.[80]

Whatever the truth of the matter, MacArthur's action highlighted an important contrast. Over the six months between December and May, the veil over the Philippines' campaign had been partial: it had shrouded the more unpleasant dimensions of this fiasco, but MacArthur had still managed to place himself at the heart of a heroic narrative. During this same period, the US Navy had worked hard to hide almost every aspect of its war in the Pacific, much to the extreme irritation of all the war correspondents stuck covering this theater.

3

Censorship at Sea

Problems in Paradise

"They used to call Honolulu 'The Paradise of the Pacific,'" noted one correspondent in late December 1941, but that was before the Japanese attack on Pearl Harbor. Now that Hawaii was at the epicenter of the US Navy's war effort in the Pacific, it rapidly proved a major disappointment to all the media reinforcements who arrived from the States.

Not that the basic ingredients of paradise had suddenly disappeared. The sun still shone, the waves still crashed ashore, and even the food remained "plentiful." For many reporters, however, these basic attributes made their daily life seem all the more incongruous. "The aura of desolation was over everything," recalled one of them, "along with the smell of burned oil and iron rust. The sense of an utter destruction was poignant and inescapable." The reality of military control only compounded the gloom. A blackout began promptly at six every evening, forcing almost everyone inside. In the big hotels, the bars and restaurants remained open for an additional thirty minutes, but after that there was nothing to do except lie in a darkened room and try to sleep. "There wasn't a flashlight battery in town," noted one frustrated visitor, "nor flashlight bulbs nor flashlights."

After a restless night, the correspondents set to work in the morning on two main tasks, but they found neither easy to complete. Looking forward, they wanted to find out how the navy planned to use Pearl Harbor to strike back at the enemy. This meant attending intermittent press conferences, although these sessions rarely produced anything of value. They were almost always dominated by intelligence officers who spent the bulk of their time explaining why they were unable to discuss future operations in any way. The Japanese still held the whip hand, they stressed. Not only must they be denied information that might allow them to launch another stunning blow, but they must also be kept guessing. "Lacking information," one officer elaborated in January, "—and especially official information—he [the enemy] cannot plan with any degree of certainty any offensive or defensive operation to meet precisely whatever we may contemplate."[1]

Stymied on this front, the more mischievous correspondents hoped to produce an exposé of what had actually happened on December 7. Anyone who had seen Pearl Harbor came away sickened by the sight. "The blackened hull of the *Arizona*," noted one, "the capsized *Oklahoma*, and the twisted corpse of the old target ship *Utah*."[2] Back on the mainland, these were just the sorts of details that many readers were craving. Navy censors had by now permitted the publication of interviews with survivors and photographs showing some of the destruction, but their generosity remained limited.[3] Whenever a correspondent produced a descriptive article about the disfigured ships that lay stricken in the harbor, he received the same blunt response: "I regret to tell you that its publication in whole or part cannot be authorized."[4]

With so little to report, and even less to do, the press corps in Hawaii quickly threatened to turn mutinous. Before long, all the reporters were frustrated and bored, but only one of them had the prestige and position to lobby hard for change: Bob Casey of the *Chicago Daily News*.

* * *

At first glance, Casey hardly looked like a military expert. Portly, with thinning hair, he has been described by one writer as "a pudgy leprechaun of a journalist." Yet beneath his gregarious manner and unmartial bearing resided a tough character hardened by years of punishing experience.

Born in Beresford, South Dakota, the son of a "nomadic tinsmith," Casey began his military career on the frontline trenches during World War I. There, he had risen rapidly from private to captain, receiving three citations for bravery under fire and the Silver Star Medal. In the ensuing years, he had followed in his father's nomadic footsteps, combining his *Daily News* duties with frequent travels to far-flung locations like Baghdad, Cambodia, and Tahiti to gather material for a series of books. When war erupted again in Europe, in 1939, he was approaching his fiftieth birthday, an age when most of his peers had long settled into staid stateside office jobs. But Casey continued to find the lure of combat irresistible. After heading to London that September, he had witnessed the dramatic fall of France the following spring, before returning to London to suffer under the German blitz. The start of 1941 had found him in the North African desert, where a Luftwaffe air raid had injured both his legs. "Capt. Casey," his colleagues had muttered respectfully on his return, "knows what war is like." Largely for that reason, he was the first person his editor turned to when word spread that the Japanese had attacked Pearl Harbor. That same afternoon, he boarded a plane to Washington, where he hoped to acquire the necessary paperwork to travel to Hawaii.[5]

For any other correspondent, trying to get the highly harassed navy to co-operate at that fraught moment would have proved impossible. But as well as his extensive military experience, Casey could play another trump card. Frank Knox, the boss of his newspaper, also happened to be the secretary of the navy, a situation that swiftly unlocked all the relevant doors. Within twenty-four hours, Casey had his accreditation. A few days later, he had also received priority boarding on the first ship departing from San Francisco for Pearl Harbor after the Japanese attack.[6]

Once Casey was in Hawaii, his privileged status as a veteran reporter whose boss held two critical roles gave him access to Admiral Chester W. Nimitz, the new commander in chief of the Pacific Fleet (CINCPAC). Nimitz arrived at Pearl Harbor on Christmas Day knowing that he had a tough job on his hands, from dealing with the material destruction that remained so visible in the port to reviving the morale of officers and men at all levels. He also had to confront the unruly press corps, although he scarcely considered this a top priority.[7]

Even before Nimitz's arrival, Casey had begun to document the reporters' biggest concerns. The inexperienced censors topped the list, for in Casey's eyes, these men "had assumed the customary attitude of the novice . . . that the purpose of censorship is to keep the press in its place." The underlying structure only magnified this problem. "It turned out to be a dual censor-ship," Casey concluded, "because the fleet press officers insisted on seeing any copy pertaining to their department before release and downtown censors—children of the intelligence section—insisted on the full exercise of their au-thority afterward. It was a blind censorship. You tossed in the copy and that's the last you heard about it until somebody at home raised a howl maybe."[8]

At first, the howls of the press corps exerted little impact on this unwieldy system. Then Knox got wind of Casey's complaints. Although willing to defer to senior naval officers on most matters, Knox considered himself an ex-pert on media relations in an organization that still prided itself on secrecy. He also recognized that he now had the perfect envoy in Hawaii. So in early January he sent Nimitz a message: Casey "will call on you. Please listen to him on navy censorship question. You can rely on whatever he tells you."[9]

Prodded by Knox to implement "a sweeping reform," Nimitz decided not only to end the system of dual censorship, but also to give the reporters a copy of their dispatches showing what had been cut. Most momentous of all, he promised them a taste of combat. Until now, the navy had only ever allowed reporters on board its ships during peacetime. In wartime, its senior officers had maintained, "the need for using all ship space for service men and materials" meant there was simply nowhere to put the members of the press.[10] In early January that changed. The reporters drew lots to decide who would go on the first trip. Although Casey missed out this time, in mid-January he joined a task force headed to the Marshall Islands, where his ship would take part in a hit-and-run raid on Japan's "fixed aircraft carriers"—the heavily fortified islands it possessed in the central Pacific.[11]

* * *

Bob Casey never really enjoyed being at sea. He suffered from excruciating headaches whenever his ship rolled in big swells. He found the heat stifling, especially when all the portholes were closed so tightly in the blackouts that no air seemed to circulate inside his cabin. During the long, monotonous hours spent traversing the thousands of miles to and from the target, he settled down to reading a string of books, but he increasingly missed a good stiff drink—an impossibility on a dry navy ship. "Hooch," he remarked, "has become the subject of a lot of wistful conversation aboard." Casey certainly felt that he needed something soothing whenever the general alarm sounded, and the prospect constantly loomed of a Japanese attack, from either planes above or submarines below. In one enemy bomber raid, he smashed his head on a bell, skinned his knees on the floor, and battered his ribs against the rails.[12]

Yet, like his fellow reporters on other ships, Casey could not fault the navy's hospitality, especially when the going got particularly rough. "Correspondents," one of his colleagues enthused, "are accorded every courtesy while covering a naval battle." On some ships, the captain even assigned a sailor to provide them with whatever they needed, from earplugs to action reports.[13] Casey himself had little doubt that he was part of something special. "It came to me," he noted after four days at sea, "that few men in any lifetime have a chance to look at such a spectacle as this": ships everywhere, giving the appearance of a fleet as formidable as anything that had so far sailed in this war. When the task force approached the Marshall Islands on February 1, Casey could barely conceal his excitement. "This," he jotted in his notebook, "is the first time in this war (save for some ack-ack at Pearl Harbor) that US guns have fired on the enemy." When the moment came to strike back at the enemy, Casey stood enthralled as, in the distance, red flames burst on the shore, followed by a massive black cloud floating skyward.[14]

Casey's problems began once he arrived back on dry land a week later. Knox had learned that no wire-service reporters had accompanied the fleet to the Marshalls. Keen to avoid allegations of discrimination, he instructed Nimitz not to release Casey's dispatches until the AP, UP, and INS correspondents had had an "opportunity to interview officers" in order to produce their own accounts. Partly for this reason and partly because of the familiar security concerns, the navy's censors held Casey's story for over a week.[15] When it finally appeared on February 13, his editor at the *Daily News* tried to compensate for the delay by giving it a banner headline and a prominently displayed advert revealing that Casey's second eyewitness article "will be published tomorrow."[16] Yet Casey still felt aggrieved. The navy, he complained, had effectively helped the "stay-at-home" reporters, while he had been at sea risking his neck. Just as bad, when his story finally appeared, Casey felt it was no longer "hot," especially as it had to compete with the news of the stunning British loss of Singapore, which had broken the previous day.[17]

After he returned from a second mission with the fleet a few weeks later, Casey's agonies mounted. Like other war correspondents traveling to a war zone, he had already pledged to submit his copy to the military censors in order to acquire accreditation. In Hawaii, this first meant a trip to see the chief naval censor, who, as another correspondent explained to his boss, was by reputation "the meanest hombre in Pearl Harbor." By the spring, it also entailed a visit to the Office of Censorship's official in Honolulu, who oversaw the voluntary code that applied inside the United States and who checked every story that was sent out by cable.[18] If this seemed like the reappearance of that old bugbear, dual censorship, worse was to come. Casey began to suspect that at least one of these censorship bodies was stopping all of his cablegrams from leaving Hawaii without informing him of this fact. When he demanded an answer, Casey discovered that his new position as a fleet correspondent, instead of making it easier for him to report, had actually placed him in an impossible position. "I was closely identified with the fleet," the censor explained to him. "Any message from me dated Honolulu would indicate that I had arrived in Honolulu and that therefore the fleet had arrived in Honolulu." For this reason, the navy decided that Casey had to be silenced. Along with the other fleet correspondents, he had effectively been "placed in a sort of quarantine or internment between voyages."[19]

At least one correspondent managed to get a story past the censor, however, and as Casey started to mull over the reasons why, his blood pressure rose still further. On his regular visits to the navy's press office in Pearl Harbor, Casey could see a letter from Frank Knox prominently displayed on the wall, and it underlined how his status was starting to shift. "Under no circumstances," the letter read, "will the representatives of the *Chicago Daily News* receive any more favorable treatment from Public Relations officers of the Navy Department than is received by the correspondents or writers of any similar newspaper under similar conditions." Knox's motives for writing were transparent. He was simply trying to protect himself against allegations of blatant favoritism. But Casey began to suspect that the Pearl Harbor PROs were overcompensating by openly helping his rivals. "Perhaps," he complained to his editor, "there should be some assurances that *Daily News* correspondents get the *same* privileges and restrictions as other correspondents."[20]

Despite this flash of professional anger, Casey often found himself sympathizing with his rivals—and not just over censorship. By this point, an illustrious group of reporters were based in Hawaii, including Ed Angly of the *Chicago Sun*, Joseph Harsch of the *Christian Science Monitor*, Foster Hailey of the *New York Times*, and H. R. Knickerbocker, who was so notorious for turning up in the world's trouble spots that a Vienna hotel manager had once greeted him with the words, "Mr. Knickerbocker, welcome. Are things really so bad?"[21] "In peace time," Casey noted, "the navy press agency department would have pinned medals on any genius who could get those lads together in one bunch on a navy story." In wartime, however, these same officers seemed to take perverse pleasure in antagonizing them all.[22]

The reporters, for their part, hated the unpredictability of fleet missions. While Casey had at least seen some action during the raid on the Marshalls, "other correspondents," he observed, "have been out repeatedly on expeditions that produced nothing. One lad found himself on a patrol that wandered over the Pacific for a couple of months without producing anything."[23]

Then there was Foster Hailey, who returned from a mission in March to find that his credentials had suddenly been revoked. Someone in the navy seemed to think that "he had avoided censorship," although the reality turned out to be much more complex. Only after weeks of protests did the navy reveal that Hailey's crime had been to send a private letter to his editor containing confidential information, an action that contravened the accreditation agreement. Hailey hastened to point out that he had never signed such an agreement, but the navy still barred him from going out with the fleet until it had completed a laborious investigation.[24]

Back home, meanwhile, newspaper bosses increasingly complained about the paucity of information the navy was releasing in the Pacific. Throughout March and April, many editorials expressed "regret" at its "belated" announcements. According to the "index of newspaper support," editorial approval crashed to 40 percent in late March, compared with its usual 70 to 80 percent, because of "disapproval over news suppression."[25] The navy trotted out all the usual excuses, chief among them the need to furnish "all information which does not give aid and comfort to the enemy," but for many this explanation was clearly wearing thin.[26]

In Hawaii, Casey certainly did not buy it. Alienated and angry, he decided that the time had come to use the cover provided by Knox's ownership of his newspaper to become the mouthpiece for all the reporters' grievances. "I am the only correspondent here," Casey wrote to his editor in the middle of March,

> who has lifted his voice in protest against the nonsense with which we have been surrounded. I suppose that is because the rest of the mob feel that maybe the colonel [Knox] would listen to me—an error to which I once fell myself. Anyway I have borne the banner and now I am considered by all and sundry to be a grouch, an agitator, and a boil on the calloused ass of progress. All I can say about that is that I admit the indictment.[27]

Yet, however hard he pushed the censor or supported his embattled colleagues, Casey never came across as totally convincing in the role of number-one "agitator." His résumé was simply too distinguished, his newspaper too closely connected to the government. A real troublemaker needed a very different background. Someone perhaps with a touch of the exotic or a slightly shady reputation. Or a newspaper boss who totally rejected, rather than embraced, the president and his foreign policy.

* * *

In the middle of March, just as he began to seriously consider resigning as a fleet correspondent, Casey suddenly bumped into Stanley Johnston of the *Chicago Tribune*. The two men knew each other well, having spent time together during the Battle of Britain eighteen months earlier. As Casey settled down to listen to one of Johnston's inimitable stories, he could have been forgiven for thinking that here was a man so different from himself that he might have come straight out of central casting for the role of principal troublemaker.[28]

The most obvious contrast was physical. The six-and-a-half-foot Johnston towered over the diminutive Casey. Both men had been in uniform during World War I, but whereas Casey had compiled an impressive combat record, Johnston had a tendency to embellish his own experiences, claiming that he had served as an Australian artillery officer, first at Gallipoli and then in Flanders, when the reality had been much less glamorous. After the armistice, Johnston had undertaken a variety of mining jobs in Asia and the Pacific before returning to Europe in 1937 by way of New York, where he had met the dancer he was soon to marry. Johnston's first experience in the media had been with Press Wireless in the Netherlands, where he had worked on a system that allowed reporters all over the Continent to phone their dispatches straight through to their main offices. This had remained his job until Hitler's armies scythed through Western Europe in the spring of 1940, and he had retreated across the channel to Britain.[29]

Johnston's initial involvement with the *Tribune* had come shortly afterward, when he had acted as "a valuable assistant on military subjects" to the paper's overworked correspondents.[30] Seasoned hands in the *Tribune*'s London bureau had appreciated his valor and knowledge, but the British authorities had viewed him with much greater suspicion. That anxious summer, with a Nazi invasion a real possibility, rumors had swirled around London that Johnston had business interests in Germany, that the "dancing girl" he had taken for a wife had family who lived in Bavaria, and that he might even be a Nazi "spy." At first, Johnston's manner scarcely helped his cause. Unlike Casey, who came across as a gregarious, grandfatherly figure, Johnston struck even his potential friends as "overly smooth." He "had a sort of 'Hollywood con-man bearing and manner,'" observed one *Tribune* editor, "and has a tendency to 'oversell himself.'"[31]

Despite this characterization of Johnston, the *Tribune*'s owner, Colonel Robert McCormick, was considering hiring him. The publisher liked the look of the man when he turned up in Chicago in May 1941 and thought he might make a promising reporter. As for the allegations of espionage, an internal *Tribune* investigation found nothing in them. The oversensitive British, a senior editor concluded, had simply taken umbrage at

Johnston's tendency, when he had worked at Press Wireless, "to take good care" of his clients "by doing them personal favors such as slipping into Germany packages of coffee etc."[32]

That the *Tribune* was prepared to recruit such a figure highlighted just how different it was from the *Daily News*. Before Pearl Harbor, McCormick had encouraged his reporters to pursue a vehemently isolationist line; afterward, he continued to express a profound suspicion of America's British ally—which helped to explain why he was willing to hire someone like Johnston, whom the British authorities appeared to dislike so intensely.[33]

For his part, Johnston knew he was being granted a major opening. Despite McCormick's isolationist tendencies, the *Tribune* boss had built an impressive "globe-straddling network" of top foreign correspondents. The colonel had also created a newspaper that people wanted to read— indeed, it consistently sold around one million copies a day, making it second in national circulation only to the *New York Daily News*. Yet the idiosyncratic McCormick also had a habit of getting embroiled in trouble. Soon after Johnston joined the paper's permanent staff in September 1941, the *Tribune* had come under federal investigation for publishing the top-secret "Victory Program" that outlined America's grand strategy in the war. Knox had been so appalled that he lobbied hard for a prosecution. That never came, but the *Tribune*'s critics were consoled by the fact that McCormick's paper was increasingly being labeled "a distorter of news" in the weeks after Pearl Harbor.[34]

As Johnston soon discovered, no one on Hawaii had much chance to produce any news, distorted or otherwise. He and Casey might be different in many respects, but they both immediately agreed that their current jobs—which had appeared so glamorous before their departure—had placed them in a journalistic dead end. "Living in Honolulu these days," Johnston cabled his editor soon after his arrival, "must be about the most dismal existence there is." It certainly took a physical toll. While Casey's blood pressure soared whenever he faced a new slight from the censor, Johnston started to feel so unwell that in early April he consulted a doctor, who suggested that he return to the mainland for a minor operation. Then the *Tribune* man suddenly got word that he had a chance of becoming a fleet correspondent. The opportunity was too good to miss, so he decided to defer his medical procedure and linger a little longer in dismal Hawaii. It proved a momentous decision.[35]

Coral Sea and Midway

Johnston was playing poker at the swanky Moana Hotel on April 14 when a porter hailed him to the telephone. A naval PRO was on the other end of the line, and without any ceremony he asked the reporter if he "cared to go to sea." "Yes," Johnston replied laconically, before returning to the game, where, in his excitement, he found it difficult to keep his normal poker face in place.

At five thirty the next morning Johnston took a cab to Pearl Harbor, where he discovered that the navy had a surprise in store for him. In yet another effort to minimize allegations that Knox was biased against the rivals of the *Daily News*, it had decided to place Johnston on the USS *Lexington*. This, the PRO explained with a large grin, was "one of the two biggest ships in the world" in its class. It was also much more—one of the first US aircraft carriers, with a legendary reputation as the forerunner of all future American designs, operations, and tactics in this crucial new sphere. Johnston was suitably impressed. "That morning," he noted, "the deck was empty, and to my eyes seemed to stretch endlessly away from me."

As soon as the *Lexington* headed out to sea, Johnston began exploring his new domain, chatting with admirals, sailors, and airmen and meticulously jotting down information in his precious black notebook. Soon, its pages were full of interesting material, from facts about the history, specifications, and maneuverability of the ship to pithy descriptions about the senior officers on board, including the executive officer, Morton Seligman, with whom he struck up a close friendship.[36]

Johnston was particularly interested in the airplane pilots who constantly took off from the deck to begin scouring the vast ocean in search of the enemy. They were at the heart of a new form of warfare, he quickly realized, that also required a new form of war reporting. Whereas in other theaters the correspondent always tried to get as close as possible to the action in order to write an eyewitness account, the sheer size of the Pacific Ocean meant that a reporter's ears were often his most valuable tool. Whenever the planes went out, Johnston would head to the radio room, where he could listen to the pilots' observations as they patrolled hundreds of miles away from the ship. If they spotted a Japanese plane heading toward the *Lexington*, the captain would immediately issue the call for battle stations, and, forewarned, Johnston could head for a good viewing position.[37]

By early May, as the task force approached the Coral Sea, battle-station alarms became increasingly common. Nimitz, acting on intelligence that the Japanese planned to attack Port Moresby, New Guinea, from which point they could threaten Australia, wanted American ships to draw the Japanese invaders into a fight. Increasingly, Johnston began to recognize the full dimensions of his own luck. As the only correspondent around, he would have the upcoming battle— the first major US naval engagement with the Japanese fleet—all to himself.[38]

On May 7, Johnston "crowded into the wardroom with officers off duty. Loudspeakers there," he wrote later, "were connected with the *Lexington's* receivers tuned to the communications circuits of the planes in the air." For a long time, no one could make much sense of the mishmash of voices, orders, and indecipherable talk between the planes, but then the voice of Lieutenant Commander Robert E. Dixon came through clearly. Dixon was the skipper of one of the scouting squadrons that had located the Japanese aircraft carrier *Shoho*. After the bombers had fatally struck this enemy ship, Johnston recorded his immortal words, as cheers echoed around the ship. "Scratch one flat-top," Dixon declared triumphantly, "—scratch one flat-top."[39]

The next day, the *Lexington* was on the receiving end. Johnston watched from the signal bridge as the Japanese planes appeared shortly after 11 a.m. and began launching wave after wave of torpedo attacks. Johnston found this part of the battle particularly hard to comprehend. With so much happening, he scarcely knew where to look. He tried to use one hand to dictate his impressions into a microphone and the other to jot down details in his notebook, but soon explosions began to rock the ship. By late afternoon, the situation on board was dire, so the captain stopped the engines and issued the dreaded order to abandon ship.[40]

Despite the flames and smoke billowing all around, Johnston was in no hurry to leave. He had already been below numerous times and had even rescued a wounded seaman, whom he had dragged to safety through gasoline flames that burned off some of his clothes. He now joined a group of pilots who were handing out ice cream on deck, and parched after hours in the intense heat with little to drink, he eagerly grabbed his share. Once refreshed, Johnston carefully transferred his surviving notes into his breast pocket, lowered himself off the *Lexington* by a rope, and after a quick dunking in the sea, climbed into a life raft. The water was warm, but that raised the possibility of a shark attack. Along with a naval yeoman, Johnston rowed around the wreckage, rescuing as many as sixty sailors. It was hazardous work, as explosions continued to shake the *Lexington*, showering steel splinters everywhere. As soon as the raft was full, the yeoman set course for the safety of a cruiser. Once the men were safely aboard the ship,

Johnston's first instinct was purely professional. He hunted around for a laundry steam presser, so that he could dry out his precious black notebook.[41]

* * *

Johnston had almost a month to peruse his notes as he slowly made his way back to the United States. His first destination was a small island of Tongatapu, where he and the 2,750 other *Lexington* survivors were crammed into two small transport ships. Johnston boarded the USS *Barnett*, where Seligman invited him to bunk down in the "commodore's quarters"—a suite of rooms that included two bedrooms and a dining area. Over the next few weeks, he would often tap away at his typewriter, compiling a series of first drafts that detailed what had happened during the Coral Sea battle. He spent the remainder of his time talking to the officers who either milled about as they waited to see Seligman or were lured into the dining room area because it was the only place to grab a coffee when the mess was closed.[42]

During these discussions, Johnston discovered many more details about the *Lexington*'s last battle. Much more controversially, he also learned about an important upcoming operation. Johnston had pinned a large map of the Pacific above his bed, and this often became a focal point for musings about future strategic developments. "During the last two days at sea," Johnston wrote a short while later, "there was a lot of serious discussion between all officers about the impending Japanese invasion attempt in the North Pacific sphere. It was natural that I should hear the discussions."[43]

Less natural, perhaps, was that he should see a piece of paper with "the names of Japanese warships and listed transports, etc., under headings of 'Striking force,' 'Occupation force,' and 'Support force.'"[44] The source of this information was the navy's greatest secret: the codebreakers in Pearl Harbor, who had managed to assemble crucial facts about the Japanese fleet's disposition and movement.[45] Seligman had worked out a procedure with the *Barnett*'s captain that gave him access to the decoded messages sent from Pearl Harbor to the fleet, including one from Nimitz on May 31 that described the Japanese order of battle for its upcoming assault on Midway. No one will ever know for certain whether Seligman deliberately showed this message to Johnston or whether, as the reporter subsequently claimed, he came across it as he was moving some "old papers" around his desk. What is not in doubt is his decision to copy the information onto another sheet of paper before leaving the *Barnett* when it docked in San Diego on June 2.[46]

* * *

Having spent many weeks out of touch, Johnston arrived at the Tribune Tower on Friday, June 5, to "the applause and hosannas of the paper's staffers." J. Loy "Pat" Maloney, the *Tribune's* managing editor, immediately ushered him into a secure office, protected from the rest of the capacious newsroom by a guard whose job was to ensure that none of the information in his stories leaked before they went to press. Johnston spent that night and all the next day at his new desk, reworking his Coral Sea material. At 9:00 p.m. on Saturday, desperate for a cup of coffee and change of scene, he strolled into the main newsroom, where he found the AP machine clattering out Nimitz's communiqué about a new naval battle near Midway island. Although the details remained patchy, CINCPAC was claiming that two or three enemy aircraft carriers had been destroyed, with one or two more badly damaged, and that the sneak attack on Pearl Harbor "has now been partially avenged." Looking around, Johnston was surprised by how calmly his fellow reporters were taking this news. So he hurried over to see Maloney, who was sitting at the "center desk" in his shirt sleeves. Excitedly, he explained to his boss that the information he had gathered on the *Barnett*, when compared with the navy's communiqués, not only demonstrated that "we had prior warning of [Japanese] intentions," but also confirmed that Midway had been a massive victory. In full agreement, Maloney instructed Johnston to go back to his secure room to compile a story based on what he knew.[47]

As a condition of his accreditation, Johnston had agreed—albeit orally rather than in writing—to submit anything he produced about the fleet to the naval censors. The fate of the copy he handed to Maloney was very different. Another *Tribune* writer had already added a sentence suggesting that the story was based on information from "naval intelligence." Maloney added a Washington dateline. The editor also decided that there was no need to submit the piece to the Office of Censorship, reasoning that its voluntary code only prohibited the publication of information about US fleet movements and said nothing about enemy ships unless they were "in or near American waters." Since Johnston's story focused on the Japanese fleet in the distant Pacific, Maloney, after talking to a couple of senior colleagues, ordered it placed on the front page, beneath a striking headline: "NAVY HAD WORD OF JAP PLAN TO STRIKE AT SEA."[48]

A "Campaign to Smear, Purge, and Intimidate"

When the Washington-based naval officers arrived for work on Sunday, June 7, they doubtless expected a party atmosphere. Six months to the day after Pearl Harbor, the navy had avenged this humiliation, while also decisively turning the tide in the Pacific. Yet the mood that morning was far from triumphant. Officers found the Navy Building "shaking" and their boss in "a white fury."[49]

Everyone knew the jokes already doing the rounds about Admiral Ernest J. King, the powerful chief of naval operations and commander in chief of the US Fleet. One wag insisted that King was the "most even-tempered man in the navy. He is always in a rage." His "idea of war information," observed another, "was that there should be just *one* communiqué. Some morning we would announce that the war was won and that we had won it."[50] On this particular morning, however, King was horrified to learn that someone else's idea of giving out war information was to reveal the navy's foreknowledge of enemy plans. As yet, the precise provenance of the offending story remained unclear. The same information had appeared on page four of the *Tribune*'s sister paper, the *Washington Times-Herald*, and because of the Washington dateline, King initially suspected the leak had come from inside the Navy Building. After frantically sifting all the relevant documents, King's subordinates soon shifted their suspicions to the *Barnett* and, by extension, to Stanley Johnston and his bosses.[51]

While this investigation proceeded, King summoned reporters to his office. His aides billed the session as a press conference, but it soon descended into an admonitory lecture. King began calmly enough. Not wanting to give Japan confirmation that the navy had broken its codes, he claimed that the advance knowledge of the Midway invasion had come from other sources—especially submarines "sprinkled" across the Pacific and an educated guess that after the Coral Sea battle the enemy "would have to go somewhere and do something." Then King went off the record. The information in Johnston's story, he scolded, "came unmistakably, from a leak that may involve very serious consequences. It compromises a vital and secret source of information, which will henceforth be closed to us. The military consequences are so obvious," King concluded, "that I do not need to dwell on them."[52]

The reporters left the room stunned. Perhaps, the more alarmist began to intimate, King was so incandescent about the breach that he "wanted to put the Marines in the *Tribune* to close the plant that Sunday night." Walter

Fig. 3.1. Two admirals: Ernest J. King (*left*) and Chester W. Nimitz (*right*).
© AP/Shutterstock.

Trohan, the *Tribune*'s Washington correspondent, quickly demolished this particular rumor, but in a confidential memo to his bosses he added another claim. "The navy was honest in its complaint against the Johnston story," Trohan concluded after doing a bit of investigative work. "When the navy first began acting it did not know the story was a *Tribune* story. Later the New Dealers moved in and directed the smear."[53]

Stanley Johnston soon became the obvious target of the government's smear campaign. Within days, Roosevelt directed the Justice Department to investigate whether he, Maloney, and the *Tribune* could be charged under the Espionage Act, which carried a maximum penalty of ten years in jail and a $10,000 fine. To this end, J. Edgar Hoover's FBI began questioning everyone connected to the case, including crew members of the *Lexington* and *Barnet*, who were scattered across the country. Meanwhile, William D. Mitchell, a former attorney general, accepted the position as "special assistant" charged with building a case against the *Tribune*.[54]

As soon as they discovered what the government planned, McCormick and Maloney began to map out their defense. One strand would be legal-istic: they would insist not only that they had no intent to injure the United States (which, their lawyers told them, was crucial to any prosecution under the Espionage Act), but also that if any rules had been broken, they were military and related to the accreditation agreement (which Johnston had never signed), and so did not come under the jurisdiction of a civil indict-ment.[55] The other component would be political. Nasty smears were already doing the rounds, intimating that Stanley Johnston "was not married to his 'wife' who is a native German with known sympathy for the Nazis" or that "Johnston is of known Nazi sympathy; that he was authorized to go on the *Lexington* without the knowledge of the FBI."[56] If such rumors became ac-cepted as fact, they could easily sway the grand jurors. So, after conducting their own internal investigation, which indicated that Johnson was "clean as a whistle," McCormick and Maloney launched a concerted publicity cam-paign on behalf of their beleaguered correspondent.[57]

The *Tribune* began this campaign with some obvious strengths. More than a month after the event, the naval censors had only just decided to re-lease news of the *Lexington*'s sinking.[58] Despite the long time lag, Johnston's graphic eyewitness story would be a major scoop. To magnify its impact, the *Tribune* hastened to emphasize that the author had been one of the battle's big heroes and had received a formal navy citation for rescuing sailors as the *Lexington* went down.[59] McCormick and Maloney also decided to offer Johnston's stories to the wire services, free of charge, for distribution to other newspapers. "We felt that the possession of the story was a public trust," the paper editorialized, "to be shared as widely as possible." That was the public justification. In private, the *Tribune*'s bosses conceded that they were not being totally altruistic. The more fame Johnston acquired as the chronicler of the navy's first big battle, they calculated, the less chance the government would have to smear, and then indict, him as a spy who was bent on aiding the enemy.[60]

This, in essence, is what happened. In nine separate stories that appeared daily from June 13, Johnston produced a compelling and fast-paced narrative of the Coral Sea battle that bulged with heroes. One was Bob Dixon, whom Johnston had interviewed in order to discover how he had helped to "scratch" that Japanese "flat-top." "It was obvious we had caught them by surprise," Johnston recorded Dixon as saying. "They had a number of planes on deck, and one was coming up from the hangar deck in the elevator. I could see it all clearly as I kept my eye on them, sighting for the release point." Other pilots, Johnston explained, "reported that Dixon's dive was perfectly made and his 500 pound bomb hit the Jap carrier amidships." Such a willingness to share credit was far from uncommon. Every pilot story, Johnston explained,

> was replete with more action, more thrills, and more destruction of planes than the wildest pulp magazine thriller ever dreamed up. But in this case every one was true. And invariably they were told in the most self-effacing manner possible by men who were proud of their flying mates, but mentioned their own deeds as impersonally as tho[ugh] they had nothing to do with them."[61]

By the end of his nine-day epic, Johnston had developed a powerful—and somewhat familiar—narrative arc. Superficially, the *Lexington*'s sinking on May 8 seemed to echo the American fate in the Philippines: a heroic tragedy that forged American individualists into team-playing fighters, but ultimately ended on a sour note. As Johnston wrote of the ship's end, "It is a tale of gallantry above and beyond the valor of men in the heat of battle. . . . It is an account of the dogged determination and unshakable courage with which the humblest and highest members of the ship's company strove together in a long, torturing, and deadly hazardous effort."[62]

Yet Johnston's series managed to close on a much higher key than anything that had come out of the Philippines, in part because he repeated the pilots' exaggerated claims of destroying "14 out of 15 warships and transports" in a May 4 strike that Nimitz had privately called "disappointing."[63] He also stressed that the Coral Sea battle had not been a reverse, even for those who had had to swim away from their stricken aircraft carrier. Not only would these sailors soon have a chance for revenge on a new carrier, the "*Lexington II*," but seen in a broader perspective, Coral Sea had been a decisive victory. "It was a battle," Johnston insisted, "that naval authorities believe may prove to have been the turning point in the Pacific phases of World War II. It was the greatest naval defeat ever dealt Japanese fleets."[64]

Across the country, the reaction was immediate. Even many naval officers recognized that Johnston's "Coral Sea stories were the best break the Navy had received in the war." Editors of small-town newspapers were especially delighted by what one dubbed a "great piece of unselfish journalism[,] releasing those exclusive stories on the *Lexington*." Behind the scenes, Johnston's bosses were equally pleased. By the end of July, Maloney believed that a front-page story by the hero of Coral Sea could add more than a hundred thousand readers to the *Tribune*'s daily circulation figures.[65]

* * *

Of course, Midway, not Coral Sea, ought to have been the biggest story. Ironically, Knox's reporter, Bob Casey, had been with the fleet at this truly decisive victory, but his dispatches had nowhere near the impact of Johnston's.

Casey's relative lack of success stemmed partly from his very different battle experience. While Johnston had produced an eyewitness account of a legendary aircraft carrier sinking, Casey spent the critical moments of the Midway battle on the bridge of his ship, munching ham sandwiches while digesting the information coming in from the attacking American pilots. These reports were absolutely stunning. Within the space of eight minutes, planes from the outnumbered American fleet managed to fatally hit three Japanese aircraft carriers; a fourth was sunk a few hours later. These strikes completely transformed the balance of power in the Pacific, but they were impossible to see, let alone describe, from a ship a hundred or so miles away.[66]

Shortly after midday, Casey caught a glimpse of the Japanese attack on an American carrier, the USS *Yorktown*, but even then he could make little sense of what was happening. "The ack-ack was ragged," he jotted in his notebook, "but the thunderheads of it blackened the horizon. We had no way of telling how many Jap planes came in on that raid," he added, "but there couldn't have been many. The blasting was short-lived." For the rest of the afternoon, Casey continued to peer anxiously up at the sky, but ultimately that was all the action he witnessed on this pivotal day. And he naturally found the whole experience disorienting. "Now," he wrote soon after it was over, "it turns out that we have fought a major engagement—one of the biggest naval battles of all time. And miracle of miracles, we have won. It was too stupendous to contemplate as we lolled in a mist of nervous exhaustion, mumbling to one another in senseless syllables, falling to sleep over our coffee."[67]

A scrupulous reporter, Casey made sure that his story of the battle was based principally on these personal experiences, and as a result it inevitably lacked drama. His account of the first skirmishes was typical. "It was in the nature of things," he told his readers,

> an attack by individuals, each of whom saw only his own little sector with his own eyes. Operational technique can be reduced to the formula of the pilot who reported: "sighted sub, sank same." As for our part in it, there

wasn't any unusual activity the night when word was received that the Navy patrol planes had located the main body of the Jap fleet. The cribbage games went on as usual.... A few nighthawks went on reading stale magazines and most of the ship's company went to sleep in the old, uncomfortable corners about the turrets, magazines, hatches, and such.

Even the climactic period of battle contained little excitement, just "the usual tense hours of waiting—waiting for our planes, waiting for theirs, nobody was quite certain which."[68] When Casey finally learned how many Japanese ships had been sunk, he found it particularly difficult to convey the reasons for this decisive victory. In subsequent years, historians would emphasize the importance of naval codebreaking, together with Admiral Raymond A. Spruance's clear, cool command of the situation.[69] With the censors placing both these factors off-limits, however, Casey diagnosed the recipe for success as little more than "old-fashioned Navy savvy, plus common horse sense."[70]

More than a week after the battle, the *Daily News* plastered Casey's eyewitness dispatch across the front page, and it did the same for a subsequent story based on interviews with the pilots who had won the battle.[71] Yet these accounts received nothing like the exposure that Johnston was enjoying from the *Tribune*—the nine-day serialization and the decision to allow other papers to run his stories free of charge—although, significantly, the *Daily News* man did not begrudge Johnston his success.[72]

* * *

Casey had decided to leave the Pacific weeks before the Midway battle. He had lost twenty-five pounds in the past six months, and although he joked that this was because the navy food did not agree with him, close observers thought it was probably due to the stress of navy life. "Nearly everyone connected with this racket in Honolulu," he observed when pressing for a move, "has lied to me at one time or another." As a veteran of countless campaigns, Casey knew that being misled by the military was an integral part of the war correspondent's lot. But he also believed that nothing came close to the dysfunctional situation in Hawaii, where, he concluded, he had "never been so unhappy on any assignment." So, after returning from Midway to Hawaii, Casey headed straight for the States, "aching," as he joked to a colleague, "for a good murder story."[73]

Instead of reporting on a Chicagoland killing, Casey immediately became embroiled in a DC espionage case. Soon after arriving home, he arranged a meeting with Stanley Johnston at a "neutral spot." This precaution was necessary, Casey explained, because the FBI had just questioned him about the *Tribune*'s Midway story, as part of its ongoing investigation.[74]

If the government thought that Casey would be an ally, it had badly misjudged the man. Over the past six months, Casey had become so disgusted by the navy's treatment of the press that he continued to act as the champion of any reporter he believed to be "getting [an] indefensible runaround."[75] Casey placed Johnston firmly in this category, and when the two men met, he could not have been more helpful. Casey explained that he had told the FBI agents that Johnston's "reputation and conduct was perfect," while also confirming that British intelligence had given him a clean bill of health over the Nazi spy allegations.[76]

Casey's positive character reference was not the government's only problem. More than thirty years later, Dixon would claim that he had seen Seligman show classified messages to Johnston on the *Barnet*. When questioned at the time, however, the man Johnston had made a hero of the Coral Sea battle refused to incriminate either a fellow officer or the reporter and his paper. As a result, Dixon was not called to testify before the grand jury, which began hearing testimony in Chicago on August 13.[77]

Inside the courtroom, Johnston stuck tenaciously to his story that he had picked up the incriminating evidence only from conversations onboard ship and a piece of paper left on his desk.[78] Outside, the *Tribune* continued to trumpet Johnston's heroism, while calling the prosecution politically motivated—yet "another move," it declared, "in the Roosevelt administration's campaign to smear, purge, and intimidate prewar noninterventionists and others now demanding a more efficient prosecution of the war."[79]

After five days of testimony, Mitchell, the prosecutor, still felt he had a chance to get an indictment, but only if navy intelligence officers testified to the potential harm Johnston's story had done to the codebreaking success—and therein lay the nub. King, although still angry at the *Tribune*, wanted to protect, above all else, the fact that the navy had broken the Japanese code. He therefore prevented any naval cryptanalyst from appearing before the grand jury as an expert witness, an action that effectively decided the outcome. "The jury has considered the case fully," Mitchell revealed on August 19, "and its conclusion that no violation of law was disclosed settles the matter."[80]

As soon as he learned of this decision, McCormick descended from his twenty-fourth-floor office in the Tribune Tower to make a rare visit to the newsroom. After the cheers finally died down, he read out a short statement.

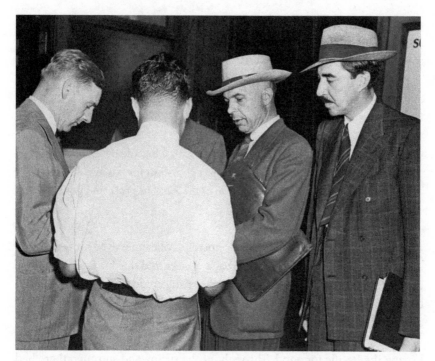

Fig. 3.2. Stanley Johnston (*right*) and J. Loy Maloney (*second from right*) are questioned by reporters after offering to appear before a grand jury in Chicago.
© Getty Images.

"Our whole effort is to win the war," the publisher insisted, "and we will not indulge in any factionalism excepting in so far as we are persecuted and have to defend ourselves." In the ensuing days, the celebrations reverberated way beyond Chicago. While congratulatory telegrams and phone messages piled up in McCormick's office, one survey found that fifteen of the seventeen newspapers editorializing on the subject welcomed the collapse of what they believed was a government "grudge fight."[81]

Such an assessment exposed the obvious tensions between the media and military during the early stages of the Pacific War. On the one hand, the US Navy had the means, motive, and opportunity to clamp down hard on reporters. It controlled access to the fleet. It needed to deny vital information to the enemy after the debilitating defeat at Pearl Harbor. And it had a press corps that was equally anxious to strike back at the enemy. Yet these same reporters, who had to file regularly to justify their professional existence, came to loathe what they considered to be the overzealous nature of the navy's censorship, even though the underlying structure of this censorship regime contained complexities that the *Tribune* exploited in June, in what became perhaps the biggest-ever crisis in media-military relations.

As for the man at the center of this controversy, fame clearly agreed with Stanley Johnston. A short while later, another *Tribune* war correspondent found Johnston

> laughing himself silly about the money he is making and about how easy it is to make it. He's amazed, too. "They pay you—just for talking," he laughs. He is cleaning up on his book (*Queen of the Flattops* [*sic*]), and got $2,000 for 2,000 words from *Reader's Digest*.[82]

As this comment suggests, many of Johnston's colleagues eyed him enviously as "a real soldier of fortune," but they also recognized that his fame had come at a cost. Most obviously, neither Knox nor King could stomach the prospect of having him report on the navy again, giving the *Tribune* no choice but to abandon its plans to send him back to Hawaii.[83]

If, for Johnston, this smacked of an exile, he was by no means unique in leaving the Pacific for good. Throughout the spring and summer, there had already been a large exodus from Honolulu, sparked by a combination of pull and push factors. In public, most correspondents stressed the attraction of Europe. "European and Russian battlefields," opined H. R. Knickerbocker, "will provide better copy in the future—that's why I came back from the Pacific theater." In private, other reporters were much more cynical, including Casey, whose own move to Europe, he admitted, was prompted largely by a desire to "write under intelligent censorship."[84]

Two further developments made it even more likely that the media would turn its back on the navy's war in the future. On the one hand, as a senior PRO observed in July, Knox "has insisted, since the Stanley Johnston affair, in going slow about accrediting new correspondents until their backgrounds have been carefully investigated." As a result, the reporters who had left the theater were not replaced for quite some time.[85] On the other hand, MacArthur stepped eagerly into the breach, luring anyone interested in covering the Pacific War to Australia. Whether they would be able to report more effectively from there remained to be seen.

4

The New Guinea Gang

"Total Censorship in This Foreign Country"

Douglas MacArthur had not enjoyed his first weeks in Australia. On learning that he had only twenty-five thousand US troops under his command—about a third of the number he had left on Bataan—he "turned deathly white," according to one account, "his knees buckled, his lips twitched." Pacing his office in an old insurance building in Melbourne, he began lashing out at the "New Deal cabal" in Washington and the "Navy cabal" in Hawaii, convinced that both groups were hatching plots to sideline him. Surrounded by perceived enemies on all sides, MacArthur sought the company of those who had been with him on Corregidor. Mostly, this meant the tight-knit coterie of officers who would soon become known as the "Bataan gang." But from time to time it also included the cluster of correspondents who had protected his reputation during the doomed Philippines campaign—the likes of Clark Lee and the Jacobys, to whom he now gave personal tips about possible breaking stories.[1]

By April, however, more than fifty additional correspondents had arrived in Melbourne, and their relationship with MacArthur soon became much more fraught.[2] Sixteen of them had traveled from San Francisco by sea, enduring eighteen days in which their ship had been buffeted by storms and had almost hit a Japanese submarine. Among this party was a group of experienced hands, including Carleton Kent of the *Chicago Times*, who had been a reporter for ten years; Robert Sherrod of *Time* and *Life*, who had been working for Henry Luce's magazines since 1935; and Lewis B. Sebring of the *New York Herald-Tribune*, who had spent more than a decade reporting for this prestigious newspaper. Even in such an august crowd, though, Byron Darnton of the *New York Times* stood out. The "plump but debonair" forty-four-year-old had served with distinction in the trenches during World War I, after which he had worked for a variety of newspapers before joining the *Times* in 1934. On the long voyage to Australia, Darnton soon acquired a reputation for fearlessness and leadership that so impressed his colleagues that they elected him their "official delegate to lead them in boat drill." It was a role he was anxious to avoid, but as one of them joked, "such campaign posters as 'Darnton for Dog Catcher' and 'Darnton is the People's Choice' gave him a mandate he could not reject."[3]

Although Darnton, Kent, Sebring, and Sherrod were all experienced reporters, none of them had covered a war before, and this set them apart from those correspondents who began arriving in Melbourne from the searing Allied defeats in Burma, Malaya, Singapore, and Java. Even at first glance, these refugees looked different. War correspondents were all supposed to wear the same uniform, adorned with a green felt armband marked with the letter "C." But with clothing in short supply in Australia, those who had come from other parts of Asia had to make do with what they had acquired during their recent travels. "So," one of them observed in late March, "you will see one man in a correct shirt and wrong pants, one man in an Australian shirt and a British cap and American pants. It is a very interesting hodgepodge altogether and arouses no end of polite comment."[4]

Comment was less polite when these war-scarred correspondents learned about the American censorship arrangements. MacArthur's new command comprised the Southwest Pacific Area (SWPA), which stretched from the western half of the Solomon Islands, through New Guinea, and up to the Philippines. With Washington still wedded to a Germany-first strategy, MacArthur's hope of an early return to Manila was firmly on hold. Instead, he had to make do with "check[ing] the enemy advance toward Australia and its essential lines of communication." In operational terms, this meant focusing on New Guinea, since Japan clearly intended to control this large island to the north of Australia.[5] When it came to censorship, MacArthur had to work closely with the Australian government, which had developed its own system. "The matter is governed by Australian law," MacArthur observed. It would be "utterly impossible," he initially believed, ". . . under the authority I possess to impose total censorship in this foreign country."[6]

In Washington, however, top officials were increasingly convinced that Australian censorship was so lax that it constituted a major threat to Allied operations. Even George C. Marshall, the army chief of staff, who had no illusions about MacArthur's penchant for using censorship to bolster his personal image, deemed the leakage of information so dangerous that he ordered the new SWPA commander to undertake a "complete revision" of censorship in his theater.[7] Reluctantly, the Australian government agreed to comply, its concerns about surrendering more sovereignty to the pushy Americans overwhelmed by the looming threat posed by the rampaging Japanese. After a short negotiation, MacArthur acquired "partial control over the Australian censorship," in addition to the "rigid and complete" jurisdiction he already exercised over information relating to his SWPA command. In practice this meant that no correspondent, American or Australian, would be able to file any dispatch relating to operational material "until after the issuance of the [General Headquarters] communiqué" covering that event.[8]

The correspondents who had been chased out of Burma or Singapore were dismayed when they learned the practical consequences of MacArthur's new system. Amid the horror and humiliation of fleeing the Japanese, these reporters had often been on the receiving end of overzealous British censorship, which, they believed, had created a misinformed home front that tended to underestimate the Japanese threat. Worse, it had also prevented the Allies from honestly considering what had gone wrong, in order to make the necessary improvements. Landing in Australia, haggard and distrustful, these refugee reporters were so appalled when they realized that MacArthur seemed bent on making the same mistakes as the British that they even forgot about their normal professional rivalries.[9]

E. R. "Al" Noderer and George Weller were cases in point. At first glance, the two men were a study in contrasts: the former a "chubby" grafter who worked for McCormick's *Tribune*, the latter an urbane intellectual who was one of the stars of Knox's *Daily News*. Their time in Singapore, however, had erased any personal or professional differences. And on learning that the British had refused to accredit Noderer, Weller had done his "best to try to persuade [the British] War Office to forgive the isolationist *Chicago Tribune*" reporter.[10]

Both men soon found themselves in Australia, where their first impressions of Melbourne were clouded by the chaos surrounding the simplest of tasks. Accreditation seemed to take forever, even for the biggest names, while the existing communications network was unable to handle the pressure created by the arrival of so many correspondents.[11] On censorship, Noderer, who worked for a MacArthur-friendly newspaper, accepted that a strict policy was "not unreasonable" given the threat Japan posed to Australia. But even Noderer was soon complaining that the censors were giving him no feedback on what they were cutting from his stories.[12] Weller was much more caustic. Privately, the *Daily News* man conceded that he could just about forgive all the wasted hours over despatches [*sic*], the administrative injustices, the passing of stories in one quarter that have been forbidden elsewhere, and the withholding from the American public of non-security information which would give them some idea of the huge task before them. One could forgive these things if there were a disposition to recognize them in military quarters. But aside from a striving on the part of the American press officers to change the administrative setup for "smoother" operation, there is little recognition here of the necessity for political education of the American people to overcome the nonsense they have been given for the first months of the war.[13]

By far the most influential "nonsense" came in the form of MacArthur's official communiqués. In the Philippines, these documents had acquired a reputation for grandiloquently extolling MacArthur's virtues. Initially, their Australian counterparts proved to be mind-numbingly dull, for the simple reason that, as one reporter put it, "after the sensational torrent of Japanese conquest in the early months of 1942, the stream of war had stagnated."[14] To the north of Australia, Japan had captured the important air and naval base at Rabaul in January, following this up by grabbing a toehold in northern New Guinea in March, but then its offensive had stalled at the Battle of the Coral Sea. As a result, a typical MacArthur communiqué during May and June said little more than "Enemy air activity has diminished" or "The enemy attacked again, at night, without effect."[15]

With so little to report, the correspondents soon began to balk at their tedious workdays. Many passed their mornings reading the newspapers or meandering around Melbourne's tidy streets. Afternoons would be spent in Diller's press office, where press conferences were held promptly at one and six. The material gathered in these sessions went into a dispatch that had to be filed with the wireless office three blocks away before ten in the evening, after which the correspondents were free. In other parts of the world, the more convivial would use this downtime for alcohol-fueled parties with close colleagues, but in southern Australia even this form of solace seemed in surprisingly short supply. Sebring, who had formed a number of close friendships on the boat over from San Francisco, found Melbourne particularly isolating. "There is quite a corps of correspondents around," he remarked in early April, "but I seldom see them except at the press conferences."[16]

When MacArthur moved his General Headquarters (GHQ) north to Brisbane in July, the situation threatened to get worse. The sudden influx of

Americans almost overwhelmed this small city, whose population had been just over three hundred thousand before the war.[17] While MacArthur moved into an apartment in the Lennon's Hotel, Diller took over three floors of a big office building, one for censors, one for wireless operators, and one for his daily press conferences. With only two elevators, the reporters soon settled into a tiresome daily routine that revolved around

> jostling and shoving to see who got into which car and which car descended first. Then there was a scramble for positions at the typing tables, and finally a race to see who could compress the day's news release into the fewest significant words and thus have his message be first checked in and sent out.[18]

Elsewhere in the city, American reporters quickly discovered a dearth of their most basic needs, including cigarettes and Scotch, with bottles of the latter costing anywhere from $5 to $32. Accommodation was at a particular premium. Diller's men helped American reporters pick up some of the better rooms—to the consternation of locals, who were even more riled when they heard the Americans complain about the primitive plumbing.[19]

Back home, what troubled American media bosses was the paucity of hard news coming out of Brisbane. Some editors even began to wonder if MacArthur had put their correspondents in the "dog house" for not being sufficiently sycophantic.[20] Others began to ask why it was costing them so much to receive so little. The AP, which many newspapers relied on for communiqué-based stories, was particularly worried about the impact on its bottom line. One AP executive calculated that his organization's costs had spiraled from $800,000 a year before the war to $1.25 million, and he laid the blame squarely on the duplication of uninformative bulletins from distant battlefields. "For instance," he complained, "the MacArthur communiqué is brought in *three ways* simultaneously, night after night. One of the ways costs 60 cents a word and the communiqué sometimes runs several hundreds of words. So that often, that one little story, of little importance that day, and given only a stick or two inside, costs $200."[21]

For reporters, the best chance both to regain a sense of purpose and to appease their bosses would be to produce battlefield stories from the front. The first real prospect of action in Australia came from the air war. US bombers had been operating from the region around Townsville, north of Brisbane, since February. The reporters who headed in this direction all checked into the Queens Hotel, which, as one of them recalled, "was a rather ramshackle affair situated on the waterfront." They then hunted for something to write about, only to encounter a variety of obstacles.

* * *

The first roadblock involved the black troops who arrived in April, commanded by white officers and under orders to begin the construction of more airfields. MacArthur hoped that by sending these men to the remote north he would "prevent friction or resentment on the part of the Australian government or people at the presence of American colored troops," but other difficulties quickly arose. The landscape in this part of the country was flat and barren. The work was often backbreaking and dull, and the men had little to do during their free time.[22]

One evening, Robert Sherrod got talking to an officer in the bar of the Queens Hotel, who told him "about the problem between the white and colored soldiers." After a recent fight in town, white soldiers had massively overreacted by rounding up more than a hundred black GIs "with bayonets and loaded guns." A much worse incident came a short while later, when, as Sherrod learned,

> a company of Negroes got their rifles and determined that they would kill their commanding officer, a Captain Francis Williams of Columbus. They fired several hundred rounds of ammunition at his tent (he was in a slit trench, later escaped without facing the almost certain death which it was his duty to face as an officer). When other officers tried to escape the camp to obtain help, they were fired upon (in a half track) with a fifty-caliber machine gun.[23]

After gathering all the details of this "mutiny," Sherrod thought he had "one of the biggest stories of the war," but he also believed it "can't be written— and . . . shouldn't be written" for publication. Instead, he compiled a private account, which he handed to a young visiting congressman named Lyndon B. Johnson to take back home to his editors. Johnson considered the report so "hot" that he destroyed the original and wrote a copy that excised all the references to himself or Sherrod. He then buried the document in his files, ensuring that the mutiny never became an issue during the war.[24]

Before long, the reporters who remained in Townsville started to fear that other stories might prove equally difficult to tell. The cameramen had the hardest time. As Joe Dearing of International News Photos told a *Time* editor,

"Absolutely no cooperation is afforded photographers by the Army or the Australians.... At Townsville," he added, "photographers are not allowed any place near the air field."[25]

Print correspondents were permitted inside the bases, only to find that they were banned from boarding a mission to bomb Japanese bases at Rabaul and in northern New Guinea. The small number of available planes, the PROs explained, were "badly worn" and "inferior" to what the Japanese were using. "The odds against them," Sherrod learned, "are terrific." After one aircraft crashed, killing a group of senior officers, MacArthur issued a direct order "forbidding correspondents [from] going on bomber raids."[26] The reporters were naturally disappointed, but in compensation they discovered a loophole in the censorship regulations that allowed them to "freely interview and quote US combat personnel."[27]

On April 11, Byron Darnton succeeded in getting the censors to pass his conversations with pilots who, having just returned from a raid on Rabaul, were anxious to strengthen MacArthur's perennial demand for more resources. "We can clean them up," he recorded one of them as saying, "if we get enough planes." Following up on this success, Darnton began to tour the various places that these young airmen called home, from rudimentary billets in the bush to bases in which the radio always seemed to play American dance tunes. "They have no illusions about the fact that the life they are living is dangerous," Darnton told his readers a month later, but, he hastened to add, their sleeping arrangements "are comfortable enough" and they "are getting pretty good chow."[28]

From late July, a confluence of factors made Townsville an even more attractive destination. First, there were the Japanese landings at Buna on the northeastern coast of New Guinea, followed by the enemy's attempt to push down the Kokoda track to capture Port Moresby in the south. MacArthur and his senior officials were so disappointed with the air force's initial response to these attacks that they talked angrily about "what a terrible state the air was in." Luckily, help was at hand. In late July, Major General George C. Kenney arrived in Brisbane to take over MacArthur's air war. A brash, feisty figure, Kenney quickly reorganized his new command, gathering together sufficient bombers "to put on a real show." Kenney's focus was on knocking out enemy "air strength until we owned the air over New Guinea," but he was also quick to exploit other opportunities, from helping to thwart a Japanese landing on the eastern tip of New Guinea in August to using his planes to ferry large numbers of US troops to the island in November.[29]

Although not part of the Bataan gang, Kenney quickly became a MacArthur favorite. He was a hit with the press, too, in a way that even MacArthur appreciated. Soon after Kenney arrived in Brisbane, Lee Van Atta of the INS visited the air commander in his office. Kenney was not yet in a position to issue a formal press statement, but he was almost certainly the major source of a story that Van Atta managed to get past the censor, which repeated a familiar MacArthur gripe: namely, that Washington was ignoring his command, while lavishing resources on the European theater. "American machines and supplies in this area," Van Atta wrote, "at present represent less than three days of production power of the United States"—a bold claim that brought a sharp rebuke from Marshall, who accused MacArthur of "objecting to our strategy by indirection."[30]

Whatever the size of Kenney's force, reporters appreciated the new drive he brought to the air campaign. For a start, it gave them something more up-lifting to write about, especially when MacArthur allowed reporters to mention Kenney by name. "He believes in hitting the enemy hard in one place," noted a typically glowing report. He also "believes in getting out and chewing the rag with his pilots. He told one group in the operational zone," Noderer revealed to his readers, "that they could win decorations by shooting Japs out of the air, but would get nothing for shooting them up on the ground."[31]

Soon, Kenney's energetic policy brought an even bigger benefit. As more planes began ferrying men across the Coral Sea, the correspondents were allowed to cadge a lift to witness the battles that promised to reverse the fortunes of war in this part of the world.[32]

"Only the Two of Us"

Despite their desperation to get to the front, many correspondents felt an understandable sense of trepidation when they contemplated heading to New Guinea. Little was known about this large island. Much of the terrain remained unmapped. The natives had a reputation for hunting with poisoned arrows and using human heads for trophies. The correspondents who had witnessed the bloody Australian effort to delay the Japanese advance along the Kokoda track returned with terrible tales of enervating heat, swarming mosquitoes, and debilitating illnesses, including malaria, dengue fever, and tropical dysentery. Osmar White was one. Having spent seven months in this hostile land, White told his American counterparts in Brisbane that the conflict with the Japanese "was almost incidental," explaining "that the real fight was an incessant battle against exhausting terrain, climate, disease, and accident."[33]

The last of these tribulations was particularly alarming to anyone about to board one of the overworked planes that were making the seven-hundred-mile trip to Port Moresby. The entire pressroom knew all about Mel Jacoby's tragic plane accident in late April: how he had been killed on a runway in northern Australia, hit by an American fighter that had careened out of control as it tried to take off.[34] Everyone heading to New Guinea also knew how the region's tropical weather systems greatly accentuated the chance of a major accident—how, as one survivor put it, a plane "skated, skidded, staggered, slithered, rocketed its way through air that was as rough and solid seeming as an angry sea." And then there was Vern Haugland's terrible ordeal, which sent a chilling shiver up every war correspondent's spine.[35]

Haugland, a gangly, six-foot-three AP man who weighed just 165 pounds, was not the most seasoned of war correspondents. He had come to Australia directly from the wire service's Los Angeles bureau, where his most eye-catching assignment had been to date Hollywood's ten most eligible ladies.[36] In comparison, he found life in southern Australia a major letdown, and so he headed north to Townsville at the earliest possible opportunity. After pumping everyone he met there for information, he soon learned that places were available on four planes heading to New Guinea. After a coin toss, he won a berth on a B-26 medium bomber that was scheduled to depart on August 7.[37]

Everything went smoothly on the long flight until the plane, as it approached New Guinea, flew into a large cloud bank. The disoriented pilot, low on gas and fearful of crashing into the mountains, ordered all on board to don their parachutes and bail out. Haugland survived the jump, but he had injured his shoulder and lost his glasses. He also had no idea where he was, had nothing to eat, and as he confessed later, knew little about the jungle except what he had gleaned from Hollywood movies starring Dorothy Lamour and Bette Davis. Teaming up with the plane's copilot, who had landed close by, he found a river and decided that following it downstream offered the best chance of getting through the "towering mountain wall." The two men separated when Haugland, with his sore shoulder, was unable to climb a cliff. Weakened by ten days of walking, he rested beside a river. Not until the end of August did he set off again. Half-starved and feverish, he made tortuously slow progress until finally finding refuge in a village. By now, he was so ill that he had little idea where he was. Nor did he remember how he made it back to Allied lines after forty-three days on the missing list.[38]

Haugland's epic ordeal had various repercussions for media coverage of the New Guinea campaign. For a start, his survival story made such great copy that as soon as the AP's editors got their hands on Haugland's diary, they circulated it to newspapers across the nation. The resulting attention

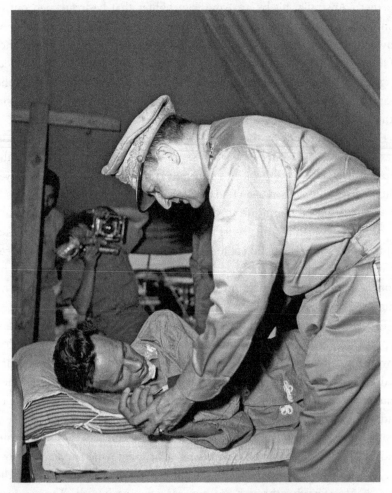

Fig. 4.1. MacArthur leans sympathetically over the hospital bed of Vern Haugland, who had just spent forty-three days in the New Guinea jungle. The general would award the reporter the Silver Star as a symbol of his "devotion and fortitude."

© AP/Shutterstock.

went a long way to framing New Guinea as a battle against the elements and terrain as much as a fight against the Japanese. Haugland's own victory over these conditions had been a pyrrhic one. He finally arrived in Port Moresby so weakened that he was in no state to carry on covering the war. New Guinea had claimed its first journalist victim, but he would not be the last, as conditions continued to hamper, if not totally sabotage, the reporting of this campaign.[39]

* * *

At least Haugland's ordeal failed to deter others from boarding a plane from Townsville. Lewis Sebring's thinking was typical. The *Herald Tribune* man had talked extensively to Osmar White about the taxing conditions he would face in New Guinea. He had also followed the story of Haugland's crash and rescue with horrified fascination, but he still decided to make the trip, driven by a familiar motive: "the fact," he wrote to his family, "that I might get more news here than on the mainland, which after all is pretty far removed from activities."[40]

Landing safely in Port Moresby, Sebring found a town ravaged by war, dust, and heat. About twenty correspondents lived "in a one story rectangular shaped hut with wallboard sides and a tin roof." Next door was their small office, kitted out with a telephone connected to the military field system and a "rough wooden table" on which to write. At mealtimes, the compulsory first course was always "five grains of quinine passed around in a bottle" to ward off malaria. To Sebring, the main compensation was the "magnificent scenery," particularly the Owen-Stanley mountains to the north and the Coral Sea to the south. He spent many a pleasant hour "on a rickety wooden balcony" gazing at the latter, "with a fine ocean breeze blowing in, and the sea sparkling beyond a screen of waving palm trees."[41]

The correspondents also spent much of their time swapping stories, chatting about the past, and considering their current predicament. Port Moresby, they all agreed, was a relatively safe posting. The main dangers came from the regular enemy raids on nearby Allied airfields and the occasional out-of-control bushfire ignited to kill mosquitoes, one of which burned down the correspondents' kitchen. Yet New Guinea, the reporters concluded, was too far removed from the normal trappings of civilization, although the isolation did foster a sense of solidarity—a feeling that the reporters were part of a close-knit gang of their own. Elsewhere, whenever the war promised to bring correspondents together, professional rivalries invariably pulled them apart. In New Guinea, with MacArthur's handpicked censors poised to gut anyone's scoop, even the most ambitious reporter soon realized there was little to be gained by going behind everyone else's back.[42]

Haugland's sudden appearance in mid-September only added to the feeling of fellowship, for it provided a timely reminder, if any were needed, that beyond the relatively safe confines of the Port Moresby press camp lay the mysterious, and highly dangerous, jungle. The reporters certainly pampered Haugland during his treatment at the local hospital. Some sent him fresh fruit, while Darnton, who had been one of the first correspondents in town, and Noderer, who had arrived in the middle of September, both visited him daily, until the time came to head closer to the fighting.[43]

* * *

By October, the Japanese were in full flight back to their northwestern base around the small beach town of Buna. To wipe out this position, MacArthur reinforced Australian forces with the American Thirty-Second Division under the command of Major General Edwin F. Harding, whose first job was to concentrate men and supplies near Buna. For this task, Harding deployed three modes of transport: foot-slogging along primitive jungle trails, an airlift into newly constructed airfields, and a ship shuttle along the northwestern coast.[44] If Haugland's epic ordeal had underlined the perils of traveling around New Guinea by air and foot, then what befell Byron Darnton when he joined the ship shuttle made it clear that a journey by sea could be even more dangerous.

Since arriving in Australia in March, Darnton had invariably been in the vanguard, making it to Townsville and then Port Moresby before most of his peers. In October, as the Thirty-Second Division moved toward Buna, he was "hot to be on the spot for the first contact of [the] American Army ground troops" with the enemy. As well as the normal desire of any war correspondent to be at the heart of the action, he had an added motive. Darnton had fought with the Thirty-Second Division on the Western Front in World War I, and he was eager to accompany it into its first battle in this new war.[45]

Pongani, a small settlement thirty miles along the coast from Buna, was Darnton's destination. Engineers planned to construct a small airstrip there, but until this was ready the sea offered the best route to the front. On October 17, Darnton grabbed a spot on one of the first two troop carriers heading in this direction. He sat alongside Lieutenant Bruce Fahrenstock, who was in charge of small-boat operations in the area, and at first everything proceeded smoothly. Then, midmorning, American planes appeared overhead. Allied air support of land and sea operations was still in its infancy. Pilots were inexperienced and overworked. They also had no way of liaising with friendly troops on the ground, and in this instance they mistook the troop carriers for enemy ships. The result was disaster. US planes dropped their bombs on the American flotilla, killing both Darnton and Fahrenstock instantly.[46]

The news sent shockwaves through the theater. MacArthur, who had met Darnton just before he left for the front, praised his "gallantry and devotion" and told his editor that he had "fulfilled the important duties of war correspondent with distinction to himself and the *New York Times*." Harding, who considered Darnton "one damn good correspondent and swell guy," confessed that he was deeply "distressed" by his death.[47] His fellow reporters were even more distraught. Darnton had been a man the rest of the New Guinea gang had looked up to, and six of them acted as pallbearers at his funeral. Slowly, somberly, they carried his redwood coffin draped in an American flag as it made its way to a resting place "under a croton tree brilliant with flaming red blossoms." "He was a fine person," his former comrades all agreed, "and such an integral part of the Port Moresby press group that it was difficult to realize he was gone."[48]

* * *

Despite the sense of loss, half a dozen reporters still headed north toward Buna over the next few weeks, including Noderer and Sebring, who arrived at Pongani's new airstrip on November 13. Almost immediately, both men received troubling reminders of the fate of Haugland and Darnton. First they spotted "two wrecked planes" on the runway. Then, after walking along a track hacked through the jungle, they hitched a ride on a troop ship that would take them to divisional HQ at Embogu, a few miles to the west. All the time at sea, they kept a "wary eye on [the] sky" for any planes, American or Japanese, that might suddenly swoop down and destroy their small, vulnerable vessel.[49]

Arriving safely at Embogu, the two reporters received a warm greeting from Harding, who emerged from his grass hut to explain that they were "free to go anywhere." Sebring decided to stay at the HQ, but Noderer pressed on eight miles closer to the front, where a small group of correspondents had established a primitive camp next to an artillery position. It proved a challenging place to live. The rain poured so relentlessly that nothing ever remained dry. The size of the insects was scarcely believable: "spiders as big as saucers that crawl inside your mosquito net," noted Noderer one night, "butterflies as big as birds, lightning bugs like flashlights." Dysentery, malaria, and "jungle rot" soon began to take a toll. Before long, conditions were so grim that even Brisbane began to acquire a rosy glow in the reporters' imaginations. One night, Noderer sat on the beach in his damp clothes with two colleagues, and they mulled over the fun they would have if they ever made it back to the Australian city.[50]

That prospect looked increasingly distant when the Japanese finally appeared and added the riskiest ingredient yet to a hazardous cocktail that already contained torrid weather, tropical diseases, and military snafus. Late on the afternoon of November 16, a flotilla of four ships, one of them containing Harding, came under sustained attack from Japanese planes. Almost instantly, the boats were in flames. Harding managed to swim to the shore, but twenty-four men were killed in the attack, including an official Australian photographer. All the supplies were also lost, which only added to the sense of gloom, for it meant that everyone, including the reporters, would have to get by on severely curtailed rations during the next few days.[51]

Noderer had watched this Japanese raid unfold from his tent on the beach. After it was over, he took out his notebook and pencil—typewriters were not much use in these conditions—and compiled an account of what had happened, including Harding's swim through shark-infested waters, although he knew that he had little chance of getting anything back to his editor.[52]

The lack of a reliable communications network became particularly troubling from November 19, when Harding launched the first in a series of fruitless attacks to wipe out the Japanese positions around Buna. With the torrential rain often reducing visibility to a minimum, the reporters had to work out what was happening from conversations with officers and soldiers who had been to the front. Even after they managed to scrawl out something on a soggy piece of paper, they had little chance of it getting very far. On one occasion, Noderer handed a dispatch to an officer who was returning to Pongani by boat, but the man jumped into the water the minute he heard the sound of approaching enemy planes. Noderer then gave his story to an Australian solider who planned to leave on another boat, but his vessel ran aground on a reef. Only when "native runners" agreed to carry a bundle of dispatches "thru forests, downstream, and along the coast in dugout outrigger canoes" did Noderer finally get something to Port Moresby, from where it was flown to Australia for radio transmission to America.[53]

Realizing that they were effectively incommunicado at their forward positions, many correspondents were already thinking of making a trip back to Port Moresby when the Japanese returned again, late in the afternoon of November 22. This time, the enemy dive bombers targeted the artillery position adjacent to the reporters' tents, pounding the area for fifteen minutes with great accuracy. The reporters dashed to their slit trenches, which, thankfully, provided sufficient protection from the bombs. But as Noderer remarked in his notebook, this was "the baptism of fire for most of the correspondents and some of them don't like it. Two of the toughest ones," he added, "are pretty terrified. One is shaking like a proverbial leaf, with sweat pouring off his brow."

After the raid was over, Noderer went off to eat some C-rations, while the other correspondents engaged in a heated debate about the wisdom of remaining so close to the front. Too many of their colleagues, the more nervous pointed out, had already become victims, and they had no desire to join the lengthening casualty lists. When the debate finally ended, Noderer asked Murlin Spencer of the AP how many reporters would still be in camp that night. He received a stunning reply. "Only the two of us," Spencer announced. "The rest have gone." "That was the last they saw of the war," Noderer observed. "Some of them went all the way to Brisbane—1000 miles."[54]

* * *

Even Noderer and Spencer did not last long at the forward press camp. That night, they moved their tents into the jungle, hoping that the dense vegetation would provide a modicum of protection if the Japanese planes reappeared. Then on November 25, they hiked for six and a half hours back to Embogu, where they hoped to get their stories out. Spencer, aware that his UP rival had already left for Port Moresby, decided to head in the same direction—and before long, he would be listed by his employer as "definitely but not dangerously ill," having caught a tropical bug.[55]

Noderer was also suffering. Exhausted from trekking around the jungle, he spent a few days at divisional HQ trying to recuperate. Then, when Harding moved his headquarters to Dobradura on November 29, Noderer summoned the strength to join him on the "hot, tiresome" fourteen-mile jungle march. Harding believed that he needed the better communications on offer at Dobradura in order to make the case for more resources, but the move only sealed his fate.[56] When MacArthur learned how badly the battle was going, he summoned Lieutenant General Robert Eichelberger, his hard-driving, charismatic I Corps commander, and instructed him to capture Buna as quickly as possible.[57]

By the time that Eichelberger arrived in Dobradura on December 1, Noderer knew that his perseverance was paying off. He was, he confided in his notebook, "the only American correspondent within 120 miles of the front," a fact that Eichelberger, who was no stranger to cultivating the press, recognized instantly.[58] "My orders are to take Buna," the general told the reporter shortly after his arrival, "or stay in the jungle pushing up the trees." He would do this, Eichelberger explained candidly, not only by replacing a number of battalion commanders, but also by instilling a new fighting spirit into the men. Noderer came away impressed. "Eichelberger," he wrote in his notebook, "is big, loud, and full of energy. He is sort of [a] cheerleader type. He is active."[59]

Just how active soon became clear. On December 3, Tillman Durdin of the *New York Times* arrived at Dobradura, disoriented, like so many before him, by an hour-long plane ride from Port Moresby that had transported him from "a world of dryish, sparsely forested hills and comparative security" to "a world of wet, green jungles and bitter combat."[60] Durdin was an old China hand, with more than ten years' experience in Asia, and Noderer was glad to have him around for company. So was the publicity-conscious Eichelberger, who invited the two men to accompany him on a trip to Buna.

The party left at 7:00 a.m. on December 5, in time to reach the frontline command post before an attack that was due to start at 10:00. The Allied planes appeared first, softening up the enemy lines, before the artillery began to fire. Soon after, Eichelberger received a call from someone at an advanced observation post, claiming that American artillery was hitting American troops. He immediately headed outside to see for himself, asking Noderer and Durdin if they wanted to join him. Their honest answer would have been no. "My own idea of covering a war," thought Noderer, "does not include going forward to see if the artillery is falling short, but what are you going to do when a General asks you if you want to come along?"[61]

Slowly, nervously, the two correspondents inched through the jungle, always on the alert for enemy snipers, until finally they reached the frontline, less than one hundred yards from enemy positions. Buna Village, and beyond that Buna Mission, were agonizingly close. Eight hundred GIs had gathered and were making nervy last-minute preparations. As soon as they launched their attack, Eichelberger ushered the two reporters into a deep trench. Here, they felt a measure of safety, as hell broke loose all around: machine-gun, sniper, and rifle fire mixed with the sound of mortar shells and then the distressing sight of wounded men returning to friendly lines.[62]

As ever, the Japanese soldiers fought stubbornly, although by early afternoon Noderer and Durdin were able to visit a recently captured enemy position. Then, a few hours later, the reporters learned that a group of riflemen led by Sergeant Herman Bottcher had managed to hold a portion of the beach to the east of the village. The cost of the day's battle had been high—roughly 150 casualties, according to Eichelberger, including two of his most valued officers—but with Bottcher leading the way, American troops had shown they could fight aggressively. Content with what he had seen, at 4:00 p.m. the general called a halt to the attack.[63]

The reporters returned to Dobradura delighted to be in one piece.[64] They also had a major scoop to write up: the first eyewitness account of a major American attack on Japanese positions in New Guinea. Although the censorship guidelines prevented the publication of Eichelberger's name, both Durdin and Noderer placed "the commanding officer's" heroics at the center of their accounts. They detailed how this unnamed general had led his troops by example, recounting his lack of concern for enemy bullets and his solicitude for their own safety.[65] The two reporters also reserved a special place for Bottcher, whose name the censors were happy to release. Bottcher, observed Noderer, was a "full-bearded San Francisco whirlwind with a wild look in his eyes." During the December 5 attack, Noderer explained, he took twelve men and "fought his way against heavy machine gun fire thru the jungle to the beach between the village and Buna mission, reaching a point which has been the allied objective for some days." "Bottcher was wounded in the hand," Noderer reported,

> but after receiving first aid he returned to the fray. As night fell he still held the beachhead—important to the Americans because it prevented the Japs from shifting reinforcements back and forth between Buna village and Buna Mission, which are separated by 500 yards of beach.[66]

Back in Chicago, Colonel McCormick was so impressed with this story that he began to place Noderer in the same exalted company as Stanley Johnston, which meant awarding him a substantial financial bonus. Maloney, meanwhile, was worried that jungle life might be seriously affecting the health of the *Tribune*'s newest star. He therefore wrote to Noderer asking if he needed a rest, only to discover he was too late. The reporter had already returned to

Port Moresby—where he was regaling his colleagues with tales about a "very frightening 18-foot bush python [that] had developed the habit of creeping in under mosquito nets and sharing blankets with terrified American soldiers"—when he received a message from Diller's office. On the basis that Noderer had been "at the front longer than anyone else," MacArthur's PRO instructed him to return to Australia in order to free up a combat spot for another news organization.[67]

* * *

With Al Noderer slated to leave, George Weller of the *Chicago Daily News* joined Durdin at the front. Each day, these two veteran reporters would watch the enemy's last-ditch resistance from various vantage points, before sending back vivid reports that finally gave the home front some sense of how vicious the fighting had been. "The bitter battle of Buna," wrote Weller on Christmas Eve, "grows harsher as it progresses. Today on the right flank," he explained, "where the prize is a mud-slogged airdrome with two wrecked Jap fighters on it, tanks again pushed our line farther up the field in what resembled a bloody gain for yardage upon some incredible football stadium of enormous size." The reason for all the gore, Durdin told his readers that same day, was simple. "The Japanese way of fighting here," he wrote,

> has made this a battle of extermination. The Japanese have made of the usual procedures of surrender and the few remaining rules of warfare, such as respect for the wounded and for hospitals, tricks to lure the enemy into exposing himself to destruction. It is only natural that Japanese treachery has provoked intense bitterness among Allied troops. No Allied soldier here now expects any humanitarian consideration or fair conduct of the Japanese.[68]

Yet, however vivid such reporting or however clear-cut this apportioning of the blame, one salient factor blunted the impact of these dispatches: only a small number of reporters were managing to survive for any length of time at the front. As a result, the vast majority of newspapers had to rely on the output of HQ-based reporters who, fed a diet of MacArthur communiqués, reiterated a familiarly upbeat tale. Some remained enthralled by Kenney's dynamism, proclaiming that his air force enjoyed complete superiority over Japanese forces in New Guinea.[69] Others emphasized just how close the Allied troops were to capturing Buna, claiming that they were "contracting" the enemy's grip on the town, using intensive artillery barrages as well as tanks. With the last remaining enemy troops trapped in a shrinking beach-head, all the stories carrying a Brisbane dateline increasingly agreed on one thing: the Japanese were doomed.[70]

"Calculated to Mislead the American Public"

The bloody fighting at Buna Mission finally ended on January 3, and the next day Marshall sent a message of congratulation. MacArthur's response revealed just how bitter he had become. "However unwarranted it may be," he told the army chief of staff, "the impression prevailed that this area's efforts were belittled and disparaged at home, and despite all my efforts to the contrary the effect was depressing."[71]

In one sense, MacArthur was correct. Although no one in America had deliberately belittled or disparaged the Buna campaign, few had paid it much attention either. This was particularly true of some of the nation's most important editors. When asked for the year's ten best stories, bosses at two of the wire services overwhelmingly placed the North African invasion in the top spot. Their other picks included Japan's victories across Southeast Asia, the battles at Stalingrad, Coral Sea, Midway, and Guadalcanal, as well as the Dieppe raid and the Cripps mission to India. Significantly, though, not one of them found a place on their list for the New Guinea campaign.[72]

Nor had the major newspapers created much space for MacArthur's offensive. The *Chicago Daily News* was the major exception. With Weller producing "first-class copy" direct from the Buna battlefield, his editor ran a major piece featuring his work, which "was reproduced in a number of the [*Daily News'*] client papers."[73] In stark contrast, most other outlets relegated this campaign to near the bottom of their priority list. *Time* was typical. "There were many issues in 1942 and 1943," an internal audit for the magazine discovered, "when General MacArthur was not mentioned at all (for example, the index only lists seven references to him in the fall of 1942)."[74] The *New York Times* was equally neglectful. Throughout December, two events dominated the *Times'* front page: the North African invasion and the fighting around Stalingrad, with 41 percent of its war stories concentrating on the former and 21 percent on the latter. Even the navy's war in the Pacific accounted for 17 percent. MacArthur, by contrast, had to make do with a paltry 11 percent, placing his campaign above only the Allied bombing of occupied Europe and the China-Burma theater, which garnered 9 percent and 4 percent, respectively.[75]

However vexing MacArthur found this neglect, it was hardly Washington's fault. The cruel jungle conditions had hampered reporting from the start. Indeed, the difficulty of travel; the friendly-fire incidents; the insects, illnesses, and weather; and, finally, the sheer danger of getting near the battlefield: all of these factors had combined to ensure that this campaign had rarely been covered by correspondents close to the fighting.

Throughout, MacArthur had tried to use his own communiqués to compensate. Each day, he would sit with a yellow pad and pencil working out what he wanted to say before handing the first draft to a typist and "then correcting, and refining, sometimes through half a dozen more versions until he was satisfied." Yet, despite all this hard work, few editors back home thought that these carefully crafted documents carried the same punch as eyewitness accounts.[76]

According to some of the battle-scarred reporters, MacArthur's communiqués also had little grounding in fact. Noderer reached this disturbing conclusion within weeks of returning to Australia. At first, the *Tribune* man focused on regaining his strength, having lost twenty pounds during his time in the jungle. Then on January 8, as Allied forces pivoted to the west to attack the final Japanese positions on the Buna front around the swampy delta at Sanananda Point, MacArthur loudly proclaimed victory. At the battlefield, Eichelberger reacted with disgust when he heard about this announcement. "Public-relations officers on General MacArthur's staff," he wrote in his memoirs, "chose to call the last phase of the . . . campaign a 'mopping-up operation.' Instead, it was a completely savage and expensive battle." From the safety of the rear, Noderer fully agreed. He even "suggested to Colonel Diller that he might be going out on a limb a little. I believe it will take a month to clean up Sanananda point," Noderer explained, "where 1500 to 2500 Japs are dug in."[77]

Noderer's mood was scarcely improved when the savage fighting of the next few weeks proved him correct. "These censors are driving me insane," he remarked privately on January 9. "I have never worked in a theater where there has been such a consistent attempt to distort and misrepresent the news, both by the political and military authorities." The only material that was passed in Australia, Noderer believed, "is untrue, and calculated to mislead the American public." After spending the next day "browbeating censors," he was at his wit's end. Then he heard that Diller planned to provide all war correspondents "with the assimilated rank of second lieutenant," and he snapped. "Maybe I am a snob," Noderer confessed,

Fig. 4.2. Al Noderer of the *Chicago Tribune* became highly critical of MacArthur's censorship policies after leaving New Guinea.
© AP/Shutterstock.

but I think it is because I instinctively resent any further attempt to control journalists. I screamed the house down at PR Sydney. . . . I am going mad! I sent Diller an urgent telegram: "Have you any openings for assimilated generals? Assimilated second lieutenant Noderer."

Unable to calm down, Noderer decided his only option was to leave. Like so many reporters before him, he believed that censorship in the Pacific had become so divorced from reality that he could no longer do his job properly in this theater.[78]

* * *

Before his departure, Noderer learned that MacArthur would finally allow Eichelberger's name to be released to the press.[79] All the correspondents realized what a good story this made, but Noderer had been one of the few who had accompanied Eichelberger around the front.[80] He also recalled how this fighting general had taken him into his confidence at the battlefield, while HQ-based officers in Australia only seemed to lie and cheat. On January 10, Noderer made his admiration plain. Eichelberger, he told the *Tribune*'s readers, "is a soldier's soldier. Running a war by remote control is something he doesn't understand. Instead of a rubber stamp, which forms the principal affirmament [*sic*] of many generals, 'Ike' carries a Tommy gun. He not only carries it—he uses it."[81]

MacArthur doubtless winced when he read these words. Not only did he hate anyone else stealing the limelight, but he was also acutely aware of the slights still being whispered behind his back, which disparaged him as "dugout Doug."[82] Recently, MacArthur had worked hard to demolish this particular slur. After moving his GHQ from Brisbane to Port Moresby during the early stages of the Buna campaign, he had made sure that the press had stressed that his new base was "only a short distance by air from the front lines."[83] When the reporters began to emphasize that Eichelberger had been much closer to the battle, MacArthur was incensed. Eichelberger even came to believe that MacArthur wanted to reduce him to colonel and send him home in disgrace. Whatever the truth of this allegation, Eichelberger never again tried to cultivate correspondents, telling one of MacArthur's PROs a short while later that he "would rather have you slip a rattlesnake in my pocket than to have you give me any publicity."[84]

Eichelberger's savvier colleagues also learned the lesson. Normally, a *Time* cover story was one of the highest press accolades available, but when Kenney discovered that this tribute would be coming his way in early January, he reacted with horror. As one *Time* editor remembered it, he said, "Here I am getting along fine with boss and if some of you people start playing me up as an important character in this campaign, you may break up my beautiful friendship and end my usefulness."[85]

If MacArthur had little trouble reasserting predominance inside his own theater, he also recognized the difficulty of getting the outside world interested in his battlefield achievements. He found it particularly galling that Eisenhower, a former subordinate, was dominating media coverage as the commander of the North African operation, but even this indignity paled next to his fears of what the navy might do. For most of 1942, MacArthur had been able to rely on the navy's heavy-handed censorship to shield the war at sea from the American public, but recently there had been signs that his big rival might be mending its ways. MacArthur's decision to declare victory on January 8, despite the existence of sturdy Japanese positions around Sanananda, was driven partly by his attempt to capture the headlines before the navy could declare victory in its own campaign on Guadalcanal.[86]

The outcome of this protracted battle had been in the balance since the summer, generating more and more media interest and, in the process, forcing the navy to slowly loosen the restrictions on its war correspondents. As MacArthur feared, it was at Guadalcanal, not New Guinea, where the shroud over the Pacific War would really start to slip.

5

The Shroud Slips: Guadalcanal

"Sparse Information"

In the weeks after the Battle of Midway, few Washington-based reporters relished a trip to the ugly, whitewashed Navy Building on Constitution Avenue. True, the Public Relations Division was headed by Captain Leland P. Lovette, a man most of them liked, even respected, mainly because of the sterling work he had done during an earlier stint in charge of PR. Lovette also possessed a foghorn voice that, as one journalist joked, "makes strong men tremble and women swoon." Yet no one was under any illusion that he held much sway over what news the navy released to the press. Admiral Ernest King saw to that. Still smarting from Stanley Johnston's Midway story, the irascible King continued to make sure that Lovette's daily briefings gave the reporters as little information as possible.[1]

When not harboring angry thoughts about the press, King spent much of his time after Midway contemplating how best to exploit this decisive success. Although Roosevelt and Marshall remained wedded to a Germany-first strategy that would lead to the invasion of North Africa in November, King believed it would be disastrous to adopt an entirely passive position in the Pacific. The US Navy, he was convinced, had to protect the sea lanes between America and Australia, which in turn required establishing "strongpoints" in the South Pacific or, at the very least, denying such positions to the enemy. When King learned that Japanese forces were busy constructing an airfield on Guadalcanal in the southeast of the Solomon chain, he lobbied for an American invasion of the island using the First Marine Division under Major General A. Archer Vandegrift. The risks were high, but King would not be deterred. Exactly eight months after Pearl Harbor, he pushed hard to ensure that American forces would be taking the offensive against Japan at long last.[2]

* * *

Inside the Navy Building, the decoders went into overdrive on August 7. Much to King's relief, the landing of Vandegrift's Marines on Guadalcanal took the Japanese by complete surprise, although enemy resistance was much stiffer on the islands of Tulagi, Gavutu, and Tanambogo to the north, where early estimates erroneously suggested an American casualty rate approaching 60 percent. The next day, the news was even better: the Marines had captured the precious airstrip on Guadalcanal, with the Japanese still offering little opposition. Then came disaster. In the Battle of Savo Island on the night of August 8–9, the Allies lost four cruisers. The admiral in charge also decided to withdraw the three American carriers out of harm's way, which meant the Marines were on their own. For the next twelve days, Vandegrift's men received only limited air cover and occasional supplies, while the Japanese navy began landing troop reinforcements on Guadalcanal to contest the tenuous American toehold around the airstrip, soon to be named Henderson Field.[3]

King took the Savo Island defeat particularly badly. When the duty officer woke him in the middle of the night with the dreadful news, King was so shocked that he asked for the message to be decoded again in case there had been a mistake. There had not: four big ships had been destroyed and more than a thousand sailors had perished. "That as far as I was concerned," King later remarked, "was the blackest day of the war."[4]

It was for him, perhaps, but not for the American public, who had little inkling either of the success of the Guadalcanal landings or the disaster around Savo Island. The navy's first communiqué set the tone. "United States naval and other forces," it declared on August 8, "have attacked enemy installations in the southeast part of the Solomon Islands in force and attacks are continuing." "Offensive operations against Japanese forces in the Solomon Islands are continuing," the navy repeated the next day. "Considerable enemy resistance has been encountered."[5] On August 10, King made a rare intervention in the public debate, but only to emphasize that Guadalcanal marked "our first assumption of the initiative and of the offensive." The rest of his statement simply reiterated that "the enemy has counterattacked with rapidity and vigor" and that "heavy fighting is still in progress."[6]

And so it continued. A week into the campaign, the navy revealed that the Marines were doing the fighting on Guadalcanal, that they had consolidated their beachhead, and that the all-important airfield was in American hands. Beyond that, Lovette provided few additional facts, let alone any great color, much to the growing annoyance of the Washington press corps. Some reporters began to complain openly about receiving "only sparse information" or "the scantiest [of] details."[7] On August 14, the AP was particularly savage. "There was no suggestion in tonight's communiqué on the Solomons," its Washington reporter pointedly observed, "that American escort craft had been in conflict with surface vessels of the enemy, nor was there any indication of the extent of American losses, whether by land, sea, or air. For this eighth day of the hard-fought action there was no substantial variation from the communiqué issued two days ago," and this had merely stressed that the Marines were "consolidating their position."[8]

For newspapers hoping to publish something juicier, MacArthur willingly stepped into the breach that same day. Never one to share the limelight, especially with the US Navy, MacArthur had originally protested the divided command in the southern Pacific, which had given him New Guinea and the admirals Guadalcanal, complaining that this setup would "result in nothing but confusion."[9] Yet, with the navy providing so little information on Guadalcanal, MacArthur quickly spotted an opportunity to benefit from this command confusion. On August 14, his censors allowed Brisbane-based correspondents to report on the role that his air force was playing in the battle. The next day, they permitted a story that revealed the number of ships involved in the campaign.[10]

King reacted with predictable fury, urgently requesting Marshall to instruct MacArthur "that such news releases be controlled as being seriously damaging." Equally predictably, MacArthur contested any suggestion of his own culpability, but he also added a sage observation about the consequences of the navy's tight-lipped information policy. "There is a growing volume of public opinion here," MacArthur told Marshall, "in complete resentment of the lack of authoritative information being released with regard to this operation. . . . It is my opinion," he concluded, "that there will be an explosive reaction unless the navy releases such details of this action as must be known fully to the enemy. Speculation always presents a worse picture than the truth."[11]

In Australia, speculation was already rife about the Savo Island disaster, partly because survivors soon began to arrive in Sydney, where they could be seen and would talk.[12] In the United States, too, senior media voices began to complain privately to the administration about what the managing editor of the *New York Times* dubbed "the dearth of news on the Solomon Islands." In their eyes, the navy seemed to be using the same playbook that it had deployed after Pearl Harbor—and, once again, a number of reporters and editors wondered whether the admirals were more interested in protecting their own reputations than in denying usable information to the enemy.[13]

Convinced that success—or even survival—at Guadalcanal required restricting news, King brushed aside all of these critiques. He also continued to seethe at MacArthur's sudden public intervention in the navy's big battle, viewing it as a major breach of both security and etiquette. Yet had King paused to consider MacArthur's press operations in more detail, he might have realized that, in essence, the two men shared a surprisingly similar approach. Indeed, both were focused on trying to control the news agenda from afar, using their own communiqués to reveal only what they wanted the public to know. As such, their press operations were totally different from those of a third actor in the theater. The US Marines, instead of churning out press releases written hundreds, if not thousands, of miles from the fighting, were in the process of developing a new initiative that would place their own PR men directly on the frontlines. Dubbed combat correspondents, these men would, on Guadalcanal, ultimately help to lift the veil that had shrouded so much of the Pacific War since Pearl Harbor

Combat Correspondents

Combat correspondents were the brainchild of Brigadier General Robert L. Denig, who had been the director of the Marine Corps' Division of Public Relations since July 1941. Until Denig's appointment, the Marines had viewed PR as little more than a recruitment tool. Denig himself had shared the corps' general suspicion of "puffery," insisting that he had never even heard of the term "public relations" before his appointment. His only prior press experience, he claimed, had come in France during 1918, "when the *New York Times* had published his letter to his wife describing the Battle of Soissons."[14]

Yet Denig proved to be a quick study. His first move was to feed Marine-based storylines to reporters and advertising agencies. Then in early 1942, he came up with his boldest idea. The inspiration derived partly from the ongoing controversy surrounding the navy's overzealous censorship, which was making the public "hungry for news." But Denig also recognized that the nature of the war against Japan called for something entirely new. "The Pacific," he explained, "was a mighty big place. . . . There was no telling where the big news would break. . . . It would be a great help to the civilian correspondents to realize if there were a competent newspaperman with at least every regiment who could cooperate with them." Despite the obvious logic behind the idea, Denig initially struggled to convince Thomas Holcomb, the Marine

Corps commandant, who focused more on the risks. How, Holcomb wondered, would the media view the military stepping directly on its turf? Would reporters relish being scooped by Marine officers? Would their editors consider the whole initiative to be nothing more than a brazen act of state propaganda? And then there was the current culture of the corps. Few Marine officers had "huckstered for publicity" before, and most were deeply "suspicious of the new combat correspondent program."[15]

In the early months of 1942, Denig brought all of his persistence to bear on overcoming the naysayers, until finally he received permission to enlist an initial group of ten men. Some of them came from the main news organizations in Washington, DC—the *Post*, the *Star*, and the *Times-Herald*—after a Marine turned up at their offices to ask if any of their staffers were willing to volunteer. Others entered the program via even more informal routes. James W. Hurlbut was one. A CBS publicist and former Marine, Hurlbut often visited Denig's office, where he would sit on a radiator to keep warm while pitching his latest story ideas. Then one day Denig offered him a job. Hurlbut jumped at the chance and soon found himself mentoring Herbert C. Merillat, whose qualifications to be a combat correspondent escaped everyone, including himself. A Rhodes Scholar and Treasury Department lawyer, Merillat had bumped into an old friend in a bar that April, who had told him about Denig's initiative. About to be commissioned in the naval reserve, Merillat was intrigued by the idea, despite never having fired a gun or written a dispatch. Nevertheless, Denig was impressed enough to recruit him on the spot.

From that point, the two men found the speed of events dizzying. In May, they rushed to Norfolk, Virginia, in time to board a boat for New Zealand. They arrived in Wellington in mid-June. Eight weeks later, they landed on Guadalcanal, on the first morning of the invasion.[16]

* * *

The Guadalcanal assault itself proved to be surprisingly straightforward, even for combat novices. The water was calm, the enemy nonexistent. The only excitement on the first day came from the chaos surrounding the unloading of supplies on the beach, as most Marines headed inland to locate the Japanese, leaving only a few men to sort out the cargo that kept arriving by boat.

Hurlbut and Merillat already knew that as well as producing their own stories, they would be acting as PROs, helping their civilian counterparts, as Merillat acerbically put it, "get stories when they are allowed to have them and try[ing] to keep them calm when they can't have them."[17]

Only two regular print correspondents would accompany the Marines when they landed on Guadalcanal: Robert C. Miller of the UP, known affectionately as "Baldy," who had spent the past two years covering Hollywood movie stars; and Richard Tregaskis of the INS, six-foot-seven and Harvard-educated, who had been about to head to Portugal when Pearl Harbor had changed his plans.[18] As their ship approached the Solomons, both men recognized that they were involved in something big and dangerous—they could sense it from the frenzied scuttlebutt, the compulsive polishing of weapons, and the almost obligatory attendance at religious services. "This is shaping up as the biggest story of the war," Miller told a PRO on August 6. "A million thanks for tipping me off to it. With good cooperation all around I think we can keep the datelines in the Solomons with the Navy and the Marines where they belong and not in Australia."[19]

Since the story was so huge, however, the two wire-service correspondents initially evinced little desire to cooperate with each other. Desperate "to score a scoop," Miller even concluded a private deal with the radio men on his ship, which enabled him to send a message at 0700 on D-Day morning. "UPBLOWING JAP SHORE DEFENSES STOP," Miller cabled, "MARINES READY ATTACK."[20]

Nimitz's PROs immediately blocked this dispatch "as being prejudicial to security." They also served Miller with a stern reminder that "the use of naval radio facilities for the transmission of press copy cannot be permitted."[21] Miller was duly chastened, but his period of disgrace did not last long. It ended as soon as the situation began to deteriorate.

The first sign of trouble came during the night of August 8–9. Everyone on Guadalcanal could hear the terrifying sounds of the massive sea battle around Savo Island. The next morning, Vandegrift had to deal with the practical consequences of this defeat, tightening his defensive perimeter against a possible Japanese landing and rationing the remaining food and ammunition supplies. He also briefed Miller and Tregaskis on what the situation meant for them. With the last US ships due to depart in the afternoon, Vandegrift explained that the reporters would "have to leave then or plan on staying there a probable six weeks without being able to get dispatches out."[22]

Both men decided to stay. Although they would be out of contact with their home offices, they also recognized that their newfound isolation came with a major upside: they no longer had to worry about what the other man was up to. Instead, they could focus on forging a bond with the Marines, which only deepened as they began sharing makeshift bivouacs and hastily dug foxholes while eating the same small quantities of C-rations.[23]

On August 12, Miller, Tregaskis, and Merillat joined three boats making an inspection trip to Tulagi, twenty miles to the north. Halfway across, the engine on Merillat's aging craft burned out, forcing him to jump into Tregaskis's ship in such haste that he left behind his shoes. Just beforehand, a sailor had spotted a Japanese submarine, which for an anxious few moments appeared to be catching them, until the thickening artillery barrage drove it away. Once safely ashore, the reporters enjoyed a memorable day. It began when they met Colonel Merritt A. Edson, who would become one of the bona fide heroes of the campaign. Talking in rapid, clipped sentences, Edson walked the three men through the horrors of the Tulagi invasion, pointing to the Japanese dugouts that honeycombed the island and elaborating on the enemy snipers' sneaky tactics. The Americans had won, but the fighting had been bloody. "The Japanese casualties were about 400," Edson revealed. "Not a single Nip gave up."[24]

None of the correspondents flinched at Edson's racist language. Such words were commonplace at the time, and in any case the men were increasingly preoccupied with their hazardous journey back to Guadalcanal, which, thankfully, proved to be uneventful.[25]

Soon after their return, the reporters learned that Vandegrift's prediction of a six-week break in communications had been far too pessimistic. One Marine had discovered a Japanese transmitter, and he managed, after five days of tinkering, to get it to work. Hurlbut, Merillat, Miller, and Tregaskis had already built up quite a backlog of stories, which they handed to another Marine, who patiently encrypted them for transmission. Once the dispatches reached Hawaii, however, the navy took over—and therein lay the main snag. The censors in Pearl Harbor were the same men who had driven Bob Casey to distraction, and they were still guided by the same restrictive instructions that had been drafted by senior officers "with a mania for secrecy of all sorts." However much copy they received, these censors refused to release a single word.[26]

* * *

After almost two weeks of furious work, Henderson Field opened for business on August 20. At four that afternoon, everyone watched as the first friendly planes prepared to land, and for a brief moment they allowed themselves to forget all about the sleepless nights, meager rations, and con-stant fear. At last, the Marines had their own land-based air support. The fol-lowing night, the situation improved further when Vandegrift's forces wiped out a major Japanese assault at Battle of Tenaru, on the eastern edge of the defensive perimeter. Tenaru was a pivotal moment, at least psychologically, because it shattered the image of Japanese battlefield invincibility, but it was not the only success. In a sea battle during the night of August 24–25, this time to the northeast of Guadalcanal, a powerful enemy fleet failed to secure safe passage for another batch of Japanese infantry reinforcements.[27]

With the situation looking brighter, the navy censors decided to re-lease the first eyewitness accounts on August 29. They gave the civilian correspondents the honor of going first. Miller, whose story focused on the initial Guadalcanal landing, found a particularly colorful lead. "Old Glory," he began, "is flying today over the first Japanese-conquered territory retaken by the United Nations in the Pacific War." Tregaskis, whose dispatch told of the desperate fighting to capture Tulagi, Gavutu, and Tanambogo, also presented an eye-catching angle. "A new crop of Marine heroes," the INS man wrote, "ranking with the most exalted, from Tripoli to Belleau Wood, was born in the 3-day knockdown, drag-out battle preceding our victory."[28]

Denig's combat correspondents, by contrast, produced much more stolid fare. Merillat had never written a dispatch before and had received no direc-tion from Denig about how to frame his stories. Unsurprisingly, his account was little more than a matter-of-fact rendition of his own experiences during the first days of the invasion. Hurlbut had more media experience, but he felt a different constraint after becoming a Marine mouthpiece. Determined to give nothing away to the enemy, Hurlbut focused his short dispatch on the disparity between the Marines' "comparatively small losses" and the "disas-trous casualties for the defending Japanese." "Heroism," he concluded some-what flatly, "is taken as a matter of course."[29]

* * *

Although the navy censors had belatedly opened the sluice gates, the initial result was a trickle, rather than a flood, of stories. Indeed, it was definitely not the case, as some historians have maintained, that newspaper extras were "screaming" out Tregaskis's heroic reports, "giving the home front its first sense that American boys would turn the tide."[30] In fact, Tregaskis got only two more stories into print during September, to Miller's four. And even Denig's combat correspondents added no more than a few extra drops to the shallow pool of Guadalcanal dispatches, with Hurlbut and Merillat publishing another four eyewitness accounts between them that month.

In short, the correspondents on Guadalcanal remained largely anonymous, as they discovered when Tillman Durdin of the *New York Times* and Tom Yarbrough of the AP arrived in early September. Both men were big hitters in their respective news organizations. Durdin, introspective and taciturn, was a man other reporters looked up to—a role model who meticulously recorded everything he saw but, as one admirer observed, "doesn't swallow everything he hears." He had learned his trade during ten years in China, making his name covering the infamous Nanking massacre in 1937.[31] Yarbrough, by contrast, had been schooled as a war reporter in Europe, where he had run the AP night desk during the long, dark months of the London blitz.[32]

The two men landed at Henderson Field convinced, as Merillat recorded, that "they were the first reporters to hit the island." When they discovered the truth, both became so "sick" that the mood among the small press corps immediately soured. Miller and Tregaskis took great pleasure in contrasting the "glamorous fresh uniforms" of the newbies with their own hand-washed clothes, stained by weeks of grime. Durdin and Yarbrough, in turn, exploited every opportunity to "take a dig" at the two rivals who had beaten them to the Guadalcanal story.[33]

This sniping was just one sign of how the dynamic among the reporters was starting to change. When Carleton Kent of the *Chicago Times* arrived a few days later, the five correspondents began to refer to themselves grandly as the "Guadalcanal Press Club." They even had a new base. Instead of sleeping in makeshift bivouacs or hastily dug foxholes, they bedded down in tents alongside Vandegrift's headquarters. When the general moved his command post inland on September 9, the reporters shifted as well. Their new position was "at the foot of a ridge, facing the jungle," and it was no safer. Everyone anticipated a major Japanese attack. "I wish I had a pistol," Yarbrough remarked to the others once it got dark on the evening of September 10. "The rest of us were nervous," admitted Tregaskis, "and not anxious to go to sleep. We kept up a clatter of conversation to help our spirits."[34]

Three nights later, they needed more than cheerful chatter to stave off their jitters. Shortly after the correspondents retired to bed, they were told to move well away from the ridge. Before long, the sound of rifle and machine-gun fire rose to a terrifying crescendo. The correspondents learned that the Japanese had launched a major attack on what would soon become known as

Bloody Ridge. Although Edson's crack troops bore the brunt of the fighting, the outcome hung in the balance all night. The next morning, their own press tent was still too close to the frontlines, with hidden enemy machine-gun positions just yards away. When Edson emerged from the jungle to brief Vandegrift, the correspondents began to breathe a little easier, for it meant the fighting had slackened sufficiently for this ferocious Marine to leave the frontlines. But they soon learned that Vandegrift had decided to move his HQ once again, creating more headaches. With no time to repitch their tents, the reporters spent another night sleeping in the open. For Kent and Yarbrough, it proved too much. Early the next morning, they boarded a boat to take them off the island.[35]

The three reporters who remained now began to exhibit the telltale signs that afflicted almost everyone on Guadalcanal: a torn and grubby uniform, black rings around the eyes, and a semi-emaciated frame. The chaos surrounding the move of Vandegrift's command post only made a bad situation worse. It took Merillat nine days to rustle up some cots for the correspondents to sleep on, and another two before he got them a new tent. Until then, they had to bed down under the stars. Small wonder that the remaining reporters also decided to leave.[36]

Miller was the next to go. When he learned that the UP was sending Frank McCarthy to relieve him, he was so delighted that he shaved off his grimy beard in celebration. Tregaskis soon followed, ostensibly because the quartermaster had no replacement boots in his size, but mainly because he was suffering from a bad bout of dysentery. When Tregaskis asked Vandegrift for permission to depart on September 25, the general smiled and said he had chosen the perfect time. "They're putting in a shower for me in a few days," Vandegrift revealed. "And when such luxuries come, the correspondents should go."[37] Tillman Durdin expected no such luxuries where he was going next—to report the New Guinea campaign—but, if anything, the Marines were even sadder to see him leave. Durdin had caused quite a splash among the men in the First Regiment for publicizing the phrase they had made their own: "Never a dull moment on Guadalcanal." Durdin, Merillat noted on the day he departed, was "one of the most intelligent and thoughtful of the newsmen who had descended on us."[38]

Making Known the "Unknown War"

These reporters left during a lull in the fighting, but for those who remained the respite did not last long. The Japanese high command was determined wipe out the US Marines on Guadalcanal. To make sure they had sufficient troops to fulfill this mission, the Japanese first needed to stop the American planes on Henderson Field from destroying the ships bringing Japanese reinforcements to the island. This calculation lay behind the massive naval and artillery bombardments that hit the airstrip on October 13. Two days later, with Henderson Field "unusable," Vandegrift's men could witness the dispiriting sight of thousands of new enemy troops arriving a short distance away. "They are landing 'em faster than we can kill 'em," Marines on the frontlines began to grumble. Although they couched their opinions in less colorful language, senior officers agreed that a crisis was at hand. When Vandegrift left Guadalcanal for a short conference with Admiral William F. Halsey, who had just taken over the South Pacific Command (SOPAC), he emphasized the poor physical and mental state of his troops after two and a half months in the jungle. "Can you hold?" Halsey asked. "Yes, I can hold," Vandegrift replied. "But I have to have more active support than I have been getting."[39]

The only historian to examine press coverage of Guadalcanal has claimed that the October crisis was a pivotal moment. "The desire to unmask the perilous situation of their countrymen on Guadalcanal to the public," argues Richard Frank, "—or as some astute observers believed, to prepare the nation for a defeat—triggered a major shift in the public information policy of the United States government and the armed services during October."[40] Frank's claim is well taken—up to a point. Lovette's press briefings in Washington certainly became much more downbeat in the middle of the month, prompting newspapers across the country to run alarming banner headlines. The *Boston Globe* was typical. "YANKS IN GRAVE PERIL ON GUADALCANAL," it blared on October 17.[41]

Yet the navy's sudden effort to manage public expectations was only one reason that coverage of the battle began to shift during the second half of October. An even more important catalyst was the mounting criticism directed against naval censorship. The reporters who trudged into the Navy Building each day were in an increasingly rebellious mood. They all knew that a major battle had been raging in the Solomons for more than two months, but the navy's skimpy communiqués had rarely given them enough information to detail precisely what was going on. To the severest critics, the shroud had become impenetrable. "An over-stringent censorship," the *New York Times* claimed on October 23, was "making the Pacific War the 'unknown war.'"[42]

As a matter of fact, just days earlier the navy had finally released news of the disastrous Battle of Savo Island, but in a manner that had elicited another storm of protest. The PROs at Pearl Harbor had been holding the eyewitness accounts by Clark Lee of the AP, Joe James Custer of the UP, and Jack Singer of the INS since the middle of August. When the Navy Department finally lifted this block on October 12, these wire-service correspondents quickly discovered that they had been scooped by the official communiqué, which was released many hours before their dispatches. The UP reacted particularly angrily. Custer had sustained a serious eye injury during the battle, which had left him partially blind. And his bosses claimed that the navy's inconsiderate handling of his story had an obvious counterpart in its negligent treatment of his wound.[43]

While the PROs in Pearl Harbor worked hard to refute this allegation, their colleagues in Washington suddenly faced another powerful indictment. On the night of October 11–12, the US Navy scored a significant success against a Japanese effort to reinforce Guadalcanal, destroying one enemy cruiser and three destroyers. Lovette quickly moved to announce this triumph, even though his account had to jostle for newspaper space with the belated release on the Savo Island defeat.[44] Many editors were deeply suspicious of the timing. More than one began to claim that the navy had held up "the story of these losses until such a time as their revelation could be accompanied by good news." It was a charge that stung Lovette into action. "Any appearance of 'cushioning,'" he told the editor of the *Chicago Times*, ". . . was purely coincidental." "Information," he insisted to another critic, "is a weapon in precisely the same category as ships themselves and fuel and food and ammunition. Military considerations must come first in determining when and if information is to be divulged."[45]

This security-first emphasis had long been King's mantra. In the aftermath of the Stanley Johnston controversy, Knox had initially been willing to go along with his restrictive news policy, but by fall he was starting to have second thoughts. More politically sensitive than King, Knox worried when senators on the Committee on Naval Affairs began asking pointed questions about the navy's excessive use of censorship.[46] He became positively alarmed when media surveys detected the intensity of editorial outrage on this subject, especially in his hometown. True to form, the *Chicago Tribune* was "exceptionally bitter in its attacks on censorship," but even the *Chicago Sun*, which had been set up explicitly to challenge the *Tribune*'s hold over the city's morning market, was condemning the navy for unnecessarily long delays in releasing war news. As for the *Chicago Daily News*, it too had become "consistently critical. A peculiar aspect of its objections," observed one official, "is that most of its criticism is directed against the Navy Department (publisher of the *News* is the Secretary of the Navy Frank Knox.)"[47]

On top of being criticized by his own paper, Knox knew that the claims of excessive censorship were merging with growing public demands for a unified command in the Pacific. "Charges of rivalry and lack of cooperation between army and navy forces in the Southwest Pacific were found in all media during October," noted another survey, with the government's most vociferous critics calling for MacArthur to be given total control over the war against Japan.[48] No one in the navy was prepared to countenance this suggestion, but Knox fretted that unless something was done to improve the navy's public relations, the political pressure might become unstoppable, especially with the midterm elections looming. Inside the administration, the newly created Office of War Information (OWI) was also pushing hard for the prompt release of naval losses. Knox decided to act. "The situation got so bad recently," he wrote to the publisher of the *New York Times* on November 3, "that I had to inject myself into it very vigorously and set up a new basis for the release of news."[49]

King was far from happy with Knox's intervention. The admiral had not even wanted to announce the Savo Island losses, convinced that—sixty-three days after the event—the enemy had still "received valuable information from that announcement." When the USS *Hornet* sank on October 27, he certainly did not want Japan to learn about the loss of one of America's two remaining aircraft carriers. Yet Knox insisted. Just days after the *Hornet* went down, the Navy Department announced that the carrier "was sent to the bottom by a United States warship when salvage was found to be impossible following two enemy attacks." King was so appalled that he briefly broke ranks to reveal what he considered to be the unsavory calculations behind this new openness. "We announced bad news prematurely," he complained a few weeks later, "because we were told that if we insisted on holding it until after the election, it would be charged that we had had political reasons for not announcing it."[50]

* * *

Even with this sudden gush of bad news, many newspapers continued to complain that the navy's communiqués gave their readers little sense of the conditions on Guadalcanal. Yet this, too, was about to change, albeit for reasons that had little to do with either managing or massaging information. Instead, the main reason frontline war reports suddenly started to appear in greater volume was much more prosaic.

Ever since the opening of Henderson Field, war correspondents had been able to get in and out of Guadalcanal with greater ease. Carleton Kent and Tom Yarbrough, who had left in a hurry after the Bloody Ridge battle on September 13, returned a month later. On the island, they found six other members of the Press Club residing in a "five-buck tent with a luxurious wood floor and a water-bucket shower bath." They also discovered combat conditions that were as grim as any they had seen during the early stages of the campaign, as well as personal relations that were becoming more fractious. "The gentlemen of the press," Merillat noted in his diary on October 9, ". . . were badly out of sorts yesterday—growling at each other, complaining about everything, after an unpleasant day at the front in a driving rain. They take it out on each other," Merillat observed, "and everyone else within earshot. Seeing men die around you, watching the stretchers bring out the wounded, with artillery and mortar fire blasting your ears and machine-gun bullets pinging all about does not promote good spirits and bonhomie."[51]

The situation became particularly hellish on October 13, when the Japanese launched their intensive artillery assault. Kent and Yarbrough reacted as they had a month earlier. Muttering ruefully about their newfound superstition of the unlucky number thirteen, both men scurried off the island the following morning, along with four other reporters, leaving just Robert Cromie of the *Chicago Tribune* and Henry Keys of the *London Daily Express* behind.[52]

Kent would later claim that he had departed because "the intense heat and the bombing jitters again took their toll," but he was being hard on himself.[53] The reporters knew that if they stayed, they had little chance of getting their eyewitness stories published anytime soon. For one thing, the situation on Guadalcanal was hardly conducive to writing good prose. "Between a perfect blackout every night," remarked Kent on October 17, "and air raids every day plus the exigencies of just plain living—meals, washing, and gathering news—I wouldn't get much chance to write."[54] Nor, for that matter, would he be able to guarantee that his dispatches made it back to the States. In early November, Kent discovered that his newspaper had received only three of the first sixteen stories he had filed from Guadalcanal. He felt so "heartsick" that he immediately cabled his editor: "Tired of getting shot at without avail. Suggest be more value back home unless you can get copy I risk precious neck producing."[55]

John Graham Dowling of the *Chicago Sun* was another reporter who had left the island in a hurry after the October 13 bombardment, and he used some of his time away from the combat zone to get to the bottom of the continued delays. "There are a number of unfortunate things that can happen to them," he explained.

> Censorship and the wastebasket for one. Lost in the mail for another. Their chances of survival and ultimate publication run the hazards of a tadpole striving to become a frog. However, we try. As for the time element—that is in the hands of God. It's a hell of a good story down here, but I'm afraid we can't tell it at the moment. Maybe later.[56]

In fact, it was not until the end of November that the British telecommunications company Cable & Wireless agreed to allow reporters to file a few thousand words a day from their station on Fiji. Until that point, the correspondents' best chance of getting something into print was to take a plane to Hawaii with their work tucked safely in their bags.[57] Of course, once they arrived in Honolulu, they still had to show what they had written to the censors. But with Navy Department spokesmen finally talking openly about the perilous situation on Guadalcanal, close observers noted that by the end of October this censorship had clearly "eased-up."[58]

* * *

Hanson W. Baldwin of the *New York Times* was the first reporter to exploit these new opportunities. A thirty-nine-year-old graduate of the Naval Academy, Baldwin normally analyzed events from afar, surrounded by books and maps in his New York office, but in the late summer he undertook a whirlwind trip to the South Pacific, arriving at Henderson Field on September 19.[59]

After clambering down from his plane, Baldwin headed to Vandegrift's command post, where he shocked the general with his candid appraisal of the public's ignorance of the Marines' exploits to date. The home front, he began, was "not getting a true picture of Guadalcanal," and as a result many Americans saw the Marines as "strongly entrenched, occupying most of the island." Baldwin then added that the top officials in both Washington and the Pacific had a very different opinion, viewing the Marines' "position with mounting alarm." Stunned by these revelations, Vandegrift responded with a robust defense of the campaign so far, stressing that it had caught Japan off guard and had revealed the enemy's "tactical blindness."[60]

Baldwin left the island convinced that he had gleaned "an exclusive story," although this did not make him entirely happy.[61] Before heading to Guadalcanal, he had met Nimitz, with whom he shared "rather emphatically" the media's mounting displeasure at the navy's obstructive press policy. On his return to Pearl Harbor, he offered some practical suggestions for improvements, including stationing censors closer to the action, which were soon credited with "bringing about changes in the Pacific Fleet's publicity policy."[62]

When he safely returned to the States, Baldwin was able to do what no one else had managed so far: produce a string of stories about Guadalcanal that caused a major splash. Some gave his readers a tour of what the battlefield looked like from the air—the devastation, including buildings that had turned into "heaps of ashes, the earth pitted and scarred." Others recorded how the Marines lived on the ground, sleeping under the stars and spending much of their time sheltering from shells. But most placed Guadalcanal within a broader strategic context. This battle, Baldwin stressed in late October, was acting like a "magnet," dragging the two navies into a series of costly battles. Although the United States had entered the war with fewer ships, Baldwin argued that it would ultimately be able to sustain its losses much better than the enemy. "We have one great advantage over the Japanese," he wrote, "— our productive superiority enables us to provide replacements far faster than Japan can hope to."[63]

In contrast to Baldwin's detached overviews, the other correspondents who made fleeting visits to Guadalcanal focused more on the human angle. John Hersey of *Time* and *Life* arrived in early October, having spent the past weeks with a "forlorn bunch" of sailors who had witnessed the destruction that Japanese submarines had wrought on American shipping.[64] Although the navy prevented him from writing about these losses, Hersey spent nine days on the island, during which time he compiled a vivid account of an average Marine's combat experience. Such a man, he wrote in *Life*'s November 9 issue,

> has an understanding of war that will take most Americans a long time
> to get. For one thing, he has lost several friends. He knows plenty about

fear—about huddling up in a foxhole and wishing his body were as small as a fox's when a big one is coming in with its ghostly, spiral noise. He has experienced the savage feeling of delight when a skirmish has been won.[65]

Hersey's written account carefully omitted what the average Marine knew about the goriest aspects of war—the dead bodies, the horrific wounds, the jungle diseases. In the accompanying photo essay, *Life* was almost as reticent, although, for the first time, it did publish images that gave the home front a glimpse of what this battle was like.

* * *

Photo magazines were at the height of their influence during the 1940s. With an estimated twenty-three million readers, *Life*, as one of its editors boasted, was "the most successful weekly the world has ever known"—a success based in large part on the two hundred or so pictures contained in each issue.[66]

The advent of war promised yet more success, as Americans clamored to see their troops in action, but the reality of combat initially generated a series of snags. The army and navy, fearing that a large influx of war photographers would clog up their transportation and communication networks, pushed the four major picture operators—*Life*, AP, International News Photos, and Acme—into creating the Still Picture Pool. This operated on a simple principle. "When the War Department or Navy Department releases a Pool photographer's pictures," explained *Life*, "his editor immediately provides other Pool members with a selection of duplicate prints, then negotiates for a suitable release date."[67]

Though the theory was straightforward, the practice proved troublesome. "There seems to be little or no evidence," griped one *Life* editor in September 1942, "that, because we are pool members, we are being given any better facil-ities than non-pool members," particularly when it came to "transportation to war areas." Even worse, the photographers employed by the other organi-zations in the pool came nowhere near *Life*'s high standards. "The Acme man whom Hersey picked up in Honolulu" was a case in point. "He is a local pub-licity photographer," complained the *Life* editor, "—who considers . . . that he achieved the picture of the year when he made a 'soft focus' shot of a girl crawling out of the hunk of a sewer pipe which had been dumped on a golf course."[68]

Luckily for *Life*, one of its own cameramen had managed to grab a space on the fleet heading toward Guadalcanal in early August. Twenty-five-year-old

Ralph Morse used his berth on the USS *Vincennes* to make "a complete photographic record of the landings," but then his luck ran out. The *Vincennes*
was one of the four cruisers sunk in the Battle of Savo Island. Although Morse
survived, he "lost all of his pictures and cameras," much to the dismay of his
editors, who not only had nothing to print in their magazine but also had to
foot the bill for his return to the States "to pick up new equipment."[69]

In the wake of these travails, *Life* began to contemplate making greater use
of artists like Tom Lea, who had honed his skills painting soldiers during the
national defense preparations the previous year. *Life* had always published
artwork, but with the picture pool suffering teething problems and battlefield
disasters destroying combat photos, its editors saw even greater potential in
this form. A skilled artist like Lea took weeks, if not months, to produce a
painting, which meant his work had to focus more on the human-interest
angle than topical breaking news. The censors liked this time lag, because
there was less chance of an illustration revealing sensitive information. They
also liked the fact that Lea, although keen to record what he saw, not what he
thought the public ought to see, was careful to omit any operational secrets,
like details about new weapons.[70]

On the treacherous seas around Guadalcanal, Lea's big moment came
after he witnessed the sinking of the USS *Wasp*. When *Life* published his
painting more than six months later, its readers could see, in vivid techni-
color, the impact of a torpedo striking the aircraft carrier, but Lea himself had
reservations about its power. "The colors," he explained in the short story beneath the two-page spread, "are poor inadequate symbols of the real tragedy,
and whether the picture shows that tragedy, I do not know. It is so strange to
put a howling inferno into the middle of a soft and beautiful sky and an un-
troubled tropic sea."[71]

The first photographs of the fighting on Guadalcanal were similarly ambiguous. In mid-October, Merillat forwarded a large batch of pictures to the
PRO in Pearl Harbor, who considered them "the best stuff of the war to date."
Life duly splashed these images over nine pages. One revealed a Japanese
soldier sprawled "in the universal and ungainly attitude of violent death."
Another showed a group of Marines examining a row of enemy soldiers who
"were probably methodically mowed down by American machine-gun fire
as they attacked."[72] Yet, even with the censors' new determination to reveal a
fuller depiction of the fighting, *Life* still drew the line at publishing the most
disturbing photographs it had received. One notable absentee was a picture
that, as a Marine officer noted, displayed "the extra large group of [Japanese]

dead—they were actually piled one on top of the other, at least 200 in one small area, and almost 1000 total." The magazine's editors felt its readers were not yet ready to see such horrors.[73]

* * *

By the end of November, the tide of battle was clearly turning in America's favor. In a series of bloody and confused naval engagements, the US Navy essentially sealed off the island to enemy shipping. Not only could the Japanese no longer send in fresh troops but, more important, they could not feed the men they had transported to the island, whose combat effectiveness diminished accordingly. Delighted, Knox hastened to share the good news with the American public. The result of these battles, he declared on November 17, "is to leave American forces in complete possession of the area . . . and to cause the enemy severe losses in ships and personnel." "I think it is fair to say," he added three days later, "that our hold on the island is now very secure."[74]

On the island itself, Ira Wolfert produced the most gripping eyewitness accounts of these battles. In a series of dispatches that would win him a Pulitzer Prize, Wolfert, an acclaimed novelist who was representing the North American Newspaper Alliance, told the home front of "a skillful, tenacious, heedlessly bloody attempt to reduce permanently our Guadalcanal salient by wiping out its sea armor and obliterating its garrisons, planes, and men." The night of November 13, he revealed, had been the worst:

> Those seven hours of darkness, with each moment as silent as held breath, were the blackest our troops have faced since Bataan, but at the end of them our Navy was there, incredibly, like a Tom Mix of old, like some hero of some antique melodrama. It turned the whole tide by throwing its steel and flesh into the breach against what may be the heaviest Jap force yet engaged in the war.[75]

Yet not everyone thought highly of Wolfert's work. Merillat, who was suffering from bouts of illness and fatigue, was perhaps his biggest critic. Wolfert, Merillat came to believe, "was given to florid and sometimes fanciful press stories, and often irritated the other correspondents. He had the nerve once to write a piece saying that a nearby shell explosion had knocked the typewriter off his lap when in fact he was sitting quietly in the press tent not far from me and no sort of bombardment was in progress." Merillat was particularly savage about his stories on the naval battles. "Wolfert and I and most of the correspondents were watching from a little ridge, about a mile inland, where the press tent was put up within the division command post," he wrote after the war.

> Out at sea all was noise and flame and smoke. All we knew was that a huge brawl was in progress; we hadn't a clue as to who was doing what to whom out there. Wolfert left the island after the last of the battles and wrote his dispatches from a base in the rear. He wrote as if he was in a position to describe, blow by blow, what had transpired. He took issue with parts of the Navy's communiqué (on which he was undoubtedly dependent for most of his story).[76]

Disgusted by the actions of one of the leading civilian reporters, Merillat at least took solace from the way that the Marine combat correspondents were finding their feet. During the first phase of the fighting, neither he nor Hurlbut had received any guidance from Denig on what type of stories they ought to be producing. Nor were they told how much play their first dispatches had received. That finally changed in late October, when Holcomb paid a flying visit to the island and "broke the news that their material *was* getting back and *was* all that they could hope—a smash hit."[77]

A few weeks later, a fresh wave of combat correspondents reached Guadalcanal. Unlike Merillat and Hurlbut, these men had been through eight weeks of basic training. They also brought with them a new handbook full of practical advice for making an even bigger smash hit. "Every battle produces a small crop of heroes about whom we hear," Denig tutored. "But almost every individual who participated is worth a hometown story, if his part in the action is related." While these stories would fill the pages of local newspapers, Denig believed that the bigger titles would be attracted to anything that discussed the "ingenuity shown by Marines in adapting their lives to tropical weather, jungle operations, lack of entertainment and comforts."[78]

Armed with this advice, the combat correspondents began providing the home front with colorful details about how the average Marine was handling the seemingly endless battle on Guadalcanal. One dispatch told of a man who "almost went crazy when he discovered what was in the pocket of one Jap he had shot": the dog tag that "belonged to his brother, a Marine at Wake Island." Another recounted the terrifying journey of five Marines who spent five harrowing nights "in a jungle infested with enemy troops" before staggering to safety. And then there was the story of perhaps the most successful patrol of the entire campaign, when forty Marines wiped out the Japanese force on the island of Malaita without suffering a single casualty.[79]

* * *

While Hurlbut and Merillat supervised the influx of new combat correspondents, the two civilian reporters who had been with them at the start of the battle never really left Guadalcanal behind. Despite suffering from exhaustion and hunger, Richard Tregaskis had felt particularly glum when he journeyed from "honesty, freedom" at the front "to red tape, inefficiency, sham" in the rear. For years to come, he would retain a high regard for American combat troops, always viewing them "as tough, human, sometimes brave, and sometimes frightened men doing a mean job that had to be done."[80]

Robert Miller, if anything, developed an even stronger attachment to the Marines, asking Vandegrift to provide a reference in case he decided to switch sides and become a combat correspondent. Vandegrift happily obliged. Miller, he wrote to Holcomb in a letter that underlined the bond that had developed between the military and the media during the early days on Guadalcanal,

> has lived a Marine's life under jungle conditions and is a good Marine. He has been on a raid with Edson, been shelled by destroyers, cruisers and subs. Has endured with the rest of us our daily bombing raids. He still thinks the Marines have what it takes. I have talked with him relative to a commission and will you please take this as my unqualified recommendation for him to join our Public Relation Section. He has a story to tell first hand that I think will interest the public. I feel that if we could get him on the air, not as a Marine but as a correspondent, who had been there, that he could do us a lot of good.[81]

Before he could broadcast his experiences, Miller hit on another idea. Vern Haugland had recently demonstrated how even the sketchiest of diaries— in his case, the few comments he had scrawled when trying to find his way through the New Guinea jungle—could be turned into a publishing sensation. After Haugland's success in September, Miller spotted a similar opportunity. His diary arrived in New York in early October, "battered and riddled by the scissors of the censors," but still containing plenty of vivid depictions of his time on Guadalcanal. His bosses at the UP, spotting its news value, distributed the best pieces to their newspaper clients on October 14. In them, Miller revealed that he had had "butterflies in his stomach" as he prepared to land with the Marines in early August. He also detailed how he and Tregaskis "lived, dodged bullets, and cursed the tropical heat and humidity." Miller's entry for September 9 was typical:

> Rained as usual. Dick Tregaskis and I spent a miserable hour in the jungle while two Jap 75's blasted at us pointblank. They were so close we thought they were mortars. There's nothing worse than lying in a jungle, wringing wet, with a war going on around you.[82]

Although Miller won the race to publish the first Guadalcanal diary, his relatively meager offering was soon eclipsed by Tregaskis's blockbuster account, which more than any other publication shaped how the home front came to view this battle. The INS man began expanding and polishing his diary notes while waiting on the island of Noumea for a military plane to take him to Honolulu. With a month to kill in Hawaii before his next assignment, Tregaskis had little to do but continue typing. Each day, he would spend hours writing in an office provided by the navy censors, who would then lock up his notebooks at night because they contained sensitive information on events like the Doolittle raid that were still embargoed.[83] Working fast, he realized on November 1 that he had completed a book. The manuscript arrived in New York ten days later, and from there the publication process went into overdrive. After his agent read it through in a day, Random House accepted it for publication within forty-eight hours and sent it to the Book-of-the-Month Club just before its next meeting. Bending its own rules, the club gave the panel members a short window to read the manuscript. They were so impressed that they convened a special meeting to make it one of their selections for February 1943, as other authors looked on enviously at "a new world record for speed in writing and marketing a best-seller."[84]

Early in the new year, as the fighting still raged on Guadalcanal, the Random House marketers went into a higher gear. Tregaskis's diary, they declared, provided an insight into the battle "more coherent, more detailed, and more honest than day-to-day headlines."[85] The salesmen were not wrong. Tregaskis's book contained colorful vignettes of what he had witnessed on the island—the death and destruction on Tulagi, Gavutu, and Tanambogo; the dangerous patrols in the Guadalcanal jungles; the close-run fight on Bloody Ridge; and above all, the courageous endurance of the many Marine

Fig. 5.1. Richard Tregaskis (*left*) of the INS became the most famous reporter of the Guadalcanal campaign. Here he is seen with two photographers, Jack Rice of the AP (*center*) and Frank Scherschel of *Life* (*right*).
© AP/Shutterstock.

heroes who defended Henderson Field against everything the enemy could throw at them. Tregaskis did not spare his audience the feelings common to anyone in the combat zone—the extreme fear, even helplessness, in the face of intense incoming fire; the enervating fatigue, even exhaustion, after weeks of sleeping rough and eating paltry rations; and the intense anger, even hatred, toward "Japs" when news filtered through that Marines had been butchered on the beach. Even so, Tregaskis's book, like so much of the reporting at the time, tended to depict the enemy as a distant, rather elusive presence. The reason was not difficult to discern. Japanese troops had fled inland on the day of the invasion, and after that they were almost always on the other side of the jungle. Tregaskis could hear them, especially when they fired guns or dropped bombs, but he rarely saw them, except when they were dead, and on these occasions he was particularly unsparing. "The stench of bodies strewn along Hell Point and across the Tenaru spit," ran his entry for August 22, "was strong. Many of them lay at the water's edge, and already were puffed and glossy, like shiny sausages. Some of the bodies had been partially buried by wave-washed sand; you might see a grotesque, bloated head or twisted torso sprouting from the beach."[86]

* * *

Despite having seen such horrors, both Tregaskis and Miller were keen to witness the end of the battle. Tregaskis headed to SOPAC, where Halsey was already proving a big hit with reporters, who viewed him as the symbol of a new, more candid navy. "Admiral Halsey," as one of them put it, "has a way of speaking his mind that appeals to most Americans."[87] It certainly appealed to Tregaskis, who delightedly reported how Halsey dominated a press conference on January 2. In place of the usual sketchy details, cautious phrases, or "no comments," Halsey predicted the "absolute defeat of the Axis forces" in the coming year, adding that the victory "must be complete—so complete that the enemy will never rise again." "We are definitely now passing to the offensive," Tregaskis reported the admiral as saying. "We're just starting."[88]

Before bigger victories could be won elsewhere, the fighting had to end on Guadalcanal. Miller arrived back on the island just as Vandegrift handed over command to Major General Alexander M. Patch of the US Army. Although the Marines had often struggled to get their story told, Patch's exploits in wrapping up the battle got even less traction back home—and not just because Eisenhower's campaign in North Africa was dominating the front pages. The War and Navy Departments did not even reveal that Patch had assumed command of the "successful offensive" to clear the Japanese from Guadalcanal until January 21, more than six weeks after he had taken over.[89]

Miller's account of the battle's last rites told of "a brilliant surprise maneuver at the enemy's rear, cutting off all means of escape." The raw numbers, he added, demonstrated just how big a victory the United States had achieved. "At least 20,000 Japanese soldiers and Marines died in the green hell of Guadalcanal's jungles," Miller revealed on February 9, "many from disease, while another 30,000 died hideous deaths aboard flaming transports and warships which were blasted by American units as they attempted to reinforce the beleaguered Japanese forces." Allowing himself a personal moment, Miller reminded his readers of both his unique relationship with Guadalcanal and his overpowering respect for the triumphant US troops. "To the only newsman present at the beginning and the conclusion of the campaign," he wrote in his last dispatch from the island, "[the victory] was a magnificent example of American bravery, tenacity, and resourcefulness which the enemy was unable at any time to match."[90]

* * *

Across the nation, the press hailed this triumph. "In area covered and numbers engaged," editorialized the *New York Times* in a typical comment, "the battle of Guadalcanal is small compared with the titanic struggles in Russia or even North Africa. But in the history of the Pacific war it will assume the same symbolic import that Verdun did in the last war, and Stalingrad in this war."[91] In other words, Guadalcanal marked the high-water mark of the enemy's advance; from now on, the tide would inexorably turn in America's favor.

As it did, the military would have more scope to lift the veil that had descended over the Pacific War since Pearl Harbor. This process would not be easy, however, for the simple reason that there had never been a coherent plan to cover up the main events in this theater. True, Roosevelt was strongly committed to a Germany-first strategy, which gave him a major incentive to counteract the domestic clamor for resources to be concentrated against Japan. Yet the White House had never wielded sufficient power over either the military or the media to ensure that they kept the nation's attention deliberately directed toward Europe. Based on faraway Corregidor, Australia, or New Guinea, MacArthur not only was a law unto himself, but also periodically bucked the prevailing trend by trying to drum up domestic support for a shift away from Roosevelt's strategy. Closer to home, King and the navy often seemed impervious to political pressure, convinced that basic military security trumped any other consideration. And the media, despite censorship and the anti-Japanese fervor of its audience, remained free to decide where to position its stories and how to produce its own headlines. Rather than part of a grand scheme, the news blackout had occurred incrementally, almost by accident, as MacArthur and the navy grappled with humiliating defeats, novice PROs struggled to devise new rules, correspondents in the jungle faced taxing conditions, and editors back home often calculated that the main story was unfolding in Europe, not Asia.

On Guadalcanal, a conscious effort to publicize the war had occurred from mid-October, but only after a complex interaction between media pressure, courageous reporting, and the intervention of politically savvy officials. As such, it offered a good guide for the future, for even as the battlefield situation brightened, there would be no straightforward path to greater openness. Indeed, throughout 1943, Roosevelt, MacArthur, the navy, and the media would not even be able to agree on how to publicize one of the most shocking stories: the atrocities that the Japanese were inflicting on American prisoners of war.

PART II
LIFTING THE VEIL

6

Atrocities

The *Gripsholm*

A large crowd had gathered along the Rio de Janeiro portside long before the *Gripsholm* was scheduled to dock. The more eagle-eyed first spotted it as a dark speck on the deep-blue horizon. As it edged closer, pulled into harbor by four tugs, the vessel clearly looked different from anything else plying the submarine-infested oceans. Instead of the usual blue and green camouflage, the ship's whitewashed sides were adorned not only with Swedish blue and yellow stripes, but also with its name boldly embossed in large capital letters. The Red Cross flag that fluttered from the top mast revealed the reason for such brazenness. The *Gripsholm* was sailing under the auspices of that neutral organization because it was carrying an unusual cargo: 1,451 passengers who had been held by Japan as civilian internees since Pearl Harbor. In August 1942, these men and women were on their way home as part of the first prisoner exchange between the belligerents in the Pacific War.[1]

For the reporters jostling for position on the Rio dockside, a major story beckoned. Until this moment, the fate of the thousands of Americans held in Japanese captivity had been one of the biggest mysteries of the Pacific War. What had happened to them? Had they survived? If so, what kind of conditions had they faced?

Rumors had been rife since the start of the year that the Japanese treated their prisoners with the utmost severity. The British government had fueled such fears in March, when Anthony Eden, the British foreign secretary, had publicly indicted Japan not only for the "wholesale murder of British officers and men after their surrender" on Hong Kong, but also for "an orgy of rape and sadism" against civilians.[2] Washington had been much more cautious, however. Roosevelt's propagandists believed that most Americans viewed all atrocity stories with a large dose of skepticism, largely because British atrocity-mongering during World War I had been discredited during the 1920s.[3] Senior military figures also considered the subject "dynamite since a wrong handling may result in the deaths of Americans" still in captivity.

In off-the-record briefings, US officials had therefore cautioned reporters to steer clear of atrocity stories. They should print only material confirmed by a "reliable American official," government spokesmen had stressed in early May, adding that the US government at that time did "not have a single case of a confirmed atrocity by the Japanese." "So far as is known," a *Time* journalist had told his editor after speaking to officials in the White House, War Department, and State Department, "the Japanese are reasonably living up to the 1922 Red Cross Treaty. They never ratified it, but since December [they] have 'adhered.'"[4]

The *Gripsholm*'s arrival in Rio offered the waiting reporters a tantalizing opportunity to confirm the veracity of this optimistic picture of Japanese behavior. Among the 1,451 passengers was Joseph Grew, who had spent the past ten years as the US ambassador in Tokyo, as well as diplomats, missionaries, and businesspeople who had tasted the bitter pill of Japanese captivity since December 7.[5] As soon as these repatriates disembarked for a day of rest and recuperation, reporters swarmed around them. The Brazilian government had obligingly lifted censorship restrictions, "to permit correspondents to file at pleasure anything pertaining to their tribulations under the Japanese," but even so, most correspondents came away disappointed. The passengers, one cabled his news desk, were tense and nervous. None of them would talk, "because they were afraid of what would happen to friends they had left behind."[6]

When the *Gripsholm* approached New York harbor two weeks later, the media frenzy intensified. The government had tried to deter a big crowd from forming alongside the American Export Line dock in Jersey City, and the five hundred or so friends, relatives, and reporters who ignored these warnings found the area protected by a large contingent of armed coast guards. Once the ship docked, those waiting discovered that the government had already diverted more than six hundred of the *Gripsholm*'s passengers to Ellis Island for extra questioning in case the Japanese were trying to use this exchange to sneak agents into the country. The reporters also learned that State Department diplomats had instructed the remainder "to speak cautiously of their experiences—out of deference to their compatriots still living in conquered countries"—advice that almost all of them heeded. According to the *New York Times*' account, "women said that they had been treated courteously, that the food had been 'not too bad.' Others said they did not know 'first hand' of any atrocity stories that had been definitively substantiated."[7]

As a result of such restraint, the *Gripsholm*'s return failed to live up to the media's expectations. Many waiting reporters had hoped to turn it into a major indictment of Japanese barbarity, but the best that they could come up with was a description of the passengers' wan appearances, especially their "thin bodies and shadowed eyes." One correspondent did get a repatriate to admit that "there is plenty to tell, and it horrible, but we can't tell it." A few also discovered that those who had been captured in Hong Kong had faced the worst treatment, thereby reinforcing the line the State Department had been peddling since the spring: namely, that the Japanese treated British imperialists worse than their American counterparts.[8] Overall, though, there was no smoking gun in any of these unattributed, somewhat muffled allegations, and so most editors buried the resulting stories deep inside their newspapers.

The Doolittle Raid

Also buried in the aftermath of the *Gripsholm* voyage was the story of the Doolittle raid, although the effort to hide this episode of the Pacific War had been ongoing for months. On April 18, 1942, sixteen medium bombers had taken off in heavy swells from a US aircraft carrier in the Pacific. Thirteen had dropped their loads on Tokyo, while three had bombed other targets. Lacking the fuel to return to the fleet, fifteen planes had flown on to China, while one had landed in Siberia.[9]

At the time, Washington had placed a complete embargo on all of these details. Naval censorship had remained incredibly tight in the weeks before Midway, and besides, senior officials wanted to keep the Japanese guessing about where the bombers had flown from. So even though a number of fleet correspondents had watched the planes take off, including Robert Casey and Richard Tregaskis, none of them had been permitted to publish what they had seen. With Washington spokesmen equally tight-lipped, newspaper editors had been forced to rely solely on Japanese accounts.[10]

Here, the psychological blow had been palpable. The first Tokyo broadcasts had told of widespread fires and asked the population "to pray for rain." Subsequent Japanese stories had greatly magnified the size of the attack, claiming that "more than sixty planes had participated in raids" and that schools and hospitals in the city had been "severely damaged." In Washington, meanwhile, senior figures had declined to provide any official confirmation for four days. Roosevelt had been quizzed on the subject in his weekly press conference, but his studied answer was designed to obfuscate. When a reporter asked him where the planes had flown from, the president, with a glint in his eye, had replied, "Yes, I think the time has now come to tell you. They came from our new secret base at Shangri-La!"[11]

Despite this lack of official information, the Doolittle raid remained a hot story. Over the following weeks, some journalists managed to piece together what had happened by talking to the pilots when they returned from China. Others quizzed those *Gripsholm* passengers who had been in Tokyo at the time, asking them what it had been like to live through a US bombing raid. In September, the *Chicago Herald-American* even proposed publishing the "Diary of Shangri-La," which would have revealed operational details about the aircraft carrier from which the Doolittle raiders had flown. Yet, significantly, not one newspaper printed a single word of what its journalists had learned.[12]

This conspiracy of silence continued even after the press had the chance to refocus the story on Japanese atrocities. In October 1942, the Japanese executed three of the Doolittle airmen who had been captured in China, while commuting the sentences of another five to life imprisonment. Tokyo openly admitted this action, claiming that the barbarous fliers had killed fifty civilians, including hospital patients and schoolchildren. Even so, the American print media said nothing about the executions. With their own government refusing to confirm the story—the White House would later claim that it did not receive definitive proof until the following March— newspapers merely reported that Japan was threatening "reprisal executions of American prisoners of war." Tokyo, explained the widely used AP account, had declared that the Doolittle airmen "would be punished for acts of inhumanity and [had] said that fliers seized after any similar raids would be tried for their lives."[13]

The media's muted treatment of such an eye-catching issue surprised even the officials charged with supervising domestic censorship. Stories written inside the United States were subject only to a voluntary code overseen by the Office of Censorship. Despite its lack of teeth, this voluntary system had worked well in this instance. "Not a single American newspaper, magazine, or radio station violated the code on the Tokyo bombing story," gushed Byron Price, the Office of Censorship's director. "The faith was kept inviolate."[14]

* * *

In April 1943, with the first anniversary of the Doolittle raid approaching, the US government debated the wisdom of lifting this embargo. George Marshall had reached the conclusion months ago that there were no longer any security reasons to justify strict censorship, and he had even gotten the navy to agree. Proponents of releasing the story also insisted that there was "a good deal of public dissatisfaction with the prolonged secrecy which gives rise to recurrent erroneous charges that the raid was not a success, that there was bungling and that many of the men were lost." But not everyone advocated openness. The White House remained firmly behind the clampdown, content with everyone continuing to believe that the planes had taken off from the mythical Shangri-La. Many intelligence officers likewise favored silence. Not only did they want to keep the Japanese guessing about where the bombers had started from, but they also claimed that publication might provoke retribution against other captured airmen.[15]

As officials continued to deliberate on this issue, they were suddenly faced with a fait accompli. Major General James H. Doolittle, who had led the raid a year earlier, was now based in North Africa, as were eleven of the fliers who had participated in the mission. Learning that these men were planning an event to mark the first anniversary, a UP reporter in Algiers did a little digging. He then compiled a story that led with the crucial fact that the Doolittle planes had taken off from an aircraft carrier in the Pacific. The North Africa–based censors, unaware that this information remained blocked, permitted the publication of the dispatch, and as one media analyst noted, they thereby "unlocked the one essential detail previously kept under key 'for national security reasons.'"[16]

Competing news organizations complained vociferously that the only thing they had gained from their yearlong restraint was to be scooped by the UP.[17] The government, in response, realized it had no choice but to release the entire story, even though this generated another potential problem. The Japanese had long insisted that the Doolittle raid had been nothing more than an indiscriminate terror attack, an allegation that completely undermined the air force's claim that US bombers only ever targeted specific war production sites, not civilians.[18] Keen to shift the public's attention away from claims of American savagery, the government decided to play its own atrocity card.

The White House led the way. "It is with a feeling of deepest horror," Roosevelt declared on April 21, "which I know will be shared by all civilized peoples, that I have to announce the barbarous execution by the Japanese government of some of the members of this country's armed forces who fell

into Japanese hands as an incident of warfare." Using words like "barbarity"
and "depravity," the State Department then divulged that it had formally
warned the Japanese government that it would bring those responsible for
this "murder in cold blood" to justice at the end of the war.[19]

The military, meanwhile, instructed many of the surviving raiders to tell
the press just how unwarranted the executions had been. In Washington,
two airmen, their voices shaking with emotion, called "the Japanese accu-
sation that the Americans deliberately bombed nonmilitary objectives and
machine-gunned civilians . . . 'a damn lie,' " explaining that they had "even
passed up such legitimate military targets as an unprotected aircraft carrier and a line of pursuit ships parked on an enemy airport" in case they
hit noncombatants. In North Africa, the fliers, who had been planning to
mark the first anniversary with a celebration, described their anger at the
unjustified executions. "The filthiest, dirtiest, and most suitable expression,"
declared one, "is the word 'Jap' itself, and that word now becomes the vilest
expression on the face of the earth."[20]

* * *

The handling of atrocities in these two instances revealed some complicated
truths about wartime information. On the one hand, the government obviously wielded enormous power over what made it into the public domain,
and not simply because of the coercive power of censorship. During both the
Gripsholm and Doolittle episodes, officials had also managed to persuade a
large number of media outlets to stay away from atrocity allegations.

Unlike the British government, which could publicize claims of "wholesale murder" by the Japanese safe in the knowledge that its home front would
never push for redirecting the war away from the looming German menace,
the Roosevelt administration always had to keep one eye on the undercur-
rent of Pacific-first sentiment. To be sure, no official ever admitted, either
in public or in private, that this public-opinion constraint underpinned
their caution. Instead, they deployed a variety of other arguments, from
the need to verify atrocity allegations to the public's innate skepticism of
this type of propaganda.[21] In important respects, these were similar to the
reasons the government advanced when refusing to say more about another
Axis atrocity—Nazi Germany's systematic extermination of the Jews—but,
of course, there was one key difference. In the Pacific, US citizens were the
actual and potential victims. And as the administration repeatedly claimed,

its reticence was driven, first and foremost, by the need to protect these American lives.[22]

Although the media bought into these claims, the government's power was not unlimited. One difficulty was trying to maintain a single, unified message in the midst of a global war. The first leak about the Doolittle raid had come from North Africa. A few weeks later, China provided Washington with another major headache. Two AP reporters had interviewed another group of Doolittle pilots, who told them of the plan they had hatched if their planes had been so badly hit they had no chance of flying to safety. Rather than bailing out and becoming prisoners, the pilots had agreed they would try "to dive on [the] emperor's palace." Senior officials were appalled by this admission. The AP story, the War Department's head of public relations complained, "received widespread attention on [the American] radio and may be seized upon by Japanese as supporting [the] contention that civilian targets were selected."[23]

While this unexpected controversy faded within days, the same could not be said for the most obvious consequence of publicizing Japanese atrocities. Within hours of the Doolittle release, commentators across the political spectrum lined up to condemn the Japanese executions as an "unspeakable piece of naïve barbarism [that] is characteristic of the essentially savage and primitive minds against whom we are fighting."[24] Many influential voices went much further. In the Senate, politicians from both sides of the partisan divide immediately stepped up their demands to wage a more aggressive war in the Pacific. The nation's military leaders, declared Senator Albert B. Chandler (D-KY), needed "to take the Pacific War more seriously, recognize Japan as America enemy No. 1, and furnish Gen. MacArthur with all the aid he needs and demands." Senator Arthur H. Vandenberg (R-MI), who was already planning to organize a presidential bid for MacArthur in 1944, wholeheartedly agreed, demanding that "the far east be given higher 'priorities' in our war strategy," with "more aid for MacArthur."[25]

MacArthur appreciated this support. Unsurprisingly, he did not agree with the way Washington was handling atrocity material. While the White House and Pentagon fretted that the premature release of such information might endanger those still in captivity, MacArthur saw publicity "as a means of securing better future treatment and ... sav[ing the] lives of those still surviving." MacArthur doubtless believed this argument, but with his Senate cheerleaders in full voice, he also recognized that news of Japanese barbarity against US fighting men gave him extra leverage in his ongoing effort to extract more men and materiel from Washington. It was a lesson he would not forget when he learned what had happened to the thousands of American soldiers who had surrendered at Bataan in April 1942.[26]

Dyess and the Death March

For more than a year, the fate of the Bataan prisoners had remained a mystery. The Japanese guarded their camps so tightly that the US government had little idea how many POWs remained alive, let alone the conditions they were having to endure. In the summer of 1942, the Red Cross had launched a Bataan Mercy Fund so that supplies could be sent to the prisoners, but communities across the nation could only live in hope that the tens of thousands of dollars they raised would get through to the survivors.[27]

Then in July 1943, William "Ed" Dyess of the air force, Melvyn H. McCoy of the navy, and Steve M. Mellnik of the coast artillery suddenly appeared at MacArthur's headquarters in Brisbane. These three officers had, with seven other men, slipped out of their prison camp in the southern Philippines back in April and spent weeks traipsing through dense jungles and malarial swamps. Their tattered clothes and emaciated frames hinted at the arduousness of this journey, but to the debriefing officers, even their haggard appearance paled next to the horrors they told about their time as Japanese prisoners of war. [28]

Speaking slowly in a Texas drawl, his sentences "colored by pungent colloquialisms," Dyess was a particularly compelling witness. In a series of interviews, he stunned MacArthur's men with details of a "death march" that he and the other Bataan prisoners had made in April 1942. The Japanese had forced them to walk sixty miles north to their first prison camp, Dyess revealed, in intense heat with no food and little water, all the while subjecting them to taunts, threats, and outright brutality. Conditions were no better when they finally reached the camp. Dyess remained particularly haunted by the sight of enemy guards brutally whipping prisoners before shooting or beheading them. Like every other prisoner, he had quickly begun to suffer from rapid weight loss. He had also succumbed to a series of illnesses, including scurvy, dengue fever, and yellow jaundice. Even so, Dyess recognized that he had been one of the lucky ones. The death rate, he estimated, had approached fifty a day among the Americans, while "the Filipino death toll had soared to 350 each twenty-four hours."[29]

MacArthur was as appalled as anyone when he learned what these men had been through. After awarding Dyess, McCoy, and Mellnik the Distinguished Service Medal, he pondered how to act. There could be no doubt that atrocities on this scale would create a renewed domestic demand for America to focus on Japan first, but this was not his only consideration. MacArthur believed that the barbarity Dyess had revealed made a mockery of Washington's muted stance, since the Japanese could scarcely step up the level of their cruelty. Perhaps, he reasoned, publicity might even make Japan pause before committing further crimes. This was certainly Dyess's view. Having watched the enemy up close for a year, the airman believed that the Japanese desire to save face meant they could be persuaded to tone down their savagery. For this reason, Dyess felt he owed it to the men he had left behind to tell his story to the world.[30]

There were only two obstacles, both of which would prove difficult to overcome. Military personnel had to submit anything they wrote to PROs for review before publication. And in this instance, the services had very different ideas about what elements of the story ought to be told.[31]

The navy, for once, was the first off the mark. After hearing McCoy's harrowing account, one of King's senior advisers approached George Creel at *Collier's* magazine. As America's chief propagandist during World War I, Creel had used atrocity-mongering to whip up hatred of the German enemy, and he immediately offered McCoy $20,000 for the magazine rights to his story. He had second thoughts, however, when he learned that Dyess had what the War Department was privately calling "probably the outstanding story that has come out of this war." As an army officer explained, Dyess was in a much better position to tell it than McCoy, since the navy man had not taken part in the death march and had arrived in the POW camp only after the Japanese guards had "inflicted their worst tortures." On interviewing Dyess, Creel agreed with the War Department's assessment, a decision that meant the two men had to agree on how to share both the money and the credit.[32]

To formulate a way of moving forward, PROs from the army and navy summoned Dyess and McCoy to a lunch meeting at the Pentagon on August 25. Once the plates had been cleared, the two sides traded blows. The navy officers attacked the army's attempt to downplay McCoy's role, insisting that their man had been the senior officer during the escape, as well as the one "chosen to lead as the only one capable of navigating to safety." When the discussion shifted to money, McCoy insisted that he wanted to "split all proceeds ten ways," while Dyess countered that "he and his squadron be given 35 percent of the proceeds,

50 percent to the other eight members of the party, and 15 percent to Cmdr. Moody."[33]

Wearied by this unseemly haggling, Dyess suffered a physical collapse soon after the lunch. His superiors sent him to a hospital in White Sulphur Springs, West Virginia, to recuperate, but he was given little chance to rest. First, General Henry "Hap" Arnold, the air chief, sent a PRO to his bedside to find out how much of the story could be written without compromising security. Then a range of news organizations, including *Cosmopolitan* and *Reader's Digest*, came calling in an attempt to outbid *Collier's* for the rights. On September 13, McCoy also phoned the hospital, only to receive a nasty surprise. Dyess revealed that he had decided to sell his personal story to the *Chicago Tribune*, which had already sent Charles Leavelle, an accredited war correspondent "with a record of notable literary achievements on war stories," to help him put his experiences on paper.[34]

Feeling betrayed, McCoy slammed down the phone. The airman, he vented, had not merely been given bad advice; he had also been "impetuous, boyish, stubborn, and not too intellectually mature."[35] Seen from Dyess's perspective, however, the deal made perfect sense. His wife owned the *Champaign News-Gazette* in Illinois and already knew Colonel McCormick, the *Tribune's* publisher, quite well. With her ailing husband tired of "talk[ing] about percentages on this, cut-ins on that, and slices of something else," she got her attorney to broker a deal with McCormick's paper that gave Dyess $21,000, a large proportion of which would go to air force relief funds and the Red Cross to help his fellow prisoners. The increased sum helped to change Dyess's mind, but the clincher came when Leavelle convinced him that the *Tribune*, with its large syndication network, could maximize the impact of his appalling story, disseminating it to a daily audience of forty million, compared with three million who bought *Collier's* each week.[36]

Yet the *Tribune's* involvement created another snag. The government still had to sanction the story's release. Even before Dyess shook hands with Leavelle, senior officials had questioned the desirability of whipping up a storm of home-front anger at this particular point in the war. Crucial strategic decisions were pending, including the all-important matter of when to launch a second front in Europe, and neither Roosevelt nor Marshall relished the prospect of a major domestic clamor to focus on the Pacific. Negotiations were also under way for the release of a second batch of prisoners on the *Gripsholm*, and recognizing that civilian internees and prisoners of war were often conflated in the public debate, neither Roosevelt nor the State Department wanted to do anything to jeopardize this fragile process.[37]

With the *Gripsholm* uppermost in his mind, Roosevelt reached a firm decision on September 9. The army and navy, he ordered, must prevent "the publication or circulation of any stories emanating from escaped prisoners until I have authorized a release."[38] Four days later, the likelihood that this authorization would ever be forthcoming seemed greatly diminished. As soon as McCoy ended his phone call from Dyess, he contacted Leland Lovette, the navy PRO, with the news that the airman planned to publish his account in the *Chicago Tribune*, of all places. Within minutes, Lovette and his team went into overdrive to ensure that the presidential ban on escaped prisoner stories would be vigorously enforced.

As they mobilized, the navy's publicists could not help but ponder the eerie parallels with earlier occasions when awkward information had seeped into the public domain. As with the Doolittle raid, too many people already knew about the Dyess story, and it would only take one of them to blurt out something and the press would be in a frenzy to publish everything. There was also the distinct possibility that *Tribune* might resort to the tactics it had used during the Stanley Johnston affair, when, the navy believed, it had played fast and loose with the rules. On the afternoon of September 13, Lovette spoke to Major General Alexander D. Surles, the War Department's director of the Bureau of Public Relations (BPR). Until now, the two services had been at loggerheads over the Dyess story. The *Tribune*'s involvement resolved their differences. Both men agreed to instruct all departments and agencies that no one was to "do any talking in any way on this thing. No writing, talks, or any deals." They also decided to warn the *Tribune* that atrocity stories were "against the public interest" and that the Espionage Act would be invoked if the newspaper breached the ban.[39]

To make doubly sure that the Dyess story did not leak, Surles sent an unambiguous order to the airman still convalescing in the hospital. "Dyess," the *Tribune*'s editors mournfully noted, "was informed that he could no longer talk to Leavelle." By way of explanation, the government stressed the delicacy of the ongoing *Gripsholm* negotiations, which were due to be concluded by late October. Privately, Lovette and Surles knew that this was only cover. The two men hoped to keep Dyess's story under wraps "far in[to] the future."[40]

* * *

An early morning mist hung over New York harbor on December 1, 1943, shielding the *Gripsholm* from the large crowd that had gathered along the "grimy and gritty Jersey waterfront." It was an apt symbol of what was to come. The day before, the navy and FBI had agreed to assign the "small army of waiting reporters and photographers" a specific space on the pier. Here they would receive an official briefing while agents checked the 1,494 passengers. Once the repatriates came ashore, the press would be able to interview them, although, as one correspondent noted, "[t]he navy's public relations officers in charge at the pier made it plain that atrocity stories are frowned upon because publication of them makes it difficult to deal with the Japanese over the release of 6,300 civilians still held in the Orient."[41]

Even so, many media organizations were more optimistic that the second *Gripsholm* voyage would yield greater returns than the first. For one thing, the passenger list this time contained many of the journalists who had surrendered in Manila in December 1941, among them Russell Brines and Ray Cronin of the AP. "Throughout internment," Brines revealed soon after his return, "we gathered information and impressions against the time, which seemed so far distant, when we would finally return to the job." Having built up a large backlog of stories, the two men found the long voyage home particularly therapeutic. They managed to wire something to New York at every port, although, as their editors were quick to note, none of this material contained any evidence of systematic mistreatment. Brines, for instance, revealed that food shortages were becoming acute in the camps, but he blamed this on "the disruption of communications and rising living costs" rather than a deliberate Japanese policy to starve the internees. Cronin disclosed that the Japanese occupiers had "executed at least fourteen Filipinos and one Chinese" after Manila's fall, but he stressed that this action had been a response to "a wave of sensational assassinations and attempted killings . . . carried out by bitter anti-Japanese elements."[42]

While many reporters came away frustrated by their colleagues' refusal to unequivocally indict the Japanese, the *Chicago Tribune* held out hope that the *Gripsholm*'s return would end the government ban on the Dyess story. Since the middle of September, the newspaper's editors had tried various tactics to encourage an official change of heart. Walter Trohan, their Washington correspondent, had met privately with Surles to stress that McCormick would not make any financial profit from the contract, explaining that every cent would go straight to Dyess "to be used by him as he sees fit for his comrades and himself."[43] When this argument fell on deaf ears, the *Tribune* resorted to a public campaign. Throughout October, its front page carried "a series of carefully documented articles recording atrocities" that revealed "the unparalleled bestiality of the Japanese military machine," including the execution of the Doolittle airmen and the shooting of stretcher bearers in New Guinea.[44]

When the *Gripsholm*'s return passed without a lifting of the ban, McCormick became so frustrated that he ratcheted up the pressure. He turned to Governor Dwight H. Green, who had ridden "a *Tribune*-generated updraft into the Illinois governor's mansion" in the last election. Green repaid his political debt by slamming Washington's continued cover-up. "The true story of the Pacific War," Green declared on the second anniversary of Pearl Harbor, "is in possession of our government. In addition to the civilians evacuated by the *Gripsholm* last month, there are military men who have made their way home after escaping from Jap prison camps. Their story should be told now."[45]

* * *

In fact, the story might never have been told had it not been for a final twist of fate. After recovering in the hospital, Dyess decided to return to active service. On December 22, he was flying over Burbank, California, when his plane developed engine trouble. According to an eyewitness, Dyess might have been able to land safely in a vacant lot had a passing motorist not been in the way. In swerving to avoid the car and save the civilian's life, he hit the steeple of a local Catholic church and crashed.[46]

As tributes flooded in, McCormick and his men spotted their chance. On December 23, they led with an AP story on the death of this "hero of the Philippines campaign." Below, they ran an account of Leavelle's meeting with Dyess back in September. In it, the reporter revealed that the airman had told him, in graphic detail, "the greatest story of the war in the Pacific and one that should arouse the wrath against the Japanese such as never had been turned against Hitler," only for the censors to refuse publication.[47] The Pentagon reacted furiously. "There is a hell of a stink swirling around on Dyess now," Trohan told his editors that same day. "Anything can happen now. Army has heard about the pieces [published] in Chicago and is screaming. I replied by pointing out that the pieces are true and released by censors."[48]

Dyess's funeral four days later gave the *Tribune* another opening to pressure the government. Leavelle headed to Texas to interview the flier's father, a former county judge, who also hinted at a grand cover-up. "My son kept his promise to his superiors not to reveal anything he said or did after the fall of Bataan," Leavelle reported Dyess, Sr., as saying. "My son told me that his story would help stir folks up to fight harder to win the war in the Pacific," but, the father added, his superiors had ordered him "upon pain of military punishment to tell nothing of the experiences he and his American colleagues had gone thru. They said the country would not understand and this story must remain suppressed."[49]

Inside the government, meanwhile, a number of civilian officials began to question why the military was persisting with suppression. In the wake of Dyess's death, Trohan met with officials from the Office of Censorship, who, already unhappy that the military had not informed them about this "blackout," told the reporter that they thought that "the dead march [sic] should be told as is." They also agreed to look over what Leavelle had written the previous fall, to see whether he had breached their guidelines. Elmer Davis, the head of the OWI, likewise believed that the story should now be released, adding an argument that had not yet been aired out loud. The time had come, Davis believed, to educate the public about the nature of the Japanese enemy so that there would be no demand for a negotiated peace in the Pacific after the war in Europe had been won.[50]

Despite this mounting pressure, the military remained obdurate. After his death, Dyess's stories had become the property of his widow, who was given no time to grieve. One reporter learned from a disgusted OWI official that

> [t]he army could not "order" her not to publish it, but it did try to prevail upon her to withdraw it and it is said that she agreed on "patriotic" grounds. The argument put forward to her was that publication might endanger the lives of thousands of American prisoners of war—both military and civilian—in the Far East.

There the sorry saga might have ended had the *Chicago Tribune* not decided to play hardball. The newspaper retained a copy of what Leavelle and Dyess had written, and the *Tribune*'s editors "threatened if Mrs. Dyess withdrew the story to have an Illinois senator or congressman read it into the congressional record on the Hill."[51] Backed into a corner, the military bowed to the inevitable, agreeing to the publication of Dyess's story early in the new year.

* * *

"US CRY: ANNIHILATE JAPS," thundered the *Tribune*'s front page on January 29, 1944. The day before, the army and navy had released a four-thousand-word statement, based on sworn statements by officers, which documented Japan's "cold-blooded campaign of savagery" against US prisoners. This paved the way for the *Tribune* to run with the headline it had been planning for months: "DYESS' OWN STORY!"[52]

Told in twenty-five daily installments, this story began with the airman's heroics during the doomed Philippines campaign. Then, from February 4—three days before McCoy and Mellnik's account of thousands of Americans dying in Japanese prisoner camps appeared in *Life* magazine—the *Tribune* began divulging Dyess's appalling account of the Bataan death march. Day after day, its audience learned of the unpredictable and unprovoked beatings, the random executions by either bullet or sword, the lack of food and water in the intense heat, and the countless dead who littered the path.[53]

Crucially, these atrocity stories were also read by millions beyond the confines of the *Tribune*'s normal market. Following the successful policy pioneered with Stanley Johnstone's Coral Sea dispatches, McCormick declared that his newspaper had a "patriotic duty" to see that the Dyess story "received the widest possible reading here and abroad." He therefore gave it "to all the newspapers outside Chicago and all the news agencies, without charge." He also allowed the radio networks to broadcast the most horrific moments. NBC came up with a particularly poignant show, using actors to dramatize the worst Japanese excesses, while its sound-effects team created whipping noises and ominous drumbeat thumps in the background.[54]

As this multimedia barrage gathered force, the nation erupted in anger. According to one poll, more than 70 percent supported the decision to release "stories of Jap treatment of American prisoners." Unsurprisingly, opinion was particularly virulent in Dyess's home state of Texas, with local newspapers, according to one government survey, expressing "without exception . . . the wrath[,] horror and intense resentment of their respective communities concerning these atrocities." Elsewhere, even stolid establishment organs joined in the chorus of disgust. "From the people in the forty-eight states," declared the *New York Herald Tribune* on its front page, "came an echo in the form of unprecedented purchases of war bonds to speed the time when, as one legislator put it in some of the most temperate language

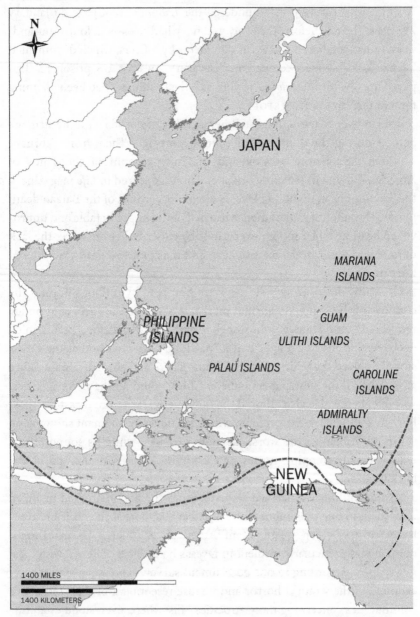

Fig. 6.1. Allied gains in the western Pacific, March 1944. Drawn by George Chakvetadze.

used during the day, the American Fleet can 'steam straight into Tokio and blow it to Hades.'"[55]

MacArthur and his supporters echoed these sentiments, although they believed that the army, not the navy, should be in charge of destroying Japan. Senator Chandler, who had returned from a recent tour of the SWPA an even more ardent fan of the general's, demanded that MacArthur be given the resources "to avenge each hero's death." MacArthur naturally agreed. Since November, he had been locked in a bitter battle with Washington, not only protesting Roosevelt's and Marshall's overarching Germany-first strategy, but also attempting to undermine King's and Nimitz's push to secure "a preponderance of resources" for their drive in the central Pacific. "To that end," observes historian Stephen Taaffe, "in late 1943 and early 1944, MacArthur brought into play every weapon in his personal arsenal," which included exploiting the Dyess story to the utmost.[56] "They are now planning to send three million more Americans across the Atlantic," the general was reported as saying in January. "Why can't some of these men and material be sent to the Pacific? The sooner we concentrate our power in the South Pacific, the quicker we will . . . spare other Americans the barbaric treatment which the zalous [sic] Japs are handing out."[57]

For Roosevelt and Marshall, the main saving grace was that this outpouring of anger came too late to influence the biggest strategic decision of all. At the Tehran Conference in late 1943, the president had promised Stalin that the Americans and British would invade France in the first half of 1944. More and more GIs were already pouring across the Atlantic in preparation for the long-awaited second front, and not even the horrific revelations about Japanese atrocities could halt this flow.[58]

Those of a conspiratorial bent doubtless believed that Roosevelt and Marshall had deliberately delayed the release of the Dyess story until it could no longer influence grand strategy. The reality was much more convoluted and, in its own way, even more sordid. Rather than a carefully considered propaganda ploy, it was a blend of tragedy and politics, of public pressure and private threats that had brought the ban to an end. Thankfully, when it came to lifting the veil on other aspects of the Pacific War, the motives and moves of the key players would be much more edifying.

7

Dress Rehearsal in New Guinea

"A Victory of Such Completeness"

Although MacArthur disagreed with Washington over the release of escaped prisoner stories, he did nothing to undermine the government's news embargo on this subject. In a normal commander, such obedience would have been taken for granted, but for MacArthur it was a remarkable act of restraint. Throughout the war, he often went out of his way to question orders he considered wrongheaded. In the months before and after the Dyess affair, he was particularly keen to publicize his part in the Pacific War in ways that rankled Washington, starting with the Battle of the Bismarck Sea in early March 1943.

After losing Buna, Japanese commanders had decided to reinforce their remaining strongpoints along the northern New Guinea coast, especially in the Salamaua-Lae region. As soon as American intelligence caught wind that a big enemy transport convoy was heading in this direction, Kenney mobilized his air force. Taking off from bases in Australia and New Guinea, 330 Allied planes launched wave after wave of attacks on the Japanese armada, often sweeping in low and "skipping" their bombs at enemy ships. The result was carnage, although it would take intelligence officers some time to establish the precise scale of the death and destruction.[1]

When Kenney woke MacArthur with the news in the early hours of March 4, the commander's impatience to announce such a massive triumph overrode the prudent dictates of verification. "I have never seen such jubilation," the airman noted. After Kenney reminded MacArthur that he would be departing for Washington in a few hours to attend the Pacific Military Conference, where the next moves in the theater would be discussed, MacArthur "said OK." Then, as Kenney recorded in his diary, he "made some wonderful remarks about what a great guy I was and started outlining his communiqué."[2]

This rapidly compiled document pulled no punches. "The Battle of the Bismarck Sea," it began, "is now decided. We have achieved a victory of such completeness as to assume the proportions of a major disaster to the enemy. His entire force has been practically destroyed." To support this grand assertion, MacArthur produced hard numbers. There had been twenty-two vessels in the armada, his communiqué claimed, and no less than twelve transports and ten warships had been "sunk" or were "sinking," taking with them fifteen thousand enemy troops who had been "killed almost to a man."[3]

Upon seeing the draft, Diller urged caution. These figures, the PRO warned, came from fliers flushed with victory, and their claims might well prove inflated in the cold light of day. MacArthur, though, was adamant. "I trust George Kenney," he replied, which was enough to close the argument as far as Diller was concerned. "It wasn't up to me to verify the communiqués," he remarked much later. Nor did the press feel the need to question MacArthur's facts. Editors simply placed his eye-catching claims on page one, beneath banner headlines proclaiming "JAP NAVAL DISASTER."[4]

* * *

By the time Kenney arrived in Washington to confer with senior army and navy leaders, MacArthur felt that his decision to release an unchecked, perhaps inflated, communiqué had been vindicated. Until that point, newspaper bosses had continued to neglect MacArthur's theater, as demonstrated by the way in which they allocated their resources. By the spring of 1943, there were sixty-one accredited American reporters in North Africa, another twenty-two in the Middle East, and no less than seventy-six in Europe, based mainly in London and Moscow. By comparison, MacArthur's SWPA housed just forty-two correspondents, while there were another thirty-one covering the Solomons in the South Pacific.[5]

Nor, as MacArthur knew only too well, was the media's relative lack of interest measured only in resource allocation. In the past nine months, the navy, which had almost gone out of its way to shield its battles from the press, had nevertheless basked in the acclamation of two major victories, at Midway and Guadalcanal, which newspapers back home had hailed as turning points in the Pacific. In contrast, MacArthur's success at Buna had been depicted as little more than a sanguinary sideshow, and the reporters stuck covering it were in an increasingly gloomy mood. "Twelve months of reporting a front where nearly every big story had been smothered by bigger news from other theaters," one noted in March, "had left many of them bored and weary."[6]

Seen against this gloomy backdrop, MacArthur's determination to luxuriate in the limelight of the Bismarck Sea success was unsurprising, and he rightly predicted that the bigger the boast the more coverage it would receive back home. For days afterward, editors not only flourished large triumphant headlines about the battle on their front pages. They also ran countless opinion pieces touting "the most clear-cut, complete, and conclusive triumph our side has won in the fifteen months since Pearl Harbor."[7]

Such approbation did more than stroke MacArthur's ego, bruised though it was after months in which other generals and admirals had garnered much more attention. Crucially, it also strengthened Kenney's hand when he began to demand more planes from top officials in Washington. Roosevelt appeared particularly receptive. Having avidly read the Bismarck Sea stories, he told an aide to clear his morning appointments so that he could give Kenney more time. The airman duly recounted to the president his own version of the slaughter inflicted on the Japanese. He then provided a detailed accounting of how few planes he had in his command. Roosevelt, in response, "grinned and said 'Write down on this pad what you need. Be reasonable about it and I'll see what I can do.' "[8]

Not content to rely on the president's word, MacArthur's allies continued to use the media to pressure top officials. Even as Kenney left the White House, reporters were handed more details on the Battle of the Bismarck Sea, including the striking claim that "five Japanese soldiers were the only survivors of 15,000 aboard the twenty-two enemy ships destroyed." Few close observers thought that the timing of this release had been an accident. "General Kenney," declared the managing editor of the New York Times in a typical comment, "has a good story to tell. His best argument, of course, is the recent outstanding victory of General MacArthur's planes against the Japanese force."[9]

Still, the use of unverified figures and extravagant claims carried obvious risks. In the perennial tug-of-war over resources, MacArthur had powerful rivals in Washington who were not frightened of pushing back hard. The navy predictably recoiled from the idea that land-based airpower could be so potent against ships, but even senior air force officers were not entirely pleased with MacArthur's public bragging. General Henry "Hap" Arnold, the air chief, was the most influential. Arnold held a single-minded strategic vision: he wanted to use the precision bombing of German industry to demonstrate that airpower could win the war on its own. Faced with MacArthur's transparent attempt to inveigle a larger proportion of precious aircraft for the Southwest Pacific, Arnold asked his officers to take a closer look at the Battle of the Bismarck Sea.

This inquiry took some time to complete, but its conclusions were damning. There had been only sixteen enemy ships in the convoy, Arnold's subordinates discovered, not twenty-two, and at least two of these had survived. "Communiqué also stated that ground forces numbered 15,000," the investigation concluded, "whereas corrected information indicates only about 8,000." Marshall, when conveying this information to MacArthur, suggested that he issue "a corrected communiqué." MacArthur, fearing for both his reputation and his demands for additional resources, refused point blank. "Communiqués issued in this area," he replied, "are meticulously based upon official reports of operating commanders concerned and I am prepared to defend both of them either officially or publicly."[10]

Burdened with much larger concerns, neither Marshall nor Arnold relished a public battle, so they quietly let the inflated communiqués stand. By brazening it out, MacArthur had avoided the humiliation of a retraction, but he did not emerge entirely unscathed. As well as having damaged his reputation with the top brass in Washington, he had to confront correspondents in both Brisbane and Port Moresby who were more desperate than ever to report the air war in graphic detail.

* * *

For the past year, correspondents had not found it easy to cover Kenney's campaign, beyond churning out praise for the air commander laced with basic facts about bombs dropped and targets destroyed. Even the Battle of the Bismarck Sea had proved a frustration. In the immediate aftermath, correspondents had hurried to airbases in Australia and New Guinea to interview the victorious pilots. George Weller of the *Chicago Daily News* had grabbed one of the biggest scoops. Using the fliers' words, Weller revealed that enemy troops had been "so bewildered by the simultaneous oblique level-bombing and medium-bombing with missiles ranging from 500 to 1000 pounds that many leapt into the sea rather than be minced by the terrible strafing attack."[11]

Although these accounts created quite a splash back home, most reporters realized that interviewing pilots was only a pale substitute for going on a bombing mission, an activity that remained strictly off-limits. A year earlier, when many aircraft had been old and decrepit, this ban had made sense. Now, the air war seemed much safer. The best proof was MacArthur's own communiqués, which repeatedly emphasized "light" Allied losses, culminating in the Battle of the Bismarck Sea, where, according to the official figures, only "one bomber and three fighters were shot down." With the risks so low and interest so high, a number of correspondents were eager for a firsthand taste of the New Guinea air war.[12]

Vern Haugland of the AP was perhaps the unlikeliest figure to be so tempted. The AP man had only just returned to the theater, having enjoyed a long stretch of stateside leave to recuperate from his earlier plane crash and jungle trek. Undeterred by this previous brush with death, Haugland decided to team up with Harold Guard of the UP and Lee Van Atta of the INS. The three men boarded an operational flight bound for the Salamaua-Lae region, where Kenney's planes were softening up the next Japanese target on the northern New Guinea coast. Their trip was uneventful, but once safely back they had no time to savor their achievement or even to write a story on what they had witnessed. Instead, Diller immediately reminded them of the prohibition against undertaking "hazardous assignments." He then expelled them from New Guinea.[13]

Other veteran reporters were shocked, though not surprised, by the punishment. Elsewhere, they knew, the military had recently begun to encourage correspondents to accompany bombing missions. The decision to enforce the ban in New Guinea, they concluded, was yet another example of the excessive censorship and control in this theater. Al Noderer had already departed from Australia in January, muttering darkly about how MacArthur's censors only passed news that was "calculated to mislead the American public." George Weller agreed, complaining to his editors in March of the "policy of cloaking unpleasant facts and damping down criticism." These two American reporters largely confined their gripes to private communications.[14] Noel Monks of the London *Daily Mail* was much more brazen. Monks, who had covered the wars in Abyssinia and Spain in the 1930s and the campaigns in France and the Middle East since 1940, left New Guinea in March in an angry mood. Reporters in the SWPA, he told anyone who would listen, had to deal with "an almost fantastic MacArthur censorship, which is the worst I have ever experienced in any war I have covered."[15]

Establishing the Template

Luckily for Haugland and his two colleagues, their ban coincided with a lull on the battlefield, as both sides recuperated, reorganized, and planned their next moves.[16] Any correspondent who had been in New Guinea since the fall was in particular need of a rest. Virtually everyone had succumbed to some sort of tropical disease in recent months, with malaria the most common ailment, and the only recourse was to spend days in a field hospital on a diet of quinine, followed by weeks in Port Moresby catching up on fresh food and sleep. Nor was it only ailing bodies that needed mending. "The jungle breaks everything down," observed George Weller in April, "typewriter, camera, papers. My glasses gave way this morning," he complained to his editor after one prolonged stay in New Guinea; "it takes so long to get things done that take hours under ordinary circumstances."[17]

While veteran reporters struggled to recover from the months they had spent working in this enervating environment, MacArthur's PROs desperately needed a breathing space for their own repair job. Even the most obtuse censor recognized that war correspondents were deeply dissatisfied by the way their copy was being handled in both Australia and New Guinea. They also knew that their boss saw publicity as a key tool for getting Washington's permission to return in triumph to Bataan, Corregidor, and Manila.[18] Attracting more headlines inevitably meant fostering a better relationship with reporters. This was one challenge. The other was perhaps more daunting. MacArthur needed to evict the Japanese from New Guinea and the Solomon Islands before he could head for the Philippines. To do so, he planned to launch no less than thirteen amphibious operations over the coming months, which meant that his PROs would have to establish a template for ensuring effective press coverage of this tricky type of battle.[19]

In addressing these dual tasks, MacArthur's PROs had the advantage of starting from a stable base. By the spring of 1943, the Port Moresby press camp had become much better organized. Durable tents lined the garden outside the old plantation house in which reporters ate and wrote. At least one jeep was always on hand to take them to the airstrip, where they could catch regular flights over the mountains to the front. Once there, the reporters were accompanied by a chaperone. "All field commanders," Diller warned new arrivals, "rigidly require that all correspondents in an area of active ground operations remain with and under the control of a press relations officer. Individual, unescorted movements of correspondents is prohibited." Back at the press camp, military regulations could be equally suffocating, encompassing almost every aspect of the reporters' daily lives, from what to wear at mealtimes to where to throw their cigarette butts; but Diller at least made some attempt to infuse this stringent supervision with a more positive spirit.[20]

Inside the plantation house, a senior PRO held a press conference at ten o'clock each night in which he revealed "everything shown in the military operational reports." With censorship still so tight, the briefing officer knew that nothing he divulged in these sessions would ever leak, but this candor also denoted a more constructive approach to press relations. PROs, as one senior correspondent observed that spring, were increasingly trying to ensure "that the proper kind of stories are produced for correspondents, as well as by them."[21]

In Brisbane, meanwhile, Diller decided to give Haugland, Guard, and Van Atta a second chance. Neither he nor MacArthur considered them to be a real danger. On the contrary, Van Atta had proved an effective mouthpiece for Kenney's demands for more planes, while MacArthur had personally pinned a Silver Star on Haugland after his forty-three-day ordeal in the jungle. Once the initial shock of their ban had sunk in, the PROs let it be known that the reporters had got off lightly, since they ought to have been expelled from Australia as well as New Guinea. Then Diller quietly laid on transportation so that the former delinquents could return to Port Moresby in preparation for the next phase of the offensive.[22]

At the plantation house, Haugland, Guard, and Van Atta encountered a group of new arrivals who had been lured to New Guinea by the prospect of more action. Five came in June alone, among them big names like Hal O'Flaherty of the *Chicago Daily News*, the "debonair" former managing editor of that newspaper, and Robert Cromie of the *Chicago Tribune*, who had been on Guadalcanal the previous summer. On landing, these reporters were treated to an interview with MacArthur, who greeted them "with a warm smile and a gracious handshake" before explaining "that he felt our work as newspaper men connected with his Office of Public Relations was an essential part of war as waged by free people."[23]

To add substance to these warm words, MacArthur and Diller turned to Lloyd Lehrbas, a lean, square-jawed former AP correspondent who had reported on both Hitler's blitzkrieg in Poland and Washington's reaction to Pearl Harbor. After receiving instructions to improve the SWPA's press relations, Lehrbas immediately arranged a meeting with Lieutenant General Walter Krueger, whose Sixth Army (known at the time as Alamo Force) would be launching the first round of attacks, scheduled for early July. Krueger's targets were the islands of Kiriwina and Woodlark to the northeast of Buna, while to the southeast Admiral Halsey would simultaneously invade New Georgia in the Solomons.

A gruff, blunt man, Krueger was the direct antithesis of MacArthur's last battlefield commander. The "smooth, polished" Eichelberger had loved the limelight a little too much for MacArthur's liking, which is why he had been shunted off to train troops after the Buna campaign.[24] Having observed Eichelberger's fate, Krueger was determined to keep his own counsel around correspondents, although he also recognized MacArthur's desperate need for publicity. So, after listening carefully to Lehrbas's presentation, Krueger agreed to find places for four correspondents on each invasion task force. The wire services, Lehrbas decided, would get the first choice of which island to cover, since their stories could be picked up by all the newspapers back home. Haugland and his UP rival chose Kiriwina, since it was closest to MacArthur's next target of Lae. Cromie and O'Flaherty had to make do with slots on the naval armada that would remain offshore.

On receiving their assignments, the men immediately succumbed to the usual pre-combat cocktail of nerves and excitement. Although Kiriwina was not currently under Japanese occupation, it was only 270 miles from the major enemy base at Rabaul, and so the correspondents in the landing parties decided to prepare for the worst. This meant getting kitted out in "camouflage green coveralls," as well as packing "the regular jungle equipment of hammocks, mosquito nets, and army rations." Then they slipped away to their embarkation points, feeling a pang of relief as they looked up at the sky. The thick, low-hanging cloud not only offered some respite from the intense heat; it would also provide a welcome umbrella from prowling enemy planes.[25]

At dawn on June 30, the landing barges chugged toward Kiriwina in an eerie quiet: no planes, no artillery, no rifle fire. Once on dry land, an officer located the colonial administrator, who had remained on the island despite the Japanese threat. The man not only confirmed the complete absence of enemy troops, but also provided a warm welcome. Indeed, rather than suffering in some makeshift jungle bivouac, Haugland and his colleague found themselves inside the administrator's impressive abode, where they enjoyed "showers under a bucket arrangement kept full by native servants and feasted on roast wild pig, tropical vegetables, and fruit while native servants plied them with iced water and tea."[26]

Despite this unexpected luxury, the correspondents knew that they could not linger in Kiriwina for long. The absence of enemy troops meant they had no war stories to file. The rudimentary communications network also left them with no reliable method of contacting their news desks. During the weeks of intensive planning, Lehrbas had tried to devise a way of ensuring that the frontline story could be told promptly. He had agreed with reporters

Fig. 7.1. War correspondents on Kiriwina. Vern Haugland is third from the left. Lloyd Lehrbas, the PRO, is next to him, on his left. National Archives 111-SC-18538.

that there would be no field censorship—everything would be checked and passed at GHQ in Brisbane—in order to speed up the process. He had also encouraged everyone to file two copies of each dispatch by a different means, so as to safeguard against things going astray. Yet, however hard he planned, Lehrbas could not alter the fundamental fact that Australia was over a thousand miles away, and even without any Japanese resistance, the ship and air couriers took between two and four days to get the dispatches to GHQ.[27]

As a result of these delays, the correspondents who had remained in Brisbane stole the story of the Kiriwina and Woodlark landings. On the day of the operation, PROs summoned them to the spacious briefing room, where they had arranged chairs in neat rows and pinned sliding map panels to the walls. Once the reporters arrived, the officers handed out "more than 3,000 words of background—geography, history, native life"—about the unfamiliar islands, and then divulged the first bare-bone facts of the uncontested landings. When the briefing ended, the correspondents hurried to their desks in the adjoining work room to begin banging away at their typewriters. In the next twelve hours, members of MacArthur's press corps produced a total of 45,700 words for four overworked censors to check. "This," wrote one of them when it was all over, "is the largest wordage and the largest number of stories written in any single day by correspondents in the Southwest Pacific. The volume subsided during the next few days but the general level of wordage was higher than during any past story."[28]

On this basis alone, MacArthur's new template for press relations appeared to be working. More reporters were churning out more words at GHQ than ever before, while their colleagues at the front were relatively happy that they had made it so close to the action. The only lingering questions surrounded who would get the public credit in this new round of battles.

Krueger had landed on Kiriwina and Woodlark with US forces, while the Australians continued to shoulder the bulk of the fighting on the New Guinea mainland. As soon as MacArthur's media machine cranked into high gear, General Sir Thomas Blamey, the Australian commander, became decidedly unhappy. In his memoirs, he complained that Krueger's attack on Woodlark "was hailed as a fine operation of the war by the news hungry," when it "was, in fact, one of the jokes of the war." Even worse was to come once MacArthur decided to sideline both Blamey and his Australian troops. For the past year, MacArthur's egotistical communiqués had given "scant recognition of the Australian efforts," even when Australian troops had outnumbered American forces. As soon as Krueger's Alamo Force went into action, the fearsome Australian "Diggers" would get fewer and fewer mentions in US coverage, while gushing stories continued to appear beneath headlines like "How MacArthur Saved Australia: The Story of His Brilliant Campaign for New Guinea."[29]

* * *

While MacArthur had little trouble consigning the Australians to the margins of the US news agenda, Halsey's SOPAC presented a greater challenge.

Since the end of the Guadalcanal campaign, war reporters had increasingly ignored this part of the world. The lack of a major battle was the main reason, but as an internal navy investigation discovered, the correspondents had also become increasingly frustrated by their inability to get in, out, and around the Solomons. Under pressure from Knox, who wanted to improve the navy's press relations throughout the Pacific, Nimitz instructed Halsey to end the ban on correspondents using air transport, which had been instituted in late

January when space on planes had been at a premium. He also assigned an officer to SOPAC "for the purpose of expediting copy from the forward areas of your headquarters" back to San Francisco and beyond.[30]

These basic improvements immediately improved the morale of the war correspondents toiling in the Solomons, but they did nothing to address the much more fundamental problem that hung over the next phase of the offensive: divided command. For more than a year, SWPA and SOPAC had jostled for scarce resources, bickered over strategic priorities, and struggled to provide coherent air and naval support for each other's battles. Liaison between the two had been rudimentary at best, while the chain of command only compounded the confusion. Halsey, who had been SOPAC chief since October 1942, remained ultimately responsible to Nimitz while also "under MacArthur's strategic direction." "No one much liked this command sophistry," one historian has observed, but since neither King nor Marshall would countenance Nimitz or MacArthur as supreme commander, the "unsound" structure remained in place.[31]

Luckily, when Halsey met MacArthur in Brisbane in April, the two men got along well. Armed with a directive from Washington, they agreed to commit their forces to a series of "mutually supporting, coordinated advances along two lines," which, they believed, would keep the enemy off balance as they moved to isolate Rabaul. When it came to publicizing the ensuing battles, however, trust was in dangerously short supply. Halsey, although impressed with MacArthur's personal magnetism, had long shared the widespread naval view that the general was a "self-advertising Son of a Bitch." MacArthur, although full of admiration for the "blunt" and "outspoken" Halsey, retained the distinct suspicion that the admiral "thinks a lot of himself" and "likes a headline."[32]

In an attempt to ensure that he, not Halsey, dominated the headlines during the next phase of operations, MacArthur took the precaution in late June of coordinating the release of all SWPA and SOPAC communiqués from his GHQ in Brisbane. Halsey's response was revealing. "This Public Relations is certainly a pain in the neck," he wrote Nimitz on the eve of the New Georgia landings. "We have immediately stopped all communiqués. I am afraid that you will hear repercussions. However, I am delighted because it saves us much worry."[33]

* * *

The reporters slated to land on New Georgia had much more to worry about than who would be releasing the communiqués. Despite repeated injunctions to travel light, many members of the small press pack boarded the boats laden with equipment—not just notebooks and typewriters, but, as one PRO complained, full "Abercrombie and Fitch outfits." Like their colleagues who were landing on Kiriwina, these reporters expected the worst, but in this case their fears had much more grounding in fact. An estimated ten thousand Japanese troops lay in wait on New Georgia, firmly ensconced in impressive defensive structures. Halsey planned three separate landings on June 30, followed by another assault on July 2 to capture the Munda airfield, the island's main prize. Even if everything went according to plan, he anticipated that it would take twenty thousand men two weeks to gain control over New Georgia.[34]

At first, everything did go according to plan. The reporters accompanying the assault on Rendova, just to the south of Munda, watched the first wave of troops land from a destroyer waiting just offshore. Henry Keys of the *London Daily Express* grabbed a worldwide exclusive when his eyewitness account "hitch-hiked a thousand miles by sea, land, and air to reach the nearest radio," from which the AP circulated it to US newspapers forty-eight hours after the invasion. Keys described how, for much of the day, "the beach was black with men and trucks and the channel in which the ships stood was pimpled with dozens of small landing boats which frequently were hidden in showers of spray as they plowed through the choppy sea." He also revealed numerous brushes with danger, including a sustained midafternoon attack by Japanese torpedo planes. By the end of the day, though, he and two reporters from the UP and the *Christian Science Monitor* were able to record a resounding success. "Now that it is over," Keys wrote that evening, "and we have gotten away with one of the most brazen attacks against the Japanese it is almost impossible to believe we have accomplished the objective."[35]

MacArthur was almost as incredulous when he read these stories, albeit for a very different reason. He deemed it bad enough that the dramatic accounts of the New Georgia invasion received many more column inches than his own uncontested assault on Kiriwina. He thought it infinitely worse when he found that the navy was releasing its own version of this battle, in contravention of his expressed instructions. Normally, navy communiqués were renowned for their drabness—it was "part of the Navy Gospel," one observer had noted a few months earlier, "that there should be no adjectives, no editorialization in the communiqués"—but this time senior navy officials added a large splash of color, with Knox leading the way.[36] The navy secretary, MacArthur fumed, even had the temerity to boast on July 2 that with a growing number "of ships, planes, and submarines" in the Pacific, his admirals had managed to launch "a real offensive."[37]

MacArthur retaliated immediately. He encouraged his Brisbane correspondents to claim that "the navy's premature announcement of the Rendova landing . . . might easily have meant disastrous results" for his own operations. He also asked Marshall to clarify, once and for all, where power resided in this matter. "Total news releases and communiqués concerning the Southwest Pacific-Solomons operations," the army chief of staff reassured him on July 9, "will be made by you except for such matters as you may authorize Halsey to release locally."[38]

This unequivocal ruling inevitably angered the correspondents covering the SOPAC battles, who, as one observer noted, were henceforth "forced to wait three to six days to release their eyewitnessers of Halsey's operations because these operations must first be mentioned in [the] MacArthur communiqués." It came just in time, however, to allow MacArthur to execute a much-needed cover-up.[39]

On New Georgia, the fighting quickly bogged down into a nightmarish stalemate that ultimately took almost fifty thousand men more than a month to end. "Tangled terrain and shrewd defenses," observes historian Thomas Hughes, "befuddled the National Guardsmen, who had arrived on New Georgia's shores" with little battlefield experience. Some units were spooked by phantom night attacks. Others struggled to hack their way through the dense jungle. Before long, exhaustion, malaria, and what one surgeon dubbed "psychoneurotic complexes" began to take such a crippling toll that Halsey decided to fire the division commander and commit a large number of reinforcements.[40] In Brisbane, however, the daily briefings never came close to revealing such a grim reality. "The Battle of Munda," wrote an AP reporter at MacArthur's HQ on July 15, "appeared to observers to have settled down to a methodical blasting of the Japanese out of their foxholes, bunkers, and strong points defending the air base of New Georgia." The American offensive, agreed Tillman Durdin, also writing from GHQ, "has been slowed up a bit, but it is far from stymied and promised soon to break all Japanese resistance in the southeastern New Georgia Islands."[41] Exposed to this rosy picture, editorial writers back home offered the strongest possible approval. "Gen. Douglas MacArthur," declared the New York Times, commander in chief of this offensive, has added to his stature. The dashing and courageous soldier of the Bataan campaign is also a strategist who can direct diverse services in the execution of a well-conceived plan. From staff officers down to the Marine private who stumbled through the bush and took part in the final attack with a broken leg, everyone in these actions seems to have earned the historic commendation: Well done![42]

* * *

By the time SOPAC forces invaded Bougainville in November, Halsey's tolerance for such puffery was wearing so thin that he lobbied hard to issue his own communiqués, but to no avail. MacArthur continued to dominate the coverage of Halsey's campaign from Brisbane, where his reporters effectively identified him with every battlefield success—although sometimes this backfired. MacArthur was particularly upset when he discovered that the UP had transmitted a story claiming he had said that the Bougainville invasion was progressing a "damned sight better than scheduled." Angered not by the sentiment, which was perfectly in character, but by the attempt "to put words of profanity in my mouth," MacArthur immediately demanded "corrective action."[43]

Meanwhile, the reporters who accompanied the invasion found conditions on Bougainville "pretty rugged." According to Gordon Walker of the *Christian Science Monitor*, the Americans had received "the stiffest resistance encountered on any of the Solomons' many beachheads." The first waves of attacking Marines, agreed George E. Jones of the UP, "ran into an inferno of grenade, mortar, artillery, and machine gun fire at the water's edge." Thankfully, Walker reported, the Japanese riposte "cracked quickly under the weight of vastly superior numbers," and American forces were able to consolidate a perimeter around Empress Augusta Bay to protect the vital airstrip. "The official description of our losses," added Jones a couple of days later, "is 'moderate,'" although the small press pack suffered more than most, with Keith Palmer of *Melbourne Herald* killed by a bomb and Ron James of the AP sustaining a wound.[44]

Over the following weeks, the survivors struggled to get their eyewitness accounts into print as the fight settled down into a series of battles to expand the US perimeter. The reasons for this failure were depressingly familiar. As a navy investigation concluded at the end of the November, the correspondents' "efforts to tell SOPAC's story to the American people [were] hampered by an utterly inadequate commercial radio service. More than

50 percent of the time this daily file of press is so delayed in transmission that it arrives in the US too late for use."[45] When dispatches did finally make it to a home news desk, many editors decided that they were nowhere near as interesting as what was happening elsewhere. William Chickering of *Time* was so angry when he discovered that his magazine had cut his story to make space for "a new batch of Russian War pictures" that he sent a cable to his editors protesting *Time*'s "desolate . . . treatment [of] Bougainville."[46]

The main saving grace was a discernible improvement in living conditions. Despite heavy rain, the Marines launched an intensive effort to tame the jungle while the Japanese attacks tapered off. Two sets of reporters stayed on the island to report this next phase of battle. One consisted of the Marine combat correspondents, who, since Guadalcanal, had been working hard to ensure that the navy's PR section was "deluged with copy from the combat area." On Bougainville, these men continued to suffer "from the oppressive heat, the continuous rain, the knee-deep mud, [and] the dark overgrown tangled forest with the nauseous smell of the black earth and the rotting vegetables," but they still managed to convey a positive image to the home front. "At this beachhead, just a month or so after the initial attacking wave," observed one Marine correspondent in a widely published dispatch, "there are movies being shown 300 yards behind the front lines. Instead of bearded figures, caked with mud, there is a colonel out of *Esquire* going by, smoking a cigarette in a six-inch holder."[47]

The other group of correspondents on Bougainville were those working for the black press, which boasted a circulation of more than 1.6 million.[48] Until this point in the war, black reporters had struggled to get close to the action. In Europe, they had largely been confined to covering the work of black service units in the rear.[49] In Asia, the situation had been even worse. For one thing, the Marines "refused to accept black recruits" in combat roles, while the navy "allowed them to enlist only as messboys." For another, many in government were fearful that the Japanese "were conducting a 'systematic campaign' to stir up black demands for equality, and that 'a good many' black leaders were receiving payments through the Japanese ambassador in Mexico." They therefore had little desire to let black correspondents anywhere near the Asian theaters.[50] The navy's attitude was typical. "We are somewhat fearful," remarked one PRO in October 1943, "of accrediting any Negro correspondent to the Navy in the South Pacific, not only because of transportation but of what he might write of the activities of Negro troops and soldiers."[51]

Yet, as the Bougainville battle bogged down over the winter of 1943–44, the situation gradually began to change. Under pressure from civil rights groups and with a presidential election pending, the administration began to encourage black newspapers to produce "constructive and accurate stories on black participation in the war." What was much more important, the War Department agreed to give combat experience to a number of black regimental combat teams, including one that arrived in Bougainville in March, just after an enemy attack on US positions. Once the Japanese had been halted, these black troops were ordered to pursue them and "enlarge the perimeter."[52] Fletcher P. Martin, a correspondent for the National Negro Publishers Association, told their story. Martin began by stressing how quickly the men were adapting. "Despite the newness of jungle fighting," he wrote in one dispatch, "our troops have dug in like veterans and hang tenaciously on to their plot of ground as artillery motor and rifle fire cloud inky night with blood curdling bursts of hell and destruction." Above all, he tried to convey the horrors of the jungle experience. "The smell," Martin reported in late April 1944, "still remains as repulsive as ever. This phase of warfare is the kind you just can't write about. Words don't suffice, pictures can't show the stench which permeates tropical air. . . . Life is measured by the weight of a small caliber shell."[53]

Dangerous Dress Rehearsals

Conditions on the ground were no better in New Guinea, where MacArthur's campaign was starting to gather pace, but here correspondents were increasingly taking to the skies after Diller relaxed the ban on flying operational missions.[54]

Robert Cromie was one of the first correspondents to exploit this new opportunity. Accompanying a bombing raid, the *Tribune* man was lucky not to encounter any enemy aircraft, but in the story he compiled on his safe return he recounted plenty of other jittery moments, from the preboarding briefing that highlighted the strength of Japanese ack-ack fire to the "anxious conversations concerning the weather . . . as the plane left the clear stretch of heavens, plunged into the soupy clouds and began to twist and buck."[55]

A month later, Cromie's rival on the *Chicago Daily News* decided to go a step further. Aware that only in North Africa had an American correspondent jumped into battle with paratroopers, George Weller asked Diller for permission to train as a "parachute infantryman."[56] The PRO took the matter to MacArthur, who decided that this "case was an unusual and exceptional one" that deserved approval. Armed with this endorsement, Weller headed off to undergo the regulation instruction, which included making no less than seven training jumps. These gave him some excellent material for a long story that told of the dangers inherent in this form of warfare: the tension as the plane took off, the rush on plunging into "the great vastness of the world," and the dread of breaking an ankle on landing. Once safely on the ground, Weller reported, the troopers had to trot off fast to reach their assembly point, often leaving the deflated 'chutes behind. "Parachutes," he explained, "are expendable and so, too, in the grim way of war, are paratroopers; [our parachutes] will be recovered by us if we win, by the enemy if we lose."[57]

By September, when these paratroopers were assigned to capture the Nadzab airstrip during a major operation in the Lae region, MacArthur decided to take center stage once again. He arrived from Brisbane just before the attack to take up residence in Port Moresby's Government House, "a huge, white, rambling bungalow" surrounded by a tropical garden teeming with frangipani, hibiscus, and palm trees. The day before the attack, he made the short drive to the airstrip, where eighty-one planes stood in neat rows. Along with Kenney and a retinue of reporters, he watched as the paratroopers checked their kits, cleaned their guns, and nervously swapped jokes. "Tell your boys I have complete faith in them in this job," he told their commander, "and that I'll be praying for them." That night, when Kenney revealed that he would be flying with his "kids . . . to see them do their stuff," MacArthur decided that he, too, would go along. Kenney tried to talk him out of such a reckless move, but MacArthur was immovable. He was "not worried about getting shot," he explained, only about suffering from airsickness and disgracing himself "in front of the kids." Appearances, he knew, mattered and placing himself alongside some of the bravest of all combat fighters would help to remove the deeply damaging stain of "dugout Doug."[58]

That same evening, Diller handpicked eight correspondents to join the air armada, and they repaid him royally the next day after ninety-six transport planes had dropped an entire regiment of seventeen hundred men on Nadzab in less than three minutes.[59] "American paratroopers, watched from a Flying Fortress by Gen. MacArthur," the AP account began, ". . . have landed behind Lae, New Guinea, to complete the encirclement of 20,000 Japanese in the Lae-Salamaua sector." "I didn't want our paratroopers to enter their first combat," another reporter recorded MacArthur saying, "fraught with such hazard, without such comfort as my presence might bring to them."[60]

After the success at Lae, many more correspondents began to accompany air missions. Eleven volunteered for a big bombing raid on Rabaul in October, but due to mechanical problems only seven reached the target. Bill Wilson of the UP flew in a B-24 Liberator and was lucky to survive an attack by several Japanese fighters. "Cannon shell burst around them," another correspondent explained, "and machine gun bullets slammed into the fuselage, one bullet cutting through Wilson's oxygen mask." For the remainder of the flight, the reporter struggled to breathe, although he remained conscious as his plane limped back to base, riddled with holes.[61]

Wilson's hair-raising experience was by no means unusual. Other correspondents returned to Port Moresby having almost crash-landed because of thick cloud or fierce turbulence. At least one boasted that his aircraft had a fuselage "like a sieve" after it had dodged through heavy ack-ack fire at the target. Yet, even in the face of such dangers, flying became an integral part of the war reporters' lot, for the simple reason that it was their only way of getting to and from a front that became ever more distant once MacArthur's troops were pushing westward along New Guinea's northern coast. Indeed, hitchhiking an airlift became so commonplace that it even acquired its own name: "The War Correspondent's Transit System."[62]

George Jones described how this system worked during the invasion of Arawe, New Britain, in December. The UP reporter had recently arrived in New Guinea from Bougainville in a bedraggled state, the incessant rain having destroyed "the contents of his wallet including his Pacific Fleet War Correspondent's Pass." As soon as he received a replacement pass, he boarded a plane to watch MacArthur's assault on Arawe, whose capture was designed to neutralize Rabaul to the north and protect the flanks of future operations in New Guinea to the south.[63] Approaching the invasion site, Jones could see dark specks below, which, he realized, were the US Marines pouring ashore. After a short while, his plane returned to a northern New Guinea airdrome, where he wrote his story. "But there are no censors or wireless sets on that side of the towering, cloud-capped Owen Stanley range," he told a colleague. So when a sergeant yelled, "Hey, there's a B-25 shoving off," he gathered together his field bag, typewriter, and camera, and cadged a ride to the closest headquarters, where, grimy and unshaven, he handed his copy to the censor for transmittal through facilities that, as Diller confessed, "are limited in capacity." "We had slept through the cold, high-altitude portion of the journey,"

Jones wrote of his dramatic day, "and our ears were still popping. But we polished off the evening with a shower and dinner."[64]

However disorienting Jones's journey, it paled next to the experience of his AP rival, who had the misfortune of joining one of the boats participating in the amphibious assault. Bob Eunson was a rookie reporter when he got chosen for Arawe. He had spent the past few weeks covering Kenney's air force from GHQ, and as he confessed later, he was a little too eager for action. In the early morning darkness, he found himself on one of fifteen landing craft filled with Marines whose job was to block the enemy's evacuation route before the main invasion landed an hour later. Eunson soon regretted joining this hairy mission. "We tried to land in rubber boats," he remembered after the war, "and didn't have any force behind us. . . . We landed under a bombardment," he added, which killed twelve troopers and wounded seventeen more. Eunson's own harrowing experience provided him with a compelling story. It detailed how he had jumped out of the boat in order to avoid the incoming fire, how one bullet had hit his typewriter and smashed it into two pieces, and how he had been saved when a landing craft that was part of the main invasion force picked him out of the shark-infested water. For the first time in his fledgling career, Eunson received a major byline on a big story, but at a cost. "It was a baptism of fire," he confessed later, "and I respected it and I learned to play it cooler after that and not to rush out and try to get killed."[65]

* * *

By early 1944, MacArthur felt no such restraint, as William B. Dickinson discovered when he landed on Los Negros, one of the Admiralty Islands, in late February. The forty-four-year-old UP man had almost fifteen years of reporting experience behind him, including a stint covering the London blitz, but like other observers, he found the naval bombardment preceding the Los Negros assault to be "frightening, awe-inspiring, and unearthly."[66] MacArthur ostentatiously courted the danger, standing so tall and proud on his boat that that he reminded one reporter of Washington crossing the Delaware. As he neared the beach, the general spotted Dickinson on a makeshift jetty. "I see the press is present," he announced before heading off on an hour-long tour of the beachhead, during which he refused to flinch when bullets whizzed close by. By the time Dickinson accepted MacArthur's invitation to join him on the journey back to New Guinea, the UP man was clearly smitten. MacArthur, he wrote in his battlefield dispatch, "showed his usual magnificent lack of concern for possible danger."[67]

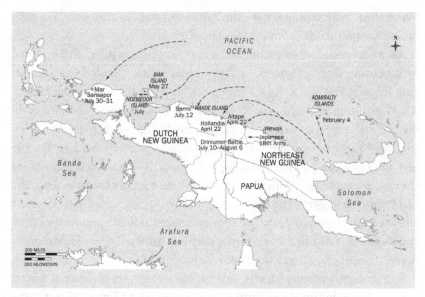

Fig. 7.2. Allied advance in northern New Guinea. Drawn by George Chakvetadze.

MacArthur's determination to be seen on an invasion beach, despite the strong protests of his senior commanders, was one of the best indications yet that he increasingly viewed the New Guinea campaign as a dress rehearsal for the main event, which, as he had constantly promised for almost two years, would be his triumphant return to the Philippines. Another sign was how his headquarters justified the Admiralty Islands operation. The timing had certainly been bold. The invasion had originally been planned for April, but when intelligence officers reported that Los Negros was lightly defended, MacArthur decided to take a gamble. He knew that the navy's offensive in the central Pacific was gathering momentum, and he feared that Washington would favor that axis of the advance over the Philippines if he did not keep pace. He also believed that, once in Allied hands, Los Negros would provide "a first-rate staging base" when the time came to assault the southern Philippines islands of Mindanao and Leyte.[68] His invasion-day communiqué made little secret of these calculations. The Admiralty Islands, it declared, "stand at the northern entrance to the Bismarck Sea," at a location "almost due south of Guam [which the navy had yet to reach] and 2,300 miles from the Philippines." Editorial writers immediately took the bait. "The gate to the shortest road to the Philippines" was now open, they declared, and

MacArthur "may soon use the Admiralties not only as a base for mopping up, but for another dash toward Mindanao."[69]

As it happened, this prediction was a little premature. Emboldened by mounting signs of enemy weakness, MacArthur decided to make his next lunge at Hollandia, New Guinea, 500 miles to the west of the present Allied position. His aim was to capture the two sheltered anchorages in the Hollandia area, as well as the Aitape airfield 125 miles to the east. With roughly 73,000 troops landing in three locations, this would be his largest and most complex undertaking so far, and the big news organizations planned accordingly.[70] Gone were the days when no more than two reporters had been able to get to the frontline of a New Guinea battle. The AP alone allocated ten correspondents and photographers to the three invasion sites, and these men used all the experience they had gathered over recent months to keep the copy flowing rapidly from the battlefield.[71]

Bob Eunson, still somewhat shaken by his harrowing experience at Arawe, acted as the point man. On April 22, he landed with General Krueger, the Sixth Army commander. He then toured each invasion site in turn, collecting the eyewitness accounts written by AP reporters who had hit the beaches with the troops. Some of his colleagues jokingly described him as a glorified copy boy, but his job was hardly risk-free. At one point, Eunson had to shelter from flying shrapnel after a Japanese plane bombed an ammunition dump. On the beach at Aitape, his final destination, he also saw a pile of dead Japanese soldiers. That gruesome sight was his cue to ask Krueger's permission to make a dash back to headquarters. With his pack bulging with his colleagues' dispatches, Eunson boarded the next plane out, arriving in Port Moresby seventy-two hours before any other reporter and thereby scoring a notable scoop for the AP.[72]

The stories from Hollandia fit the pattern that had been established over the past eight months. They invariably began by recounting the tension of boarding an assault vessel bound for an enemy-held shore in "the blackness of a tropical night." They then told of the stunning success of the landings, with the loss of surprisingly few men. Finally, they described the central role played by MacArthur, who was starting to make an invasion-day appearance on the battlefield one of his signature moves. "MacArthur," observed Murlin Spencer, "wore his customary braid-covered peaked hat and carried his gloves. After listening to reports from officers, MacArthur strode around among the men. As the general moved over to the edge of a muddy road one soldier turned to his comrade and asked, 'Did you see MacArthur?' 'Yes,' was the reply. 'I never thought I would see him in a hole like this.'"[73]

Once the invasion-day excitement had abated, seasoned war correspondents faced a dilemma. They knew that their assault stories would be the ones to make it onto the front page. After that, the interest of most editors would start to wane, even though the campaign would invariably drag on. The Japanese normally regrouped and dug in, turning the relief and euphoria of the first day into a slow, grinding bloodbath to obtain the ultimate objective. The reporters recognized that if they departed from the battlefield before this second phase, the home front would receive a skewed picture. Yet they also had to consider not just the dangers associated with remaining at the front for any length of time, but also the difficulty of organizing repeated airlifts of copy back to GHQ. Since MacArthur always seemed to have another operation pending, most correspondents decided that the savviest course was to get out quickly in order to recover and prepare for the next invasion, even if this meant that the home front would learn about the remainder of the battle from MacArthur's overoptimistic communiqués.[74]

When American forces invaded the island of Biak on May 27, MacArthur was in a particularly bullish mood. "For strategic purposes," his first communiqué announced the next day, "this marks the end of the New Guinea campaign." Enemy resistance, another bulletin stated on June 1, was "collapsing," and a mop-up operation, added a third on June 3, was "proceeding." Unfortunately, the reality soon proved much bleaker. Biak contained more than ten thousand Japanese troops, who used the island's airstrip as a bait to lure US forces onto low ground surrounded by high ridges. To break out of this trap, the Americans launched a series of grinding attritional battles, made worse by the intense heat and lack of freshwater. Only when Eichelberger arrived to reprise his Buna performance did the Biak battle start to go better, but he had learned enough about the perils of publicity to keep a low profile. As a result, the Biak story continued to be written from MacArthur's distant GHQ, where reporters admitted to "bitter fighting," with "Japanese resistance . . . increasing every yard," but produced few details about the savagery of a campaign that dragged on into late August at a cost of more than four hundred dead and two thousand wounded.[75]

As the engineers moved in to turn Biak into a forward base for MacArthur's next offensive, another menace appeared. More than a thousand men succumbed to a vicious scrub typhus, which peaked in August, killing about a dozen of them. Unsurprisingly, MacArthur remained studiously silent about this development, while offering some happy news about another deadly disease. Malaria, one of his communiqués confessed, had been "one of the major contributing causes of Bataan's surrender," but after more than a year of intensive study and treatment in New Guinea, this foe had been largely vanquished in "one of the greatest victories General MacArthur has won in the Southwest Pacific—a victory by Science and discipline over the anopheles mosquito."[76]

* * *

Eighteen months earlier, MacArthur's boasts had often been met with dismissive scorn from his war correspondents, who had viewed them as part of a deliberate ploy to distort the news. According to a private assessment undertaken by *Time*, at that stage "about three out of four of the correspondents out there [in Australia] . . . disparage him."[77] During the first half of 1944, however, the mood among MacArthur's reporters started to shift. While some were noticeably grateful for the tangible improvements he had made to the way they could cover the string of daring and tricky battles, others publicly praised Diller's men, stating that "generally speaking, the censors were fair."[78] Many more were genuinely impressed that the commander was willing to risk his neck to witness battles firsthand. A few even became such avid MacArthur boosters that they believed the general would make the perfect Republican candidate in the upcoming presidential election.[79]

Correspondents working for the MacArthur–loving *Chicago Tribune* knew that promoting the general's political prospects was almost part of their job description, but even some of those who worked for less partisan papers caught the MacArthur bug. Frank Kluckhohn was one. The *New York Times* reporter had acquired a reputation as a troublemaker in North Africa, where he had been banned from the frontline for violating the censorship code.[80] Arriving in the SWPA in the middle of 1943, he spent more than six months covering the New Guinea campaign, including watching the Arawe invasion from the invasion fleet's flagship. During that time, Kluckhohn became so captivated by the commanding general that he even sent his publisher a private protest when the *Times* publicly questioned MacArthur's presidential bid.[81]

While this improved relationship was one outcome of MacArthur's new template for press relations, the other consequences were more mixed. By the summer of 1944, MacArthur had clearly forged an effective system that was primed for use when he finally made his big return to the Philippines. Indeed, the logistics of getting correspondents to and from distant battlefields; the various methods of speeding copy from the beachhead; and, above all, his own star performance on invasion day—these were all important innovations that could be readily transferred from the dress rehearsal to the main event later in the year. More immediately, however, the higher visibility of MacArthur's New Guinea campaign did not always have the impact on the home front that he desired. It certainly failed to boost his political aspirations, which faded so quickly during the spring of 1944 that MacArthur was forced to renounce his presidential ambitions just days after the Hollandia invasion.[82]

Nor was this the only problem. From Buna to Biak, via the Bismarck Sea, MacArthur's trademark bombast had been partly due to his gnawing fear that the navy would grab all the headlines, which would in turn strengthen the admirals' case for focusing on the central Pacific rather than the Philippines. For much of 1942, MacArthur could at least take comfort from the fact that the navy's press policies were even more restrictive than his own. A year later, he also knew that his own improvements had far surpassed anything the navy had been able to achieve. As Tom Yarbrough of the AP observed privately in July 1943:

[T]he difference between Admiral Halsey's headquarters and General MacArthur's headquarters regarding the work of correspondents is the difference between a crossroads country store and a big city department store. One is slick and streamlined, provides a large amount of usable information promptly and has a properly authorized machine to expedite the movement of press copy from the field. The other is lumbering, timid, and operated largely by thumbs.[83]

These advantages undoubtedly helped MacArthur when he lobbied Washington for a return to the Philippines, for the politically sensitive Roosevelt was extremely reluctant to alienate his media-savvy general with a presidential election looming. Yet MacArthur was also acutely aware that these advantages were rapidly evaporating. The navy had long taken umbrage at what it disparaged as MacArthur's "propaganda plan."[84] Toward the end of 1943, Nimitz was finally in a position to start launching his own series of invasions against three island belts in the central Pacific: the Gilberts, the Marshalls, and the Marianas. When it came to publicity, Nimitz was determined that his reporters would encounter an operation not only as slick and as streamlined as MacArthur's, but also, in crucial respects, very different from the SWPA's, with less focus on the commander's brave exploits and more attention on the hellish, bloody nature of the fight against Japan.

8

Bloody Battles in the Central Pacific

Preparations in the Pacific

In the eyes of many war correspondents, Commander Waldo Drake symbolized everything that was wrong with the navy's press relations. Tall, gaunt, and with a slight speech impediment, Drake had served for nineteen years as an editor at the *Los Angeles Times* before becoming the PRO in Pearl Harbor in early 1941. Unlike so many others who had switched from the media to the military, Drake exhibited little liking for his former colleagues. He stood aloof from the correspondents he did not respect and was positively rude to those he disliked, even if they worked for the most prestigious news organizations. His feud with Bob Casey had become so bitter during 1942 that editors at the *Chicago Daily News* believed that, a year later, Drake still held a deep grudge and "that, as a result, our service has suffered." His animosity toward Foster Hailey was much worse. Senior managers at the *New York Times* even began to suspect Drake of imposing "unreasonable" restrictions on Hailey's "movements and his communications," which in turn meant he could not produce "anything approaching a day-to-day or even a week-to-week picture of developments in the Pacific area." Reporters for other newspapers increasingly hoped, if not lobbied, for Drake's relief or reassignment.[1]

The PRO's position looked particularly precarious in the early months of 1943. Worried that the toxic press setup was obscuring the navy's battlefield achievements, Frank Knox called for an audit of media relations ahead of a big conference to be held in Washington on April 26. Any reporter who thought that this meant the end of Drake was soon in for a rude awakening. Nimitz trusted and liked his PRO. The two men played tennis every day, and the admiral had come to appreciate Drake's "loyalty to and his understanding of the navy and the press." Rather than getting rid of him, Nimitz decided to give Drake the job of working out what had gone so wrong.[2]

Before flying all the way to Washington, Drake embarked on a tour of Pacific bases, covering more than fourteen thousand miles in fourteen days. The sheer size of the theater provided one major clue to why the reporters were so unhappy. They felt isolated, with only tenuous links to their news desks and a slow, arduous journey whenever their assignment was changed. Drake jotted down these complaints, which, he knew, would be much easier to address than the obsession that many admirals had with secrecy, although even here there were some grounds for hope. The taciturn King had already started meeting reporters in Washington, providing them with off-the-record briefings about upcoming operations. With Nimitz's fleet about to take the offensive at long last, some of King's subordinates agreed that the time had come to ease a few of the more onerous restrictions, which had been essential a year earlier when naval resources had been stretched so thin.[3]

By the time Drake arrived in Washington, expectations were running high. Knox and Lovette had invited more than a hundred PROs to the conference. They had also asked editors to file any complaints ahead of time, so that, as one officer put it, the navy could "brush up on a lot of things to settle every squawk by the press in the field."[4] Drake opened the proceedings by explaining the improvements Knox had instructed him to make, including allowing correspondents to travel around the South Pacific by plane and charging an officer with the task of "expediting copy from the forward areas" to the United States. He also revealed that his own press office in Honolulu would be expanding from two to nine officers and that he would be reviewing his theater's press relations each week in an effort to resolve fresh problems as they arose. Above all, he emphasized that his team would be working hard to foster a new spirit. "The entire conference," remarked one observer, "reflected the navy's willingness to scuttle any arbitrary practices of the past which have irritated the press . . . and to work wholeheartedly with the press through its PRO to cover the war at home and abroad with more thoroughness and efficiency by ironing out all misunderstandings that hamper their mutual and colossal job."[5]

* * *

Few correspondents would benefit more from this new cooperative spirit than Robert Sherrod of *Time* and *Life*. The thirty-three-year-old had endured a long, hard apprenticeship before joining Henry Luce's expanding magazine empire in 1935, starting with a stint on the *Atlanta Constitution* and ending with a series of unsatisfying jobs in depression-wracked New York City. In 1937, he had become part of *Time*'s Washington bureau, where he had forged connections with some of the most powerful figures in government, but as soon as the Japanese attacked Pearl Harbor he had demanded an overseas posting. "I can think of nothing less interesting than sitting out the war in Washington," he had remarked in early 1942. "There is too much history being written where men are dying."[6]

So began a restless attempt to find the ideal place from which to cover the war. *Time* first sent Sherrod to Australia, which he soon found even more boring than the American capital. After six months in Brisbane and Townsville, he came to the conclusion that MacArthur was "the world's greatest actor," a man preoccupied with his own "heroic elevation." He also thought that the overly restrictive PR operation in the SWPA ensured that Americans back home had not "the slightest idea of what a hell of a long, hard bloody war we're in for." Desperate to awaken them to the brutal reality, Sherrod pressed his bosses for a combat assignment in 1943. Initially, he ended up on the cold, foggy islands of Attu and Kiska in the North Pacific, covering the savage fighting, where, he reported, the chances of survival were fifty-fifty, at best. But he quickly tired of "groping my way over tundra-covered mountains without being able to see more than thirty feet in any direction." He also learned that Nimitz would soon be launching a major offensive in the central Pacific, built around the new *Essex*-class aircraft carriers that had recently been arriving in the theater. After successfully pushing for another transfer, he arrived in Honolulu in October, in time to grab a berth on "the largest carrier task force ever assembled."[7]

As Sherrod prepared to depart, he had little trouble detecting the new mood among CINCPAC's press officers. His colleague in the Hawaii bureau of *Time* and *Life*, Bernard Clayton, had, like so many other correspondents, been on the receiving end of Drake's "bluntness, his frankness, and his ability to give a hard 'No.'" But Clayton also recognized that Nimitz's PRO had been working hard to turn promises into policy since the April conference, even if in his opinion other factors were just as important in improving press relations. One of these, Clayton observed that fall, was the healthy respect between the navy and the media "springing from two years of close fraternity in Guadalcanal foxholes, sinking ships, riddled landing-craft, and so forth." The other was a new offensive mentality, which incentivized the admirals to share their likely victories with the world. Whatever the cause, the consequences were easy to spot. Just look at the early preparations for the upcoming offensive, Clayton stressed. Drake had already rounded up twenty-seven correspondents from various locations in order to forge "the largest press force ever assembled for one operation in the Pacific."[8]

In October, Drake set off on a tour of the staging posts for the new operation in an attempt to identify ways of speeding the flow of copy when the
battle began. He left Ken McArdle, his deputy, in charge in Hawaii. It was
McArdle's job to provide the war correspondents with a new kit containing
"special envelopes, air mail press copy stickers, and orders signed by
CINCPAC, ordering the press material to be routed past field censors." The
hope, McArdle explained, was that all of this distinctive stationery would
"expedite news stories and pictures back to Pearl Harbor for transmission
to the mainland." If this failed, he added, Nimitz had instructed every officer
"to keep a sharp eye out for press copy, to rush it through by aircraft, ship, or
landing craft."[9]

When the briefing officers began to outline the battle plan, the war
correspondents realized why so much time had been spent addressing these
logistical challenges. The next targets were Makin and Tarawa, two tiny atolls
in the Gilbert Islands, two thousand miles from Hawaii.[10] Tarawa would "be
a bigger show." Here, the Second Marine Division had the task of capturing
the all-important airstrip. Sherrod was so disappointed when he learned that
he would be covering the army's attack on Makin that he appealed the assignment. Earlier in the war, the navy might have ignored the distress of a senior
correspondent, but in tune with the new obliging spirit of the times, McArdle
switched Sherrod and two other correspondents to the Tarawa force. "You
don't know how lucky you three are," the PRO added as they departed—a
comment they would often ponder ruefully in the weeks to come.[11]

* * *

Sherrod certainly felt lucky to begin with. After boarding an old battleship
for the first leg of the long journey, he marveled at the number of destroyers,
aircraft carriers, and scout planes in the fleet. He felt so secure, he joked,
that it was almost like being on a prewar pleasure cruise. Soon, however,
boredom set in. There was little to do each day except read book after book
before repairing to a communal area to drink a nonalcoholic beverage. Then
Sherrod discovered four British sailors on board. The US Navy knew so little
about the Gilbert Islands, especially the times and depths of the tides, that it
had recruited these men to help with navigation. Sherrod spent an increasing
amount of time pumping them for information before compiling a long background story that he sent to his editors in preparation for the day of battle.[12]

On arriving at the island of Efate, Sherrod hooked up with the Second
Marine Division, and his mood began to improve. In the evening, he sipped

excellent cocktails in the officers' club. The next day, he met with Merritt Edson, the hero of Guadalcanal, who was the division's chief of staff. Edson tried his best to prepare the correspondents for the troubles to come. It was doubtful, he explained during an hour-long lecture, that the naval bombardment would kill most of the enemy troops on the island. "Neither," he added, "can we count on taking Tarawa, small as it is, in a few hours." Along with William Hipple of the AP, Sherrod learned that he would be landing in the middle sector, which, the two men joshed, increased their chances of getting "shot at from both sides." Even so, Sherrod remained hopeful that the attack would be little more than a cakewalk, a hope that hardened into an article of faith when he learned that a B-24 scouting mission had reported no signs of enemy activity on the atoll. "Try as I might," he recorded long after the battle was over, "I never got over the feeling that the Japs had pulled out of Tarawa."[13]

On leaving Efate, the invasion armada sailed toward its destination. Sherrod spent the long, hot days observing the Marines as they went about their final tasks, from compulsive rifle cleaning to endless letter writing. The night before the attack, he made his own preparations. He decided that his typewriter would be too cumbersome for this mission, so he left it in his cabin. Into his pack went two notebooks, some rations, a couple of canteens of freshwater, morphine, and a small bottle of medicinal brandy. Just after 8:00 p.m., he tried to sleep. Still awake when the alarm went off at midnight, Sherrod headed for the mess to breakfast on steak and eggs. Then he went outside to get ready for the dawn. As he knew from numerous briefings, this would be the cue to board a landing craft to accompany America's first large-scale assault in the central Pacific.[14]

"The Hard Facts of War"

Even before the sun rose on the morning of November 20, the sky was awash with brilliant, orange-red flame as shell after shell from the American armada arced toward Tarawa. Sherrod's first thought was that this horrific rain of destruction was payback for Pearl Harbor. His second was that, surely, "no mortal men could live through such destroying power." Then he saw a shell splash close by. The Japanese were returning fire. Not only were they on Tarawa, but they had also survived the pre-invasion bombardment. By the time that Sherrod clambered onto his landing craft to join the fifth attack wave, his optimistic illusions were in tatters.

The problems had started with the bombardment, which, despite appearances, had not been sufficiently sustained to eradicate the impressive Japanese defenses. The currents and the tides caused the next set of troubles, the former pushing the invasion craft too far to the south and the latter preventing many of these boats from entering the shallow lagoon when they finally reached the right place. As enemy fire intensified, the Marines could get near the shore only by boarding amphibian tractors (known as amphtracks) and "many of these vehicles were in poor mechanical condition." As Sherrod waited for one, shells burst all around, filling his landing craft with countless pieces of shrapnel. When an amphtrack finally arrived, the driver was scarcely reassuring. "It's hell in there," he shouted, motioning toward the beach. "They've already knocked out a lot of amphtracks and there are a lot of wounded men lying on the beach." The last seven hundred yards proved particularly harrowing. Sherrod and fifteen Marines jumped neck deep into the water, while Japanese machine-gun bullets fizzed close by. Somehow Sherrod survived. Spotting a pier, he sheltered in the rocks beneath it while he recovered his breath. Then he dashed from shell hole to disabled tank, trying to find a place of relative safety to gain his bearings. Thus far, the Marines had managed to secure only about twenty feet of sand and coral in front of a seawall that provided a modicum of cover. The situation looked bleak.[15]

Sherrod could see dead bodies everywhere. Those who had survived were desperate to know if their buddies had made it. Sherrod asked a number of Marines if they knew anything about the other war correspondents, but without luck. Only after the battle started to settle down did he come across Bill Hipple, as well as Richard W. Johnston of the UP and Frank Filan, an AP photographer. Amid so much death and destruction, these reporters immediately forgot their professional rivalries. Here, Sherrod recalled, "everyone was glad to see anyone he knew, because the chances of not seeing him were so heavy." Besides, none of them had any prospect of telling their story anytime soon. Sherrod did not even have a usable notebook; the two in his pack had become so saturated that he had to dry them "on the hub of an amphtrack."[16]

Life during the three days the reporters spent on the island was both traumatic and exhausting. Filan had already become something of a hero, having damaged his camera while rescuing a Marine. Johnston, for his part, could scarcely believe he had survived, having presented such an inviting target when wading ashore with his typewriter clutched above his head.

Many Marines had not been so fortunate. Sherrod and Hipple estimated that American casualties had to be around 30 to 40 percent. When Sherrod joined a burial party, he almost gagged at the numerous corpses left by this awful battle. "Some are bloated," he observed, "some have already turned a sickly green. Some have no faces, one's guts are hanging out of his body. The eyeballs of another have turned to a jellied mass, after so long a time in the water."[17]

By now, the correspondents were anxious to return to their ships. After hitching a ride on a transport heading back to the fleet, Sherrod borrowed a navy typewriter and sat down in the comfort of a cabin to begin tapping away. At first, the words did not come easily. Sherrod had barely slept in three days. He had also seen many incidents that would, he cabled his editors, "in themselves make momentous news stories," but the sheer number made it difficult to find a frame. Sherrod decided to start with "the most gruesome sight I have seen during the two years of this war," although when he tried to write, the words did not come. So he put his typewriter to one side in order to get a good night's sleep before attempting a "second take" the next morning.[18]

Even then, Sherrod and his colleagues had no idea if the censors would allow them to focus on the bloody nature of the fighting. In recent weeks, Drake and his team had gone to great lengths to guarantee that news copy would be sped from the distant battlefield to big-city news desks. These PROs had said very little, however, about whether the censors would cut anything they deemed too graphic, and as Sherrod knew, the navy did not have a great track record on this matter. Until this point, he believed, "our information services had failed to impress the people with the hard facts of war." Not only had the communiqués been too optimistic, but "the stories accompanying the communiqués gave the impression that any American could lick twenty Japs." Nowhere had there been any room for the war's unsavory side. Would that change now?[19]

* * *

The simple answer was yes. In recent months, senior officials in Washington had become increasingly concerned that the home front was far too complacent about the prospect of an early victory. With opinion polls revealing a sharp spike in the number of those who thought the fighting in Europe would be over in months, Roosevelt had pushed for a change in the way the media dealt with battlefield stories. The president, according to one of his aides, was now convinced "that the lethargic elements should be aroused" by harder-hitting stories demonstrating that the war "is not all beer and skittles for the country's soldiers, sailors, and airmen."[20]

The army had already begun to permit a more realistic depiction of the fighting in Italy, while Roosevelt had recently allowed *Life* to publish a photograph taken a year earlier of three dead American soldiers on the beach at Buna.[21] Knox, who fully backed the need to confront complacency, decided to follow the same path in the central Pacific, although his senior admirals did not initially appear to agree with him. The first word Nimitz received from the Tarawa beaches suggested that the fate of the invasion might be in doubt. Calling his chief PRO into his office, he reacted in a predictably prudent way. "Drake," he instructed, "we've got to keep this thing to ourselves until we find out what's going to happen."[22] When Nimitz finally learned that the danger of defeat had passed, he released only the blandest of statements. "Army troops and Marines, aided by the greatest fleet ever assembled in the Pacific," his headquarters declared on November 22, "have established beachheads on Makin and Tarawa atolls and fighting is now going on."[23]

With none of the correspondents on the beachhead yet in a position to transmit an eyewitness account of the carnage, there seemed a real danger that, once again, the home front would receive a distorted picture of the battle. So Knox summoned members of the Washington press pack to a conference a couple of days later. "You can't capture a well-defended island fortress without heavy losses," he explained to them. "It was bitter, hard fighting. The first waves of troops had to take a lot of punishment."[24] The battlefield reports that Drake's team subsequently shepherded into print described precisely what this meant. "Alongside the jetty in the water," recounted one, "lay shattered landing boats on their sides, draped with the battered bodies of Marines; light tanks which didn't get ashore; smashed oil drums and debris, and forever silent Marines whose limp forms floated on lifebelts they'd inflated wading ashore." "The smell of death," insisted another, "literally permeates the blasted shell-torn beaches."[25]

Compared with newspaper reporters, Sherrod was in a privileged position. The next issue of *Time* would not appear until December 5, and his editors were almost certain to clear a large space for such a dramatic story. After overcoming his brief bout of fatigue-induced writer's block, he produced a truly shocking piece. It culminated in an account of a post-battle inspection trip in which he found Tarawa "bloodier than the stockyard abattoirs of Chicago," reeking "with the stench of thousands of blown and twisted and charred bodies." The navy's censors happily passed this cable. In New York, however, Sherrod's editors decided that their readership was not quite ready for such an explicit description. Excising the more disturbing sentences, they ensured that the worst thing *Time*'s massive audience would read about was the fate of one Marine unit. "Many were cut down as they waded in," Sherrod reported, "others drowned. Men screamed and moaned. Of 24 in one boat only three reached shore."[26]

Despite this editorial trimming, Tarawa quickly became known as a place of death. When Nimitz visited the atoll on November 27, he told reporters that "he was afraid that the American people were not sufficiently impressed with the toughness of the battle for Tarawa because it was over in three days." He need not have worried. The release of the official casualty toll a short while later revealed that 1,026 Americans had been killed on the atoll and another 2,557 had been wounded, which, according to one spokesman, were "the heaviest [losses] in any operation in the Pacific."[27] Nor did the Marine combat correspondents pull any punches. Sergeant Jim G. Lucas, who had landed in the second wave, admitted that Tarawa had seen "the bitterest, costliest, most sustained fighting on any front." He also revealed that "something appeared to have gone wrong." In a press conference on November 30, Major General Holland Smith, the corps commander during the battle, acknowledged what this had been. Smith's role during the operational phase of the battle had been "ambiguous" to say the least—he had been, in essence, a frustrated observer with no actual command control, which perhaps explained why he was prepared to be so candid in his criticism. "Tarawa," Smith told reporters, "might have fallen at less cost had there been longer naval gunfire and aerial bombings."[28]

This admission that military mistakes had caused excessive casualties immediately sent Washington-based reporters dashing to their more indiscreet off-the-record sources. "Tarawa," noted Walter Kiplinger, the influential editorial writer, "was a very bad blunder—the loss of life may have been 3,000 instead of the 1,000 published." "The operation," Kiplinger concluded after talking to a number of officials, "was undertaken on orders from someone higher up (no names mentioned at all)[,] maybe the White House in order to make a showing for political reasons."[29] Thankfully for the government, no one was prepared to commit such incendiary allegations to print, but the usual critics did spot an obvious opportunity. The *Chicago Tribune* led the way, calling for a public inquiry into the purpose, tactics, and cost of the invasion. The "severity of the casualties," it thundered, meant that "evidence should be developed to determine whether better planning and conduct of the plan might not have avoided some of them."[30]

Throughout December, senior officials launched a spirited riposte. Knox worked hard to shift public attention away from American errors and onto the impressive nature of the Japanese defenses. Meanwhile, Lieutenant General A. Archer Vandegrift, who was about to become the new Marine Corps commandant, used Tarawa to make a deeper point about the nation's morale. "No one regrets the losses in such an attack more than does the Marine Corps itself," Vandegrift declared in a public statement. "No one realizes more than does the Marine Corps that there is no royal road to Tokio. We must steel our people to the same realization."[31]

In subsequent weeks, anyone trying to steel the nation for what lay ahead continued to concentrate on Tarawa's bloodiness. Robert Sherrod was the most influential. The *Time* reporter returned home in December full of praise for his treatment by the navy since the reforms earlier in the year. "I believe a lot of reporters," he wrote to one of his editors, "use the censorship fog and the poor-public-relations as an excuse for their own shortcomings. I can honestly say that the censors have never caused me any trouble, except in the case of a few minor points which did not matter much."[32]

Yet, despite the obvious PR improvements, Sherrod found the nation still dangerously ignorant about the Pacific War. So he decided to produce a book about his experiences. A self-confessed pessimist, he did not think his volume would sell anything like the numbers of Richard Tregaskis's *Guadalcanal Diary*, which had become the benchmark for success. But along with his publishers, Sherrod still managed to emulate Tregaskis's astonishing speed of production by completing the writing and editing process in a little over ten weeks. The book that appeared in early March began with a description of the Marines' supreme self-confidence before the invasion. It then recounted the chaos and carnage they experienced during the assault and, ultimately, the horrific death toll. "The Marines floating in the water," he wrote of his last tour of the battlefield, "are now pitiful figures. Many of them have had their hair washed off their heads by this time."[33]

Even amid such gore, Sherrod had witnessed some stirring sights. The most poignant was a Marine "leaning in death against the seawall, one arm still supported upright by the weight of his body. On top of the seawall," Sherrod recalled, "just beyond his upraised hand, lies a blue and white flag, a beach marker to tell succeeding waves where to land. Says Holland Smith,

'How can men like that ever be defeated? The Marine's duty was to plant that flag on top of the seawall. He did his duty, though it cost him his life.'"[34]

* * *

The strong bond that Sherrod had forged with the Marines on Tarawa also cast a profound influence over how the home front came to see images of this battle. While on the island, Sherrod had watched the Marine combat photographers go about their work. Sixteen of them had landed on invasion day under the direction of Staff Sergeant Norman T. Hatch. Walking around the battlefield "upright, holding their precious equipment overhead," these men had presented "perfect targets for the withering Japanese machine-gun fire." Even so, they had still managed to take more than nine hundred still pictures, some of which impressed even Life's finicky editors.[35]

Life had pioneered a form of photojournalism that "used related pictures in a logical sequence to report a particular event. To get these news picture-stories," one of its editors explained, "the magazine has had to develop its own corps of photographers, trained not only in the art of getting one or two or three first-rate pictures that show the highlights of a news story, but also in the art of getting an entire series of outstanding pictures that tell the story visually from beginning to end as completely as a newspaper article might tell it."[36] That other news organizations often failed to provide such sequential shots was one reason Life regularly grumbled about the Still Picture Pool, but on Tarawa it had no complaints about the work of the Marine photographers. "These fellows," Life's photo editor remarked on December 7, "who weren't even in Life's school, did a better job than any of us has ever done"—a judgment that lay behind the decision to publish thirteen of their photos across nine pages of the December 13 issue.[37]

Norm Hatch had once attended a Luce school organized by those who ran the March of Time newsreel, and on Tarawa he used this training to stunning effect. During the battle's first phase, the civilian newsreel cameramen had been stranded offshore. Hatch, by contrast, had waded onto the atoll through enemy fire, and after making a series of running repairs to his camera, had shot nearly four thousand feet of film. When fashioned into a nineteen-minute movie, these images presented such a disturbing depiction of the battle that the decision on whether to release it to the public went all the way up to the White House. When pondering what to do, Roosevelt turned to the reporter who had become synonymous with Tarawa. Sherrod's response was categorical. "Gruesome, yes, Mr. President," he replied, "but

Fig. 8.1. The home front saw graphic images of the Marine dead on Tarawa. National Archives 80G 57405.

that's the way the war is out there, and I think the people are going to have to get used to that idea."[38]

As a result of this conversation, *With the Marines at Tarawa* went on general release in March 1944. Its message was as shockingly moving as Sherrod's bestselling book. "These are the Marine dead," the narrator intoned at one point, as the camera panned across bodies lying on the sand and bobbing in the shallow sea. "This is the price we have to pay for a war we didn't want, and before it's over there will be more dead on other battlefields."

* * *

Opinion pollsters struggled to gauge the impact of such images. In one of the first-ever focus groups, academics at the Social Research Library at the City College of New York tried to explore the reaction of 224 people. Exposure to "realistic war pictures," they concluded, "increases the favorable attitudes toward a realistic news policy, although no change in the degree of identification with the war could be seen after one brief exposure to realistic war pictures. There was little evidence of revulsion toward the pictures." If this result was far from conclusive, the government found another set of results truly alarming. Despite its conscious effort to depict the war in grittier terms, one national poll discovered that only 57 percent of Americans in the spring of 1944 thought the "government is releasing as much news as it should," down from 74 percent in February 1943. Even worse, a mere 38 percent thought the information provided was accurate, while 44 percent believed it "made the situation look better . . . than it is."[39]

The only upside was that by early 1944 few people were questioning whether Tarawa had been worth the cost. The strategists had always intended the campaign in the Gilberts to be a staging post on the way to the much more important prizes in the Marshall and Mariana Islands. Tarawa, these officers concluded, had been an important learning process, revealing a number of flaws while confirming that US amphibian operations could prevail against a strongly defended coastline. At a more practical level, it had also resulted in the capture of an important airstrip two thousand miles to the west of Pearl Harbor, which would prove invaluable in the upcoming operations in the Marshalls, scheduled for early 1944.[40]

"What He Does Find Out Will Scare Him"

At first glance, the USS *Rocky Mount* looked like all the other small supply ships packed into Pearl Harbor. Inside, however, it was a marvel of modern technology, with room after room jammed full of up-to-date communications equipment, essential, so the navy now recognized, for directing the "vast and complicated" operations involved in amphibious warfare. During the pending Marshalls campaign, the ship would serve as the headquarters of the Joint Expeditionary Task Force. It would also house the correspondents who would be joining the mission, all of whom were delighted to discover that they would have access to these state-of-the-art facilities.[41]

This delight soon disappeared when the reporters found out who else was on board. Admiral Richmond Kelly Turner, the task force commander, inspired fear, even loathing, among his subordinates, who called him "Terrible Turner" behind his back and complained that he could be "irascible, if not actually mean." Holland Smith, the Marine general who was again serving as the corps commander with no actual command control, was equally fearsome, his aversion "to a sloppy or inept performance" earning him the nickname "Howling Mad" Smith. On board the *Rocky Mount*, the two navy men got along tolerably well, but Smith became his usual cantankerous self whenever he encountered Major General Charles H. Corlett, the army commander of the Seventh Division.[42] Indeed, the Marine officer struggled to mask his deep-seated distaste for the army's tactical prudence. He also bristled at his lack of authority during the amphibious phase of the upcoming battle, his ire becoming almost uncontrollable when Corlett threatened to place him under arrest if he attempted either to control Seventh Division troops or to go ashore once the fighting started.[43]

For a battle-hardened reporter like Keith Wheeler, Waldo Drake's presence on the *Rocky Mount* only promised to make the mood even more toxic. The bespectacled Wheeler had learned his trade in Chicago's tough school, where being loud and aggressive was often a prerequisite for success in the newsroom. His war dispatches in the *Chicago Times* reached only a small audience, but he seemed determined to compensate by trying to get as close to the action as frequently as possible. "No correspondent," observed his friend and colleague Robert Sherrod, "had seen more of the Pacific War. Wheeler was along when Admiral Halsey raided the Marshalls and Gilberts in early 1942. He was aboard the cruiser *Charter* when it took a Jap bomb. He went to the Aleutians in late 1942, stayed to report the winter-long bombing of Kiska and Attu through weather that birds wouldn't fly in." He had missed only one major sea battle, and it still rankled. Wheeler continued to blame Drake for "intentionally" sending him off on an irrelevant mission at the time of Midway. As the fleet headed to Kwajalein and Namur-Roi in late January, the forceful correspondent was determined that the navy PRO would not pull another fast one on him.[44]

For his part, Drake was in a surprisingly buoyant frame of mind, and not just because Tarawa had seen all the hard work of recent months reap rewards. As the *Rocky Mount* approached the next target, he found to his surprise that Turner was much less terrible than he had feared. "Despite the fact that he has been as busy as 20 men," Drake wrote to McArdle, Turner "has been most cooperative on press problems and has kept his eyes open constantly for press operations." The admiral's motives were not entirely altruistic. A workaholic, Turner would, during the battles to come, "read nearly all the stories written by war correspondents and filed through his flagship" as part of his voracious desire "to know what the writers thought about the things that were going on." On balance, though, Drake believed that the reporters would value his personal input, for it gave them even more confidence that their eyewitness stories would be sped back to their home offices in record time.[45]

* * *

The initial landings on the Marshalls turned out to be a welcome contrast to Tarawa. With the wire-service reporters taking turns transmitting eight-hundred-word stories, the home front soon received a story of major triumph—of the Japanese caught by surprise, operational goals quickly "exceeded," and US forces encountering only "spotty, sporadic resistance."[46]

Yet Wheeler and Drake still managed to have a major row. Just before the attacks on Kwajalein and Namur-Roi, the PRO spelled out what could and could not be reported, telling the correspondents that they could mention the use of field artillery, but not the caliber of weapons. "The only other prohibitions," he explained, "are: (1) damage to pillboxes, etc; (2) rockets; (3) demolition teams; (4) detailed description of our weapons."[47] When Wheeler returned from Kwajalein with a dispatch "mentioning rockets and identifying the infantry regiments, etc.," the bad feeling between him and the PRO immediately bubbled to the surface. Drake was particularly angry that Wheeler wanted to give credit to the army's artillery for "pulverizing" enemy positions, insisting that most of the destruction had been inflicted by the navy's firepower. He also reacted badly when Wheeler composed an angry letter "objecting to the radioed press procedure."[48]

When the Marines and the army invaded Eniwetok, to the northwest of Kwajalein, a couple of weeks later, Drake had more to worry about than possible censorship infractions. Enemy resistance, although much lighter than on Tarawa, remained a constant worry. The captain of the transport ship that took two AP correspondents to the beach allowed them only ninety minutes on the island, "so that they had to dash ashore, get what they could on the run, and then bring the stuff immediately to the flagship for forwarding." These men turned out to be the lucky ones. A group of correspondents, including Hal O'Flaherty of the *Chicago Daily News* and Harold Smith of the *Chicago Tribune*, found themselves about 150 yards behind the frontlines when American planes began to strafe enemy positions. Inching forward to inspect the damage, they suddenly came under sustained mortar fire. Smith dashed to a small coconut stump, where O'Flaherty had already burrowed a makeshift shelter. Then he felt the sharp stings of a mortar wound in his right eye, so he and O'Flaherty made a desperate dash back to the beach, where they skidded into a shallow shell hole for cover. "We slid down," Smith recalled soon after, "just as Capt. Waldo Drake . . . appeared, blood streaming from a two-inch cut above his right eye. Drake, completely disregarding his own wound, insisted on accompanying me and Correspondent Merle Miller of *Yank* [magazine] 300 yards back to the beach landing area for a stretcher and medics."[49]

However grim the reality was for war correspondents on the ground, newspaper readers back home continued to receive stories of stunning success. Nimitz's communiqués led the way, hailing the fact that American forces had suffered only 282 deaths on the Marshalls, compared with the 8,122 Japanese fatalities. At a time when news of the Bataan death march dominated the headlines, most editorial writers took this asymmetry as "America's direct and instant answer to . . . [the] revelation of enemy atrocities."[50]

For the war correspondents who braved the battlefield, success had another dimension. For more than a year, they had been waging a losing battle against their colleagues covering the European theater, whose reports on the invasions of North African, Sicily, and Italy had invariably dominated the front page. In early 1944, with the Italian campaign bogged down in a grisly stalemate, the correspondents in the Pacific finally had the front page all to themselves. Wheeler's bosses gave his eyewitness stories particularly lavish treatment. "SEIZE 10 MARSHALL BEACHHEADS," the *Chicago Times* blared on February 2. "TIMESMAN WHEELER TELLS EPIC ATTACK." The articles that accompanied such headlines showcased the navy's new determination to permit a grittier depiction of the fighting. "War on this desolate ruin of an island," Wheeler told his readers of the Kwajalein battle, "is compounded of dirt, weariness, hunger, thirst, sweat, stink, rage, fear, and pure fascination." O'Flaherty's page-one story in the *Chicago Daily News* revealed why the navy was prepared to be so open. "Japan's defenses in the Marshall Island Group," O'Flaherty wrote on February 3, "—its naval strength, its air force, and its military force in the area—have been obliterated. In this entire operation, not one Japanese plane has been sighted; not one submarine has attacked our gigantic fleet; not one shot has been fired from a Jap naval ship. . . . Here, amid the dismembered bodies surrounded by chaos, can be found the poignant truth that Japan is an inferior nation, misguided and misgoverned. . . . Its doom is sealed."[51]

* * *

For the next few weeks, both sides of the military-media divide basked in the afterglow of these triumphs. The navy contemplated the award of medals to correspondents like Sherrod who had "shown great courage under fire in the pursuit of his profession," while even Drake's biggest critics respected his bravery on Eniwetok and applauded his subsequent promotion to captain.[52] Nor could the press corps complain about how the victorious navy was handling its copy. The time had long since passed when fear of defeat had led to delays and excessive censorship cuts. "We've got so much stuff and power now," boasted one AP correspondent to a colleague after the Kwajalein landings, "we don't have to give much of a damn what we tell the Japs. What he does find out will scare him."[53]

Yet there remained a few dark tinges to take the edge off this rosy picture. For one thing, war correspondents continued to face extreme danger in the Pacific. Astonishingly, every reporter on Tarawa had come through unscathed, but the Marshalls had been much bloodier. As well as the wounds sustained by Smith, Miller, and Drake, there had been the tragic loss of the columnist Raymond Clapper, who became the sixteenth reporter killed at the front after his plane crashed during the initial stages of the Kwajalein invasion.[54]

Interservice rivalry also continued to plague operations. The central Pacific was the navy's war. Alongside the major improvements that Drake had instituted, which had greatly facilitated the civilian reporters' coverage of the operations in the Gilberts and Marshalls, the Marines' combat correspondents had continued to provide a constant source of additional information. The AP estimated that by early 1944 it was placing 95 percent of the Marines' copy on the wires, with "50 to 55 percent of it being distributed on a nationwide basis and the rest being used for regional purposes." Denig, the Marine Corps' publicity chief, was naturally "very well pleased" with the way his innovation was working. "We have tried not to beat the people who make their living as correspondents," he told a *Time* reporter, "but to assist them."[55]

The army saw the situation quite differently, however. Back in November, its battle on Makin had inevitably been overshadowed by the Marines' bloodbath on Tarawa. In early February, by contrast, the army's Seventh Infantry Division had toiled for four days on Kwajalein, while the Fourth Marine Division had captured Namur-Roi within forty-eight hours.[56] Most correspondents had duly headed to Kwajalein, but with Drake excising Wheeler's praise for the army's artillery, tensions quickly grew. On board the *Rocky Mount*, one army PRO even confronted Drake, complaining that "it is Makin and Tarawa all over again, the Marines are getting all the big news breaks."[57]

Drake was never known for his diplomacy. Like almost everyone else in the navy, he begrudged the way that MacArthur had been belittling the navy's operations in Bougainville and New Georgia. To calm the army PRO down, he only offered a few soothing platitudes. Some of his superiors did not bother to do even that. Holland Smith told reporters shortly after Kwajalein that the Seventh Infantry's attack had been far too slow—an allegation that Corlett brushed aside with the acerbic comment that Smith had no basis on which to make such a judgment "since he was shipboard the whole time." The censors immediately placed this exchange off-limits, but the warning signs were clear. The upcoming operation to capture Saipan would require even more intense cooperation as the two services fought side by side for weeks in order to capture an island that dwarfed anything in the Gilberts or Marshalls. Whether the censors could continue to paper over the cracks remained to be seen.[58]

The "Brush Off"

After spending his stateside leave writing the Tarawa book, Robert Sherrod arrived on Eniwetok in early June. He was glad to reunite with his old friend Keith Wheeler, whose bravery and brashness underpinned his honest and hard-hitting reporting, but during his time in New York, he had reached a bleaker verdict on some of his other colleagues. "I must admit," he had written his editor in February, "that the public relations people have a lot on their side when they say: 'Why do they keep sending those half-ass reporters out here? What kind of reporting do they expect out of the $40-a-week police reporters and $50-a-week sports writers. . . . The press associations, in particular," Sherrod concluded, "cannot take any bow for their coverage of this war. They have sent out young, green reporters who systematically overwrite, without any sense of news evaluation."[59]

Thankfully, there was no longer anything amateurish about the navy's own PR work. Everywhere on Eniwetok, Sherrod found a hive of activity, from the constant construction that bulldozed away most signs of the recent combat to the continued efforts to improve the reporters' lot, which, as Drake boasted, meant that press relations had "jumped overnight from a corner drugstore job to a big-league enterprise."[60] Recreation facilities were also getting better all the time. On the evening of June 6, Sherrod settled down to watch that night's movie. As the projectionist loaded the first reel, a young lieutenant stood in front of the audience to announce the latest news, including the liberation of Rome and the fighting on Biak. Then, after stepping away from the stage, he reemerged and called for quiet. "Here is a piece of news that has just come in," he stated calmly, "—the invasion of Europe has been announced." While the Marines, soldiers, and sailors uttered a brief cheer, Sherrod and his colleagues began to calculate how this would affect their upcoming dispatches from the Marianas. No one was optimistic, for they realized that the Normandy campaign would be the biggest story of the war.[61]

For some reporters, the main consolation was the prospect of another easy victory in the Pacific. Those who had covered the Marshalls operation felt that the Japanese were now a spent force, although Sherrod, who had missed that battle, feared that Saipan would prove a tough fight. Once again, he would be accompanying the Second Marine Division, and this assignment immediately rekindled memories of the slaughter on Tarawa. On board the *Rocky Mount*, he encountered Holland Smith, and the corps commander gave him another reason to fret. "We are through with the flat atolls now," the general told the reporter. "We learned to pulverize atolls, but now we are up against mountains and caves where the Japs can dig in. A week from today there will be a lot of dead Marines."[62]

* * *

Fires from the pre-invasion bombardment dotted the dark horizon in the early hours of June 15. As the sun rose, Mount Tapotchau emerged as an imposing silhouette. The first landing craft began bobbing toward it shortly after 7:00 a.m. Sherrod's boat was not due to hit the beaches for a few more hours, so he spent much of the morning trying to "construct some kind of picture of what was happening ashore." This was no easy task, for the smoke and dust rising from the beaches became so thick that Tapotchau soon faded from view. Only when Sherrod finally landed did he discover that Holland Smith's gloomy prediction had proved correct. Touring the shallow beachhead, he saw dead Marines lying in the sand; one, he noted, "had had the top of his head nearly carved out, evidently by a shell fragment, and his brains had run out on the sand." "It was no trouble at all to find out why our casualties were so high," Sherrod concluded after spending his first night on Saipan. "The Japs from their mountainside dug-outs were looking down our throats. Not only were our front lines being pounded. Our beaches were still crowded with shore parties unloading supplies."[63]

By midmorning of the second day, the situation had become sufficiently stable for Sherrod to return to the *Rocky Mount* to pound out an article. On board, Drake's press operation appeared to be working smoothly. Richard Johnston of the UP had already transmitted the first story, telling the home front that the Marines were involved in "a savage land battle after surviving the fight for the beachhead." "I saw the assault waves claw their way over the barrier reef," Johnston reported, "and move on to the beaches, supported by naval guns, flaming rockets, and the automatic weapons from landing craft." The navy's communications team was immensely proud of what happened next. "Aside from a minor hitch occurring in the Western Union office," noted one officer, "Johnston's excellent pool story reached all hands [so] expeditiously . . . that the people of the States were treated to spot-news over their breakfast coffee—today's dateline *today*."[64]

That Americans on the home front would get this glimpse of the invasion just hours after it had happened was indeed a major achievement, but it was also the closest they would get to the Saipan battle for another week. The cause had nothing to do with Drake's preparations and everything to do with the vagaries of combat. The naval strategists who had planned the battle were hoping that the invasion of such an important island would lure the Japanese fleet into the open seas, where the formidable American carrier force could destroy it in a single strike. Four days after the first Marines waded ashore on Saipan, this hope turned into reality. The resulting Battle of the Philippine Sea did not go entirely according to plan. Admiral Raymond Spruance, the senior commander, saw his first task as protecting the invasion force, and so he refused to let his ships dash too far from Saipan in order to chase the Japanese fleet. Even so, Spruance had sufficient firepower at his disposal to shoot down 330 of the 430 Japanese carrier planes in what became known as the "Great Marianas Turkey Shoot."[65]

"Quiet" and "discreet" by nature, Spruance usually "shied away from publicity as if it were a booby trap," observed Sherrod, and on those rare occasions when he did come into contact with reporters, he made little secret of his feelings. "Gentlemen," he would begin, "I wish you'd hurry this up. We have men here who want to get back and get along with this war." In the aftermath of the Battle of the Philippine Sea, Spruance ran true to form, providing the correspondents accompanying his fleet with so little information that the story could be written only from Nimitz's distant headquarters in Hawaii.[66] This was one consequence of the big naval battle. The other was far worse. As soon as Spruance set off to intercept the Japanese fleet, Turner decided that his own ships sitting just off Saipan presented too vulnerable a target. On June 17, two days into the invasion, he therefore retired his task force to the east, where it remained for almost a week.[67]

The result was little short of disastrous for the war correspondents wanting to tell the story of the unfolding battle. Days into the campaign, those on Saipan had established their press camp in "a middle-class Japanese duplex, a stucco affair." A victim of friendly fire, "it stood with gaping openings" after its windows and doors had been blown out, but two serviceable rooms remained intact and the electric lighting still worked. On June 20, the correspondents gathered here hoping to get some rest after camping under the stars for the past five days. When an artillery barrage made sleep impossible, they began to talk about their shared plight. "The consensus of this sweaty, bearded, and bedraggled group of newspapermen just back from the foxholes along the frontlines," recorded Howard Norton of the *Baltimore Sun*, "was that we have not yet come against the main Jap force on the island." While they all feared that there would be thousands more casualties before the battle ended, their principal professional concern was the "fact that after six days no press dispatches had yet been sent out of this area."[68]

Sherrod understood the reason for this major delay. Returning to Saipan shortly before Turner's ship headed east, he began filling his notebook with troubling observations. "Bitter fighting," he wrote, "with gain often yard [*sic*] (of ten yards) marked the first two days of fighting for Saipan." "US casualties," he estimated, "probably outnumbered [the] Japs[']," and for the first time the Japs were using artillery extensively, chiefly three-inch guns and mortars which the tremendous preliminary bombing and shelling had been unable to silence." Yet none of this information made it off the island. "Due to the naval tactical situation," Sherrod explained to his editors when communications were finally restored, "no copy has gone out of Saipan in the first week of fighting except one or two direct Radio Press Association dispatches written by men who had not been ashore."[69]

In Hawaii, McArdle tried hard to look on the bright side. "I'm plenty glad we got Dick Johnston's initial pooler through before you had to knock off transmission," he remarked to Drake on June 25. "It established the setup, and when radio silence set in everybody understood why."[70] Unfortunately for Drake, "everybody" did not include senior figures in Washington, who would soon make him the scapegoat for the difficulties of getting press copy off Saipan. Nor did it include the battle-fatigued reporters, who were finding conditions on Saipan particularly grueling.

Fig. 8.2. Robert Sherrod (*right*) on Saipan.
© Getty Images.

"The heat," one of them recalled, "the sugar-cane flies, and the constant bursts of warm rain made slogging up to the companies of the 2d [Marine] Division harder."[71] When learning that all this effort was for naught, Sherrod, who had already reached a scathing judgment about the "communiqué commandos" based in Hawaii, alerted his editors to the fact that the reporters in the rear were regularly distorting what was happening on Saipan. "One day," he alleged, "when we lost a thousand men, mostly Marines, the Pearl Harbor boys were writing (and the headline writers compounding) that 'Yanks are mopping up Japs on Saipan.'"[72]

Sherrod thought this misrepresentation would make "a good press story." To drive home the point, he sent to New York a long letter written by Keith Wheeler, who was even more savage in his condemnation. "Correspondents in Pearl Harbor," Wheeler had complained to his own editor, "writing from a 10-line communiqué and feeling a terrible compulsion to produce prose, pump their stories full of pure fancy and balderdash." While the frontline reporters had been left incommunicado, Wheeler charged, those at head-quarters "wrote with beautiful enthusiasm of American troops swamping the Japs, sweeping up Saipan's beaches, blasting blithely through its defenses, sprinting to the island's biggest airport, largest town, and highest mountain. They wrote with such smug confidence that no reader and no editor could doubt that Americans were engaged in a picnic of no consequence."[73]

As a matter of fact, the dispatches written at headquarters tended to be bland rather than buoyant. A good example came five days into the invasion, when the home front learned nothing more than the fact that US troops had "driven all the way across Saipan Island to the shore of Magicienne bay, while an estimated 300 Japanese planes attacking the American carrier task force were destroyed in the greatest Pacific air battle since Midway."[74] In subse-quent days, as a combined army and Marine offensive bogged down against enemy positions that acquired a range of emotive names—Death Valley, Purple Heart Ridge, and Hell's Pocket—the public continued to receive a lack of vivid reporting. "Jap infantry resistance," reported a typical account on June 27, "stiffened all along an island-wide [line] from this morning as Marine and army forces reached a sector possibly chosen for the beginning of a last-ditch defense of Saipan." "Two hundred enemy troops," noted an-other story the next day, "were killed two days ago in a small sector of the island at the extreme southeastern point where they made a lunging counter-attack and broke through our lines above Nafutan Point."[75]

Hidden in this brief description was one of the most controversial episodes of the Saipan campaign. Frustrated with the pace of the offensive, Holland Smith suspected that the army's Twenty-Seventh Infantry Division under Major General Ralph Smith was underperforming, both in the mopping-up operation at Nafutan Point to the south and in helping the Marines break the stubborn Japanese resistance in the north of the island. On June 24, having consulted Spruance and Turner, Holland Smith decided to relieve Ralph Smith, a move that immediately exposed the fissure underlying the two services. Army officers in the theater were first to react, convening a board of inquiry that focused on Holland Smith's prejudice against the army and concluded that his decision to fire Ralph Smith had been unjustified. Nimitz, King, and Marshall worked hard to keep this bitterness under wraps, but on July 8 the story leaked. The *San Francisco Examiner* erroneously attributed Ralph Smith's relief to a tactical difference, with the "Marines seeking a swift decision at a high cost, while the army moved deliberately—at lesser cost." The *Examiner* was part of the Hearst chain that had long supported MacArthur. In subsequent stories, it further inflamed the situation by calling for MacArthur to be placed in charge of all Pacific forces, on the basis that he eschewed strategies that resulted in a "reckless and needless waste of American lives."[76]

The correspondents on Saipan initially shied away from the Smith versus Smith controversy on the practical grounds that Nimitz's censors would never pass a story about interservice conflict. But once the guns fell silent on Saipan and the reporters returned home for a rest, the situation began to change.[77]

During the battle, Robert Sherrod had spoken frequently to Holland Smith, who had justified his decision in the starkest terms. As historian Harry Gailey points out, Holland Smith had, "without any reconnaissance by members of Corps staff, decided that it was not the entrenched Japanese who were responsible for the Army attack lagging behind the Marine advance on either flank: it was the fault of . . . [the Twenty-Seventh Division] with which he had had previous firsthand experience." To Sherrod, he offered a particularly explosive justification for his action. "I've just lost 7,000 Marines," he insisted shortly after firing Ralph Smith. "Can I afford to lose back what they have gained? To let my Marines die in vain. I know I am sticking my neck out—the National Guard will be down my throat—but I did my duty." Having no doubt where his sympathies lay, Sherrod bristled when "the Hearst press began a campaign of denouncing the Marine Corps." He became positively offended when he read an AP report on September 10 that attacked Holland Smith for "relieving the commander of an exceptional army division."[78] Letting his anger take over, Sherrod wrote a blistering reply that appeared in *Time* a week later. In a key passage that, as Gailey observes, presented battlefield rumor as fact, he argued that "Ralph Smith's men froze in their foxholes. For days, these men who lacked confidence in their officers, were held up by handfuls of Japs in caves."[79]

"I suppose," Sherrod observed to his editor a few weeks later, "there has been more hell raised over 'The Generals Smith' than any story we have run since the war began." Officers attached to the Twenty-Seventh Division were naturally the most upset, arguing that the article combined "falsehood, cal-umny, and libel." Over time, Sherrod would accept that he "went too far in questioning the courage of the Twenty-Seventh's soldiers," especially given that he had made no more than a brief visit to their sector of the front. After undertaking "a most thorough investigation of all the ascertainable facts," his bosses suffered no such doubts. "Bob Sherrod," Henry Luce wrote to anyone who complained, "a highly competent war reporter, saw the things of which he wrote with his own eyes. In other words, he was there."[80]

Yet not everyone was appeased by this defense. Having warned Sherrod before he left the theater not to publish anything on the matter, Nimitz advo-cated the suspension of his credentials. Luckily for *Time*, the War Department was more cautious. "I do not believe that Sherrod is biased against the army," Surles, the BPR chief, wrote to Marshall, "but is rather over-whelmed by his last two experiences with the Marines. . . . If we take drastic action," he added sagely, "he will be forced to defend himself vigorously and in print as he has a high reputation as a war correspondent." It was much safer, Surles and Marshall concluded, to "work on Sherrod's basic fairness by explaining the damage he has done."[81]

* * *

Another major story that remained unpublished while the Saipan battle raged concerned the enemy's suicidal behavior. Some correspondents learned of instances when the Japanese military beheaded civilians and dynamited those penned inside caves. Others knew of a desperate banzai charge on July 7, which ended with enemy bodies stacked in tiers. Almost every reporter on the island witnessed the most horrifying spectacle of all: the hundreds of Japanese civilians, including whole families, who died on July 9, either by detonating hand grenades or by jumping from high cliffs.[82]

At first, the navy placed a complete block on all of these stories—not, as Drake and McArdle hastened to explain, because of their own restrictive impulses but due to a Joint Chiefs of Staff order dating back to February. In fact, the two PROs thought there was "a hell of a lot of good propaganda for us in these stories." In the absence of a policy change from above, how-ever, all they could do was forward them to Washington "for review and disposition."[83]

By the time this had been completed, Sherrod was back in New York, where he wrote a story that was published in August. "Some of the Jap civilians," Sherrod revealed, "went through considerable ceremony before snuffing out their own lives. The Marines said that some fathers had cut their children's throats before tossing them over the cliff. Some strangled their children." When Wheeler returned home in the fall, he was able to put a figure on the scale of the carnage. "Out of Saipan's civilian population of 25,000," he reported, "we had possession of 14,000 living souls a month later. More than 10,000 were dead, mostly by their own hands. Out of a civilian garrison of 25,000, all but a skimpy handful were dead."[84]

Wheeler's editors published this story to great fanfare, labeling it a major exclusive, but the reporter remained upset. It was not just the initial news blackout or the overlong block on suicide stories that bothered him. The problem, he believed, ran far deeper.

During the battle, Wheeler had composed a series of stirring eyewitness accounts. He had told of how the Marines considered the Saipan campaign the "most difficult" amphibious operation of all, partly because of its distance from American bases and partly because of the fanaticism of the enemy resistance. He had detailed the Marines "who live in holes and share their burrows with death," describing them as "a strange people for whom, dirt, discomfort, sudden hazard, and the sudden loss of friends are normal." In one tour de force, he had vividly recounted his own fears at the front. "If you are still on your foxhole in the morning," he had written,

> you can find out what happened during the darkness but at night all you can do is cleave to the bottom of your foxhole and keep your fingers crossed.... You hear a shell whistle in and you think it's going to land in your pocket. Your stomach contracts, there's a splintery crash and stuff seeps across the sandbags around your foxhole. Slowly, very slowly, the wrinkles come out of your stomach.[85]

When these stories finally began to appear in late June, Wheeler bristled at their treatment. Often, he complained, his dispatches were "cut, rewritten, and in some cases fragments of two stories were jumbled to make one day's issue." Even worse, his editors invariably buried them on pages ten and eleven. Such treatment, Wheeler charged, confirmed what many in the Pacific had long believed: their war was getting nothing like the amount of press attention being lavished on events in Europe.[86]

Reporters like Wheeler and Sherrod found this state of affairs infuriating not merely because they had risked their necks to cover the fighting. Those who had endured the horrors on Taiwan or Saipan had forged a particularly

Fig. 8.3. Keith Wheeler (*left*) and Bill Hipple of *Newsweek* (*right*) pose outside of the Governor's Palace on Guam, August 12, 1944.
© AP/Shutterstock.

close bond with the men they had seen suffer so much. Yet, although this turned them into team players, their new status posed obvious problems. For Sherrod and Wheeler, the Marines were their team, with the result that they sometimes cast aspersions on the role of the army—most notoriously in Sherrod's account of the Twenty-Seventh Division after the Smith versus Smith controversy. Sherrod also adopted a condescending attitude to the "young, green reporters who systematically overwrite," especially those stationed in faraway Hawaii, while Wheeler was particularly scathing about both Drake, against whom he bore a grudge, and his editors, who, he felt, continued to place a shroud over battles in the Pacific.[87]

In recent months, to be sure, Drake's improvements had helped to give the navy's dramatic battles on the Gilberts and Marshalls much more visibility back home, but Saipan had been a reversion to the bad old days. With no timely descriptions from the front, editors had relegated this battle to a less prominent place in the pecking order at a time when the news agenda was particularly crowded because of Eisenhower's invasion of Normandy. Wheeler could just about understand being knocked off the front page for this big battle, but the brutal truth was that editors had given it a much worse "brush off" by playing it a "very bad fourth" behind "the flight of B-29s to Japan and the Republican National Convention."[88]

The Pacific War, in short, remained something of a sideshow, although it was nowhere near as forgotten as another part of the sprawling conflict against Japan: the campaign being waged in the distant China, Burma, India (CBI) theater.

9

The CBI

Building Up Stilwell

Major General Alexander Surles was not known for his hands-on approach to public relations. A former cavalryman who yearned to swap his safe Washington berth for a taste of real action, he saw his job as the head of the army's BPR in simple terms. "Communiqués on combat operations," he believed, "should originate in the theaters where they are handled by newsmen on the scene or at the most a few miles from the actual fighting." That left his own organization with more mundane tasks like processing accreditation requests and finding shipping space for the hundreds of correspondents bound for distant battlefields.[1] Only rarely did Surles look up from all of this administration to intervene in bigger strategic questions, but these moments could be highly significant. One came on May 30, 1943. Sitting at his desk in the Pentagon, Surles penned a request to his subordinates. "Extensive publicity of Stilwell highly desirable," he wrote. "Important that prestige of Stilwell be built up."[2]

Surles had various motives for seeking to bolster the standing of Lieutenant General Joseph W. Stilwell at this point in the war. As the senior American commander in the China-Burma-India (CBI) theater, Stilwell had been placed in an unenviable position. Roosevelt recognized that China was crucial to the war effort in Asia, if only because it tied down so many Japanese troops; but whenever he had to allocate resources, he invariably relegated China to the bottom of his list.[3] One of Stilwell's tasks was to break the unwelcome news to Chiang Kai-shek, the Chinese leader, but this was by no means the only difficult part of his complex job. Stilwell commanded all US forces in China and India, a dubious honor given that Washington consistently refused to supply him with the American infantry divisions he demanded. He was also meant to be improving the efficiency of the Chinese army and, if possible, leading Chinese troops into battle, but here he encountered the reluctance of Chiang, who, Stilwell believed, neither wanted to develop strong forces that might undermine his own rule nor relished the prospect of offensive action in Burma after the Japanese victory there in the spring of 1942.

This defeat had been particularly disastrous because Burma had long been the main conduit for bringing American supplies into China. Until its recapture, the only remaining route was by plane over the notorious Himalayan "Hump," which, as the official historians observed, was "as villainous and forbidding a stretch of terrain as there was in the world." Because of a shortage of transport planes, the materiel that actually made it over the Hump was initially a tiny fraction of what Chiang was expecting, which only intensified Stilwell's problems. The general, whose prickly persona was so notorious that he had acquired the soubriquet "Vinegar Joe," increasingly faced a Chinese leader who felt slighted and ignored.[4]

Surles hoped that by boosting Stilwell's public image he would give the general more clout in these increasingly bitter battles with the Chinese government, but this was not his only concern. A year earlier, war correspondents had portrayed Stilwell as one of the few heroes to emerge from the horrific Burma retreat, but since then the CBI theater had become a backwater in the eyes of many Americans, who were receiving little news on what was happening there.

* * *

That the situation had been so different a year earlier had been partly a matter of pure chance. As Japanese forces swept across vast swaths of Asia during the early months of 1942, American editors had little control over where their reporters ended up. No less than six of them happened to make it into Burma in time to cover the demoralizing collapse of British imperial rule, including Leland Stowe, whose personal experience typified the prevailing chaos. The *Chicago Daily News* reporter had been trying to escape the crushingly restrictive censorship regime in Chungking, Chiang's capital city, for some time. He had initially planned to fly to Hong Kong on his way to the Soviet Union in early December, which, he ruminated afterward, would have almost certainly meant ending up in a Japanese prisoner of war camp. Instead, for reasons he could never fully explain, he headed to Burma, just in time to report on the Japanese invasion of that country.[5]

Some of the American correspondents Stowe encountered over the next few weeks had more calculated reasons for covering this battle, especially those working for *Time* and *Life*. Henry Luce, the owner of both magazines, had long been convinced "that without China we cannot achieve victory."[6]

It was hardly a coincidence, therefore, that when Stilwell traveled to Asia to begin his mission in February 1942, he was accompanied by Clare Boothe Luce, Henry's wife, who planned to write a series of stories about her experiences. Nor was it surprising that Henry Luce had recently put Jack Belden on his payroll, since Belden was fluent in Chinese, had been covering the war in this region since 1937, and had developed a close personal relationship with Stilwell when the latter had served an earlier stint as US military attaché to the Nationalist government.[7]

Soon after her arrival in Chungking, Clare Boothe Luce introduced "Uncle Joe" Stilwell to the American public as a modest family man who enjoyed the utmost respect of his soldiers. This popularity, she wrote in a long essay that appeared in two installments of *Life*, "is based on a fine mixture of his extraordinary consideration of them, his lack of brass-hat pomp, and his tough insistence that his orders be obeyed instantly and with the maximum of efficiency." Stillwell, she added, also had the ability to think beyond the narrow confines of his command, for although a Chinese expert, he saw how his own theater fit into the global war. "Every hour that Burma holds," the general told Luce in April, "saves America an hour in Australia and the Philippines."[8]

By that time, Burma looked like it might fall to the Japanese any minute. Belden headed to the front, along with Darrell Berrigan of the UP and Daniel De Luce of the AP. Although a Japanese bombing raid had recently knocked out the telegraph station that the press had depended on to transmit stories, the three reporters managed to get Allied pilots to fly out a number of their dispatches. At first, these were surprisingly positive. Indeed, aware that the Chinese authorities in Chungking were fashioning a relentlessly upbeat message, which maintained that "strong" Chinese forces had sent the enemy "reeling back toward Burma in a rout," De Luce was constantly on the lookout for something constructive to report. He found it at Toungoo, where stubborn Chinese resistance held up the Japanese advance for ten days. De Luce had no doubt where to place the credit for this battle. Stilwell, he wrote in one dispatch, had personally directed the Toungoo campaign "with all the shrewd serenity of a chess master"—a conclusion that Stilwell himself found deeply troubling. "The worst has happened in the press," he wrote with disgust in his diary. "Before I have had a chance to get my feet on the ground, a flood of crap is released. . . . What a sucker I'll look like if the Japs run me out of Burma."[9]

As defeat loomed, the War Department worked hard to "play. . . down the prominence of General Stilwell," lest he get the blame for the unfolding disaster, while the reporters at the front presented a more downbeat picture.[10]

The British had decided on a scorched earth retreat as they headed north and west to the safety of India, and Belden recorded it all in searing detail—the lack of food and water, the overpowering sense of fear and exhaustion. One of the worst moments came when he found himself encircled by Japanese forces during the bitter battle at Yenangyaung. "It was necessary to break through or die," he reported, "—die either through thirst or hunger while slowly being cut to bits by the closing-in enemy."[11]

Belden survived this trap, only to face an even more dire crisis when he joined up with Stilwell at Shwebo, just north of Mandalay. By now, the formal order had come to evacuate Burma. "It looks like we're getting out of here," Stilwell announced. "To India most of you. A plane is on the way now, but it can't carry all of us. I'm going to Myitkyina. That's where most of the Chinese troops will be, and I'm going with them." Stilwell soon learned that the Japanese were so close to Myitkyina that he, too, had to head for India, while Belden, when offered the chance to escape on the plane, turned it down. "The desire to stick with General Stilwell and see the war through to the end," he recalled, "was too strong."[12]

During the fifteen days Belden spent trudging north through the jungle alongside the 140 other members of Stilwell's polyglot party, he often found himself thinking about Dunkirk. That epic evacuation, he mused, had taken place "across the narrow English Channel under the eyes of the whole world, with the aid of the British Navy and the enthusiastic assistance of hundreds of offshore sailors." By contrast, the harrowing retreat from Burma "was carried out on a lonely jungle road, with only forests and their denizens as witnesses, without much help from the rear, and across a low mountain range which separated India from Burma."[13] In the dispatch *Time* published once he had escaped, Belden singled out one hero. "Stilwell," he wrote, "who is noted for his wiry toughness, stood the trip better than the youngest private and performed every task that any other member of the party performed." On arriving in Delhi, the general immediately added to his own emerging myth. "I claim we got a hell of a beating," Stilwell declared in a less pithy but earthier paraphrase of MacArthur's sentiments about the Philippines. "We got run out of Burma and it is humiliating as hell. I think we ought to find out what caused it, go back and retake it."[14]

* * *

Going back would take time, however, and the activities that replaced these dramatic battles were not always of the type to capture the media's attention. Indeed, rare was the reporter who showed an interest in the jobs that dominated much of Stilwell's time during the ensuing months: his efforts to revamp various components of his complex command, his moves to build up supply dumps in India, and his attempts to turn the Chinese troops in India into a new force by training them in a camp at Ramgarh.[15]

Even the more newsworthy stories contained problems. By the end of the war, fifteen thousand US engineers would be involved in constructing a new road that ran from Ledo into northern Burma. About 60 percent of them were black, which was scarcely surprising given that the army shunted the vast majority of black draftees into segregated service units that had no combat role. The vibrant black press was intensely interested in telling their story, but it was unable to get any black reporters close to the action. The War Department, fearing that the Japanese were stirring up demands for racial equality, instituted such a restrictive policy that no black American correspondent was allowed into the CBI until October 1944.[16]

Until then, only a few white correspondents reported on the activities of the black engineers. Archibald T. Steele, who wrote for the *Chicago Daily News,* was the most notable. "The colored soldiers who are stationed here," Steele wrote on one occasion, "are proceeding to conquer the jungle while fighting the Japs." Many of them, he added, were risking life and limb for their country, including Roy Lee Smith of Lexington, Kentucky, who in his first three months in Burma "cheated death twice and is credited with saving the lives of two Chinese soldiers." Smith's comrades, Steele reported, thought that he deserved "some kind of special recognition," but the only attention he received came in black newspapers like the *Atlanta Daily World* and *Chicago Defender,* which purchased Steele's stories from the *Daily News* and splashed them across their front pages. For the most part, the white media ignored the heroics of the black engineers who were toiling away on the Ledo road.[17]

The same could not be said for the ongoing air campaign. Many reporters had spent the early months of 1942 regaling their readers with the activities of the so-called Flying Tigers, an intrepid volunteer force commanded by Claire Chennault.[18] These "air knights," as *Time* dubbed them, had been one of the few success stories during the Burma retreat, but when Stilwell rearranged this command in the summer of 1942, creating the China Air Task Force, most pilots refused to sign up for the new organization, leaving Chennault feeling increasingly isolated. The airman became particularly angry when he concluded that Stilwell and the War Department were starving him of planes, fuel, and experienced fliers. So he hit back hard. Convinced that with sufficient bombers he could destroy the Japanese in China, he told every reporter he encountered that he must have more planes, for at present his was "the world's smallest air force operating in the largest territory."[19]

Chennault was not the first or the last flier who hoped to pressure Washington for more resources by launching a publicity blitz. But he did hold one important advantage over rivals like Kenney: Henry Luce's passionate interest in China. Over the coming months, *Time* duly ran a string of articles claiming that Chennault planned to use his bombers to open a second front in China, although until more reinforcements arrived, the magazine stressed, he had to do "the best he can, with the little he has." In August 1942, *Life* lavished no less than eight pages on a Belden story about the Flying Tigers. Chennault, Belden told his readers, "has vaulted over all theoretical barriers to throw a small group of American pursuit and bomber pilots into the battle, to hold off, beat back, and weaken the numerically superior Japanese aerial armada pouring back from conquests in the South Pacific to bases in China."[20]

Few inside the War Department were happy with this media barrage. Senior air force commanders always disliked efforts to pressure them into sending more of their precious planes to one of the war's sideshows. Surles, for his part, reacted angrily to many of the details in the *Life* essay. "Belden story objectionable," he cabled Stilwell after its publication. "It invited Japanese attack by indicating that our plane strength was pitifully small." After an intensive investigation, Stilwell discovered that the problem had not been with Chennault's publicists. The Chinese government wanted more planes, and its censors, he believed, had cleared the dispatch without ever showing it to the relevant American authorities.[21]

Whatever the truth of this claim, Stilwell would countenance no such censorship laxity when it came to the other element of his theater's air campaign. The Air Transport Command (ATC) was charged with sending thousands of tons of supplies over the Hump every month, after the fall of Burma cut the land routes into China. This was no easy task. Many of its aircraft were old and slow, while the new C-46 transports turned out to possess structural flaws that were brutally exposed when they tried to ascend more than 15,000 feet over the Himalayas, where air currents were "so turbulent they could break up an airplane." Before long, the ATC would lose, on average, thirteen planes a month, and the last thing its commanders wanted was to alert the Japanese so they could add to this terrible toll. The enemy, one officer observed in early 1943, "is not fully aware of the extent or nature of our transport operations at this time." Desperate to keep the Japanese in this state of ignorance, Stilwell instituted a total news embargo. The policy, the war correspondents were informed, "holds that any publicity of any sort which directly or indirectly calls attention to the operations and activities of this Wing is to be firmly suppressed."[22]

Back in Washington, Surles dutifully reinforced this policy, working on the guiding assumption that the theater commander knew best about security matters, but he also had to live with the obvious consequences. "Newsgathering is becoming quite a problem," observed one correspondent in the theater that spring, "because there's no news to gather." Unsurprisingly, when bosses back home pondered where to send their reporters, few looked to the CBI. The *Chicago Tribune* was typical. As Al Noderer prepared to leave Australia at the start of 1943, having wearied of MacArthur's censorship of the New Guinea campaign, he briefly contemplated heading to Chungking, but his publisher had other plans. As Maloney, his editor, told him, no one could "sell Colonel [McCormick] on [the] idea."[23]

* * *

About the only big name who could be sold on the idea was a thirty-year-old CBS broadcaster, although he was an unlikely recruit.

Dignified and urbane, Eric Sevareid had made his name in Europe three years earlier as one of the famous Murrow boys, the small band of radio pioneers recruited by Edward R. Murrow, who had told the American home front about the London blitz. After leaving Britain, Sevareid had become head of CBS's News Department in Washington, which meant juggling a large number of administrative responsibilities as well as making regular broadcasts, but it was a role he found deeply unfulfilling. "I felt I was no more than a war profiteer," he admitted, with his cushy office job and lavish salary, while other men of the same age were dying for their country. In the grip of "a personal moral crisis," Sevareid was desperate to see some more action, but not in Asia. The fight against Japan, he confessed to Murrow, failed to attract his interest.[24]

The US government had other ideas, however. In the wake of Surles's call to bolster public interest in the CBI theater, Stilwell had suggested the production of a series of radio shows, photo essays, and print stories that would, in the absence of a major land campaign, "give [the] public a better understanding of activities, personnel, problems, objectives, and accomplishments" in the area under his command. While this idea made its way slowly through the War Department's bureaucratic machinery, one of Roosevelt's close friends approached Sevareid with a similar suggestion: why not "go to China, see as many people as possible, and come back to write and broadcast" what he had learned?[25]

After accepting this offer, Sevareid spent days scouring the Washington shops for the kit he would need for such an exotic posting. It then took him weeks to traverse the 12,000 miles to India—and the worst leg of the journey was still to come: a further 650 miles over the Hump, followed by another 450-mile flight from Kunming to Chungking.

Shortly after breakfast on August 2, Sevareid, sixteen other passengers, and four crew members boarded one of the new—and untrusted—C-46 planes for the passage over the Hump. Once airborne, Sevareid found it too noisy for conversation, so he began drafting an outline of the article he planned to publish on his return. After about an hour, a young corporal interrupted his writing. One of the engines had failed, the man shouted. Not long after, a crew member ripped open the plane's door and screamed, "All passenger baggage out!" Sevareid's first reaction was anger at losing all the expensive equipment he had spent so long purchasing. His second was alarm as he watched the other passengers grabbing parachutes from a pile. By the time he had buckled his own, he was truly terrified. He had never jumped before, but with little choice, he tumbled out of the ailing plane, feeling the sharp rush of air before the pull of the parachute suddenly jerked him upward. Landing safely, if clumsily, in dense brush, he joined the other survivors—only one had been killed—and, almost immediately, he thought that he might make it out alive. An Allied plane circled overhead, noting their position. Members of a friendly tribe appeared and offered them shelter in a local village.[26]

So began an adventure that was to last almost a month. Sevareid and his party spent half that time in their makeshift camp, waiting for members of a rescue party from India. Meanwhile, back in America, bosses at CBS had learned, to their relief, that Sevareid was still alive. They were also told that to make it back to Allied lines, he would need safe passage through an area controlled by the "fierce Naga headhunter tribe." This detail added a further dash of spice to an already piquant story, and CBS bosses began "screaming" for permission to publish an account of it, only to find that the censors had placed all information on Hump flights strictly off-limits. The AP did manage to circulate a short item on the crash on August 9, but this only prompted the authorities to establish even "more strict censorship."[27]

Sevareid and the other survivors finally made it through the jungle to British lines at the end of August, after an exhausting 140-mile trek. They were met by a small group of reporters, who told them that they were "big news back home." Sevareid took this as a cue to begin planning for perhaps the biggest broadcast of his career, only to encounter the crushing control of the censors. They would permit him to write only a brief account for the press, as long as it was confined to "personal experiences of people who jump from a lone plane and make their way through the jungle to safety." Everything else remained off-limits, on the grounds that it might endanger the ATC's ongoing operations.[28]

* * *

Undaunted by his brush with death, Sevareid made a second attempt in mid-September to cross what pilots increasingly dubbed "the Skyway to Hell." On arriving safely in Chungking, he immediately discovered plenty of additional reasons for the lack of media interest in the CBI. Living and working conditions in Chiang's wartime capital were far from ideal. The Americans who had been there for any length of time had already grown weary of the noise and heat, the filthy smells and rat infestations, the overpopulation and hyperinflation.[29] Sevareid, although relieved to have reached his destination in one piece, was soon compiling his own catalog of miseries. The press hotel, he observed in his notebook, "is a rectangle of odds and ends of buildings, of unpainted wood here and black brick there." The dining room, which sometimes doubled as the press conference room, contained "three round tables which sag if an elbow is placed upon it [sic]." Here, he noted, "they bring us the soggy, limp mimeographed sheets of central news releases and official government statements."[30]

Sevareid quickly learned to treat these official Chinese documents with a large dose of skepticism. After one typically direct interview in mid-September, he became convinced that Stilwell was the only honest source in town.

Stilwell began his conference with Sevareid by wondering if the Chinese leader had bugged the room. He then sarcastically dismissed Chiang's recent statement that the war would be over in a year, before moving on to another bête noire. Chennault's bombing campaign, he averred, was nothing more than a "purely opportunistic" attempt to strike the Japanese in the areas where they were already weak. The best way to fight the war in this theater, he continued, was to construct an efficient Chinese army that would take the war into Burma. That was the goal of the Ramgarh training camp, Stilwell stressed, but the main lesson Sevareid learned from the session was Chiang's unwillingness to fight. "BASIC POINT," he noted: the Japanese "are not being drained and weakened"; on the contrary, "China is still a great source of *strength* to them; they are gaining not losing by their presence here."[31]

Sevareid knew that experienced reporters like Brooks Atkinson of the *New York Times* and Theodore White of *Time* and *Life* had already reached a similar conclusion. No one had been able to tell the American public, however, because Chiang's government kept such tight control over any information leaving China. "Everybody has his censor story," ran one saying doing the rounds in Chungking. "It has elbowed aside the weather or even the war as a main topic of conversation."[32]

Sevareid's own censorship story began not long after his chat with Stilwell. Whenever he planned to broadcast, a guard would wake him in the middle of the night and accompany him on the short walk to the local radio station. There, Sevareid would "sit at a high dais, peering in the fitful light" at his script. After an early success, in which he favorably compared China to India, he discovered that most of his broadcasts were not getting through. Initially, he blamed this blockage on various technical faults: "the atmospheric troubles which always occur at this season" or the failure of "the transmitter's power plant." Then, when he tried to broadcast "a rather pithy piece, saying that the American public had an exaggerated idea of the amount of fighting in China," he detected the real source of the problem. The Chinese censors had no intention of allowing him to utter such heresy. One of them even entered the studio and tried to tell him what he "*ought* to write." It was an intervention that violated the most basic tenet of Sevareid's code of journalistic ethics, coming as it did from a representative of a regime that, he believed, not only hid the truth from its own people but also divulged important secrets to the enemy. Refusing to cave in, he managed to get the censor to agree that he could state on air that there would be "no major action [in this theater], *in the immediate future*."[33]

Other American reporters in Chungking considered this a significant victory under the circumstances, but the confrontation left Sevareid, already suffering from a heavy chest cold, weary and disillusioned. He was certainly in no mood to be lectured to by a "humorless young lieutenant, ex-New York lawyer," on the lengthy list of subjects that the American military censors considered off-limits, from the types of planes that Chennault's pilots were flying to his own escape story.[34] His blood pressure rose still further when he learned that the State Department was also trying to suppress his copy on political grounds.

The genesis of the State Department's intervention dated back to the period just before Sevareid left for China, when he had been asked to write an in-depth article for the *Reader's Digest*. Sevareid had told the magazine that he would not be able to produce anything until he had been to China and formed a view, so he had agreed that, instead, Hanson Baldwin, the *New York Times* military analyst, would produce a short "icebreaker" while he was away. The *Reader's Digest* published Baldwin's piece in August, but rather than break the ice it threatened to place a deep freeze on all stories about the Chinese political situation. Baldwin claimed that Chiang's regime had been "oversold," that his army was weak, ill-disciplined, and poorly led, and that Japan would have to be conquered from the Pacific rather than the Chinese mainland. Senior State Department officials were appalled. Predicting a full-blown "diplomatic incident," they immediately launched an investigation to try to identify who Baldwin had talked to.[35]

The State Department considered the article that Sevareid wrote on his return just as bad. It was "directly and outspokenly" critical of China, concluded one official, and was bound to alienate Chiang's government unless it was significantly redrafted, if not shelved altogether. Furious at this response, Sevareid could at least see the irony of the situation. "Important men in Washington," he concluded, "had helped to get me to China to find the truth; now it appeared that equally important men in Washington had decided that the truth should not be told."[36]

Yet, as the dust settled from his trip, these important men also recognized that Sevareid wielded so much influence that the time had come to reassess their censorship policies. The State Department's review came soon after it learned that other big-name reporters, including Theodore White, had written similar pieces castigating the nationalist regime, which even a Chiang booster like Henry Luce found difficult to suppress. Rather than get drawn deeper into a public row, the State Department decided to remove itself from the censorship business altogether. "Correspondents," one of its officials observed,

> have come to the erroneous assumption that anything they write concerning China must receive the approval of the [State] Department before

publication. It is the Department's view that this is highly undesirable, both from a domestic standpoint since it has no authority to censor such articles, which is the function of the Office of Censorship, and from the standpoint of our relations with China, . . . since the Chinese authorities will themselves begin to believe that the views of the authors correspond to the official attitude of this Government.[37]

Inside the CBI theater, meanwhile, US military officers had already launched their own rethink. They had been pressed into action by Sevareid's colleagues in New Delhi, who had issued a "strong protest" over the handling of his survival story, before lobbying for the relaxation of the most onerous restrictions on covering the Hump.[38] In response, the War Department agreed that the time had come to ease off a little. "Definite types of stories which may be published," it decreed in October, "are general personality news on the personnel, and their experiences in that area, without mentioning specific fields or definite locations of the regular air route the ATC is using."[39] This ruling paved the way for the publication of a more detailed version of the Sevareid crash story, which the War Department finally released on November 20.[40] By this time, Surles had pushed Stilwell to "exploit stories and personal items about personnel," hoping that the CBI theater might emulate what was happening in Europe, where Eisenhower's command had managed to get small-town newspapers to publish thousands of such pieces each month.[41] The censors also agreed to release more news on some of the positive dimensions of Stilwell's command, including Chiang's decision to airlift Chinese troops into India so that they could attend the training camp at Ramgarh—a ruling that, as one reporter observed, "lifted the veil on one of the most daring enterprises in this theater of operations."[42]

Most American reporters had no doubt about Stilwell's ability to use these troops to maximum advantage. Even before Surles's decision to build him up, the foundations of what one historian has dubbed the "Stilwell myth" had already been laid.[43] The Luce reporters had constructed the basic framework with their depictions of him as a no-nonsense all-American hero. In the wake of his China mission, Sevareid provided additional ballast. "There could only be one General Stilwell in this war," he declared to his large CBS audience; "they must have destroyed the pattern after he was made."[44]

* * *

That Stilwell had acquired such a big name back home was important be-cause he had created a number of powerful enemies in the theater. Chennault was one. The airman believed that Stilwell's reluctance to provide him with a larger proportion of the supplies coming over the Hump was the main reason he was unable to fulfill his grandiose promise to defeat the Japanese on his own. Stilwell's stinginess, Chennault repeatedly warned, prevented him from launching a series of decisive blows, forcing his operations "to be severely curtailed."[45]

Chennault threatened danger to Stilwell because his views struck a chord with Roosevelt, but Chiang promised to be a much more potent foe. After a series of bitter arguments, the Chinese leader finally handed Stilwell con-trol over the Chinese divisions being trained at Ramgarh in late 1943, but he remained suspicious of the Americans, fearing they would leave him to fight the Japanese alone once Germany had been defeated. For this reason, Chiang's central focus was to secure as much of the materiel that was coming over the Hump as possible. At the same time, he had come to hate the man who not only referred to him as "the Peanut" in private, but could also be blunt and rude in his presence. "He disgusts me," Chiang remarked of Stilwell on one occasion. "I despise him: I've never met anyone like that!"[46]

At various times, both Chennault and Chiang pressed Washington to re-call Stilwell, without success. Marshall believed him to be the best man for the job, while Surles's strategy of building him up had placed obvious polit-ical costs in the way of his removal. Roosevelt, instead, agreed to the British proposal to create a new Southeast Asia Command (SEAC) under Admiral Louis Mountbatten, with Stilwell serving as deputy. If the aim was to stream-line the military hierarchy, it failed disastrously. Although Stilwell became Mountbatten's number two in late 1943, he did not relinquish his other posts, which, as one historian has noted, meant that he "reported to Chiang, Marshall, and Mountbatten, all at the same time, depending upon which hat he was wearing at the time." This tangled command structure might have proved tolerable had these powerful men shared the same vision, but they did not. While Stilwell's central goal remained pushing the Japanese out of northern Burma in order to open the supply route to China, the British directed their gaze southward, to Sumatra and, above all, Singapore, which they were desperate to recapture in order to erase the memory of their most humiliating defeat of the war.[47]

Mountbatten's rank and choice of headquarters epitomized Britain's prior-ities. The forty-two-year-old admiral was a noted enthusiast of amphibious operations. He also made his base in Kandy, Ceylon, which not only had the obvious attractions of cool air, botanical gardens, and a golf course but, crucially, was the best place from which to control an amphibious assault of Sumatra and Singapore. Mountbatten's goal was to convince London and Washington to send him landing craft so that he could ship as many troops as possible across the Bay of Bengal. The acerbic American, for his part, was soon dismissing Mountbatten as a mere "Glamor Boy," but he also realized that policy, not personality, lay at the root of his problems with his new superior. "The 'feud' between Louis and me," he noted privately, "is really the conflict of Br. and US policy. That's all."[48]

Well, not quite "all," because their feud also encompassed competing visions of how to deal with the media. In the European theater, it was not uncommon for the British authorities to adopt a more regimented approach to public relations than the Americans, but in SEAC the situation was particularly extreme. The handsome and dashing Mountbatten had an eye for PR and soon proved adept at improving the morale of the British under his command, partly through the creation of an army newspaper.[49] When it came to selling his campaign to a domestic audience, however, Mountbatten had to deal with yet another entity—the British India Command in Delhi—which seemed to hate releasing any news to the press. At a time when British imperial rule on the subcontinent faced monumental political, social, and economic challenges, this restrictive policy made some sense, but it naturally affected SEAC, for, short of trained officers, Mountbatten initially relied heavily on India Command personnel for both censorship and propaganda.[50]

In stark contrast to Delhi's parsimony with the press, the Americans seemed bent on hogging the headlines. Mountbatten strove hard to have all information released only by his headquarters, but well into the spring of 1944 his advisers complained that the Americans were continuing to disseminate their own news.[51] Since Stilwell had a habit of keeping his plans secret from SEAC, Mountbatten often had to await the publication of one of Stilwell's press releases to learn what the Americans were up to. Worse, when reading American newspapers, the British admiral also got a sense of what Stilwell really thought about him.

The first negative story appeared in the February 14 issue of *Time*, which revealed "hints of friction" between the two men, especially the American general's rejection of the British focus on Sumatra and Singapore. Stilwell, under strict instructions from Marshall to "get along" with Mountbatten, admitted that he had made the comments *Time* attributed to him, albeit in a top-secret staff meeting. He immediately ordered a hunt for the leaker, only for his subordinates to divulge a similar point to the press when they arrived for a conference in Washington a few weeks later. Stilwell, the *New York Times* reported, was "disappointed at the failure to launch a large-scale campaign to retake Burma." His younger officers were even more frustrated, the newspaper added, and they were stating openly that "Admiral Mountbatten, regarded in the European war as a commander of great initiative and resourcefulness, was proving a disappointment in his new post."[52]

Deeply upset by these comments, Mountbatten became yet another of Stilwell's powerful enemies, although for the time being Stilwell scarcely cared. Always happiest when he was with his men at the front, by the end of 1943 Stilwell finally had sufficient forces to head back to Burma. His plan was to push south through the Hukawng Valley to take the strategic prize of Myitkyina, whether Mountbatten liked it or not.[53]

"An Inherent Inability to Deceive Either Himself or Anyone Else"

On learning of Stilwell's destination, James Shepley of *Time* felt a sharp pang of fear. The Hukawng Valley, the reporter cabled his editor in early 1944, "is shaped significantly like a death's head." And, indeed, death seemed to lurk everywhere in this remote part of northern Burma—in the climate, which was an uninviting mixture of "intense moisture and summer heat"; in the terrain, which the sun, rain, and humidity had turned into "the worst jungle in the world"; and in the gory remnants of the galling retreat two years earlier, which had left thousands of skeletons scattered along the punishing hiking trails. Back then, Stilwell had emerged from these hills and valleys vowing to "go back and retake" Burma. With the Chinese divisions trained at Ramgarh under his command, he was at last in a position to fulfill this promise.[54]

Shepley was one of ten correspondents who had gathered to join him. Some members of this press pack were seasoned battlefield veterans, like Tillman Durdin of the *New York Times*, who had survived both Guadalcanal and Buna, and Frank Hewlett of the UP, who had been one of the last reporters out of Corregidor. Others had spent more than a year in the CBI, trying desperately to find something newsworthy to cover, including Archibald Steele of the *Chicago Daily News*, who had written about the engineers toiling away on the Ledo road, and Toby Wiant of the AP, who was known as "the flyingest war correspondent in this theater," having survived seventeen bombing raids over Burma, Thailand, and Indochina.[55]

From the outset, Stilwell left none of these correspondents in any doubt that he wanted the Chinese troops to be the stars of the show. And the correspondents, at first, needed little convincing. Most of them set off alongside a Chinese regiment, enjoying the amenities Stilwell had laid on—three cooks, a radio team, and a designated PRO—and they inevitably concentrated on the men they were spending so much time with. "After seeing him fight," noted Shepley in an early cable, "eating with him, washing with him in the little north Burma streams, and bivouacking with him, I am of the strong conviction that the Chinese soldier is a good joe. So are all the other Americans who have seen him fight." "One of the happiest developments of the past weeks," agreed Durdin, "has been a further demonstration of the fact . . . that American and Chinese combat forces in the field can fight and work together efficiently and harmoniously."[56]

Before long, however, the American reporters found themselves inexorably drawn toward the exploits of the first US ground forces to fight in the theater. Not that these men necessarily looked the part. Frank Merrill, their leader, suffered from poor eyesight and a heart condition. The three thousand troops under his command had answered the call for anyone with jungle experience and "a high state of physical ruggedness," but not all of them fit this bill. Many had come from the Southwest Pacific and suffered from the affliction so common in that area: malaria. Others had volunteered from Trinidad, where they had served in a division that was "considered a dumping ground for all the misfits and low IQs in the army." "We expected picked troops," complained one medical officer. "Instead we found many chronically ill men . . . also numerous psychiatric problems."[57]

In the correspondents' dispatches, however, all of these weaknesses faded into the background. Thus, Merrill became a dogged striver whose self-effacing demeanor was a key battlefield strength. "Quiet, shy, [and] studious," observed Shepley, he had all the qualities to "make himself one of the great shock troopers of the war like the Marines' Edson."[58] His men, according to reporters, were equally impressive: "battle-seasoned veterans from Guadalcanal, New Georgia, and New Guinea, and trained jungle troops from Panama and Trinidad." Even their name got a major upgrade. They went into battle under the official designation of 5307th Provisional Regiment, which, as one of them complained, "sounds like a street address in Los Angeles." After a short while in the jungle, they emerged in the pages of the nation's press as "Merrill's Marauders," a name Shepley coined but Durdin first put into print.[59]

The Marauders set off on February 24 for what would be the first of three long hikes deep into the enemy's rear. At Walawbum two weeks later, they confronted a major Japanese attempt to wipe them out, but they held firm during a bitter battle lasting thirty-six hours. Hewlett, who was the only correspondent to go along on this mission, returned with a major story, which the censors released on March 10. "This isn't battle out here in the Burma jungle," Hewlett declared, "—it's wholesale slaughter. Even the toughened veterans who call themselves 'the Guadalcanal ruffians' sickened at the mass killing," when Japanese troops, "howling and screaming," were mowed down as they tried to assault the American position.[60]

When Merrill arrived in Stilwell's little bamboo camp shortly after, the general summoned his small band of reporters to an on-the-record press conference. The scribes sat on the ground in a ring as Stilwell gave his interpretation of what had happened so far. "I believe we have killed two thousand

Fig. 9.1. Stilwell (*center right*) and Toby Wiant of the AP (*seated on Stilwell's right*) take cover in a deep ravine in northern Burma, March 1944.
© AP/Shutterstock.

Japanese in this operation," he began, "which should be good news in any language except Japanese. I wish to stress the fact," he added, "that the Chinese and Americans fought and died side by side. They fraternized, shared their food, their comforts and their hardships. It is not an exaggeration to say they have virtually formed a mutual admiration society."[61]

Despite Stilwell's transparent attempt to shift the focus onto the Chinese, the correspondents could not be dissuaded from concentrating on their own objects of admiration. These included not just Merrill and his Marauders, but also Stilwell himself. While their colleagues in India and China continued to complain that their copy was forever being cut, Stilwell adopted a completely different approach in the Burma jungle. "His censorship policy is liberal," observed the UP bureau chief. "In accordance with his liberal concepts of the role of the press," agreed Durdin, "General Stilwell makes a personal effort to see that war correspondents in his theater get the fullest possible information." Filled with gratitude, the reporters lavished yet more praise on the commander. "An inherent inability to deceive either himself or anyone else is a fundamental part of the Stilwell character," wrote Durdin. "Related to this downrightness is a simple unpretentiousness. Although in a war area as commander, General Stilwell surrounds himself with no pomp or ceremony."[62]

* * *

April, by common consent, "was the cruelest, and certainly the hottest, month in Burma."[63] Most members of Stilwell's press corps had already spent weeks in the jungle, walking many miles each day with a twenty-pound pack, camping night after night in an increasingly grubby uniform, and trying to sleep as the damp penetrated through their "two blankets as if they were made of tissue paper." As the offensive continued south, some of them departed for a well-earned break. The lucky ones, like Wiant and Hewlett, managed to grab a berth in "a bamboo-walled, thatch-roofed hut" at SEAC's newly opened headquarters in Kandy. From there, they could write more detached overviews, acclaiming Stilwell's forces for having apparently "broken the back of Japanese resistance in Northern Burma."[64]

For the correspondents who stayed at the front, by contrast, this became the most depressing period of the campaign, and not just because of the enervating temperatures. They also witnessed sights that raised genuine questions about whether Stilwell was, in fact, deceiving not just himself but also his reporters—and, by extension, the American home front.

The travails began in late April, when Stilwell decided to press on to Myitkyina, the crucial position in northern Burma, despite the impending onset of the monsoon rains. This last leg was a tough ask for the Marauders. Only fourteen hundred of the original three-thousand-strong force remained on frontline duty, and even those still standing were starting to sag from a mixture of sores and fever, hunger and exhaustion. These men were also under the impression that they had been promised a well-earned leave, but Stilwell had other ideas. He ordered the Marauders to march the last hundred miles to Myitkyina, traversing a six-thousand-foot mountain range along the way. Once there, they were to grab the airstrip so that Chinese reinforcements could be flown in to secure the town.[65]

The result, at first, was a stunning victory. The Marauders captured Myitkyina's main airfield on May 17. That afternoon, Stilwell ordered the first regiment of Chinese troops to be airlifted in. He then spent a restless night at his command post, in which he failed to sleep because of a combination of "ants and worry," before boarding a plane to Myitkyina the next morning. No less than twelve reporters traveled with him, and on landing, they watched admiringly as Stilwell and Merrill hugged and laughed. Caught up in the triumphant mood, these correspondents were full of praise for Stilwell's "brilliant stroke." All too soon, however, disillusion crept in. Although the airfield had fallen, the town remained in enemy hands, and the Japanese quickly poured in reinforcements to defend it. Then the monsoon rains arrived, interrupting the airlift of Chinese troops and turning the battlefield into a bloody quagmire.[66]

The reporters who remained for this grim final phase initially had little choice but to shelter inside hastily dug foxholes along the edges of the airfield. After two days of what Durdin dubbed a "separated and disorganized existence," they gradually, almost spontaneously, decided to relocate to the shattered remnants of a transport plane, which at least provided a modicum of shelter from the persistent rain, if not the Japanese artillery. The plane served as such an attractive camp—at least compared with anything else in the vicinity—that the correspondents soon had to establish a defensive perimeter in order to protect it from the "covetous eyes" of Chinese troops who wanted to take it from them. This was one worrying sign. Another was the steady evacuation of between seventy-five and one hundred American soldiers each day due to sickness, including Merrill, who was felled by a heart attack soon after he flew in to celebrate what looked like the pyrrhic victory of the airfield's capture.[67]

1. T/Sgt. Dave Richardson (Yank Magazine), 2. Capt. Clancy Topp, 3. T/Sgt. Warren Bechlen, 4. Sgt. David Quaid, 5. Cpl. William Safran, 6. Pvt. Joseph Razkowski, 7. Pvt. Daniel Novak, 8. Tillman Durdin (N.Y. Times).   Myitkyina Airstrip, May 19, 1944.   Photo by B. Hoffman

Fig. 9.2. Tillman Durdin of the *New York Times* (*right*) sheltering from Japanese fire on the Myitkyina airstrip, May 19, 1944, with his typewriter close at hand. Private collection.

As the rain poured, the siege continued. When attacks by inexperienced Chinese troops petered out against strong Japanese positions, Stilwell desperately hunted around for any American reinforcements, pressganging into action not only support units in the rear but even a number of ill and exhausted Marauders in convalescent camps. The response came close to outright mutiny. Embittered troops called Stilwell "bloodless and cold-hearted, without a drop of human kindness." At least one openly contemplated what would later be known as "fragging." "I had him in my sights," boasted an enlisted man. "I coulda squeezed one off and no one woulda known it wasn't a Jap that got that son-of-a-bitch."[68]

Such sentiments had the potential to inflict enormous damage on Stilwell's hard-earned reputation if they made it into print, a prospect that became more likely when the media flew its own reinforcements into Myitkyina. Toby Wiant was one such "pinch hitter." The UP man had last seen Burma in early April, when he had departed "with a terrific stomachache and slight fever." His first reaction on his return was fear: the airstrip, he noted, was even more dangerous than the jungle had been, with incoming fire bursting all around. His second sensation was frustration at the difficulty of telling this story. "At Kandy," he observed, "we had fast communications—only an hour and a half on urgent stuff to NYC, not more than four hours on stories at the regular press rates. . . . Here in the jungle," by contrast, "communications are slow and unreliable. . . . On the average, it takes 12 hours for one of my stories to reach Delhi; an hour or so to go through censorship there; and 12 additional hours to reach NYC."[69]

These delays at least gave Stilwell some time to control the story, as Jack Bell found to his cost. Bell had been a machine-gunner in the last war, when his bravery had resulted in the award of the Distinguished Service Cross and the Croix de Guerre. After many years as a sports reporter for the *Miami Herald*, he had created the "Town Crier" column in 1941 as a "place where appeals were made for all sorts of items for service men."[70] At Myitkyina, Bell's concern for the well-being of the fighting man led him to compose a particularly incendiary dispatch. The replacements Stilwell had thrown into action, he wrote, were

> not a well-trained infantry outfit fully equipped, but an assortment of cooks, quartermaster men, artillery men, signal corps men, band men, and some infantry men from one division. They tell, and bitterly, too, how they were herded onto the ship, not knowing who their officers were with no semblance of organization. . . . They got off planes at Myitkyina with Jap snipers and machine gunners everywhere—and many of them didn't know how to put a clip of shells into a rifle.

The combat engineers that Stilwell rushed in from the India-Burma border were equally ill-prepared. "Actually," claimed Bell, "they were combat troops in theory only. They knew nothing of jungle fighting, and the wily Japs against whom they marched were masters at trickery and ambush."[71]

Bell believed he had to tell this story "so that those responsible for the murder of many American boys—it was no less than murder—should pay the penalty." The censors, inevitably, disagreed. They quickly moved to stop Bell's dispatch, on the grounds that, as one explained, it "is based on partial facts, is written with a definite bias, and is extremely inflammatory."[72]

Yet, as Stilwell was acutely aware, Bell was not the only person to commit such explosive conclusions to paper. Colonel Charles N. Hunter had led the task force that had captured the airstrip on May 17. Just over a week later, he handed Stilwell a letter that accused "higher headquarters" of a "don't care attitude" and stressed that the Marauders were "practically ineffective as a combat unit." Stilwell found these charges more difficult to dismiss than the jottings of a journalist, and so he ordered an investigation. This remained under wraps until early August, by which time Myitkyina had finally fallen. Then, with the war correspondents writing enthusiastically about this big victory, Stilwell's PROs released to the press their own version of what had happened.[73]

The official account carefully sidestepped Stilwell's heavy reliance on American troops, lest this raise questions about the effectiveness of the Chinese forces that had been trained at Ramgarh for the past two years. It also remained silent on the experiences of both the engineers and the replacement troops, which had been at the heart of Bell's censored story. Instead, Stilwell's PROs focused solely on the temporary breakdown of morale among Merrill's Marauders, tracing this to "ill-advised promises" that the men would be given leave after ninety days and a "faulty hospital procedure that sent convalescents back to the firing line." To defuse the situation still further, the PROs insisted that Stilwell had "wept when he heard that [the] recall of several hundred men to active duty when physically unfit had resulted from a misunderstanding of his order that all possible able-bodied personnel be thrown into action."[74]

Such a highly spun version carried obvious risks. Stilwell could probably rely on Hunter's discretion, but to make doubly certain, he sent the colonel home by ship, which kept him away from the press for weeks.[75] The correspondents themselves were less malleable. They were also starting to return to the States by plane, where they would be able to write up their accounts of this battle without having to worry about compulsory military censorship. The publication of Stilwell's investigation had already prompted some newspapers to start talking openly about a "mutiny" of the Marauders, during which, as the New York Daily News acerbically commented, "Stilwell's tears don't seem to have helped much."[76] Perhaps, Stilwell fretted, these same editors might now be tempted to publish accounts like Bell's, which was so at odds with his own carefully crafted story. To head off such a possibility, one of Stillwell PROs sent Surles a begging letter. "The story," he wrote,

is known both to military personnel and to war correspondents returning to the States from this theater. There is a distinct possibility that it will leak out in the same garbled and inflammatory form taken by the Bell article. Request that in the event the story does leak in the States, the Bureau [of Public Relations] take what action is necessary to prevent the publication of garbled and biased hearsay under the guise of facts.[77]

Ultimately, Stilwell and his PROs need not have worried. The correspondents who stayed in Burma to the bitter end knew from Bell's experience that they had no chance of getting the story past the censor.[78] So they put the delay in winning the battle down to a familiar factor. "The defenders of Myitkyina," wrote Tillman Durdin in the New York Times, "achieved a state of hysterical fatalism characteristic of Japanese troops in some circumstances and apparently early in the Myitkyina battle had resolved to die at their posts."[79]

Back home, meanwhile, most media organizations bought the official interpretation, while reserving yet more praise for Stilwell. "In the long history of warfare," concluded Time, "good outfits have disintegrated before, but seldom has their commander swallowed his pride enough to tell the whole story. Last week, in an official report, frank, honest, 'Uncle Joe' Stilwell did just that. He told the world what it was going to find out in the long run, anyhow." As for Merrill, he described the whole episode as nothing more than a "storm in a tea pot." He was also on hand when his boss was promoted to full general that same month and was even given the honor of pinning the fourth star on Stilwell's uniform.[80]

"Stilwell Is on the Defensive"

To Stilwell's rivals in the theater, the muted coverage of Myitkyina appeared to be a major missed opportunity to get rid of their nemesis at a time when they each had problems of their own. These stemmed from two Japanese offensives designed by the military in Tokyo to shore up its position on the Asian mainland now that the American offensive was gathering pace in the Pacific. In Operation Ugô, eighty-five thousand Japanese troops pushed from northwestern Burma into British India, while Operation Ichigô took place on an even larger scale, with half a million men scything into central China in an attempt to create a land corridor linking the Japanese empire in Manchuria and East China with Malaya, Singapore, and Thailand.[81]

Ichigô was a particular blow to Chennault. In recent months, the airman had never relented in his campaign for more planes and more supplies.

Whenever reporters had made the trek to the Fourteenth Air Force base in Kunming, he had invited them into his "modest tile-roofed adobe cottage on a gentle slope overlooking the airfield." Once inside, he would sit them down, light his pipe, and then provide what one of them described as "plenty of good quotes." "Our action against the enemy," ran a classic Chennault comment, "is less difficult and less expensive than head-on blows which we can deal at the end of his lines in the South Pacific and Burma. We are after his shipping and we can strike at his soft belly."[82]

Yet even before Ichigô, Chennault had found it increasingly difficult to get the press interested in his daily operations. The enemy was largely to blame. Japanese broadcasters at Domei, the Tokyo news agency, had started to release their own assessment of the American raids almost forty-eight hours before the Fourteenth Air Force's communiqués. Although Chennault's PROs considered the Domei reports to be "inaccurate and biased to the point of being ridiculous," most US newspapers ran them anyway, for the simple reason that they had deadlines to meet. When Chennault's out-of-date offerings finally arrived, they were, as one PRO complained, "naturally relegated to unobtrusive positions in the papers . . . thereby being missed by many who merely glance at the headlines."[83]

Ichigô made a bad situation much worse. As the Japanese offensive gathered pace, Chennault's censors, desperate to deny valuable information to the rampaging enemy, clamped down hard. They began by bringing to a complete halt all references to the numerical designation of squadrons. Then, with the important city of Hengyang under threat in early August, they instituted a series of restrictions that, according to one editor, were "more drastic than exist in any other theater." John Hlavacek of the UP was the only reporter who remained to cover the story. Already suffering from a bad bout of dysentery, he soon had reason to wonder why he was bothering to risk his neck. Hlavacek managed to write a vivid eyewitness dispatch, which, his editor believed, "paid high tribute to the courage, tenacity, and efficiency of the officers and men who handled the difficult task"—just the kind of dispatch, in other words, that Chennault would normally have welcomed. This time, however, air force censors had other ideas. They suppressed everything Hlavacek wrote, to the disgust of his bureau chief, who sent "a vehement protest . . . against the abusive use of censorship and the negligence of the Fourteenth Airforce PRO."[84]

Struggling to make himself heard in the press, Chennault resorted to other methods to push his interests. He had long been angling for Stilwell's job.

That was never a realistic proposition, not with Marshall and Arnold both vehemently opposed to a man they considered "a show-off and a charlatan." Yet with Stilwell repeatedly refusing to provide more resources for the defense of Hengyang, Chennault and his aides stepped up their efforts to get Stilwell replaced, knowing that they had powerful allies in Kandy and Chungking who were equally desperate to help them achieve this goal.[85]

* * *

Mountbatten had never favored fighting in the jungles of northern Burma, but with the bulk of the landing craft heading for Europe, where they would be used in the Anzio and Normandy invasions, he was forced to shelve his plans for an amphibious assault to the south. Then came Operation Ugô in March, which gave him no choice but to beat back a Japanese invasion that threatened the whole British position in India.

The British strategy was to lure the enemy westward so that the fighting would take place on a plain closer to their own supply lines. The result was a series of bitter and bloody battles around the towns of Imphal and Kohima. The Japanese initially appeared to hold the whip hand, especially in the places they besieged, but the British and Indian troops fought back fiercely, helped by supply drops from the dominant Allied air force.

With the battlefield situation so fluid, any censor would have been leery about releasing detailed news, but those working for the British India Command appeared bent on eviscerating all but the most anodyne of dispatches. By mid-April, the patience of five British correspondents finally snapped. Convinced that "their messages [were] constantly tampered with for no apparent security reason," they presented a story on the Kohima battle to the India Command censors in Calcutta, only to be told that it would "killed . . . on the ground that it revealed weakness of our position at that time." As a matter of fact, this bloody battle was still in the balance, so the censors had sound reasons for their crackdown, but the reporters saw the situation in a much darker light. Angry after months of high-handed treatment, they refused to send any more dispatches until the censorship was eased, an action that soon led to pointed questions being asked of Churchill's government in the House of Commons.[86]

The American reaction to this effective blackout took a somewhat different form. When Toby Wiant arrived in Kandy in April, he discovered that his AP bosses in New York believed that excessive British censorship was "creating in America uneasiness and a feeling that the true picture is being withheld." Some US commentators were even worried that the likely British defeat at Kohima would have a disastrous impact on Stilwell's "drive toward Myitkyina."[87]

Mountbatten retaliated swiftly. To appease the striking British reporters, he moved to ease the most onerous censorship restrictions. His PROs also promised to make it easier for correspondents to get closer to the action, providing them with mobile radio transmitters near the battlefield and laying on special aircraft "to convey correspondents rapidly to distant parts of the Burma front."[88] To quell the American concerns, Mountbatten offered the AP some reassuring comments about the battlefield situation being nowhere near as bad as the speculation suggested. He also decided that the time had come to release all the information in his theater from Kandy, although here he encountered strong resistance.[89]

At first glance, Stilwell and his PROs seemed willing to allow Mountbatten to publish a single daily communiqué, but their surface acquiescence masked a subtle strategy. Convinced that the British, left to their own devices, would consign the American campaign to the sidelines, Stilwell's PROs reserved the right to send their own press notes to Chungking, where they could be radioed to the United States without any British interference.[90] With no unified control and a notable absence of trust, both sides began vying to take public credit for the victories that started to unfold during the spring. Stilwell set the tone. "Will this burn up the Limeys," he wrote gloatingly in his diary after capturing the Myitkyina airfield. Mountbatten certainly smarted at his rival's success, but what really inflamed him was Stilwell's treatment of a British long-range penetration force known as the Chindits.[91]

Under the flamboyant leadership of the eccentric Orde Wingate, the Chindits had been one of Britain's great propaganda successes during 1943. In their first campaign, they had probed deep behind Japanese lines in Burma, an action that Churchill had lavished with extravagant praise. Wingate had launched a similar mission in February 1944, only to be killed in a plane crash a month later. After much debate, Stilwell eventually took control of the Chindits, just as he was seeking to end the siege at Myitkyina. The plan was to use these troops to support Chinese operations around the important town of Mogaung, but the result was nothing short of disastrous. Stilwell had never been an admirer of Wingate, he had not wanted to command the Chindits, and with his hands full trying to win Myitkyina, he was indifferent to the plight of these men, who, exhausted after months in the jungle, were beginning to succumb to malaria, dysentery, and typhus. Not only did he refuse them a furlough, fretful of the signal that such an action would send to the near-mutinous Marauders, but he also studiously avoided giving them any public praise, even after their epic battle at Mogaung.[92] Indeed, when reporters asked Stilwell about the Chindits' exploits, his first reaction was to go off the record; his second was to dismiss their contribution, explaining that because "they were very run down and could not do anything," they had been "confined to patrolling and keeping an eye on the Japanese."[93]

The Chindits had, in fact, won a significant victory at Mogaung at the cost of eight hundred casualties, and Stilwell's scornful statements only served to infuriate Mountbatten, who became increasingly convinced that "his so-called deputy would have to go."[94] Yet the admiral also feared that Stilwell boosters, like James Shepley of *Time* and *Life*, were plotting to print a "savage attack on Mountbatten and the British generally," accusing them "of 'sabotaging' the Stilwell campaign [in Burma], which would have already succeeded if it were not for the special motives and interests of the British for delaying the outcome of his campaign." "Stilwell," concluded one British official, whose suspicions made their way to Surles, "is on the defensive with the American Army High Command and this is his counter-stroke."[95]

* * *

In Washington, senior officials were equally mindful of Stilwell's capacity to launch a counterstroke, although this was not their first consideration. As Stilwell's enemies circled, Marshall continued to shield the man he considered the only true fighter in the theater, agreeing to remove Stilwell from SEAC—and therefore Burma—but only in order to promote him to the command of all Chinese armed forces. For Chiang, this was a step too far. Hating the prospect of Stilwell taking over his army, the Chinese leader mobilized his supporters inside the US government, and on October 19, the president finally agreed to order Stilwell's relief.[96]

As expected, Stilwell pushed back hard. His PROs began by briefing reporters that "Stilwell is a symbol of tough resistance against the Japanese" and that his "recall is disappointing to the American public and indicates grave problems in China."[97] Soon after, the general met with Theodore White and Brooks Atkinson, who, he knew, were sympathetic to his cause.[98]

Ushering them into his office, Stilwell opened with an audacious offer. The two men, he said, could "read the 'eyes alone' cables the commander of the theater received from Washington," so they would be better able to make the American public understand what had happened. The reporters immediately accepted, although they realized they faced a major problem. Spencer Moosa of the AP had just composed a long story on Stilwell's recall, only to find that when he submitted it to the authorities "the American censor excised 388 words and the Chinese censor 104 words," leaving only half a sentence intact: "Stilwell is known to have taken formal leave of Chiang. . . ."[99] With the War Department also blocking the publication of any stories written in New Delhi, the two correspondents decided that one of them would have to return home in order to tell the public what they had learned from Stilwell's private correspondence.[100]

Atkinson's sudden arrival in New York at the end of October presented the government with a major dilemma. Few officials relished a major controversy, especially with the presidential election only days away. But with Atkinson careful to ensure that nothing he wrote violated the voluntary censorship code, the government had little choice but to allow the *Times* to publish.[101]

The story that appeared on the front page on October 31 revealed that Stilwell's recall had been the culmination of a long dispute between the general and the Chinese government. Stilwell, Atkinson stressed, "is commonly regarded as the ablest field commander in China since 'Chinese' Gordon." In 1942, he had been forced to retreat by the Japanese; now, his eviction "was not from the enemy but from an ally. The decision to relieve General Stilwell," Atkinson argued,

> has the most profound implications for China as well as American policy toward China and the Allied war effort in the Far East. It may mean that the United States has decided from now on to discount China's part in a counter-offensive. Inside China it represents the political triumph of a moribund anti-democratic regime that is more concerned with maintaining its political supremacy than in driving the Japanese out of China.[102]

Over the next few days, many of Atkinson's former colleagues echoed the same arguments. Toby Wiant was typical. The AP man had arrived in London in September convinced that "the Northern Burma offensive was . . . a strictly one-man show." When he heard that this man had been ousted, he immediately produced his "comprehensive analysis" of what had been going on. "For years," Wiant declared on November 1, "China has been falling apart. Why hasn't the American public been kept informed? First, because of Chinese censorship. Second, because

Washington held out hope that the mess could be cleaned up. Washington, through Gen. Joseph Stilwell, gave Chiang every assistance possible under the circumstances. But the mess became so bad that Stilwell finally was recalled to Washington."[103]

Desperate to clear up their own political mess on election eve, the White House and War Department offered a very different version of events, telling reporters that Stilwell's recall was merely the result of a command reshuffle.[104] In an effort to maintain this fiction, the administration placed Stilwell in an effective quarantine the minute he touched down in Washington. Marshall even sent an aide to the airport to hustle him into a waiting car before he could say anything to the press. He then had Stilwell smuggled into guest quarters close to his house, where Surles was waiting to "warn. . . him not to talk."[105]

Bitter about his treatment, Stilwell did not find it easy to heed this advice. Expecting a hero's welcome, he found himself being treated no better than a common criminal. On discovering that reporters were camped outside his house in California, he began to feel like a prisoner. "I did not mind hiding behind trees in Burma," he cabled Surles, "but here I cannot even exercise the dog except after dark in smoked glasses." Yet Stilwell never contemplated disobeying his orders. At heart a fighting soldier, he hankered for another battlefield command, which, he knew, would be forthcoming only if he complied with Marshall's and Roosevelt's clear wishes to say nothing about China before election day.[106]

Besides, the media's interest in him soon faded. Stilwell had been news when he was fulfilling his pledge to "go back and retake" Burma, but even then, he had never captured the imagination in quite the same way as Douglas MacArthur, and the reasons were revealing. Both he and Stilwell had paid close attention to press relations since the start of the war. Both had also demonstrated the knack of attracting loyal support from correspondents in their theater—although Stilwell had, in fact, been much more effective, garnering a good press from virtually every US correspondent he encountered, whereas many of the reporters based in Brisbane had initially been deeply disparaging of MacArthur. Yet MacArthur had much deeper resources at his disposal. While Stilwell had to rely on Surles's efforts to build him up inside America, MacArthur enjoyed the support of powerful cheerleaders from the *Chicago Tribune* to the Republican Right. After the general's presidential bid fizzled in the spring of 1944, he even developed an uneasy alliance with Roosevelt. Ever since Pearl Harbor, Roosevelt's main political vulnerability had been the Republican charge that he had prioritized the European war at the expense of defeating the Japanese. In October, just as Stilwell was arriving home almost incognito, MacArthur was poised to refute this charge once and for all by returning to the Philippines in triumph.

PART III
ENDGAME

10

The Return

The Best-Laid Plans

"It's beginning to look like a publicity junket for the opening of a super-colossal movie," remarked John Graham Dowling in the middle of October. Dowling had been covering the Pacific War for the *Chicago Sun* since the opening weeks on Guadalcanal, but he had seen nothing like the feverish preparations being made for MacArthur's next big battle. More than seven hundred ships had been assembled in nine bases stretching from New Guinea to Hawaii. Their destination was Leyte, an island in the central Philippines. The navy believed it been left "wide open" to attack, providing MacArthur with his big opportunity at long last. For two and a half years, he had repeatedly pledged that he would return. With this promise about to be fulfilled, reporters were flocking to be at his side—no less than fifty-eight of them, which, as one noted, was "the largest conglomeration of war correspondents yet seen in the Pacific."[1]

After the repeated dress rehearsals in New Guinea, MacArthur's PR team was confident it had the capability to handle this large number. Once again, MacArthur would be presiding over a complex command structure. Halsey's Third Fleet, which remained ultimately responsible to Nimitz, was given the dual role of supporting the invasion while also seeking to "destroy enemy naval and air forces in or threatening the Philippines area." Vice Admiral Thomas C. Kinkaid's Seventh Fleet, under the direct control of MacArthur, was responsible for the invasion itself.[2] On the basis of past experience, MacArthur agreed with Nimitz that the SWPA command would issue the main communiqués, with the proviso that the commander of the "covering or supporting forces" (that is, Halsey) would be able to brief the press on battles involving his ships.[3] Using the innovation that had been tested at Kwajalein, Eniwetok, and Saipan, Kinkaid would make a radio ship available to reporters just off the beachhead. Diller also planned to land on Leyte an hour after the first combat wave came ashore. With him would be a team of five PROs, including, for the first time, a radio officer. Once ashore, these men would establish a makeshift press camp, and from there they could send censored copy to Hollandia, which had a commercial radio station that could relay stories to America.[4]

Yet, even before the fleet set sail for Leyte, a number of problems had begun to bubble to the surface. Many members of the large press pack were new to the theater, and the excessive red tape they had encountered when trying to leave America had already soured them on the military. As Surles explained to anyone who complained, aspiring war correspondents normally had to wait three to four months for accreditation from request to departure date. The frustratingly long process began with obtaining a draft deferment and getting all the necessary inoculations. Next, there was a personal security questionnaire to fill in, which took Surles's BPR six weeks to check. Then the theater PRO had to decide whether he could accommodate any more reporters, which took a further two weeks, and after that there were yet more delays, including, on average, a week to be issued travel orders by the adjutant general, ten days to obtain a port call, and another week at the port to receive a sailing date.[5]

Lindesay M. Parrott was one of the many reporters who had begun to wonder whether he would ever get to see any combat. In the spring of 1944, Parrott's bosses at the *New York Times* had decided to send this Scottish-born, forty-three-year-old Princeton graduate to cover MacArthur's war in place of Foster Hailey, their long-suffering Pacific correspondent. Despite enduring the endless delays, Parrott was at least greeted with enthusiasm by Frank Kluckhohn, with whom he would be partnering over the coming weeks. Other men new to the theater tended to get the cold shoulder from seasoned hands, as the press corps cleaved into two distinct groups. On one side were reporters whose war experience had been leading up to this climactic moment, men like Frank Hewlett, fresh from the Burma jungle, who was desperate to see the recapture of Bataan and Corregidor, and William Chickering, who had covered MacArthur for *Time* magazine since 1942. This group did not take kindly to the sudden appearance of a set of "unlikely characters" from unfashionable newspapers, ranging from the *Ohio State Journal* to the *Fort Worth Star Telegram*. Chickering summed up their mood. "Although the situation is still maintained at a joshing level," he observed in mid-October, "veteran correspondents from New Guinea to the Marshalls were secretly grumbling last week, wondering why the War Department allowed accreditation to men who by great age, slight knowledge, or irksome dispositions could easily gum up the efforts of more experienced correspondents. Both the army and navy tried to be meticulously fair to all," Chickering added, "but often the swollen ranks meant quotas, and PROs in desperation resorted to drawing straws to see which correspondents were assigned to which ships or divisions."[6]

Inevitably, some correspondents bristled when they lost out in this lottery to colleagues working for news organizations they considered less prestigious, even unworthy. "We both feel, frankly," Kluckhohn and Parrott complained to their editor in New York, "that the *Times* has not been given the consideration it normally receives because of its standing and its large syndicate of important papers." This was not simply a matter of status. Kluckhohn also complained that the influx of interlopers would place undue pressure on the fragile communications system. He initially hoped to sidestep this problem by devising a simple division of labor in which he, the veteran, would head to the front, while Parrott, the rookie, would remain in Hollandia, where "filing conditions were at least fair." Yet the two *Times* men did not factor in MacArthur. The general had long bemoaned the media's neglect of his theater. With so many correspondents finally in tow, he was determined that they would all witness his big moment. So, when Kluckhohn approached Diller with the idea for Parrott to remain behind, the PRO turned him down flat. "The army," Kluckhohn informed his editor, "ordered all correspondents to move up on the show."[7]

* * *

MacArthur's part in this big show began on the early afternoon of October 20. Donning a crisply pressed uniform, sunglasses, and a cap, he climbed down a ladder of the cruiser *Nashville* and into a whaleboat, smiling to his party as he remarked, "Well, believe it or not, we're here."

MacArthur's critics would long claim that what followed was part of a well-planned publicity stunt. They were wrong. Only once MacArthur got into the boat did an aide discover that the beach's gentle angle would prevent the whaler from taking the general directly onto dry land. The aide phoned the beachmaster, asking him to provide a smaller vessel for the final leg of the journey, but the man was so preoccupied with trying to bring order to the battlefield chaos that he replied angrily, "Let 'em walk." MacArthur's biographer believes that the discomfort of getting his trousers wet accounted for his "grim expression" at this moment of triumph. It was not to be the last indignity. On the beach, which the planners had codenamed Red, at least one soldier noticed a group of men wading ashore, the most prominent smoking a corncob pipe, and shouted, "What the hell are they doing here?" Even some war correspondents were unimpressed. One yelled to a GI, who thought he wanted to point out MacArthur, but the reporter was much more interested in an enemy pillbox that had been knocked out twice but was "coming back to life."[8]

Behind the scenes, meanwhile, Diller's best-laid plans were already going awry. He was scheduled to come ashore an hour behind the first combat troops, which looked like a good idea on paper. In practice, the Japanese— who were present in larger numbers than some intelligence estimates had predicted—let the first waves land before pouring sustained mortar fire on those that followed.[9] Diller's landing craft was hit at least five times, killing his radio officer. Jumping into the water, Diller and the surviving PROs managed to wade ashore carrying their cumbersome equipment above their heads. On the beach, they found a small bamboo shack on stilts, which they turned into a press camp. "We were meant to cover General MacArthur's coming ashore from the cruiser *Nashville*," recalled one of the PROs, "but because of erratic fire from the Japs, we had to stay put." Amid the gunfire bursts and mortar thuds, Diller's men focused on setting up their equipment in the shack, including a bulky teletype machine. Then they sat back and waited for the first copy from the correspondents who would be landing at various points along the coast.[10]

It turned out to be a long wait. The fate of a PBY plane symbolized the turmoil unfolding on invasion day. The plane was meant to pick up the images that photographers had captured of the early action, including MacArthur coming ashore, but it was forced by a Japanese air raid to land more than twenty miles to the south and departed empty-handed. On Red Beach, the signal corps did manage to set up a radio transmitter in a weapons carrier so that MacArthur could deliver his prewritten speech to the people of the Philippines, announcing that "I have returned."[11] But the PROs had no way of relaying the speech live to America, so the first word that the home front received of this historic moment came from the dispatches written by the wire-service reporters on board MacArthur's command ship, which were light on battlefield details but filled with praise for MacArthur's bravery. "His disregard of personal danger," wrote William Dickinson of the UP from the *Nashville*, "stemmed from an implicit belief that it is his destiny to liberate the Philippines and that nothing can happen to prevent it."[12]

Leyte

As MacArthur's troops extended their beachhead on Leyte, forty-five American correspondents came ashore. "Some of these men," observed Kluckhohn, "have made so many landings that the sight of the dark shape of an island looming up through a dark night, the roar of a naval bombardment, the flash of rockets and a fleet of small boats carrying green clad men to shore is most familiar." Other reporters were rookies, who were unused to the unnerving conditions on a battlefield, while even the hardened veterans found it difficult to cope with the primitive and dangerous situation they found on Leyte.[13]

Communications were the biggest professional headache. With the beaches still under enemy fire, many correspondents struggled to locate Diller's bamboo shack. Those who did discovered that their dispatches were often lost by the couriers who made the treacherous journey to the radio ship. Then, for a time after October 21, the whole press pack learned that anything that reached New Guinea got backed up there after a violent storm damaged the commercial wireless transmitter at Hollandia.[14]

Living conditions on Leyte only compounded the misery. On October 21, a heavy mist shrouded the invasion sites, forcing the correspondents, as one of them noted, to eat their "10-in-1 rations gloomily on the beach while equipment rumbles ashore from the landing craft."[15] As darkness fell, rest became almost impossible. Sheltering in a foxhole, Kluckhohn, like most of his colleagues, initially "averaged about two hours sleep a night amidst frequent bombings and difficult conditions."[16] When MacArthur moved his headquarters to a large two-story house in the town of Tacloban on October 23, the press pack followed closely behind, taking over a number of houses and hoping for some respite. If anything, the situation deteriorated. The monsoon rains poured, turning the streets into mud lakes. "It's a gloomy hole," reported one correspondent of Tacloban, "and if the mud suddenly were hardened to brimstone, and the odor of pigsties sweetened by Sulphur, you would get an adequate picture of hell." The devil—in the guise of the Japanese—also appeared with a vengeance, sending thousands of reinforcements to Leyte and launching hundreds of air raids on Tacloban.[17] Shortly before dawn on October 25, a bomb struck one of the correspondents' houses, killing Asahel "Ace" Bush of the AP, Stanley Gunn of the *Fort Worth Star-Telegram*, and John Terry of the *Chicago Daily News*. Four other reporters were sleeping in the same house at the time and were lucky to survive. Many more were bedding down in a building less than fifty yards away, which was "rocked by the blast." The survivors, Dowling reported, "were left with the memory of a bad dream, and the fine way the guys took it, and the small comfort that Ace never knew what hit him. And with it all was a new hatred of the Japs."[18]

However grim and dangerous the situation in Tacloban, the correspondents initially struggled to escape the town as the "skimpy macadam veneer" of the roads "broke like eggshell under the stress of military traffic." Two *Chicago Tribune* reporters did achieve a degree of mobility when they acquired "the island's biggest car, a Packard limousine," which had previously been owned by a Japanese general. But most of their colleagues remained stuck in the second-floor room of the old post office, which served as the new press camp. Here, surrounded by "cans of food and bottles of whisky," their main amusement was to peer out of the window whenever they heard a jeep approaching, waiting for it to plunge into the large sinkhole in the road, which lay below a layer of mud and water.[19]

When Diller's team managed to restore the radio link to the outside world, this constricted view naturally affected the reporting. Instead of filing eyewitness copy of a fight that was already starting to bog down in the Leyte valley, most correspondents resorted to two alternatives. Some penned positive portraits of the "group of colorful military and naval personalities" in charge of running the battle, including Lieutenant General Walter Krueger, commander of the Sixth Army, who, as one account put it, "is master of four European languages and is fluent in several Filipino dialects," and Thomas Kinkaid, "who except for his admiral's stars might be mistaken for a college professor."[20] Most simply regurgitated MacArthur's daily communiqués, which were even more upbeat than usual. "Our forces have made extensive gains in all sectors," Diller announced on October 25. "Our ground patrols are ranging freely in all sectors," he declared four days later. Relying on these official statements, the correspondents on Leyte could do little more than provide a catalog of triumphs. Leyte, reported Dowling, "was an invasion of vengeance led by Gen. Douglas MacArthur, who had kept his word to the people of the Philippines and the heroes of Bataan." The battle, his wire-service colleagues added, could not have proceeded more smoothly, with the Japanese defenses "disintegrating" under American hammer blows. By the end of October, these reporters were even telling their readers that in just ten days MacArthur's men had seized two-thirds of the island, including all the important towns and roads.[21]

Fig. 10.1. MacArthur and the tight-knit coterie of officers known as the "Bataan gang" on their return to the Philippines. LeGrande Diller is on the extreme left.
© Getty Images.

Back home, Roosevelt could not have been more delighted. On November 7, he would be seeking an unprecedented fourth term as president. Not wanting to be tarred as a shameless opportunist, Roosevelt prohibited his aides from handing out any reports on the Leyte battles on his "political" campaign train. But he remained opportunistic enough to focus on MacArthur's success in a major speech on October 27. "And speaking of the glorious operations in the Philippines," Roosevelt concluded exultantly, "I wonder—whatever became of the suggestion made a few weeks ago, that I had failed for political reasons to send enough forces or supplies to General MacArthur?"[22]

MacArthur reacted ambivalently to Roosevelt's effort to cash in on his positive communiqués. The general had been tempted to run for the highest office himself, of course, and close observers in Tacloban thought they detected "some jealousy of Roosevelt" in him at this time. As the fighting on Leyte began to stall, MacArthur also came under pressure from some war correspondents who, as one recalled, "protested vigorously" against what they considered the series of "misleading" press releases. In response, one of MacArthur's PROs "let the cat out of the bag," telling the reporters in strict confidence: "The elections are coming up in a few days, and the Philippines *must* be kept on the front pages back home." No one will ever know for certain why MacArthur's press team was willing to help Roosevelt in this way, but the general's most distinguished biographer has suggested that the two men had probably reached an implicit agreement earlier in the year: Roosevelt would throw his weight behind a strategy focused on recapturing the Philippines if MacArthur effectively boosted his reelection chances by issuing press releases that "would portray great battlefield successes stemming from increased Washington support."[23]

* * *

MacArthur's overoptimistic press releases were not the only distraction from the emerging stalemate on Leyte. On October 24, one of the biggest naval battles of the war began to unfold around Leyte Gulf.

The Japanese commanders, viewing the landings as a chance to annihilate the American fleet and isolate MacArthur's army, developed a complex plan. One group of ships would try to lure Halsey's powerful Third Fleet away to the north, while central and southern forces attempted a pincer movement through the San Bernardino and Surigao Straits that would destroy Kinkaid's Seventh Fleet. Halsey fell for the trap. Convinced he had a chance to destroy the bulk of the Japanese fleet and believing it would be "childish . . . to guard statically [the] San Bernardino Strait," he dashed north, failing to leave any ships to protect against the enemy's central thrust. For a short time, disaster beckoned. On the morning of October 25, however, a small group of US destroyers and escort carriers did enough to turn the Japanese back at the Battle off Samar. A few hours earlier, Kinkaid had organized a more powerful force against the southern thrust, which won a shattering victory against the Japanese in the Battle of Surigao Strait.[24]

After the war, Halsey's actions would be the subject of increasingly strident criticism, with *Life* claiming that the admiral's judgment had been "questionable," while the navy's semiofficial historian publicly alluded to "Halsey's blunder."[25] At the time, however, the home front got little inkling of the controversy. Roosevelt was partly responsible. The president received a one-page "flash" about the battle late on the afternoon of October 25. With the election a fortnight away, he was naturally keen to divulge the good news as soon as possible. Only half a dozen reporters remained in the White House when Stephen Early, the president's press secretary, appeared. "Come quick," Early announced, clapping his hands for emphasis. Inside the Oval Office, the reporters found the president smiling broadly. Picking up the piece of paper, he read them the news slowly and dramatically. Halsey, Roosevelt revealed, had "defeated, seriously damaged, and routed" the Japanese fleet.[26]

Over the next few days, the war correspondents in the theater struggled to flesh out the story. Most had headed for dry land as soon as the invasion succeeded and so had only the vaguest notion of what was happening out at sea. "Around the beaches," reported William Dunn of CBS on October 26, "I found hundreds of Americans talking about the great battle which they were sure was raging to the south, because of the great flashes of light which were still visible."[27]

Even the reporters who remained with the fleet found it difficult to comprehend what had happened, including George E. Jones, who had recently joined the New York Times from the UP. As he sat at the typewriter, Jones realized that all he could write about were "odd fragments of battle scenes re-run in my memory after forty-eight hours of an unending stream of action."[28] At least he managed to cable something back to his editor. Some of his colleagues complained loudly about the difficulties of getting their dispatches radioed to Hawaii, while William Hipple of Newsweek seethed with anger when he learned that the navy had managed to lose his eyewitness account of the battle.[29]

In theory, the correspondents back in Pearl Harbor had a better chance to piece together the full picture of the confused clashes fought over 450,000 square miles. But they were also completely dependent on Nimitz, who issued only four communiqués on the battle between October 24 and 29, "the first of which," as one reporter complained, "was merely that contact had been established, and where."[30]

In fact, the pressroom in Nimitz's white, concrete headquarters on Makalapa Hill was oddly quiet during these tumultuous days. "There was no briefing by the Senior Officer Present," an NBC correspondent explained to his boss, "and only one meeting with a senior officer, which lasted twenty minutes and was mostly off the record. There was no information, background or other-wise, from any of the PROs." Some correspondents excused this neglect on the grounds that the navy had much more important things to worry about during such a big battle, but there was also a deeper cause. Senior officers were already starting to question Halsey's actions during the battle, suggesting darkly that he had given a "free gift of passage" to the Japanese. Neither Nimitz nor King was prepared to go this far. Both men also wanted to avoid handing out information that might prompt a major public inquest. They therefore took refuge in the fa-miliar navy habit of saying as little as possible.[31]

Nimitz's final communiqué followed this pattern. On handing it to the press corps, navy PROs stressed that it would not be released for at least twelve hours. This interval did not bother the newspaper correspondents, who went off to write stories gloating about how "Japan has been reduced to a third-rate sea power."[32] For radio reporters, however, the delay proved problematic. Not knowing when Nimitz would finally announce his side of the story, radio bosses decided not to disrupt their existing schedules, which would mean offering refunds to advertisers. Instead, the editors in New York merely incorporated the battle into their next regular news bulletin, thereby deadening its impact. The radio reporters in Pearl Harbor were so appalled by this outcome that they protested to Nimitz's PROs, whose response was revealing. "We forgot all about radio," muttered one apologetically, "but this won't happen again." "This is encouraging," remarked the NBC correspondent, although he knew that the navy's promise had come too late. Stories like the Battle of Leyte Gulf, he con-cluded acidly, "come far and few between."[33]

The only compensation was that, shortly after, the navy decided to permit radio correspondents to broadcast live from the invasion fleet in the middle of an operation. Before Leyte Gulf, navy PROs had repeated the same two reasons for maintaining the ban on such broadcasts: "one is military security, the other is the need for radio silence." After the neutralization of the Japanese fleet, how-ever, they agreed that secrecy was no longer essential. John Cooper of NBC made the first live broadcast from the Third Fleet on November 13, reporting that Halsey believed that the Japanese leadership now knew that "the hand-writing is on the wall."[34]

* * *

While the navy's big success saved the Leyte invasion, the island still had to be conquered. As the rain continued to pour, this proved no easy task. By the middle of November, the American focus was on capturing the port

of Ormoc, which meant penetrating fortified Japanese strongholds along
Breakneck Ridge. Although the bulk of the fighting was raging ten to twenty
miles west of Tacloban, the island continued to feel claustrophobic. Every
member of the large press pack, noted Dickinson, was effectively "living in
the front lines. There has been no rear area where they could withdraw for
rest and relaxation and the opportunity to analyze the campaign thought-
fully." Coping mentally was tough enough, but the physical dangers provided
the biggest challenge. Even hardened veterans found it tough going.[35]

Few were more hardened than Homer Bigart. The thirty-seven-year-old
New York Herald Tribune reporter had built an enviable reputation during
his eighteen-month stint covering the European war, having, among other
things, accompanied a highly dangerous bombing raid over Germany and
survived the grim stalemates at Cassino and Anzio. Bigart's first dispatch from
the Pacific recounted Krueger's punishing attempts to capture the Ormoc
Valley, the crucial position that ran down the western side of Leyte. In one
sense, he found the Japanese a much less impressive foe than the Wehrmacht.
Their artillery, he concluded, was much weaker than Germany's, and they
were nowhere near as thorough in laying mines—but the result, paradox-
ically, was to make life much more dangerous for him and his colleagues.
"Here," Bigart told his readers,

> you can drive right up to the front line in broad daylight without drawing
> a storm of artillery or getting blown sky high by Teller mines. And that is
> precisely why more correspondents have been killed here than in any com-
> parable period in the European theater. The newcomer gets a false sense
> of security. Hearing none of the usual din of battle, he comes jeeping
> along, admiring the scenery, when—ping—a sniper's bullet shatters his
> daydreams.[36]

Two days before Bigart made his trip down the Ormoc road, Frank Prist,
a photographer for Acme, had fallen to a sniper, making him the fourth
press fatality in a campaign that was not even four weeks old.[37] Shortly after,
Lindesay Parrott became another victim of the Japanese bombers. The *Times*
man had adapted well to the grueling conditions, maintaining, as one colleague observed, "a calm indifference to danger while collecting material
for his reports." Then on November 26, a bomb hit the house where he was
sleeping, spraying out metal fragments that tore a hole in his chest. Parrott

had to be evacuated by plane, and although desperate to "return [to] Leyte immediately," he remained away from the front until the new year.[38]

In earlier campaigns, losses at this level would have resulted in an effective blackout of eyewitness combat stories. MacArthur had attracted so many correspondents to Leyte, however, that even the terrible attrition rate did not ultimately affect the scale of coverage, although the result was not always to his liking. With the fighting bogged down, correspondents like Chickering provided the home front with a vivid sense of how tough it was to finish the job. "It was a lot different," he observed in *Time* at the end of November, "from the way hopeful US soldiers had imagined it after the US steamroller in the first week of the invasion. The enemy intended to dispute possession of Leyte; hard fighting was ahead." This battle, agreed Dowling in the *Chicago Sun*, "has been one of weary, soaked doughboys sweating up and along ridge after ridge in a series after series of sudden, vicious gun fights and bloody, hand-to-hand work with the elusive Jap troops. And it has all been under an endless, torrential tropical rain."[39]

Bigart joined the Thirty-Second Division for this tough phase of the battle. "It seems to be the fate of this division," he wrote at the start of December,

to be thrust into a campaign during the clean-up stage when the operations have already been written off in the public mind as an easy, glorious success. The slow, brutal slogging that must now come in the face of the enemy's fire doesn't make exciting reading. There's nothing very dramatic about an attack that gains maybe 100 yards of jungle scrub and liberates twenty desolate palm-thatched huts. Generally it isn't mentioned in dispatches because it is a commonplace—it's 99 percent of the infantryman's war.[40]

With correspondents back at headquarters continuing to base their reports on MacArthur's rosy proclamations, the war news from Leyte increasingly acquired a schizophrenic feel. The *New York Herald Tribune* exemplified the trend. Each day, it would publish Bigart's grim, ground-eye version of the battle alongside the accounts written by Frank Kelley at HQ, who told how US troops were "tightening their viselike grip on the thousands of Japanese trapped" in a small pocket or had "eliminated" the enemy's defensive line and "destroyed" thousands of enemy troops.[41]

MacArthur's most grandiose boast came in late December, after he had relieved Krueger's Sixth Army so it could prepare for the invasion of Luzon, replacing it with the newly created Eighth Army under Eichelberger. In announcing this change, MacArthur claimed that the Leyte campaign "can now be regarded as closed except for minor mopping up." Eichelberger bristled at this language, just as he had done at Buna. "I never understood the public-relations policy that either he or his immediate assistants established," Eichelberger remarked after the war. "It seemed to me, as it did to many of the commanders and correspondents, ill advised to announce victories when a first phase had been accomplished without too many casualties." As for the phrase "mopping up," he thought it only "produced bitterness among combat troops" left with this unpalatable task, which on Leyte resulted in more than seven hundred fatalities in the coming weeks.[42]

This time, however, MacArthur's boasting clearly had an impact back home. For one thing, although a number of senior columnists and editors were expressing "deep doubts" about MacArthur's communiqués, believing them to be "sometimes rosier than the facts warrant," their mounting skepticism played directly into MacArthur's hands by ensuring that his name remained at the heart of the story. "Because of this general distrust of MacArthur's communiqué figures," one editor explained to Henry Luce, "*Time* has been pretty careful to attribute all figures directly to MacArthur."[43]

MacArthur always enjoyed seeing his name in print, and from late October he had the added pleasure of finding his campaign invariably featured on the front page. Two years earlier, Buna had barely rated a mention on the media's list of top stories. Leyte, by contrast, came in third in the UP's poll of the biggest news events of 1944, behind only the D-Day invasion of France and Roosevelt's election to a fourth term. Perhaps even sweeter for MacArthur, his triumphant return to the Philippines came well ahead of the navy's battles in the central Pacific, which ranked no more than eighth on the list.[44]

Bataan Revisited

When the massive fleet assembled again during the first days of 1945, an anxious excitement pulsed through the decks as everyone contemplated recapturing the places in Luzon that had become seared into the nation's consciousness since the terrible defeat three years earlier.

On board one ship, John Graham Dowling sat all night with senior officers "drinking endless cups of coffee" and speculating about what would unfold in the days to come. "There is a certain nervousness growing now in the operations room," he noted, "and it is evident in the number of cigarettes being smoked by all hands." Frank Kluckhohn had been allocated a place on a ship that was scheduled to launch a pre-invasion bombardment on January 6. As the target came into view, his thoughts, like so many others, drifted back in time. "Low on the sun-beaten horizon," the *Times* man observed from the deck, "was a fleecy cloud lazily enfolding Mount Maravelas at the southern end of historic Bataan, where our overwhelmed forces fought so gallantly at the start of the war."[45]

Then, all of a sudden, a new menace interrupted Kluckhohn's reverie. Japanese suicide planes—the terrifying kamikazes—had first appeared in late October. Viewed with strategic detachment, they were a despairing last-ditch effort by the Japanese. For anyone on the receiving end, however, detachment was impossible. It was not just the physical damage these planes could inflict on the American fleet, which had no parallel since the costly naval battles at Guadalcanal. It was also the psychological impact of knowing that Japanese men were prepared to take their own lives to kill Americans. A veteran like Dowling found the experience so harrowing that after one attack he threw up his lunch in the captain's washroom. Having survived, he and his colleagues recognized instantly that this new form of warfare made for a terrific story.[46]

Information about the kamikazes had first seeped into the public domain in November. *Time* had grabbed the biggest scoop, with a short account of how an enemy dive bomber had "sailed over a US escort carrier as though for landing, then the pilot pushed his stick forward, dove into the carrier and sank it."[47] Now on January 6, Kluckhohn was desperate to tell his readers what it was really like to be under attack by suicide pilots: the enemy planes speeding toward the ship, dodging the defensive machine-gun fire; the top-side burning with "ammunition-jammed steel casing threatening to explode and many of our controls temporarily gone"; and the medics helping the wounded, some of whom "stagger past, burned to the waist or all over." "It is not hell," he wrote; "it is worse than hell."[48]

Yet the navy was not keen for this story to be told. With the kamikaze planes making "one-way trips, the Japanese had no way of estimating their achievements," and the last thing that King and Nimitz wanted was to let them know how successful they had been.[49] In the wake of *Time*'s story on the suicide attacks in November, navy PROs had contacted the magazine's editors, giving them "an awful lot of trouble . . . about having published that paragraph." After learning of this telling-off, Kluckhohn's bosses warned him against "breaking censorship" on the kamikaze issue. Kluckhohn therefore had no choice other than to rewrite his story in order to obscure exactly how the Japanese planes had managed to inflict so much damage on his ship.[50]

Then Kluckhohn learned that there had been a terrible irony to the fact that *Time* had scooped its rivals on the kamikaze story. About noon on January 6, an enemy plane carrying a five-hundred-pound bomb struck the bridge of the USS *New Mexico*, killing thirty men. Among them was William Chickering, the twenty-eight-year-old *Time* reporter who had been in the theater for more than two years. His colleagues were devastated. They remembered him, according to one obituary, as "a tall smiling man who never seemed to think about death or danger." MacArthur appeared particularly distraught. Chickering had long been one of his big boosters, and when he heard the news, he immediately called Carl Mydans of *Life* to the quarterdeck of his ship. The photographer found the general pacing up and down. As Mydans approached, MacArthur told him "how Bill Chickering had meant so much to him and how much . . . he felt the loss . . . of a correspondent and then he walked silently for a long time back and forth."[51]

* * *

After the tragedy of the bombardment came the triumph of the invasion. Since November, Diller had been working hard to ensure that newspaper reporters enjoyed better working conditions than those on Leyte. His most important innovation was "the establishment of floating press headquarters on three small ships . . . whereby correspondents, PROs, censors, and a transmission set-up were able to move in just behind the assault waves and begin functioning immediately." Diller envisaged that his team would have the ability to transmit 170,000 words out of Luzon during the first week of the campaign, and if this system broke down he had arranged a series of special courier facilities.[52]

MacArthur, meanwhile, wanted radio "to give the American public realistic, front-line coverage" of his big moment. So he requested almost two thousand tons of specialist radio kit, including voice transmitters, control gadgets, and mobile transmitting equipment. He also made sure that George Folster of NBC was one of the correspondents who was with him when he made his historic landing on Lingayen Gulf, shortly after 2 p.m. on January 9.[53]

"His Leyte wading scene," writes MacArthur's biographer, "was unintentional, but this one seems to have been a deliberate act of showmanship." To make sure it reached the biggest possible audience, Diller's men expedited

Fig. 10.2. MacArthur wades ashore at Lingayen Gulf, January 1945. National Archives 80G 299235.

the transmission of the first wire-service accounts, which were suitably dramatic. MacArthur, as Yates McDaniel of the AP wrote, "left Luzon furtively in the dead of night aboard a small torpedo boat. He returned today proudly and jubilantly, standing at the rail of an American warship in broad daylight." Once the radio equipment had been set up, Folster broadcast directly to the home front. "When General MacArthur examined our beachheads," the NBC broadcaster told the many millions listening, "I went with him. He found no beach defenses worthy of the name. And when I stopped and talked to the natives, they told me that the Japs had fled inland three days ago when our naval vessels started shelling."[54]

The other correspondents were equally struck by the lack of enemy resistance. On invasion day, reported Dickinson of the UP, "only a few sneak raiders disturbed the routine of pouring in supplies and men." Thereafter, the war correspondents recorded a buildup that proceeded with barely a glitch, as some units penetrated almost six miles inland. Frank Kelley observed that the amphibious teams were setting "a new record for landing of troops, supplies, and equipment." "Roads leading from the beaches were left in good condition," added George Jones of the *New York Times,* "and traffic was rolling to the front."[55]

Manila was a little more than a hundred miles away, over the same plain where MacArthur had organized his fighting retreat three years earlier. As the offensive surged forward, the correspondents accompanying the troops concentrated on trying to convey the panorama of victory. Jones, for instance, described

> columns of dusty, greenclad troops passing through country villages while lines of natives hold up two fingers in the V sign and call out "Veectree, Veectree!"; ... long line-ups of vehicles patiently waiting their turn to cross a shaky bridge or ford a stream past placidly wallowing carabou [*sic*]; ... construction crews and telephone linesmen parked along roads; ... small landing craft dashing around waters off the beach; ... the vibrant whirl of an American shell overhead, and the occasional splay of an enemy shell landing behind our lines.[56]

There were still moments of danger, although even these sometimes contained elements of comic relief. One night, an exhausted group of correspondents, including Dowling and Jones, decided not to dig a fox-hole, reassuring themselves with the thought that they had encountered no snipers, artillery, or air raids all day. Almost as soon as they bedded down, however, Japanese shells started falling close to their position. "We had been sleeping in our clothes," Dowling reported, "but poor George Jones of the *New York Times* is in his underwear. A GI going by us like a bullet mumbles something about a hole and we get off the ground and race after him through the dark." Jumping in, they discovered that the hole was a local garbage pit, although the intensifying shelling quickly dispelled their squeamishness. "We bury our faces in a mixture of canned eggs and cheese," Dowling joked, "while Jones burrows among the sardine cans and old spam, and makes noises like a dog with a can tied to his tail."[57]

The correspondents who remained close to Diller's press camp faced no such indignity. Instead, buttressed by MacArthur's habitually optimistic communiqués, they began to sense that they were part of one of the war's most spectacular triumphs. By the end of January, their reports boasted that American troops were "astride thirty-seven miles of main highway to Manila ... and have practically severed the Japanese forces in northern Luzon from those in the southern part of the island." "It looks like we're back with a vengeance," one radio broadcaster quoted MacArthur as saying, "and the entrances to Manila, Corregidor, and Bataan are virtually in sight."[58]

As MacArthur contemplated the campaign's culmination, he doubtless hoped that the liberation of Manila would be the Pacific War's counterpoint to the liberation of Paris. That stunning event the previous August had seen the enemy collapse after weeks of costly stalemate, which had resembled the fighting on Leyte. As the Germans evacuated the undamaged city, war correspondents and GIs had dashed into a tumultuous Parisian reception: surging crowds, impromptu parties, improbable reunions, and organized festivities. Almost a month into the Luzon campaign, MacArthur believed he was about to enjoy a similar triumph. On February 4, he let the press corps report that he had given the First Cavalry Division and the Thirty-Seventh Infantry Division the go-ahead to "dash to Manila," an order that "developed into a neck-and-neck race, with the First Cavalry winning." Two days later, his communiqué announced that "[o]ur forces are rapidly clearing the enemy from Manila." Shortly after, he instructed Krueger and Eichelberger to plan a "grand 'victory parade'" through the city's streets to mark his long-promised return, having already sanctioned a detailed PR "plan for entry of the commander-in-chief and official party into the city."[59]

Unlike what occurred in Paris, however, the enemy decided to contest every street and every building, including impressive strongpoints like the old walled city, which had housed MacArthur's headquarters in 1941. The result was a long, bloody slog, made worse when strong winds fanned a major blaze along the port and in the working-class residential districts. As the battle ground on, American forces sustained heavy casualties, but the Filipinos suffered the most, with an estimated one hundred thousand dying over the ensuing weeks. Many civilians were caught in the crossfire between the two armies, but a large number were simply massacred by doomed Japanese troops who adopted the attitude "If you are not for us, you are against us."[60]

This was not the type of victory MacArthur had envisioned. Quietly shelving his plans for a triumphant parade, he immediately discovered another way to mark the success of his campaign.

* * *

MacArthur had always been a proponent of publicizing atrocity stories. As well as pushing for the release of Dyess's account of the death march, his New Guinea campaign had produced some of the most horrific images of the war. Back in

May, for example, the same issue of *Life* that had shown an Arizona war worker with the skull of a Japanese soldier had also contained a stomach-turning picture of dead "starved laborers" at Hollandia.[61] In late January, with US forces in the process of recapturing the region where so many Americans had surrendered three years earlier, the fate of those who had been forced to toil away in Japanese prisoner camps was uppermost in everyone's mind, including the war correspondents.

Those plodding toward Manila encountered the first death march survivor on January 21, although at this stage they faced a familiar obstacle. The censors were under firm instructions to be careful about how the POWs' ordeal was reported.[62] The day before the Luzon invasion, Surles had even reminded MacArthur that "official releases of atrocity accounts shall not be issued or cleared without coordination among the War Department, Navy Department, and Department of State."[63]

The death march story was too big to contain, however, especially after the reporters learned that Camp O'Donnell—"one of the most notorious pestholes maintained by the Japanese for war prisoners"—had been liberated on January 24. Homer Bigart and Arthur Veysey of the *Chicago Tribune* were among the group of correspondents who hurried to the scene. In his dispatch, Bigart reminded his readers that this camp had served as "the terminus of the 'death march' from Bataan in April, 1942, and thereafter the detention center for thousands of American prisoners of war." The Japanese had long since evacuated the last POWS, so all that was left for the reporters to see were the makeshift graves. "It is hard to tell just how many Americans died here," reported Veysey. "The crosses which they erected are scattered. Hundreds are piled in one hole. Only a few have the dog tags of the men whose bones they mark. One carries a half dollar into which a soldier had scratched his name."[64]

Reporters finally had the chance to interview a large group of Bataan survivors a week later when a ranger unit made a bold dash to liberate a camp near Cabanatuan. Everything they learned confirmed what Dyess had divulged a year earlier. Bigart told his readers that many of the men had succumbed to dysentery during the death march, that Japanese soldiers guarding the artesian wells had struck parched prisoners who tried to snatch a drink, and that at the bitter end there were only eighty "living skeletons" left in Camp O'Donnell before the final evacuation. His AP colleague recounted a harrowing interview with men who were "prematurely old, with gray hair, sunken eyes." "They talked in low tones of Japanese brutality and the death march of Bataan," Jones reported in the *New York Times*, "of the final terrifying week of bombing and bombardment that hit Corregidor, of men dying like flies, of disease, of ten hours daily in prison camp under the hot sun, or waist-high in water of rice paddies under hard eyes, of frequent beatings and shootings."[65]

No one read such accounts with more anguish than Frank Hewlett. The UP man had last seen his wife, Virginia, on New Year's Eve, 1941, when he had made a snap decision to hurry to Bataan to cover the war, while she had remained in Manila to await capture by the Japanese. Since then, Hewlett had manically buried himself in work in order to blot out thoughts of what Virginia might be suffering. Indeed, after earning the distinction of being one of the last reporters off Corregidor in 1942, he had traveled "at least 50,000 miles in continuous coverage of the war," including a stint in the CBI theater, after which he had gone to Goa in 1943, hoping that his wife would be part of the second exchange of civilian internees. When the *Gripsholm* docked, he had been distraught to discover that she had been too ill to travel, but he never gave up hope of finding her, even when the fortunes of war seemed to be stacked against him. Hewlett's most recent trial had come when his ship had been ordered away from Lingayen Gulf shortly before the invasion. After ten anxious days at sea, he had finally made it make to Luzon, and at long last his luck began to change.[66]

The rangers' successful sprint to Cabanatuan emboldened MacArthur to sanction a daring raid to free the prisoners held at Santo Tomas, some sixty miles behind Japanese lines. This camp housed many of the civilian internees captured in 1942, and Hewlett was determined to accompany the mission. Brushing aside his boss's objection that it was "too big a risk to take," he declared he was "going in with the cavalry." After boarding a jeep that would be in the vanguard of the attack, he grabbed another reporter by the arm and revealed the only thing that was on his mind. "Tell me you think she's there," he demanded.[67]

The dash to Santo Tomas initially encountered "only scattered resistance from the astonished Japanese," but the fighting became fiercer as the mission neared the camp. After a tank smashed through the front gate, the members of the rescue party edged their way inside, before finally locating 3,700 civilian prisoners, 2,500 of them American. At first, Hewlett failed to recognize his wife—she was so frail and weighed only eighty pounds—and when they finally embraced he found it difficult to express his emotions. "It was a reunion," he wrote in a short dispatch the next day, "after years about which I do not want to think. The other patients, nurses and doctors and my old friend Father James J. Hurley of Boston, shared our joy."[68]

Over the next few days, Hewlett's colleagues focused much of their attention on the liberated nurses, calling them "the Angels of Bataan" on account of the way they had cared for the wounded during the bitter siege of 1942. As media interest mounted, the War Department sought to control this story. At a time when there was such a "critical shortage of nurses in combat areas," Surles's PROs decided that "the heroic part played by the nurses captured on Bataan would be an inspiration to stimulate the voluntary recruitment of American women for service as nurses." So, just days after the liberation of Camp Santo Tomas, the War Department laid on "four giant planes" to bring the "Angels of Bataan" back home, where, under close supervision, they told the officially sanctioned version of their time in captivity.[69]

One survivor refused to join the returning party. Vivian Weissblatt had spent the past two years in charge of the internment camp diet, with the near-impossible task, she told one reporter, of "feeding several hundred small children and trying to keep them nourished out of the small variety of available foods." She had last seen her husband, Franz, in Manila in December 1941, shortly before he had been captured by the Japanese on Bataan. Since then, she had received no news of his whereabouts, but at the start of February events moved quickly. The day after Vivian's liberation, Doc Quigg, also of the UP, found Franz in the dark recesses of another camp. " 'I'm Quigg, United Press,' " he recalled saying at their first encounter. "The Dr. Livingston of Bilibid prison grasped my hand fervently. 'I'm Weissblatt, United Press,' replied the correspondent who had been wounded and captured by the Japanese more than three years earlier."[70]

During his time as a prisoner, Weissblatt had kept a careful record of everything that had happened, which, within days of his release, he used as the basis of a story. Weissblatt calculated that about six thousand US prisoners had died in captivity on Luzon, a figure that did not take into account the sixteen thousand Americans who had been transported off the island and for whom he "was unable to obtain any knowledge whatever." Many of the dead, he wrote in a dispatch that the UP circulated on February 19, "were victims of the infamous 'Bataan death march,' and there were many others who did not survive wounds or disease they had incurred during their hopeless last stand." Once he was freed, Weissblatt's thoughts, like those of so many other Americans, turned to retribution.[71]

* * *

The obvious starting place was to continue liberating the places synonymous with all the brutality. At dawn on February 16, MacArthur and a small retinue of aides jumped into several jeeps and headed to the Bataan front. Here, American troops were making swift progress against wilting Japanese opposition, but this success made the journey all the more dangerous. MacArthur, anxious to get a glimpse of the attack on Corregidor, which would be assaulted from the sea and air, pushed his small convoy forward until it had gone nearly five miles past "the most forward American road blocks and was in Japanese-infested territory." The general had invited Franz Weissblatt along for the ride, and the reporter was profoundly moved by revisiting "the scenes indelibly graven in his memory in those terrible days of 1942."[72]

Weissblatt was particularly impressed by the general's courage. When one officer tried to persuade him to turn back, on the basis that the area ahead had not yet been cleared of enemy troops, MacArthur revealed his strong sense of destiny. "Oh, I don't think they'll hit us. After all, this is my homecoming and I want to go all the way." As MacArthur and his party reached the 1942 defense line, Weissblatt reported on the reception they received from the locals, who, "clad in their Sunday best, lined the street, waved, cheered, and gave the V-sign."[73]

In Manila, meanwhile, there were no celebrations, just carnage. The correspondents heading in this direction knew that the censors still recoiled from unsubstantiated atrocity allegations, so they documented the horrific sights they saw with great care. "In the final hours of their defense of south Manila," wrote Frank Kelley in the Herald Tribune on February 17, "the Japanese are machine-gunning, bayoneting, and butchering civilians as they flee from their burning homes and attempt to cross into American lines. We have investigated and corroborated reports of many atrocities," Kelley explained. "Victims' bodies have been photographed and evidence has been collected about the perpetrators of these crimes." And yet the slaughter continued. Kelley learned that the Japanese had also "bayoneted or burned alive 436 men, women, and children" in a southern Luzon town, while inside Manila the situation was, if anything, even more horrific. "The once picturesque Spanish city," he reported on February 24, as the fighting came to an end,

> with streets and shaded plazas was a shambles, with not a building intact and scarcely a stone upon stone. . . . Dead and dying women lay heaped in the rubble. Some had been dead several hours, while others lay groaning on blood-drenched pallets and clutched handfuls of maggoty rice. One woman with her right leg blown off turned her eyes piteously up at me and asked after her baby. I couldn't tell her that her boy lay near by, his back laid open like raw beefsteak.[74]

* * *

By the time the guns fell silent in Manila, the war correspondents had left no one in any doubt about how they viewed the enemy. Although they had once again placed MacArthur at the center of their narrative, their dispatches had also revealed "a new hatred of the Japs."[75] The intense danger was one reason, since the bombing of Tacloban and the terrifying kamikaze raids had left many reporters mourning the death of close colleagues and friends. Japanese savagery was another, not just the slaughter of civilians on Manila's streets, but also the treatment of the American prisoners who had surrendered three years earlier.

Yet the War Department was still not entirely comfortable with the publication of atrocity stories. Nor, for that matter, had MacArthur wanted to draw attention to the Manila bloodbath, for it had dashed his dreams of a victory parade. Back home, though, editors devoted numerous column inches to dispatches that told of innocent victims and emaciated survivors. Headline writers used words like "wanton," "horror," and "hell" to describe Japanese deeds, while editorialists called for retribution against such a vicious foe. The Luzon campaign, declared the *Washington Post* in a typical comment, "has an emotional value which may be even greater than the strategic. It means that the 'Battling Bastards of Bataan' are to be avenged at last."[76]

Americans on the home front were inevitably enraged by all of these stories. According to one Gallup poll conducted that winter, the American public took "a far sterner attitude toward the Japanese" than it did toward the Germans. No less than 33 percent of respondents favored destroying Japan as a political entity, while 28 percent advocated strict supervision and control after the war, and 13 percent wanted to "Kill them all . . . Wipe them off the map. Clean them off the face of the earth . . . Sink the whole damned island."[77]

In returning to the Philippines, MacArthur had finally achieved his vindication. In the bloody battles that ensued, the press and public had witnessed so much savagery that they were seeking vengeance against the fanatic Japanese enemy—and this was before the navy and Marines launched their invasion of a small volcanic island called Iwo Jima.

11

Flying the Flag

An Open-Door Policy

The war had not been kind to Hawaii. By the second half of 1944, the Japanese threat had long since receded, but the correspondents still found the islands a major disappointment. "Honolulu was a mess," noted one in his diary. "The narrow streets boiled with sailors. Shops seemed to be mostly cheap rackets, souvenir dives, gimcracks, boob catchers; a penny arcade atmosphere just like the pin-ball, peep show honky-tonks on West Forty-Second Street. Restaurants were hot, dirty, crowded [and the] service was terrible." Boredom was still a curse for those who traipsed up Makalapa Hill each day to visit Nimitz's headquarters. For these correspondents, the main professional challenge was to concoct something interesting to say from the navy's often sketchy communiqués.[1]

In September, six of them had a chance to swap this daily grind for some real action when they joined Waldo Drake to watch the First Marine Division's invasion of Peleliu.[2] It turned out to be a miserable experience. "Peleliu," wrote Robert Martin of *Time*, "is a horrible place. The heat is stifling and rain falls intermittently—the muggy rain that brings no relief, only greater misery. . . . Marines are in the finest possible condition, but they wilted on Peleliu. By the fourth day there were as many casualties from heat prostration as from wounds."[3] William Hipple of *Newsweek* agreed. He had "covered almost every major action" in the Pacific, his new bosses boasted after he left the AP to join them, "—from the flight decks of big flat-tops, from the cockpits of bombers, from invasion barges, foxholes, and stinking island jungles"—but he rarely had been as frightened as he was on Peleliu. Along with Lisle Shoemaker of the United Press, he spent more than two hours of the invasion day frantically digging a makeshift shelter for the night. "We pressed into the hole," he reported,

and waited, very scared. We heard heavy fighting in the direction of the airfield. As the Jap tanks kept coming, our armored amphibious tractors and a few Sherman tanks moved out to meet them. . . . It was cold and wet in the hole during the long night and we were continuously picking off 3-inch black worms and fleas which were crawling over our faces and bodies. Jap snipers infiltrated within 50 yards but there was no large-scale counterattack. We were glad to see the sun this morning.[4]

Although the war correspondents were even more delighted when they finally escaped the island, for Drake the return to Pearl Harbor provided little solace. Before departing for Peleliu, he had left a large "Do Not Enter" sign hanging above his office door. He came back to discover that this had been removed. Much worse, another officer had taken his place as the CINCPAC PRO. Enraged, Drake immediately stomped off to seek an explanation from Nimitz, while reporters began compiling lurid stories on "the controversy over the management of Captain Drake."[5]

Then everyone got to know the new PRO and their attitude changed. Captain Harold B. Miller had not wanted the promotion. His background was in naval aviation, and after a stint as the naval attaché in London, he had craved a combat mission, not another desk job. Yet from the moment he formally replaced Drake, Miller scarcely put a foot wrong. His first move was to hold an impromptu press conference, explaining why the removal of the old sign over Drake's former office was so symbolic. "It will be our policy while I am here," he said, "to tell you just what the hell is going on. If national security is involved, we will tell you that, too, and try to explain why. My office has three doors, and all of them will be open all day."[6]

This new ethos immediately worked wonders on those reporters who had become disheartened by the false paradise they had found in Hawaii, but it was not the only positive change. Alongside the open-door policy, Miller immediately began "beating the bushes frantically for qualified talent."[7] The result was a massive expansion of staff levels. By the end of 1944, the CINCPAC PRO had 128 officers and 239 enlisted men, and these numbers were projected to rise to 205 and 419 by the following summer.[8]

Some of these men were old hands, including Herbert Merillat, who had returned to the theater for the first time since leaving Guadalcanal in December 1942. Merillat immediately recognized how much had changed, recalling that three years before "no one had the vaguest idea what I was to do. Now," he observed, "most outfits not only have a pretty definite idea what a PRO is supposed to do, but tend to expect miracles from them. This applies to all branches of the services. No one is more sensitive about the public credit he gets for his achievements than the fighting man, though he is very reluctant to admit it."[9]

To get as much credit as possible for the navy, Miller demanded the utmost efficiency from his subordinates, instructing them to answer any question from a reporter as soon as possible. He also placed a premium on translating into workable policy the ideas of the man who had elevated him to this position—a man who had very clear and strident opinions about public relations.[10]

* * *

James V. Forrestal had become the navy secretary in the spring of 1944 after the sudden death of Frank Knox. As Knox's undersecretary since before Pearl Harbor, he had closely followed the navy's efforts to shed its reputation for excessive secrecy.[11] Then came Saipan, which had convinced him that an even more fundamental change had to be made in the way the navy interacted with reporters. This bloody battle had generated numerous complaints about how long it had taken to get copy from the battlefield to the newsroom. Forrestal had immediately launched an investigation, which singled out Drake as the chief culprit on the grounds that he "was not trying to move news along but was trying to slow it down."[12] This judgment was, in fact, deeply unfair. Drake had provided the media at Saipan with exactly the same facilities that had worked so well during the invasion of the Marshalls. It had not been his fault that a tactical battle maneuver had sent the radio ship away from the island, leaving reporters without transmission facilities for almost a week.

Whatever the rights and wrongs of the case, Forrestal decided to replace Drake with Miller in the late summer of 1944. He then began bombarding the new PRO with a barrage of ideas. "One of the major objectives for Public Relations in the Pacific," Forrestal wrote in November, "is personalizing the war there, that is, getting back to the people at home stories about the individual officers and men who are fighting in the Pacific." Miller responded by requesting a hundred naval men with journalistic experience whom he could turn into "enlisted correspondents." Their job would be to board various ships, get to know the sailors, and then write short, four-line stories that would appeal to the countless local newspapers across the country.[13]

When developing this program, Miller leaned heavily on the Marines, whose combat correspondents (CCs) had acquired enormous experience in publishing "Joe Blow" stories that ignored "the big picture" in favor of recording the deeds of the average fighting man. There was only one snag: the Marines had come to favor a relaxed approach that was decidedly at odds with Forrestal's prescriptive instincts. "We do not want the CCs to feel that someone is breathing down their necks for stories," one senior officer wrote in early 1945. "In brief," the Marine reporters were told, "—if you have a good yarn, write it as well as you can. If there is no story—don't try to write one."[14]

Forrestal was prepared to accept a degree of reticence from combat correspondents, but he wanted the PROs to pull out all the stops when trumpeting the navy's exploits. With the end of the war looming, Forrestal believed this was essential because of the bitter budgetary battles that were bound to ensue after demobilization. "If we can't get something done about our public-relations in the Pacific," he told Miller before he left for Hawaii, "I can't go to Congress. We'll get no funding, no allocations, or anything."[15]

While Forrestal was already casting one eye toward the postwar world, he had his other eye fixed firmly on MacArthur. This fit a long-standing pattern. For the past three years, one of the main factors pushing the navy toward greater openness had been its disgust at MacArthur's shameless attempts to grab the bulk of the headlines. This dynamic only intensified after October when MacArthur returned to the Philippines and Forrestal began to worry that the general's publicity machine was drowning out the navy's part in the war. "Activities in the SWPA," one navy PRO observed in mid-December, "have lead [sic] many to believe that the Navy is of minor importance and that in reality this is a foot soldier war. They must be shown that 'the Navy had to be there first.'"[16]

When raising the navy's profile, Forrestal was not afraid of exposing the uglier side of the fighting. Privately, he believed that there would be "no short cut or easy way" to defeat Japan, and he wanted Americans to understand this basic fact. He was therefore happy to continue the policy, instituted at Tarawa, of revealing the extent of the blood and gore in battles to capture small Pacific islands. But he also knew that easing censorship was only a partial solution. It counted for nothing if the reporters were unable to get their stories out of the theater.[17]

Miller spent much of his initial time in Hawaii dealing with the perennial problem of communications. Only two years earlier, veterans recalled, "stories had to be flown back to Pearl Harbor, to Australia, or long distances to ships that were far enough out of range of the Japs to break radio silence before they could be transmitted. Often, planes were not immediately available for this courier service," with the result that it "was usually a matter of days before the stories reached the US and found their way into print." For the big battles of 1945, the navy planned to lay on "the most elaborate facilities yet provided in the Pacific." Print correspondents would be able to relay short bulletins from the beachhead directly to the States in about an hour, and full stories within a couple of hours. To reduce the possibility of "over-loaded facilities," Miller established four separate radio channels on Guam. At least one of these would be made available to photographers, who would emerge as the biggest winners of the new system being developed in the Pacific.[18]

Over the previous year, a number of brave cameramen had captured some fine images of the navy's war, especially on Tarawa. In the wake of that battle, pictures taken by Marine combat photographers had ended up in a *Life* photo essay, while Frank Filan of the AP had won a Pulitzer Prize for his after-action shots. In both instances, as journalism scholar Susan Moeller has observed, "the range and tonality of the images because of the harsh tropical sun gave a clarity to the subjects that few pictures from the European theater captured."[19]

Despite this success, Miller's team believed that not enough pictures were getting published. Resource allocation was partly responsible. From February 1943 to August 1944, only between a quarter and a third of the photographers in the Still Picture Pool were assigned to the vast areas covered by Nimitz's and MacArthur's commands. Those who did make it faced conditions that were far from ideal.[20] "Photography in this climate," observed one Marine cameraman in 1943, "is a long, sad story." The humidity tended to turn film moldy if it was not used within a day of being loaded into a camera. And the light changed so rapidly that instead of employing a meter, photographers would "just guess and hope like hell."[21] Even if they did manage to capture a good shot, cameramen still faced time lags that threatened to make their images out of date by the time an editor came to decide whether to publish them. Here the navy's ethos was partly to blame. Drake had been particularly critical of the stubborn tardiness of the navy's chief photo officer on Saipan, complaining that "he hangs on to everything photographic like a bird dog hangs on to fleas."[22] After taking over, Miller concluded that the cumbersome censorship operation also contributed to the inexcusable delays.[23]

The new PRO was determined to turn this situation around. He had originally been sent to the Pacific "in connection with public relations photography" because he had acquired some experience in what one of his superiors called the "use of photography for illustrative purposes." After his promotion, Miller continued to believe that images provided one of the most compelling ways of selling the navy's war.[24] "The demand for pictures," his office declared in December 1944, "is greatly increasing because they tell the story much more completely. Pictures are required on all 'Joe Blow stories' as well as action shots during engagements."[25]

To make pictures speedily available, Miller established a laboratory on Guam. His aim was to fly in negatives from the battlefield and then have them "developed, censored, and radio-photoed to San Francisco." If successful, the navy would have the capacity to show the home front images from the Pacific battlefield on the same day that they were photographed, something that could have scarcely been imagined even a year earlier.[26]

* * *

While Miller and his PROs busied themselves with these improvements, the correspondents in Hawaii began to contemplate the next battle. Those who had been with the navy for any length of time knew just how bad the carnage had been on Tarawa, Saipan, and Peleliu, and they were not slow to share the worst with their colleagues. The reporters who had just arrived listened intently. Many had spent months, even years, covering the European war, but they remained decidedly edgy about their new posting. Some landed in Hawaii still bearing the mental scars of spending too much time sheltering from German bullets and bombs. Others fretted that combat out in the Pacific would be quite different from anything they had yet witnessed: more brutal, more random, more dangerous. After all, there had to be some reason the correspondent casualty toll was much higher in the war against Japan.[27]

As soon as these correspondents joined the fleet that departed from Hawaii in late January, their sense of foreboding grew apace. During the first days at sea, briefing officers spoke only of a mysterious destination dubbed "Island X." Then after the fleet rendezvoused around the Marianas, the mystery was cleared up. Thirty reporters were summoned to the officers' wardroom of the main radio ship on February 16. There, they encountered Admiral Turner, in charge of the amphibious operation, General Holland Smith, in the new position of commanding general, First Marine Force, and in a big surprise, Secretary Forrestal, who wanted a firsthand view of the upcoming battle. The senior officers began by describing the target. Iwo Jima, the reporters learned, was only nine square miles in size. It was dominated on its southern tip by Mount Suribachi, "a sheer-sided volcano rising 556 feet." And it had a fearsome reputation. "The defenses are thick," explained Turner. The island was such a "tough proposition," agreed Holland Smith, that casualties among the first waves might easily be as high as

40 percent. The mood in the room, Robert Sherrod recalled, became "rather emotional . . . —there was a sort of pit in the stomach emotion that one feels when he knows that many men who love life are about to die." Peering over his glasses, Turner asked if there were any questions. From the back of the room, one reporter asked, half in jest, "When's the next boat to Pearl Harbor?"[28]

"The Miracles of Modern Transmission"

Most radio reporters had decided not to accompany the fleet to Iwo Jima, prefer-ring to remain in Guam, where the speed of transmission would partially make up for having to recite dull communiqués over the airwaves. These broadcasters boasted an audience approaching ten million on the East Coast alone, and they were baffled, and more than a little annoyed, when they discovered that the re-cent PRO reforms had ignored many of their requirements. Forrestal was largely to blame. "Personally," he remarked to Miller on one occasion, "I don't listen to the radio and I don't think a lot of people do. Radio news goes in one ear and out the other. What appears in the small-town papers is what interests me."[29]

As the clock ticked by on invasion day, February 19, the radio reporters in Guam were left in little doubt that Forrestal's ethos had permeated down the chain of command. In their eyes, the navy's biggest blunder was to delay the release of the first official communiqué until 2:15 a.m. on the East Coast, by which time every station had closed for the night. Not until 8:15 the fol-lowing morning did CBS score a notable scoop, carrying the observations of Webley Edwards, who had flown over the invasion site and had seen "plumes of dust and smoke . . . rising where the shells from the warships were landing." Meanwhile, the other radio correspondents were left lamenting their treatment. "Every break radio had on the Iwo job," complained NBC's Robert McCormick, ". . . was made by radio itself, often at considerable cost to the networks."[30]

To the reporters heading into battle, the cost proved much higher. Sherrod spent much of invasion day on his boat waiting for the order to land. In the late afternoon, he saw Keith Wheeler of the *Chicago Times*, who had already been on the island and was returning to file his invasion story. "There's more hell in there than I've seen in the rest of this war put together," Wheeler told him. "The Nips have got the beaches blanketed with mortars. There are dead Marines scattered from one end to the other, and it looks like nearly every boat is getting smashed before it can pull out."[31]

Despite the bloody bedlam on the beach, print copy flowed rapidly back to the States, revealing in stages what was making Iwo Jima so hellish. First, there was the intensity of the Japanese resistance. Pillboxes and caves seemed to be spewing deadly fire from all directions as enemy troops demonstrated their determination to fight for every inch of the island. "Things got very tough, indeed, on D-day afternoon," noted John Lardner of the North American Newspaper Alliance, "which most of us in the beach neighborhood spent hugging the sand very warmly." Before long, veterans began to consider this to be the worst battle yet. At Tarawa, observed Robert Trumbull of the *New York Times*, the hardest part had been getting ashore. "Here the trouble begins after you have set foot on land.... On Iwo, not as on Tarawa, the Marines are fighting an enemy who holds high ground and knows how to use it."[32]

Even without the enemy, nothing about the island looked inviting. "Iwo Jima," according to the account in *Life*, "conveyed a sullen sense of evil to all the Americans who saw it for the first time. The cold wet winds loaded with fine volcanic dust, the blazing tropical sun, the shifting volcanic sand that slid back into foxholes and clouded firing mechanisms."[33] Lardner decided to ditch his pack after walking just thirty yards inland because it was making him sink knee-deep into the sand. That was the easiest problem to solve. The tiny beachhead became increasingly cramped as more and more Marines came ashore, to be faced with barrage after barrage of mortars and shells. "There is no front line on bloody Iwo," reported Morrie Landsberg of the AP on February 21. "The whole island is a battle zone."[34]

As the carnage mounted, official and semiofficial voices reinforced the scale of the challenge. The invasion beach, wrote one Marine combat correspondent, "is a scene of indescribable wreckage—all of it ours."[35] Three days after the first troops had made it ashore, Holland Smith repeated the same message. "We are up against a very tough proposition," he told reporters; "we anticipated a severe battle and we are making slow progress.... It must not be forgotten," he added, "that the Japs consider Iwo Island as the homeland. There is every indication that our fanatical enemy will fight to the bitter end."[36]

Back in Washington, senior navy officers were already starting to reveal what this fanatical resistance meant to the Marines: no less than six thousand casualties in the first five days, making it even more costly than Tarawa.[37] War correspondents were inevitably suffering as well. Days into the campaign, those on the island had established something approaching a routine. It began in the foxholes they had dug into the crumbly sand to shelter from an anticipated Japanese counterattack. All night long, a constant naval barrage helped to fend off this threat, but it also made sleep impossible. At dawn, the weary reporters would shake the "coarse ash" off their uniform, take a swig of medicinal brandy, and then start a tour of the slowly expanding beachhead, stopping at the various command posts to see where the frontline resided. With Japanese troops firing from a multitude of concealed positions, every part of this journey was fraught with danger.[38]

Veterans like Sherrod and Wheeler soon began to question why they were taking such risks. Pride, Sherrod decided, was one reason. Sympathy with the Marines was another. Then there was their earlier criticism of those "communiqué commandos" who wrote so authoritatively about battles from the safety of the rear. Sherrod and Wheeler realized the hypocrisy of emulating on Iwo Jima what they had attacked so vigorously at Saipan. But their high-mindedness came at a cost.[39]

Wheeler was standing in a shell hole, watching three American tanks smolder from enemy fire, when a Japanese sniper bullet hit him in the jaw. He would probably have bled to death had there not been a doctor close by, who gave him plasma, clamped his throat, and directed him to a hospital ship. Once safely off the island, Wheeler was immediately overcome by "a feeling of unutterable, golden relief. The knots and tensions that I didn't know were there," he wrote afterward, "and the long corrosion of repetitious fear and loathing ran out of me in a flood."[40] Wheeler's recovery was helped by the actions of his colleagues. As he recuperated in the hospital, a PRO provided him with a typewriter and visited him twice a day to pick up his copy. Even his rivals at the *Chicago Tribune* made every effort to rally to his side, for they, like everyone else on Iwo Jima, appreciated the risks of covering the fighting there.[41] Indeed, a couple of days later, Lardner was struck in the groin by a rock sent flying by an enemy sniper's bullet, making him "the seventeenth casualty among civilian and Marine combat correspondents in the first two weeks of fighting on Iwo." Some did not make it, including Marine reporters William T. Vessey, killed by shellfire, and John H. Barberio, who died from a severe wound.[42]

* * *

Joe Rosenthal had been much luckier than most. The thirty-three-year-old AP cameraman knew from past experience that the best invasion-day photographs were normally taken during the second, third, and fourth hours of the landings. He therefore lobbied hard for such a berth, telling a PRO, "It's the difference between getting the pictures I want and not getting them." As it happened, the chaos on the D-Day beaches meant that he did not arrive until noon, after more than five hours bobbing uncomfortably on a landing craft that circled just offshore, waiting for an opening. When that moment came, the incoming fire was so intense that Rosenthal could scarcely believe that he had made it through alive. "It was like walking through rain," he recalled, "and not getting wet."[43]

Survival quickly brought rewards, however. When his landing craft beached, Rosenthal snapped a picture of Marines charging over a ridge. As in any invasion, it was no easy task getting film off the battlefield. Rosenthal spent nineteen hours darting from landing craft to landing craft before he finally reached the command ship that sat three miles offshore. From here, Miller's PRO team had arranged for seaplanes to collect the negatives, and although "a landing on the rough water broke the tail on the first one out," a second aircraft picked up Rosenthal's images and flew them back to Guam, dropping them by parachute near the island's new darkroom facilities. Within a matter of hours, the photographs were developed, censored, and radioed to the United States in time for editors to place the most dramatic one on the front page of their February 21 issues.[44] "MARINES CHARGE OVER A CREST ON IWO ISLAND," blared the caption in the *New York Times*. On the inside pages, the editorial writers marveled at what the home front could now witness. "Even in these days of swift communications," declared the *Times*, "it seems almost incredible that newspapers reporting the first landing of Marines on Iwo Jima could simultaneously publish pictures of the landing itself. . . . To watch a battle fought in midocean halfway across the world from the moment it begins ranks still among the miracles of modern transmission."[45]

For two days, Rosenthal had no idea that he had scored such a big triumph. Instead, he continued to suffer as a cold and heavy rain fell alongside the constant enemy fire. Rosenthal returned to the command ship at regular intervals with a fresh batch of photographs, but these trips were rarely easy. On the morning of February 23, he slipped when transferring to a landing craft and plunged overboard. Still shivering from his cold dunking in the sea, he managed to grab a few pictures of Forrestal, who was making his first inspection of the beachhead. He also learned that a small Marine patrol had climbed to the top of Mount Suribachi—that "ugly brown lump," as Rosenthal described it, "stuck by unthinking gods on the end of the island"— and he decided to take a look.

Halfway up the mountain, Rosenthal encountered a group coming down that included Louis Lowery, a photographer working for *Leatherneck*, the Marines' magazine. Lowery told Rosenthal that he was too late. A patrol had already "raised a flag at the summit, and that he had photographed the flag raising." Rosenthal decided to continue his ascent anyway, and on reaching the top, he discovered a group of men carrying a long iron pipe. "What are you doing?" he asked. "We're gonna put up this bigger flag and keep the other for a souvenir," one of the Marines replied. Rosenthal backed away about thirty-five feet, piled up some stones on a sandbag to give himself a platform, and then snapped a picture as the six men raised this second flag.[46]

After scrambling back down, Rosenthal hastily ate his lunch and then made the familiar journey to the command ship. Luckily, he arrived just in time for the courier plane, which sped his film to Guam, where the PRO—who had been an AP photo editor before the war—looked at his flag-raising image and realized, "Here's one for all time." The PRO swiftly transmitted the picture to San Francisco, where, because of the time difference, it arrived in time for publication on the day it was taken.[47]

The reaction was remarkable. Only hours earlier, Rosenthal's bosses had cabled him about the success of his invasion-day work. "Your pictures got

Fig. 11.1. Joe Rosenthal's photograph of the Iwo Jima flag raising. National Archives 80G 413988.

tremendous play throughout the country," they revealed. "Metropolitan members played them eight columns.... Most captions credited you by name and we had requests for wire story about you." Now the flag-raising shot almost immediately transformed this budding celebrity into a major star. While editors across the country lined up to praise Rosenthal for taking "the greatest picture of the Pacific War," a Democratic congressman from Florida introduced a bill authorizing the erection of a monument in Washington as a tribute to "the heroic action of the Marine Corps."[48] Forrestal, who had watched the event from the beach, was particularly delighted. "The picture of planting the flag on Mount Suribachi," he joked, "would keep the Marines in existence for the next five hundred years if nothing else did."[49]

It was not difficult to see why Rosenthal's photograph grabbed the nation's attention. Mount Suribachi had dominated war reports from the beginning of the invasion, with correspondents comparing it to "a black, fire-spitting dragon."[50] Although its capture did not guarantee the end of the battle—which would, in fact, drag on for weeks, claiming more and more lives, including three of the six men who had raised the flag—Rosenthal's photograph gave the home front hope that victory was in sight. It also became a fitting tribute to the average fighting man bearing the brunt of what was becoming the harshest of battles. As such, it stood in sharp relief to the images coming out of the rival SWPA theater, where MacArthur, in his sunglasses and cap, had made himself the focal point of the picture show. Forrestal had recently pushed for the navy to shy away from this type of publicity, calling instead for personal stories about the ordinary sailor or Marine. Rosenthal's photograph was the perfect fulfillment of this goal, although its impact was only so large because of the other set of changes Forrestal and Miller had introduced.[51]

As Rosenthal recalled after the war, the success of his photograph depended on the actions of a large support team—from the darkroom technicians to the picture pool coordinator—who ensured that it reached the States not only in one piece but also with stunning speed.[52] Again, the contrast with the Philippines was particularly stark. It must have irked MacArthur that he had to wait eleven days before newspapers published photos of his triumphant return to Luzon, while Rosenthal's Iwo images were published the day they were taken. Nor did MacArthur appreciate how his own flag-raising ceremony was treated back home. In early March, newspapers across the nation received a picture of MacArthur and his officers standing rigidly to attention while the Stars and Stripes were hoisted over Corregidor. A staged affair, it had none of the combat drama of Rosenthal's image. It was also old news by the time it got to America, so most editors decided to bury MacArthur's big moment on an inside page, where it sat next to many more pictures of Marines winning their battle on Iwo Jima.[53]

Death in the Pacific

In the central Pacific, however, not everyone was happy about the fate of Rosenthal's photograph. Louis Lowery, the *Leatherneck* cameraman who had captured a shot of the first flag raising, was particularly upset by the acclaim being lavished on his AP rival. "Rosenthal's photo," he told Robert Sherrod, "was a set-up, posed, a phony." This incendiary claim intrigued the *Time* man, although, as he later confessed, he should have talked to Rosenthal before repeating it. Instead, he sent a cable to his editor, alleging that Rosenthal's work was "photographically great but historically it is slightly phony. The planting of the flag didn't quite happen that way, and the historic picture was a post facto rehearsal."[54]

Rosenthal's bosses at the AP were so angry when they discovered what Sherrod was suggesting that they threatened a million-dollar lawsuit if *Life* aired these claims in print. Deterred, the magazine ultimately decided to run a piece that merely compared Rosenthal's now-famous image with the shot that Lowery had taken for the *Leatherneck*. The closest it came to questioning Rosenthal's work was Sherrod's wry observation that on other parts of the island, Texas and Confederate flags "were raised in pictorially unrecorded and spontaneous bursts of enthusiasm."[55]

Despite this prudent act of self-censorship, *Life*'s overall coverage of the battle focused less on flag-waving triumphalism than on Iwo Jima's "grim" reality. Over the following weeks, the magazine's editors published their own cameraman's "powerful photographs of explosions, injured soldiers, and casualties." *Time* also printed Sherrod's stark account of the battle in full. "Along the beach in the morning lay many dead," he wrote in the March 5 issue.

> About them, whether American or Jap, there was one thing in common. They died with the greatest possible violence. Nowhere in the Pacific war have I seen such badly mangled bodies. Many were cut squarely in half. Legs and arms lay 50 ft. away from any body. Only the legs were easy to identify—Japanese if wrapped in khaki puttees, American if covered by

canvas leggings. In one spot on the sand, far from the nearest clusters of dead men, I saw a string of guts 15 ft. long.[56]

With the cost mounting by the day, Sherrod visited a battlefield hospital "built low into the embankment beside the airfield, to afford maximum protection" from incoming enemy fire. He was particularly struck by the horrible stench inside the tent, a pungent mix of cigarette smoke, sweat, blood, and dirt. He was also staggered by the doctors' workload. On one day alone, Sherrod reported, they had seen no less than 183 patients before breakfast, many of whom had the most horrific of injuries: a Marine with his foot blown off at the ankle and another man with a thumb-sized hole in his stomach. The main consolation was that the medics' valiant work meant that only a small proportion of the Marines listed on the lengthy casualty lists would never return home.[57]

*　*　*

Some of the survivors would have their photographs taken by Dickey Chapelle, one of the first women correspondents to report on the Pacific War. During Drake's tenure, the navy had told prospective female reporters that it did not have the facilities to accommodate them outside of Hawaii. Under Miller's tutelage, Nimitz decided to relax this informal restriction a little. Although still opposed to having women in "forward areas to cover spot news and technical subjects," he told Forrestal in November 1944 that "certain stories (such as those concerning Army or Navy nurses) can best be handled from a woman's point of view." Nimitz therefore directed Miller to construct living quarters on Guam that could house up to eight female reporters.[58]

Chapelle arrived just in time to benefit from this policy change. Accredited to *Life Story*, a popular women's magazine, she was under instructions to write "eight or ten lead features" from as close to the front as possible.[59] On arriving in Guam, she discovered that this task would not be easy, for Miller "did not propose to send women war correspondents to an active front or to an extremely advanced base until officer women personnel, such as army and navy nurses have been established. It is perfectly obvious," the PRO told her, "that the presence of one woman among a great group of men would be certain to cause them great inconvenience, in manner of dress if for no other reason."[60] So instead of heading to Iwo Jima, she ended up on a hospital ship, where she focused on blood donations, the subject of a current propaganda drive.[61] Chapelle duly set about this harrowing task with grim determination, trying hard "to keep out of the way of the stretcher bearers and to keep on focusing, framing, lighting, and shooting pictures." "There must be something better that a woman could do with these men," she wrote at the end of her first day, "than to photograph them. I haven't cringed at their wounds, but at my lens."[62]

When Chapelle learned that the navy was finally allowing camerawomen to visit battlefield hospitals, she left the ship for Iwo Jima, arriving just as the fighting was coming to an end. She spent her first hours on the island with the medics, taking pictures of scenes similar to those that Sherrod had described in print. Then, ever restless, she headed off in search of the front, two anxious Marines tagging along as informal guides. She found the terrain far from photogenic—just sand ridge after sand ridge. Clambering to the top of one of these mounds, she set up her camera, before standing up to look for the best angle. Behind, she heard one of the Marines shouting at her to keep down. "Do you realize," he roared angrily, "that if you'd gotten yourself shot, I'd have had to spend the rest of the war and years after that filling out fucking papers?"[63]

* * *

After the fighting on Iwo Jima finally came to an end, Sherrod tried to make sense of the slaughter. "19,938 casualties," he noted, "is a high price to pay for eight square miles of the world's least fertile land," but, he added, the island's capture was crucial to the next stage of the war, which was bound to be even bloodier. The Japanese strategy, he observed, was "to send American casualties soaring until the Americans sicken of war and call it off." "I for one," he cabled his editor on March 17, "hope the people at home can take it with the fortitude and resolution shown by the living and dead of the 3rd, 4th, and 5th Marine Divisions."[64]

Sherrod's own fortitude was starting to ebb. He was "very tired and very homesick," he wrote to his wife, and hoped to return home soon, before he joined the mounting casualty toll.[65] In the meantime, he went to Guam to enjoy some welcome respite from the battle. Nimitz had recently made his forward headquarters on the island, setting up his office in a two-story wooden building that was close to the circle of cottages where he and his subordinates lived. Miller's provisions for the press were almost as impressive. In an effort to deflect attention away from MacArthur's ongoing battle in the Philippines, his PRO team had prepared a series of huts for reporters to live in, replete with welcome comforts, including running water and proper beds. "The mess hall," Miller boasted, "is not far distant and the food, while nothing to write home about, is more than adequate. The beer hall is open from 5:00 until 6:30 p.m.," and correspondents were even provided with a bottle of liquor each, although, as Miller joked, there was "considerable doubt as to whether the amber fluid is whisky."[66]

During his eleven days on Guam, Sherrod struck up a friendship with Ernie Pyle, who he immediately recognized as a kindred spirit. Convinced that these two star reporters could raise the navy's profile, Miller's office gave them "the purple treatment," including privileged accommodation, exclusive interviews with top officers, and in Pyle's case a "personally assigned public relations officer to shadow him." But in becoming a star reporter, Pyle, as much as Sherrod, had seen so many harrowing sights that he found it difficult to shed the "awful inner horror" at the prospect of heading back into battle. "I'm getting too old to stay in combat with these kids," he remarked to Sherrod, "and I'm going home, too, in about a month."[67]

Despite these deep-seated fears, the two veterans still felt the strong gravitational pull of the next battle, on Okinawa, which was scheduled for April 1. They would be part of a large press contingent, which included seventy-one civilian reporters and ninety combat correspondents.[68] "We had a huge turkey dinner," noted Pyle the night before the attack. "Fattening us for the kill, the boys said" after learning that senior officers were predicting that Japanese resistance would be "most fanatical." "Keep your head down, Ernie," someone shouted as he departed. "Listen, you bastards," Pyle joked to a group of correspondents on his ship, "I'll take a drink over every one of your graves."[69]

What happened next was almost surreal. "You wouldn't believe it," Pyle wrote from the beachhead on the first morning. "There was some opposition to the right and left of us, but on our beach nothing, absolutely nothing." The Japanese had retreated into the interior of the island, which gave the newly formed Tenth Army a chance to dash inland and seize two key airfields.[70] "This," cabled Sherrod the next day, "was the kind of beachhead landing every correspondent who knew the Marines had wanted to cover. Particularly the reporters who had been at Iwo Jima [and] were sick of blood, sick of seeing almost every friend killed or wounded."[71] When Pyle returned to his ship, he met a PRO to whom he remarked, "Guess my premonition back on Guam was pretty silly. I haven't run into anything real hot yet."[72]

Fig. 11.2. A group of American correspondents about to embark on a ship for the Okinawa invasion. Ernie Pyle is fifth from left, seated. National Archives 80G 321043.

Instead of danger, even death, Pyle and his colleagues faced a novel problem. In earlier campaigns, the invasion had been the most newsworthy part of the battle. On Okinawa, the war correspondents initially had little to report except exhilaration at discovering so little resistance. Sherrod headed north with the Marines, who made the biggest gains. With Japanese resistance light, he found himself writing about what had failed to materialize. "Where was the withering machine gun fire?" he asked on the first day. "Where were the 320-millimeter mortars, the 9-inch rockets? Where were the Japs?" Before long, he moved on to reporting the less glamorous aspects of war, from the role of the engineers to the importance of the bulldozer. As for Pyle, his appearance on so soft a mission seemed like such a good omen that "one hulking Marine sergeant wanted to wear Ernie around his neck like a good-luck charm."[73]

To the south, the two army divisions quickly encountered much stiffer opposition. Here the terrain around the main objectives of Naha, the island's capital on the west coast, and Shuri Castle, a strongpoint in the center, was perfect for defense: a range of ridges running from east to west, which the

Japanese had turned into an impressive series of positions, underpinned by an extensive tunnel system, from which to conduct bloody, attritional warfare. At first, Lieutenant General Simon Bolivar Buckner, "the burly and forceful" commander of the Tenth Army, was not fully aware of the extent of these Japanese fortifications. Between April 8 and 23, he therefore launched a series of "furious American onslaughts" at considerable cost.[74]

The correspondents who covered Buckner's offensive struggled to make this battle as attention-grabbing as Iwo Jima. The lack of progress was the main reason. When Homer Bigart watched American infantrymen fail to force their way past one particularly impressive Japanese position, he was left groping for analogies from the European war. "The Japanese command," he reported on April 12, "has achieved what the German communiqués like to call 'a defensive success.'"[75] If this was hardly the most felicitous phrase, the absence of major landmarks only made the search for an eye-catching frame even more difficult. While Iwo Jima had Mount Suribachi, the correspondents discovered that Okinawa contained only nameless "crags" or numbered hills. Rather than a bold dash by brave, flag-carrying Marines to the top, they witnessed a seemingly endless attritional slog. "We reduced it," wrote Harold Smith of a three-day battle to capture one such position, "gun port by gun port, with the tools we brought these thousands of miles—machine guns, flame throwers, tanks, self-propelled guns, artillery, and bombs."[76]

Nor were these stories about the "cruel Okinawa battle" accompanied by the same sort of graphic photographs that had poured out of Iwo Jima.[77] The fault lay primarily with a series of communications glitches, including overcrowding on the radio circuit between Guam and San Francisco, which meant that the navy's efforts to send radiophotos were, according to one AP manager, suffering "terrible results."[78] The photographers on the island also found the going tough, including W. Eugene Smith, whose editors dubbed him "the topnotch daredevil on *Life*'s photographic team." In the second half of May, Smith was working on a picture spread to be entitled "A Day with a Front-Line Soldier" when a shell fragment hit him in the head, "cutting both cheeks, injuring his tongue, and knocking out some teeth."[79]

Dickey Chapelle, meanwhile, managed to get embroiled in a big controversy on Okinawa, which showcased the difficulties women correspondents continued to face when trying to cover this theater. Before the battle, she had come up with a plan to "follow a substantial shipment of whole blood . . . to the medical unit ashore where it is to be expended, and to photograph its ultimate use." Miller had rejected this proposal, however, adding that under no circumstances was she to set foot on Okinawa.[80] Once again, Chapelle found herself stuck on a hospital ship, but this time there was nothing to photograph: the first days of the invasion saw so little fighting that she spent her time chatting with the medics while they waited for the first casualty. Bored, Chapelle decided to visit the communications ship, where she encountered Commander Paul Smith, Miller's deputy, and pleaded with him for authority to interview doctors on the island. According to Smith, Chapelle stated that she had oral orders for such a mission and, besides, "CINCPAC public relations has been urging full coverage of . . . blood bank story." So Smith relented, allowing her to spend an afternoon on Okinawa talking to doctors, as long as she returned to the hospital ship that night.[81]

There the matter might have ended, but for two developments. One was the hostility of the male correspondents she met on Okinawa, including John Lardner, who wrote a brief account of meeting this "petite young woman with glasses and a helmet" in a dispatch that he sent to the command ship. Turner, who read everything that came across his desk, immediately scrawled an angry reply in red pencil, demanding an account of what had happened. The simple answer was that Chapelle had gotten caught up in the unfolding combat chaos and had stayed on the island beyond the allotted time. The longer she remained at large, the angrier Turner became. "Her instructions," Smith briefed him at one point, "were specifically to return to her ship before late afternoon. She represents a thing called 'Life Story,' a pulp magazine—and apparently has gone AWOL for the purpose of being a sensation."[82]

When, after four days, a military policeman finally caught up with Chapelle, she discovered the trouble she was in. "Ma'am," the Marine warned, "the admiral is so mad that at first the order was to shoot you on sight." Thankfully, nothing so drastic was in the offing, but Chapelle still had to report to the nearest division headquarters, where she found that her credentials had been canceled. Soon after, she flew to Guam and then back home to the United States.[83]

* * *

While Chapelle was departing from Okinawa in official disgrace, Pyle returned to the command ship after a week at the front, covered in mud but "too tired to wash." He planned to spend the time on board catching up on his columns, but he came down with a cold and checked into the hospital quarters instead. Here he learned that the Seventy-Seventh Division would be landing on Ie Shima, to the north of Okinawa, on April 16.

Pyle had neither the energy nor the inclination to risk yet another D-Day landing, so he waited until April 17 before taking a look. The island remained dangerous, with mines and sniper fire the main hazards, but Pyle, as one close observer noted, "was in his element—the infantry. His cold was gone; his fears had abated; things looked good." The next morning, he hitched a ride in a jeep to visit a regimental command post. On hearing a burst of Japanese machine-gun fire, Pyle and the other men jumped into a ditch. Then he raised his head for a brief moment, and a round from a further burst struck him in the left temple.[84]

Grant MacDonald of the AP was on Ie Shima when the news filtered back to headquarters, and he immediately filed a story that generated a wave of profound sadness across America. Generals, politicians, and fellow correspondents lined up to extol Pyle's virtues as the reporter who, more than anyone else, had described what the war was really like. Radio networks broadcast tributes, newspaper editors published special sections, and those who knew Ernie best wrote about how he had written "in his blood—there with the foot soldiers whose dangers it was his self-imposed lot to share."[85]

The correspondents on Okinawa grieved for Pyle as well. Those able to escape the battle became so desperate to attend his funeral that for three days running they hassled Paul Smith, the PRO on Turner's command ship, for information about the event. Each time, Smith replied that the navy had tried to contact army officers on Ie Shima, without luck. He also promised that they would be the first to know the timing and location of the service, adding that because he did not yet have enough hard facts, he had "instructed all censors to permit no speculation as to where or when Ernie would be buried." In the wake of these assurances, the reporters felt betrayed when they discovered on the afternoon of April 21 that Grant MacDonald and John Hooley of American Broadcasting had filed a story on Pyle's burial. The reason for this snafu was simple enough. Major General Andrew D. Bruce, in command of the Seventy-Seventh Division on Ie Shima, had decided to preside over a hastily arranged service without informing anyone up the chain of command of his decision. Smith took the news surprisingly well. "The burial party itself," he noted, "came under mortar fire just prior to the actual internment. From his [Bruce's] point of view I can understand why it did not occur to him to make a Donnybrook of the affair." The reporters, however, saw the matter quite differently. They were "distressed," Smith observed, "because

(1) they were roundly scooped by Hooley and MacDonald, (2) because they too wanted to be eyewitnesses. . . . Everybody is 'mad' at everybody else," the PRO concluded ruefully on the evening of April 21, "and nobody can do anything that will in any way retrieve the situation."[86]

* * *

The reporters got even angrier when they began to learn how their editors were treating stories about the ongoing battle.[87]

No one involved in the Okinawa campaign doubted its size and importance. More than half a million US troops had crammed onto sixteen hundred ships to invade the island. "In firepower, troops, and tonnage," wrote author Robert Leckie, "it eclipsed even the more famous D-Day in Normandy on June 6, 1944."[88] As the battle ground on, US casualties mounted alarmingly, promising to make this a far bloodier island than Tarawa, Saipan, or Iwo Jima. Back home, however, Americans remained fixated on other stories. First, there was Roosevelt's death on April 12. Even the most hardbitten correspondents realized why this news dominated the headlines for days: Roosevelt was the only president that younger Americans had ever known, and as one reported, many men fighting on Okinawa had reacted with "shocked dismay" at his passing.[89] But the correspondents who were risking their necks in the muddy escarpments around Naha and Shuri became far less understanding when they discovered that lesser stories were knocking theirs off the front page. Perhaps the worst moment came when their editors told them that the San Francisco Conference, which was giving birth to the new United Nations organization, warranted more column inches than the Okinawa battle.[90]

The end of the European war only pushed events in the Pacific further down the news agenda. Even the *Chicago Tribune*, which had been the most vociferous advocate of a Pacific-first focus, sent its correspondents on Okinawa a revealing message on May 12: "UNNECESSARY WRITE DAILY STOP SPACE TIGHT."[91]

What made space so tight was not just Nazi Germany's unconditional surrender, but the way that the AP prematurely broke this story. Ed Kennedy, the AP's Paris bureau chief, had grown increasingly upset at the high-handed behavior of Brigadier General Frank A. Allen, the chief PRO in the European theater. When Allen placed a daylong halt on the news that Germany had finally capitulated, Kennedy became so angry at what he considered a political, not military, decision that he bypassed the censor and radioed his dispatch directly to New York. The result was an uproar. Allen expelled Kennedy, while the media and military heatedly debated the ethics of his action.[92]

The subsequent inquest traveled all the way to Okinawa. Here navy PROs were shocked that many reporters believed "there was considerable justice on Mr. Kennedy's side." Miller's response revealed how much the navy's confidence in its PR outfit had grown in the past six months. "There is no question in my mind," Miller told his subordinates on Okinawa,

> but that the Kennedy incident was merely the visual evidence of stupid press handling by General Allen. . . . I do not condone Kennedy's action, but neither do I agree with Allen's handling of his Public Relations set up. In short, I believe it could not possibly have happened in our bailiwick. All of which shows the worth of our particular policies and demonstrates the value of the good will and compatibility which we have developed at our headquarters with the correspondents.[93]

The navy's newfound self-confidence in its public relations marked a major change from its attitude at the start of the war, when its use of excessive censorship had often alienated the press. Under Forrestal and Miller, the new ethos that had started to emerge by the end of 1943 came to full fruition. Driven largely by a desire to grab headlines from the army, the navy went to great lengths not only to get reporters closer to the action but, what was more important, to speed their articles and images from the battlefield.

This new policy could not have been better timed, because with the end of the European war the media's attention was bound to become fixated, at long last, on the Pacific—not just the ongoing slog on Okinawa, but also the intensifying bombing campaign as the air force sought to bring Japan to its knees before the final invasion of its home islands.[94]

12
Toward Tokyo Bay

Fiascos and Fanaticism

It would take weeks, perhaps months, for the reporters from Europe to arrive in the Pacific. In the meantime, those who had been on Okinawa since early April really began to suffer. Many correspondents were fortunate enough to occupy a tent with a wooden floor, which was considered a "great luxury," albeit a necessary one as soon as the rain began to pour, turning the ground into a sea of mud. "Today," observed one PRO in the second half of May, "no one goes out of the tent unless he has to. The roads are rivers and transportation is cut down to a minimum." Mealtimes provided little solace, since the mess was "execrable," the menu invariably offering just one option: canned "bully beef."[1] Although the weather sometimes prevented the correspondents from getting to the battle, the battle still had a way of finding them, in the form of incessant artillery attacks and periodic air raids. With nerves frayed and Ernie Pyle's death still casting a pall, veterans like Homer Bigart began to wonder whether the time had come to take a rest.[2]

Most found the incentive to remain too strong, however, for despite the desolate conditions, Okinawa had suddenly become the big story. The end of the European war had freed up space in all newspapers, big and small. With editors no longer imploring their reporters to exercise restraint, the navy's hometown distribution center suddenly saw a major spike in stories from Okinawa, up from 2,261 a week at the end of April to 6,023 a week by the middle of May.[3] While most of these dispatches provided the readers of local newspapers with personal information about the boys from their own area, the star correspondents increasingly saw their reports plastered across the front page. Bold banner headlines became the norm, even when the news was dispiriting. "US ATTACKS FAIL ON OKINAWA," proclaimed the *New York Herald Tribune* on May 19. "INCH ON IN BLOODY OKINAWA," blared the *Chicago Tribune* on the same day.[4]

The stories below these headlines told the home front about the renewed offensive the Tenth Army launched on May 11. Before the attack, General

Buckner had met with reporters to warn them of what lay ahead. "The opening phase," he explained, "was unlikely to produce anything spectacular."[5] Buckner was wise to manage expectations, given the formidable nature of the Japanese defenses. Bigart had already criticized leading officers for underestimating the strength of this system during the first phase of the battle. He now pointed out that Buckner's new assault would be twice the size, but the same old problems persisted.[6] Bigart joined the Sixth Marine Division, which was making repeated efforts to capture Sugar Loaf Hill, a position that blocked the way to Naha, the island's capital. "Sugar Loaf," Bigart told his readers, "was admirably adapted to rear-slope defense. It was studded with horseshoe tombs and caves, and there were huge underground passages with reinforced concrete entrances from which scores of Japanese soldiers poured as the tanks approached." After seven assaults, the Marines finally won the hill in what Bigart called "one of the most desperate and costly actions of the Pacific War," which "decimated" two battalions "in futile assaults." "They shot the hell out of us," conceded one officer. When Bigart toured the battlefield afterward, he could see what this meant:

> Sugar Loaf Hill, topped by a dozen mutilated trees and slashed bare of vegetation by weeks of shelling, looked down on a graveyard of American tanks. Our dead have been removed—and our losses were heavy on Sugar Loaf— but the air still was heavy with the odor of death. Open fields rolling up to the northwest slope were littered with helmets, canteens, and other equipment abandoned by the Marines in six retreats from the hill.[7]

Such carnage raised doubts about Buckner's decision to repeatedly assault near-impregnable positions. Bigart thought an amphibious landing in the rear would have won Naha and Shuri at a much lower cost, and on May 29 he said so in print. "Our tactics were ultra-conservative," Bigart charged. "Instead of an end-run we persisted in frontal attacks. It was hey-diddle-diddle straight down the middle."[8] Back home, David Lawrence, a columnist for the *Washington Evening Star*, picked up on this claim, adding two highly provocative twists of his own. In one piece, he revived unhappy memories of army-navy tensions during the Smith versus Smith episode on Saipan, claiming that Buckner's unimaginative leadership was yet another example of an army general "not carrying on the operation with significant speed to win the objective." In another, he called the Okinawa battle a "military fiasco" that eclipsed even Pearl Harbor.[9]

The navy considered these incendiary allegations to be spectacularly ill-timed. Plans were currently afoot for the final invasions of Kyushu and Honhsu, tentatively scheduled for November 1945 and March 1946, which would necessitate the army and navy working even more closely together. Navy PROs were already beginning to contemplate the practical problems that this would involve, including getting the two services to standardize their codes for dealing with the press, treating all correspondents as "equally accredited to the army and navy in a 'combined theater,'" and ensuring that one overall commander took ultimate responsibility for "transmitting and censoring the news." "If we adopt any other method," argued Captain Fitzhugh Lee on May 11, "we will be placing ourselves in a terrible pickle whereby the press will try to play the army against the navy, and vice-versa, to get the fullest possible advantage that they can drive in any aspects of news reporting."[10]

Against this backdrop, the navy scarcely relished another enervating public spat with the army over military tactics, and so it launched a vigorous PR offensive. Forrestal not only "emphatically disputed" the idea that the army had bungled the Okinawa campaign, but also released a letter from Turner that categorically rejected the criticism from "kibitzer" sources like Lawrence. Nimitz went even further in a press conference attended by Bigart. "New landings," the admiral insisted, "would have had to be made over unsatisfactory beaches against an alerted enemy defense. They would have involved heavy casualties and would have created unacceptable supply problems." Lawrence's column, Nimitz added, was "so badly informed as to give the impression that he has been made use of for purposes which are not in the best interests of the United States." Bigart, for his part, stood by the claim that an amphibious landing ought to have been tried, but he also agreed with Nimitz that "to call the campaign a 'fiasco' is absurd. This writer," he concluded acerbically, "covered the Anzio and Cassino actions, and he knows what a fiasco is."[11]

* * *

If it was not a fiasco, Okinawa nonetheless offered some sobering lessons for the final phase of the war. This was the thrust of a series of stories that began to appear in May and June. Bigart concluded that the terrain, combined with the Japanese decision not to contest the beachheads but to retire to formidable inland defenses, meant that "Shuri was tougher than Iwo." "There is no reason to believe," he added, "that the coastal areas of the Japanese homeland will come any easier." In the pages of the *New York Times*, Bruce Rae agreed. "Chief among the things we have learned," Rae concluded, "is that the invasion of Japan and the fighting that lies ahead will be without qualification the hardest we have to face." The skillful way the Japanese had used their weapons was one reason. "The thing that clinches it," he maintained, "is the topography of the main islands of the enemy empire, which is Okinawa magnified and multiplied."[12]

As well as tenacity and terrain, there was another obvious reason the fighting was proving so tough: Japan's fanatic determination to resist, illustrated by the repeated instances of suicide instead of surrender. At the start of the Okinawa campaign, Bigart reported the discovery of two hundred Japanese men, women, and children who "had been driven to attempt mass suicide by fear that Americans would violate and torture Japanese women and slaughter the men."[13] As the battle ground on, other correspondents told how Japanese soldiers were turning themselves into "human bombs" in an attempt to slow the American offensive.[14] Above all, there was the alarming rise in successful kamikaze attacks on the US armada, which resulted in the loss of fifteen ships by April 18, another five sunk in one day in early May, and naval casualties topping five thousand during the first month of the battle.[15]

Although Nimitz's communiqué finally admitted that enemy planes were launching "suicidal attacks on American amphibious forces off Okinawa" in the middle of April, this news was initially submerged beneath the outpouring of grief at Roosevelt's death.[16] Then on April 27, the censors finally lifted the restrictions on reporting the "origin and details of the Kamikaze corps" and allowed suicide attacks to be "treated in the same manner as attack with any other weapon," although the navy still struggled to shed its more restrictive instincts.[17] For weeks to come, reporters continued to complain that PROs "were still feeding out the story of the Japanese Kamikaze attacks in small doses"; some even claimed that the navy had "buried" the worst news.[18]

Yet enough information was seeping into the public domain to make the home front take notice. By late May, reporters were observing that a new word had entered "Americans' war vocabulary, Kamikaze, [which] means literally 'Divine Wind.'"[19] If this term imparted a mystical quality to the Japanese pilots, the eyewitness accounts of being on the receiving end told a much darker story. Perhaps the most disturbing centered on a Japanese suicide pilot who machine-gunned and then crashed his plane into a "well-lighted, unarmed United States naval hospital ship." "Tempers ran high in naval circles," observed William Lawrence of the *New York Times*, "at this premeditated and cold-blooded attack upon the hospital ship, which was proceeding alone with full illumination, including powerful searchlights that lighted up huge red crosses painted on the sides, superstructure, and stack."[20]

Tempers also ran high back home, where the attack was viewed as only the most recent in a long litany of Japanese atrocities.[21] The censors did nothing to soothe the rage. On the one hand, they let Gill Robe Wilson observe in the pages of the New York Herald Tribune that the "Japanese label us as devils, and we think of them, after bitter experience, unworthy of the classification of human beings. This is, therefore, a war of kill or be killed, which suits every American down to the ground."[22] On the other hand, they clamped down hard on anything that presented the Japanese point of view, as another New York Herald Tribune reporter found to his extreme annoyance.

Emmet Crozier had come across a letter Rear Admiral Toshinosuke Ichimaru had written to Roosevelt just before he committed suicide on Iwo Jima. "You may slander our nation as a yellow peril," the admiral had declared, "or a bloodthirsty nation, or maybe a protoplasm of military clique. Though you may use the surprise attack on Pearl Harbor as your primary material for propaganda, I believe you of all persons know that you left Nippon no other method in order to save herself from self-destruction." Crozier compiled a dispatch based on this letter on April 4, but the censors immediately blocked it. "He is very hot under the collar on the subject," a PRO based in Guam warned Washington more than two months later, "and he will probably do his best to get the story broken after he arrives in New York."[23]

When the navy finally released Crozier's story in the middle of July, even his own editors dismissed Ichimaru's message as "mystical nonsense."[24] With the rest of the media more interested in Japanese barbarity than Japanese justification, it was small wonder that, according to one survey, the view had taken hold that the Japanese were "dirty fighters, suicidal in battle," while only eight out of fifty-seven editorials that described this enemy failed to use terms like "vicious, cruel, barbaric." "Americans had to learn to hate Germans," editorialized Life magazine in May, "but hating Japs comes natural—as natural as fighting Indians once was." With levels of animosity so high, opinion polls recorded that three-quarters of the country remained fully behind the policy of unconditional surrender—a figure that approached 90 percent in some regions.[25]

Officials planning the invasion of Japan found such findings heartening. Ever since learning of the mass Japanese suicides on Saipan, Marshall had been convinced that this fanatical enemy would surrender only after a massive assault on its home islands. With the end of the war in Europe, he also worried that "a general letdown in this country" might make it difficult to sustain domestic support for such an attack.[26] Seen in this context, stories of a fanatical enemy committing yet more atrocities had obvious value, for they helped to steel the nation for a fight to the bitter end. This was one consequence of the war reporting from Okinawa. The other pointed in a very different direction.

As correspondents like Bigart and Rae emphasized, Okinawa showed that an assault on the Japanese home islands would not be easy. The kamikazes offered perhaps the most ominous glimpse into the future. This suicidal resistance, editorialized the New York Times in a typical comment, "is a strategy of attrition, a fanatical fight for every foot of ground or mile of sea. It is a strategy whose objective is to drag out the war so long and make it so costly that out of weariness and revulsion the Allies might settle for a compromise solution."[27] It was also a strategy that was enjoying a measure of success. "Jap suicide plane attacks on US warships," the UP reported at the start of June, "have brought this country up against a situation so critical that, Manpower Chief Paul V. McNutt said tonight, 'the end of the war may be seriously delayed.'"[28]

As the Okinawa battle reached its bloody conclusion, the army and Marines announced casualties totaling 36,588, which was far in excess of those in any other Pacific campaign. Even Buckner became a victim, killed, according to one news report, when a shell fragment ripped "a large hole in the left side of his chest."[29] Such losses scarcely augured well for the final campaigns on Kyushu and Honshu. Some reporters predicted that "between 500,000 and one million more American fighting men would probably die before the war's end," which raised the obvious question: would the public stomach losses at this level?[30]

The new president was not so sure. By early June, Harry Truman was "very much perturbed" by the massive casualty projections he was reading. As the Joint Chiefs of Staff developed their invasion plans, he asked for "an estimate of the losses killed and wounded that will result from an invasion of Japan proper," ahead of a major White House conference on June 18. At this meeting, Truman said he "hoped there was a possibility of preventing an Okinawa from one end of Japan to the other." Marshall, recognizing the direction in which the new president's mind was heading, withheld MacArthur's estimate of a hundred thousand or more casualties during an invasion of Kyushu. He also reminded his inexperienced commander in chief "that there is not an easy, bloodless way to victory in war and it is the thankless task of the leaders to maintain their firm outward front which holds the resolution of their subordinates."[31]

Faced with Marshall's forceful presentation, Truman reluctantly endorsed the Kyushu invasion plan. As a prelude, there would be a two-pronged effort to exert maximum pressure on Japan in order to destroy its war economy and undermine civilian morale. The navy blockade formed one prong—although the submarine fleet, which "comprised just 2 percent of the total of US manpower, but . . . accounted for 55 percent of all Japanese shipping losses," remained off-limits to reporters throughout the course of the war.[32] The other prong would come under the direction of a new actor, the Twentieth Air Force, which had been intensifying its strategic bombing campaign since the start of the year and which took center stage in the pages of the nation's newspapers and magazines over the summer of 1945.

Destruction from Above

For war correspondents, covering the bombing campaign had long meant one of two extremes. A brave few had accompanied a daylight bombing mission over Germany, suffering the cramped, alien surroundings inside a plane, followed by an acute sense of vulnerability as enemy fighters swarmed around and flak darted up from the ground. After Robert Post of the *New York Times* was killed over Wilhelmshaven in February 1943, many reporters and most editors had cooled on the idea of taking such risks to produce another "how-I-almost-got-killed-today" story. So instead, covering the European bombing campaign had settled into a safe and monotonous routine, with reporters stuck for long periods at an English air base, where their job consisted of counting the returning planes before heading off to hear briefing officers describe how much damage had been inflicted on distant enemy targets.[33]

When the air force finally acquired the capability to start bombing Japan from China in the summer of 1944, eleven correspondents opted for the highly risky method of air-war coverage. They were motivated partly by a desperation to escape the only other story in the CBI—Stilwell's deadly advance on Myitkyina, where strict censorship prevented them from revealing the extent of the debacle and any stories that did make it home tended, by June, to get buried beneath the deluge of copy on the second front in France.

They were also attracted by the brand-new weapon that made an attack on Japan possible. The air force had kept the B-29 Superfortresses under tight wraps for the past year. But after months of preparations, it had sixty-eight of them at bases in China. From there, they would head for the coke and steel plant at Yawata on June 15.[34]

No one was more excited by the prospect than Toby Wiant of the AP, who had clocked seventeen bombing raids over Burma, Thailand, and Indochina before joining Stilwell in the jungle. This, he wrote his parents on the day of the raid, was "the mission for which I've yearned since coming abroad nearly two years ago. It's an unforgettable thrill, one for which I don't think I'd take any amount of money." Wiant's delight only grew when he got his first glimpse of a Superfortress, which he described as "a dream plane come true. Longer than a Pullman," he noted after looking inside, "twice as big as a Flying Fortress, with gasoline capacity almost equaling a railroad tank car, it provides flying comfort and safety such as I've never experienced before."[35]

Unlike the Doolittle raid, the first B-29 mission would be no propaganda stunt. Rather, as Wiant reported, it marked "the beginning of a military plan to hit the Japanese again and again, where it hurts the most," their major industrial centers. Wiant found the airmen "supremely self-confident" as they went through the pre-takeoff routine. Once airborne, he jotted down the names and home towns of the men on board while observing the calm, professional way in which they navigated the initial dangers, from getting the big plane airborne to steering it through a series of dark storms. [36]

The fliers faced a long trip. Tillman Durdin of the *New York Times*, who was on board one of the planes, divulged that the men had been fed a diet of "benzadrine [*sic*] and sulphate tablets as an aide to wakefulness," although they needed only pure adrenaline once the B-29s reached the business end of the trip. Searchlights, Durdin reported, "jerked us into a state of alarm.... We could see the ground flashes of ack-ack now and processions of tracers arching into the sky." Amid the mayhem, Durdin revealed that the so-called precision bombing of enemy industry often amounted to little more than rough guesswork. "The bomb bays were open," he wrote of the culminating moment,

> and after what seemed an interminable and agonizing minute word came that bombs were away. It looked like a true lay. A glowing fog and smoke covered the area, ringed with guns and searchlights. . . . It seemed certain

that the bombs would smash something down there in the close-packed precincts of Yawata's Imperial Iron and Steel Works.

From his bomber, Wiant recorded similar scenes. "We looked back to a firebug's dream," he wrote of the moment his B-29 dropped its load. "Flames are shooting high from two huge fires. Smaller fires are blazing up rapidly."[37]

Despite a transmission glitch that stopped Wiant from grabbing a well-earned scoop, his bosses were delighted with his work. "Yawata story was enthusiastically received," they cabled him. "Heartiest congratulations and greetings." The AP man needed this acclamation, because the minute the thrill of the raid wore off, he "folded up" with exhaustion and had to check into a hospital to convalesce. He turned out to be one of the lucky ones. William T. Shenkel of *Newsweek* did not make it back at all. It was a loss that the *New York Times* could relate to. Still suffering from the death of Bob Post, bosses at the *Times* remained leery of this type of reporting. From now on, whenever one of their correspondents raised the idea, he would get the same terse response: "Publisher opposed you going on bombing mission says 'been done before and unnecessary risk.'"[38]

Significantly, even the air force entertained doubts about the Yawata coverage. At the CBI bases, many of the returning air crew were "greatly disturbed" by the amount of detailed information that had been published on targets, names, and losses. Senior officials in Washington were equally concerned, concluding that these dispatches had been "detrimental to the war effort for two primary reasons." For one thing, they argued, the Yawata stories had provided the enemy with "information of value which they could not otherwise get except at great cost and trouble if at all," including the command's target priorities and "mechanical details and capabilities of the B-29." For another, they added, the Yawata reporting had contained too much emphasis on "the importance of the Twentieth Air Force to a point where its complex and friendly relationships with other commands and services . . . are subjected to possible rupture due only to jealousy or misunderstanding of the publicity accorded to the Twentieth Air Force."[39]

As a result of these reservations, PROs in the Pentagon recommended that "the present high-pressure publicity be curbed." Arnold agreed, deeming it prudent "to prevent the B-29 from being overvalued in the public mind." The air chief was responding partly to the concerns of his subordinates, but he also knew that the crews in China were struggling to follow up Yawata with missions on a similar scale, largely because of the logistical difficulties of getting fuel and equipment over the Hump to the US airbases.[40]

There the matter rested until November, when the Marianas finally opened for business. From there, the B-29s had the ability to strike almost anywhere on the Japanese home islands, including the six largest cities, which contained more than half the enemy's industry. This was the real start of the strategic bombing campaign, and air officials spotted a major opportunity. "In the public mind," observed Lauris Norstad, Arnold's chief of staff for the Twentieth Air Force, "the Pacific War is an anti-climax. The glamour surrounds Europe." With big new bombers primed to hit most major targets in Japan, the air force now had the chance to sprinkle a little of its own glamour over the war in Asia.[41]

* * *

Brigadier General Haywood Hansell, who was in charge of the new XXI Bomber Command of the Twentieth Air Force, had not had an easy time converting Saipan from a battlefield into an air base. When Vern Haugland first visited in the late summer, he discovered "a hot, rainy, fly-blown, muddy tropical island." The engineers were working so frantically on the runway and hangars that they had little time to construct durable living quarters. Gradually, however, the situation improved. By mid-November, Hansell had gathered more than a hundred B-29s near "the white coral surface of the longest, broadest, strongest runway the Pacific had ever seen." His command had also attracted more than thirty correspondents, who were housed in a neat row of tents "on the bluff over the sea, a few hundred yards from the air strip."[42]

Hansell's plan was to send the Superfortresses to bomb Tokyo on November 17, but heavy winds over both the Marianas and Japan forced repeated postponements. Finally, on the afternoon of November 24, the planes prepared to take off. It was a dramatic moment. No one knew for sure how robust the Japanese defenses would be or how the US pilots would cope with the long journey over the mostly enemy-controlled ocean. When the bombers finally returned, the reporters who had been on board hurried to locate a censor. Mac Johnson of the UP led the way with a story that told of "perfect bombing conditions," an "outsmarted" enemy, and the destruction of a Japanese aircraft factory. "Our bombs were right in the target," Johnson recorded one of the crew announcing. "I saw many flashes as the bombs exploded among the buildings."[43]

As a matter of fact, the Tokyo mission had been nothing like the success Johnson had described. On the contrary, in the words of one historian, it actually served "as a primer on the obstacles the command was to face," from mechanical failures to bad weather.[44] Nor were the teething problems confined to operational matters. William Hipple of *Newsweek* was already in a foul mood, believing that the navy had "completely lost" his eyewitness account of the Battle of the Leyte Gulf. After risking his life on the Superfortress mission to Tokyo, he became almost apoplectic when this story also went astray. As a subsequent investigation uncovered, the air force PRO had made provisions for it to be cabled to Hawaii, but an officer had erroneously given it "the unfortunate classification of 'Top Secret,'" which had resulted in a major delay that denied Hipple his big scoop.[45]

Shortly after, the correspondents covering the air war transferred to Guam, which enjoyed a more efficient communications network and offered numerous creature comforts. Before making his tragic last trip to Okinawa, Pyle had spent a number of weeks at this base and had been particularly impressed, praising the plentiful food and pleasant climate. He had even managed to write seventeen columns in one day, equaling his "alltime world record." While most of this output had been a boon to the air force, with descriptions of the "great long macadam airstrips," the buzz of efficient activity, and a B-29 bomber fleet "which will grow and grow and grow," Pyle had been prolific only because he had so few colleagues around to interrupt him.[46] Almost every other reporter, as one PRO observed, had been motivated by the prospect of joining "some forthcoming land-and-sea operations, leaving . . . only [Pyle and] three journalistic snowbirds from the three big wire services to pick up the crumbs of news provided by each succeeding B-29 mission to Japan."[47]

Over the winter, these crumbs had not included accompanying a bombing mission. Even though the B-29s were relatively capacious, Norstad concluded that "the weight of an additional individual must be absorbed in less fuel or reduced bomb load. Therefore," he ordered, "male correspondents are permitted to participate in combat flights only when the mission is of particular significance and interest to the American public."[48] The rest of the time, the Twentieth's PROs were under clear instructions "to focus the attention of the public on a few important points," which would then be "quoted and commented upon editorially and are bound to have a good effect. This system," Norstad explained, "is opposed to that which formerly prevailed in which we threw out a lot of news of a questionable quality which left little but confusion in the minds of the public."[49]

The trouble for reporters was that there was hardly anything of importance in the missions the XXI Bomber Command managed to launch during the long weeks after the first big attack on Tokyo. Arnold became so impatient for better results that in January he replaced Hansell with Major General Curtis E. LeMay, viewing the gruff, cigar-chomping thirty-nine-year-old as a "big-time operator."[50]

Yet even LeMay struggled to exert an instant impact from the Marianas. The weather remained a major problem. As well as dense cloud cover, a powerful jet stream over the target areas made it difficult to bomb accurately from high altitudes. Although Japanese air defenses were nowhere near as impressive as Germany's, the B-29s began to encounter a growing number of enemy fighters whose pilots were prepared "to ram their planes into the big invading bombers." Losses soon started to mount, depressing morale among the crews. And it did not take long before Arnold, convalescing from a recent heart attack, began hinting that LeMay might suffer the same fate as Hansell unless the situation began to improve.[51]

Under intense pressure, LeMay came up with a bold gamble. He proposed the low-level firebombing of Japanese cities at night. The advantages, he explained to skeptical subordinates, were various. By coming in at five to six thousand feet, the B-29 engines would be subjected to less stress and so would suffer fewer mechanical problems. The planes would also have to carry less fuel, thereby freeing up more space for bombs. These would be incendiaries, which earlier raids on Kobe and Tokyo had shown to be remarkably effective. LeMay was not entirely comfortable with the prospect of slaughtering thousands of civilians. He also knew that his crews did not relish the risks involved, especially as he proposed removing the guns and gunners from the planes to provide even more room for bombs. Yet LeMay recognized that his own career, and perhaps even the future of strategic bombing, was on the line if he failed. So he decided to give the go-ahead for more than three hundred planes to strike Tokyo on the night of March 9.[52]

As luck would have it, Guam was packed with war correspondents, most of them recuperating from their recent exploits on Iwo Jima. That afternoon, as the crews prepared to take off, St. Clair McElway, LeMay's PRO, invited more than fifty of them to a press conference. A New York–based essayist before the war, the "slightly impish" McElway got on well with reporters, who not only appreciated his keen mind but also enjoyed swapping stories about his prewar exercise regimen, which had consisted of nothing more vigorous than walking from a Fifty-Second Street bar "to a taxi at the curb."[53] On March 9, after McElway called for silence, the correspondents listened intently as he unveiled the new ground rules. Because the forthcoming attack was just the first in a series of planned low-level missions, he ordered everyone to maintain the fiction that "weather or miscalculation had caused this unexpected innovation," in the hope that the Japanese would fail to alter their defensive tactics. "Otherwise," McElway added, "the story could be told in full except for one or two technical matters involving bomb-load figures and air tactics." As soon as the session ended, the reporters headed to the airfield to watch the planes take off. Then they went to their huts to write their first stories, which the censors would hold until the pilots radioed from over Japan that the attack had gone according to plan.

Although LeMay held a low opinion of Japanese air defenses, he knew that success was far from a foregone conclusion. "I'm sweating this one out myself," he told McElway as the hours dragged by. "A lot could go wrong." LeMay's mood began to lighten only when the pilots radioed in their first reports. "Bombing the primary target visually," one reported. "Large fires observed. Flak moderate. Fighter opposition nil." Even after digesting this news, LeMay remained cautious. "We can't really tell a damn thing about the results," he remarked to his senior aides, "until we get the pictures tomorrow night." By the time these arrived, sped by jeep to LeMay's tent shortly after he had retired to bed, he was in no doubt that the gamble had paid off. Motioning his cigar over a photograph of Tokyo, he pointed to the vast damage. "All this is out," he explained to his subordinates. "It's all ashes—all that and that and that."[54]

LeMay's press statement described this damage in chilling statistical detail, revealing that the area "totally destroyed" covered 422,500,000 square feet and included "eight identifiable industrial and urban targets." The correspondents who accompanied the mission added some color. "Fires were raging in several multi-block areas," reported Martin Sheridan of the *Boston Globe*, "and creating almost daylight conditions. In addition, there were hundreds of blazes throughout the waterfront area, the most densely populated area in the world."[55]

Unable to see much more than the glow from the conflagration before his plane banked away, Sheridan remained silent on the fate of the thousands of civilians trapped in the firestorm. So it was not until American newspapers picked up Japanese and Soviet accounts almost a week later that this harrowing story began to emerge. These reports suggested that thousands of people had been killed, that Tokyo's hospitals were "overcrowded with sufferers," and that the survivors "had been thrown into a panic beyond the authorities' ability to control." Domei, the Japanese news agency, "referred to the mass attacks as 'carpet bombings.'" "Hitherto," it claimed, "the enemy's targets have been essential factories, airdromes, and harbor installations; now, heedless of the objective, he has started to bomb city streets, secluded mountain areas, and transportation systems indiscriminately."[56]

The air force was highly sensitive to these allegations. Since the start of the war, it had gone to great lengths to emphasize that it engaged in the precision bombing of industrial targets only. A few weeks earlier, news stories about the destruction of Dresden had created the impression that this policy had changed, prompting Pentagon officers to deny that they were deploying "deliberate terror bombing." In the wake of the Domei's claims, these same officers believed that American commentators were "having [a] field day searching for implications . . . which imply that this is area bombing and speculating whether this means a departure from policy of precision bombing." They therefore instructed McElway to counteract "editorial complaints . . . about blanket incendiary attacks upon cities" and "guard against anyone stating this is area bombing."[57]

This was no easy task. After a pause to support the Okinawa invasion, the XXI Bomber Command intensified its assault on six of the seven largest Japanese cities, ultimately killing more than 120,000 people and destroying almost 1.5 million dwellings during the following weeks.[58] All the while, LeMay provided reporters with a series of juicy quotes that made little effort to obscure the scale of the carnage. In mid-April, he confidently predicted that the "destruction of Japan's industry by air blows alone is possible."[59] In early June, he openly admitted that the B-29s had inflicted so much damage on Tokyo that it was no longer an important military target. "We have destroyed the five largest cities in Japan," LeMay told reporters a few weeks later. "We have done this with less than half of the strength we will have in the Pacific. We have the capacity to devastate Japan and we will do so if she does not surrender."[60] To drive home the point still further, LeMay began talking about running out of targets by Christmas. He also became so confident that his planes could bomb anywhere at will that he warned more than 1.3 million people living in twelve Japanese cities to evacuate immediately, as they were next on the B-29s' target list. The aim of this ploy, LeMay announced in late July, was to make the enemy "realize [that] further resistance is senseless."[61]

Alongside these grandiose boasts, senior officers still tried to insist that XXI Bomber Command was engaged in what McElway dubbed "pin-point, incendiary bombing from a low level." When asked whether there had been a change in "the basic policy of the Air Forces in pin-point bombing [and] precision," Norstad responded simply, "None." The targets of LeMay's campaign, his PROs stressed, were industries and homes, not lives. The ultimate goal, they added, was to win the war quickly, not to wreak vengeance.[62]

When McElway returned to the States for a brief leave in June, he proudly noted that the nation's press was filled with the hundreds of thousands of words he and his censorship staff had cleared on the intensifying bombing attacks. "Yet," he concluded, "I don't think people here at home even now understand exactly how great, how devastating these raids were." McElway put this down to the difficulty of absorbing what it really meant to destroy square mile after square mile of Japan's densely populated cities, but there were other reasons for this lack of comprehension.[63] The constant stories of Japan's fanatical resistance, together with its many brutal deeds, had inured much of the home front to news that enemy citizens were now suffering. As historian Michael Sherry has argued, many newspapers simply described the attacks as "'the bombing of factories and plants' undertaken against 'a fanatical foe prepared to fight for the death.'" When correspondents did accompany a bombing mission, they tended to return with little more than a triumphalist account of specific targets going up in flames. Meanwhile, their colleagues on Saipan or Guam were bombarded by official facts and figures that provided little insight into the human tragedy unfolding on the ground. As a result, the staggering destruction wrought by LeMay's bombing sparked no controversy on the home front. On the contrary, as the only opinion poll conducted on the subject concluded that summer, "The people are sold on peace through air power."[64]

Hiroshima and Nagasaki

Tinian lay just across a narrow channel from Saipan. McElway described it as "green and flat, a stationary and roomy aircraft carrier of an island."[65] William L. Laurence of the *New York Times* recognized that it had another attribute. "It lent itself," he wrote after the war, "better than Saipan or Guam to the maintenance of strict security." This was crucial because by the summer of 1945 Tinian was home to the 509th Composite Group of the Twentieth Air

Force. Commanded by Colonel Paul W. Tibbets, the 509th's mission was so sensitive that Laurence was the only correspondent allowed inside the special quarantined base. "It was an island within an island," Laurence recalled. "The inhabitants of the inner island lived in a world apart, completely isolated from the other contingents," because they were involved in one of the war's greatest secrets: the atomic bomb.[66]

Laurence had been interested in uranium fission since 1939, but like many other journalists, he had shied away from the story since Pearl Harbor. A lack of sources had initially underpinned this silence, as editors of scientific journals quietly removed articles "that might have military value," while leading physicists associated with the atomic bomb project dropped completely out of public view. Then, after the AP had published a story in April 1943 about "heavy water" providing the basis of a possible weapon, the Office of Censorship had tried to steer editors away from anything related to atomic power, with only limited success. One officer counted no less than seventy-seven leaks between June 1943 and September 1944, although none of these breaches had divulged anything specific about the atomic bomb project.[67]

With the first atomic test looming, the military decided in April 1945 that it needed a reporter "to explain the intricacies of the atomic bomb's operating principles in laymen's language." So General Leslie Groves, in charge of the bomb's development, invited Laurence to "come to work with us." His main job was to help with the preparation of the official handouts that would be released soon after the first bomb was dropped, which in turn meant he was given privileged access to the Trinity test at Los Alamos on July 16. Shortly after, he flew to Tinian, arriving three days behind schedule but in time to see Tibbets's plane, the *Enola Gay*, take off at 2:45 on Monday morning, August 6.[68]

"We waved him goodbye," Laurence remembered after the war, "and wished him luck." Tibbets had a three-thousand-mile journey ahead of him, and Laurence found the wait little short of "purgatory." All sorts of questions flew through his mind: "Would the bomb work? Would it live up to expectations? Would it explode as expected, or would it, God forbid, be a dud, giving our secret away to the enemy? Would our fliers return safely or would they be forced to bail out in enemy waters?" Finally, at nine thirty, Tibbets transmitted two words to Tinian: "Mission successful!"[69]

Less than six hours later, Laurence watched the *Enola Gay* return. He was struck by the "beauty" of the sight, as the plane's "great silver body" shimmered in the sun, the deep blues of the sky and sea providing a vivid

contrast. Then, two nights later, it was his turn. Just hours before the scheduled takeoff, Laurence was told that he would be joining the next mission as
the "official reporter." He considered it a major honor, especially as he har-
bored few qualms about the ethics of what he would be involved in. "Does
one feel compassion for the poor devils about to die?" he asked himself
during the long journey to Nagasaki. "Not when one thinks of Pearl Harbor
and of the Death March on Bataan." As the plane approached the target, he
became too preoccupied with the operation to mull over the morality of what
was about to unfold. With thick cloud cover over the target area, the pilot had
to circle around and around for more than three hours, hoping for "a small
peephole." At noon sharp on August 9, an opening finally appeared. The
second bomb was dropped, and Laurence and the crew headed for Okinawa,
which they reached with their plane's gas tanks almost empty.[70]

Despite his privileged access, Laurence found himself in an awkward professional position during the next tumultuous days. On the one hand, he
could scarcely believe his luck, for as he wrote later he was sitting on "the
world's greatest story." Yet, although he held the title of "official reporter," he
was unable to file any copy. With the military retaining a tight control on
all atomic bomb information, Laurence's experiences—including his vivid
description of the mushroom cloud above Nagasaki appearing like a "mon-
strous prehistoric creature with a ruff around its neck"—would have to await
the book he was planning to write after the war.[71]

Laurence's consolation prize came in the form of the work he had done before leaving America, when he had prepared "the pounds of official reports
and bales of War Department 'handouts.'" These were released as part of a
choreographed PR campaign minutes after President Truman made the first
atomic bomb announcement on the morning of August 7, and they shaped
how the media initially framed the story.[72]

The documents Laurence had written divulged that the United States had
been in a race to acquire the bomb before the Nazis, a race that had been won
only because of a massive scientific and industrial effort that had cost $2 bil-
lion. They also confirmed that the outcome had been astounding. The atomic
bomb, Truman revealed, had harnessed "the basic power of the universe. The
force from which the sun draws its power," he continued, "has been loosed
against those who brought war to the far east." This enemy, the president
stressed, had rejected one recent ultimatum to surrender. "If they do not now
accept our terms, they may expect a rain of ruin from the air the like of which
has never been seen on this earth."[73]

On Guam and Tinian, censorship remained so tight that editors back in America started cabling impatient messages throughout August 7 asking "why no story there tonight on atomic bombing."[74] The dispatches the censors finally released purported to offer "the local color angles," although in reality they merely gave the air force a chance to put its own spin on the story. Tibbets, who made the short trip to Guam to meet with reporters, was the main star. In a special press conference, he did his best to provide a calm and factual account of the Hiroshima mission. "The trip to the target was uneventful," he told the assembled audience. "There was no disturbance from flak or fighters." After dropping the bomb, he added, there was a "tremendous cloud of smoke and the city was obscured by a black cloud." LeMay, who followed Tibbets, explained that even four hours after the blast, a photographic reconnaissance plane had "found the city still blanketed and obscured by smoke from the atomic bomb." Only when the briefing officers appeared did the reporters get some sense of what the mushroom cloud had hidden. The first atomic bomb, they revealed, had eradicated 60 percent of Hiroshima "with such awful thoroughness that it was as if some giant bulldozer had swept across the buildings and houses."[75]

Coverage of the second atomic attack on Nagasaki three days later followed the same template, although it had to compete for column inches with the news that the Soviet Union had entered the war against Japan. Senior air force officers on Guam made the initial announcement. Nagasaki, the wire services then reported, had been "struck by the same type of weapon which crushed buildings like match boxes at Hiroshima and killed almost every living thing within its range."[76]

In case there were any qualms about the deaths of so many civilians, senior officers stressed that the bomb would shorten the war and thereby save American lives. In one press conference, LeMay even told reporters that D-Day in Europe would not have been required had the Allies possessed the bomb before June 1944, implying that this new weapon would make a similar invasion of Japan redundant.[77] Besides, his subordinates added, both Hiroshima and Nagasaki were, first and foremost, military targets—the latter was an important shipbuilding center, while the former not only had spawned reactionary ideologies but also contained industries that "represented aggression." "If ever a place needed to be wiped off the map," one officer told a *Time* correspondent, "that place was Hiroshima."[78]

When reporters interviewed returning veterans, they found little sympathy for the enemy. "I only hope we can get a lot of them [bombs]," announced one spokesman for a large group of southern Californians, "and use them quick. Those people who are raising objections because of the destructive power don't know what is going on in the world. If they could see what the Japs are doing to our American boys they wouldn't do any kicking." Truman provided another justification. "The Japanese," he declared, "began the war from the air at Pearl Harbor. They have been repaid manifold."[79]

Significantly, the vast majority of his compatriots agreed. According to one poll, "only 5 percent of respondents opposed the atomic bombing of Hiroshima and Nagasaki, and a significant minority wished that the United States had dropped *more* A-bombs on the Japanese."[80]

* * *

While many on the home front applauded the use of the atomic bomb, the reporters in the Pacific felt a strange sense of déjà vu, for the war's end-game seemed, in two crucial respects, to be eerily similar to its start. As had happened after Pearl Harbor, the sudden transformation of the battlefield situation caught reporters by surprise, with many of them far from where they felt they ought to be. Luce's team of "harassed and frustrated correspondents" was typical. One was "bivouaced [*sic*] in an inaccessible spot on the large island of Okinawa" and so did not get a series of urgent messages. Theodore White "felt like such a goddam fool at being trapped in Manila for such a long and critical period" when he was meant to be in China. To cap it all, *Life*'s highly trained photographers were "deployed all over the place."[81]

When it came to reporting on the atomic bomb, the chaotic disposition of war correspondents scarcely mattered, because as with Pearl Harbor, this was a story largely written in Washington on the basis of official handouts. For those scattered across the Pacific, the main compensation was that the two attacks, when combined with the Soviet entrance into the war, sparked a flurry of diplomatic activity, leading to Truman's announcement on August 14 that Japan had surrendered. Whereas Pearl Harbor had marked the start of a suffocating censorship, the atomic bomb seemed likely to herald its end. This, at least, was what the army and navy were both promising, and the press initially had good reason to believe them, for the simple reason that neither service could now claim a pressing security rationale for blocking copy.[82]

Even so, the transition from censorship to autonomy would be far from smooth. The surrender announcement had itself generated a measure of friction, for it fit an unwelcome pattern. A number of major events during the last year of the war had been foreshadowed by a premature bulletin, including an AP announcement of the invasion of Europe on June 3, 1944, and Ed Kennedy's revelation that the European war had ended on May 7, 1945. With everyone primed to grab the scoop on the Japanese surrender, it was the United Press's turn to jump the gun, by issuing a "flash" two days before Truman was in a position to make an official announcement. To their intense chagrin, many radio networks broadcast the erroneous news, despite knowing from past mistakes that "a false dispatch is a very dangerous thing for radio stations, but not necessarily dangerous for newspapers where it can be killed before publication." As an NBC inquiry found, very few local networks had a safety system in place whereby breaking news was announced only after confirmation by two or more wire services. But it was the UP that inevitably faced the closest scrutiny. Agents from both the FBI and the Federal Communications Commission launched their own investigations, which, according to Earl Johnson, the UP's news manager, concluded that the UP's wire had been tampered with. "Somebody," Johnson announced, "slipped into some uncovered spot" and sent the premature message. This person, he added, was "a drunk, a crank, or was involved in a malicious plan."[83]

In the Pacific, meanwhile, some veteran reporters were convinced that malicious forces in the navy were up to their old trick of using censorship to cover up bad news. One particularly brazen example came after the tragic loss of the USS *Indianapolis* on July 30. This heavy cruiser had only just carried components of the first atomic bomb to Tinian when it was torpedoed by a Japanese submarine, with a large loss of life. While navy officers took time to establish the exact number of fatalities, their PR colleagues were in no hurry to announce this tragic event. In fact, as William Lawrence complained to his boss at the *New York Times*, the navy held the news until "two hours after President Truman had announced the Japanese acceptance of allied terms, thus making it certain that the [American] people did not know too much" about the high casualty toll. Nor was this Lawrence's only gripe. A few days later, he finished "an exclusive about the fleet losses in the Okinawan campaign," which he handed to the censors with the wry remark "that if they had to hold it for some reason I hoped they wouldn't pick some time of release when the news in it would be buried." His words, as he half expected, turned out to be in vain, because the navy decided to release the story on September 2, "when it couldn't hope to compete with the signing of the surrender aboard the [USS] *Missouri*."[84]

By this time, officials in Washington were also clamping down hard on another matter. Dr. Harold Jacobson, a technician who had worked with the navy, gave reporters the first inkling that the atomic bomb was an even deadlier weapon than the air force had let on. The explosion over Hiroshima, Jacobson told one reporter on August 7, "would leave killing radioactivity behind for seventy years." Although the Office of Censorship passed this story, the army was so alarmed that it immediately went into retaliation mode. The next day, agents from both Army Military Intelligence and the FBI visited Jacobson's house, where they questioned him for several hours before encouraging him to issue a public retraction. Dr. J. Robert Oppenheimer, the director of the bomb project, also issued a statement on August 8, which claimed "there was no appreciable radioactivity on the ground at Hiroshima and what little there was decayed very rapidly."[85]

Yet the story would not go away, not with Japanese sources claiming that radiation was continuing to cause countless deaths. The government therefore redoubled its efforts. Senior generals insisted that most of the Hiroshima fatalities had come from the blast, not the radiation, adding that "eleven days after the bomb had pulverized Hiroshima there was much less than the tolerance dose, which means . . . 'you could live there forever.' "[86] When correspondents were finally permitted to file eyewitness reports from the destroyed cities, the censors kept a particularly careful lookout for any mention of radiation.

* * *

George Weller acquired the distinction of being the first American to venture into Nagasaki after it was bombed. Slipping away from a closely supervised trip to northern Japan, the *Daily News* reporter flew south to Kyushu in early September, where he boarded a train for what he found to be a "scene of flattened destruction."[87]

Even with this traumatic vista in front of him, Weller went out of his way to "give the MacArthur command the least possible excuse to hold up my research. I eschewed all horror angles," he wrote long after the event. In one story, he even reiterated the air force claims of precision bombing. "The atomic bomb," he wrote, "may be classified as a weapon capable of being used indiscriminately, but its use in Nagasaki was selective and proper and as merciful as such a gigantic force could be expected to be." Yes, he conceded, at least twenty thousand civilians had been killed, but the principal reason for this large number was Japanese unpreparedness. "Civilian shelters," he explained, were "remote and limited," while "the Japanese air warning system was a total failure."[88]

Despite these carefully crafted phrases, Weller could not avoid touching on the one subject that the censors were never going to pass, however sensitively handled. He called it "this mysterious 'Disease X,'" and having interviewed Japanese doctors, he discovered that a month after the bomb had been dropped, at least ten people a day were still dying from it.[89] Unknown to Weller, MacArthur had already disaccredited Wilfred Burchett, the Australian correspondent of the London *Daily Express*, for producing similar stories about the radiation effects in Hiroshima. Burchett had at least got his account into print.[90] Weller's fate was quite different. He received no formal punishment from the US military; instead, the censors simply suppressed his Nagasaki dispatches, while he headed off to Guam and then Manchuria to cover postwar developments. The carbons that he retained would not see the light of day for more than half a century.[91]

* * *

During the long years of war, the military had become so adept at chaperoning reporters around the front that it found the habit hard to break, especially at a time when Weller and Burchett were causing so much trouble. So PROs from the air force planned one more trip after the guns fell silent, inviting a small number of veterans on a "vacation tour."[92]

Among the party was Clark Lee, who had been on Corregidor and Bataan at the start of the war before heading to Guadalcanal to cover the air battle; Vern Haugland, who held the dubious honor of having received both a medal and a reprimand from MacArthur; John Graham Dowling, who had reported on a string of campaigns, from Guadalcanal to Luzon; and Homer Bigart, who had seen some of the war's bloodiest battles, including Cassino and Anzio, Leyte and Okinawa. To make sure everything went as smoothly as possible, the air force laid on two B-17 Flying Fortresses, one for travel and sleep, the other for transmitting stories through state-of-the-art communications equipment. It also provided two smaller aircraft for "low-level sightseeing trips" and no less than six transport planes "to haul baggage, supplies, gasoline, jeeps, etc."[93]

For every member of this handpicked press corps, the highlight came when the planes flew over Nagasaki and they could, as Dowling put it, see "at close range and with conviction the reason the Japanese quit the war." For once, quipped Bigart, the correspondents hoped their plane might develop some engine trouble so that the pilot "will have to put down on empire soil and give us the first dateline from Japan." As it turned out, they had to make do with jotting down their observations from the aircraft window, but even from here the view was harrowing enough. "The gigantic force of the atomic bomb can hardly be described," wrote Bigart, "because it is so much more fearful than familiar agents of destruction such as floods, cyclones, and fires." "We saw half a city laid waste," added Dowling, "not in ruins as after an ordinary bombing or shelling, but smashed flat. Even the ground and stones were turned into dust and still burning, still stinking of death, weeks after the atomic bomb was turned against them."[94]

Despite witnessing such horrors, the reporters enjoyed numerous lighter moments. Major Richard R. "Tex" McCrary, a former tabloid journalist, was the PRO in charge. "Loud and raucous," he led the expedition through a series of escapades that, as one of the reporters remarked privately, could easily have resulted in "half a dozen courts-martial offenses." In fact, the expedition had something of a light valedictory feel, which impressed even those who had become highly critical of military censorship, including William Lawrence. The *New York Times* man had left Guam in mid-August still lamenting the navy's heavy-handed handling of his Okinawa stories. After two weeks in McCrary's company, he began talking happily about the fun he was having on "a newspaperman's dream junket."[95]

It would not be the last such expedition, for as August gave way to September, the army and navy were intensifying their plans for biggest junket of all: to watch the formal Japanese surrender in Tokyo Bay.

Conclusion

"The Most Thoroughly Covered Story"

Low-hanging clouds drifted gently across Tokyo Bay on the morning of September 2, 1945, while a faint mist percolated up from the sea. But on board the USS *Missouri*, everything gleamed amid the gloom, the result of days of frenzied preparation. Soon a series of flags would be raised up the ship's masts, including Nimitz's and MacArthur's fluttering side by side and another that, some said, had flown above the US Capitol on the day of the Pearl Harbor attack. On the ship's deck, expectant soldiers and sailors were packed tightly together, including the biggest names of the past few years, from Richmond Kelly Turner, who had commanded so many of the invasion fleets in the central Pacific, to George Kenney, who had propelled MacArthur's air force to complete domination in New Guinea, and Joseph Stilwell, who had dominated the CBI theater until his relief. Also in attendance were more than three hundred correspondents, broadcasters, and photographers, some hanging from gun turrets, others standing on a raised platform, each of them desperate for the best view of the old mess table covered with green felt cloth that had been placed as if at the center of a stage. Here MacArthur would summon the Japanese delegation to sign the surrender documents that would end World War II.[1]

As they waited patiently for the ceremony to begin, the more seasoned war reporters had a chance to ponder how this moment contrasted with the previous three years and eight months of bitter fighting. The most obvious difference was the sheer size of the assembled press corps. The war's early battles had often been covered by just a handful of correspondents—Hewlett, Jacoby, and Lee in the Philippines, Miller and Tregaskis on Guadalcanal, Durdin, Noderer, and Weller at Buna. As the American offensive had gathered pace, the size of the press corps had steadily grown too. No fewer than fifty-eight reporters had accompanied MacArthur's invasion of Leyte in October 1944, while seventy-one correspondents had landed on Okinawa in April 1945. Even so, this media presence paled next to the size of the press pack gathered on the *Missouri*, which, an AP reporter concluded, would make the Japanese surrender ceremony "the most thoroughly covered [story] of the war in all theaters."[2]

Nor was it only the large number of those gathered on board the *Missouri* that impressed the veteran reporters. Everywhere, symbols of American power abounded, from the 250 US warships gathered in Tokyo Bay to the 400 Superfortresses that were being readied for a ceremonial flyby.[3] The prospect that all of this military hardware would be used in celebration, not anger, generated an obvious frisson of joyful excitement among even the crustiest of officers, including "Vinegar Joe," who could be seen "in an animated conversation" with Kenney, and "Terrible" Turner, who swapped jokes with his fellow naval officers.

When MacArthur and Nimitz appeared after 8:00 a.m., a hush briefly descended until the two men strode off to join Halsey in a cabin to await the Japanese delegation. The arrival of these eleven diplomats and officers was the big moment, and it brought yet another change in the mood. "Stilwell," observed Theodore White, "bristled like a dog at the sight of the enemy. . . . Kenney curved his lips in a visible sneer." Then "The Star-Spangled Banner" rang out over the public-address system as MacArthur reappeared, flanked by Nimitz and Halsey.[4]

The reporters who had been around for any length of time recognized this as a rare moment of interservice unity. Until this moment, the vast expanse of the Pacific had meant that correspondents had effectively been covering two separate campaigns against Japan—or three with the inclusion of the CBI theater. Only a few weeks earlier, with plans still being honed for an invasion of Japan, the underlying rivalry between the services had been as intense as ever. The navy had tried to open a dialogue with MacArthur's headquarters, hoping to get its agreement on a single, united regime for all war correspondents, but Diller had initially refused even to meet. By late July, one Marine officer complained, "nothing had been done" to harmonize "censorship, the collection of press copy, the transmission of that copy, and the distribution of news stories, still pictures, and motion pictures." A Marine PRO finally arrived at MacArthur's HQ on August 1, but he continued to find little desire to cooperate on an agreed-upon system. Instead, MacArthur's position was that "all policies covering Public Relations would be determined and executed by General Diller."[5]

News that the Japanese would surrender had rendered MacArthur's attempted power grab irrelevant. "The airtight compartmentalization policies of the army and navy," observed Yates McDaniel, "which had long forced AP and other news services to organize their staffs into separate teams in the Pacific was well on the way to being broken down when Japan gave up the fight. But there was enough of the divided command idea still alive to force us to organize for the final surrender act in Tokyo Bay along parallel lines." While one set of reporters joined MacArthur as he departed from the Philippines, another came with Nimitz from Guam and Hawaii. Once everyone had arrived in Tokyo Bay, Diller quietly shelved his plans for dominance. With the navy controlling communications and the air force intending to allow its accredited reporters to accompany the flyby, he had no choice but to allow these two rivals to censor everything that their own correspondents wrote, except direct quotes from MacArthur.[6]

Once the ceremony began, however, MacArthur left no one in doubt that he was the star of the show. As Nimitz and Halsey took their places alongside other senior officers, MacArthur, standing erect before the microphone, delivered a short speech. He then summoned the Japanese representatives to sign the instrument of surrender, before broadcasting to the world. "Today," he began, "the guns are silent. A great tragedy has ended. A great victory has been won." As MacArthur referred to "the long, tortuous trail from those grim days of Bataan and Corregidor, when an entire world lived in fear," attention turned to the man standing just behind him. General Wainwright appeared gaunt, with sunken cheeks, "his neck scrawny and leathery" after years in captivity, but he was not the only former prisoner on board the *Missouri*. General Arthur E. Percival, who had surrendered the British garrison on Singapore in 1942, was also there, adding an Allied flavor to the proceedings.[7]

After the Japanese delegates had signed the surrender, MacArthur and Nimitz affixed their own signatures, followed by officers representing China, Britain, the Soviet Union, Australia, Canada, France, the Netherlands, and New Zealand. This procession underscored that the United States had not won the war on its own, even if the role of these allies had rarely formed part of the American news narrative. In the SWPA, MacArthur had successfully monopolized most of the headlines while increasingly shunting the exploits of the Australian "Diggers" into the distant background. In the CBI, Stilwell had set the tone for American coverage of the Burma campaign by dismissing the role of Mountbatten and the Chindits. Likewise, when the Royal Navy had finally started to play a bigger role in the Pacific after Germany's defeat, US navy PROs had tried to limit the amount of publicity it received. "Frankly,"

Fig. C.1. Surrounded by representatives of the Allied powers, MacArthur reads his speech before the Japanese surrender on the USS *Missouri*. National Archives 80G 332694.

remarked Harold Miller, "I have no desire to have the British correspondents convey to the world press the thought that they have won the Pacific War."[8]

Although these allies were given a supporting role in the surrender ceremony, MacArthur enjoyed the last word. This was fitting, for the Japanese occupation would be solely an American affair and he was about to become its head. Mindful of his new role, MacArthur took care to end on an uplifting note. "It is my earnest hope," he intoned, "and indeed the hope of all mankind, that from this solemn occasion a better world shall emerge out of the blood and carnage of the past."[9]

From One War to the Next

After the ceremony, many Americans headed across the bay into Tokyo, where they found the extent of the carnage truly shocking. "Everything has been flattened," observed Russell Brines. "Only thumbs stood up from the flatlands—the chimneys of bathhouses, heavy house safes and an occasional stout building with heavy iron shutters."[10]

Amid the rubble, MacArthur set about remaking Japan. As well as meting out "stern justice" to war criminals and demilitarizing the economy, he planned to turn the Japanese polity into a fully functioning democracy, which meant allowing a free press to flourish. "There shall be an absolute minimum of restrictions on freedom of speech," one of his first directives stipulated, as long as anything spoken or written "adhered 'to the truth' and did not disturb 'public tranquility.'"[11] When it came to dealing with American reporters, however, old habits died hard. Rather than treat them in the new spirit of openness, Diller introduced a quota system, which aimed not only to curtail the number of US reporters working across the Far East, but also to make those who remained dependent on the military for food, accommodation, and transportation. A howl of protest forced MacArthur to ditch this plan. The correspondents who stayed in Tokyo then established their own base in an old five-story building "located in a narrow alley in the central business district, within a few minutes' walk of the major Occupation offices." But the fundamental dynamic between the two sides remained unchanged. From his quiet office in the Dai Ichi building, MacArthur worked hard to cultivate a small "palace guard" of docile reporters while imposing a range of sanctions on any press critics, from verbal abuse to outright expulsion.[12]

Few of the big-name reporters lasted long in this hostile environment. Many had already departed during the first exodus of 1942–43, complaining loudly about the excessive censorship, including Bob Casey, Al Noderer, and Richard Tregaskis, who all went on to cover the European war. Many more left Japan soon after the surrender, although some wanted to remain in Asia, among them John Graham Dowling, who headed to Singapore, Vern Haugland, who went to Indonesia, and Tillman Durdin, who returned to China. Others left for home to take up new challenges, like Frank Hewlett, who worked briefly in the Pentagon, and Robert Sherrod, who, while still on the *Time* payroll, wrote a memoir about his experiences in Saipan, Iwo Jima, and Okinawa.[13]

Homer Bigart was one of the few Pacific War veterans who returned when another conflict erupted in the region in the summer of 1950. Having survived Cassino, Anzio, Leyte, and Okinawa on his way to winning the 1945 Pulitzer Prize for Distinguished Reporting, he found his first stint covering the Korean War "the roughest ten weeks I've ever lived." When China's intervention flung US troops back down the Korean peninsula in December,

Bigart became particularly outspoken. This reverse, he told his readers, was "the worst licking Americans had suffered since Bataan."[14]

Bigart was perfectly aware that this jibe would sting MacArthur, who commanded US forces in Korea, but he also knew that the general was surprisingly powerless to retaliate. Although strict control over the media had been the hallmark of both his campaign in the Pacific and his occupation of Japan, MacArthur initially refused to institute censorship when correspondents flooded into the region to cover the Korean War. MacArthur claimed that he lacked trained censors. He also knew that the media would dislike being formally controlled, especially when it came to a small-scale "police action" against a North Korean foe that, he believed, would be swiftly beaten.[15] But his decision quickly backfired. While Bigart used the absence of censorship to bait MacArthur about Bataan, other correspondents challenged the general's misleading communiqués, exposed his tactical mistakes, and reported the long retreats of July and December 1950 in harrowing detail. Only after the Chinese intervention threatened disaster did MacArthur finally reverse course and, under pressure from Washington, introduce a censorship regime. When correspondents complained that the new rules were unparalleled in their severity, MacArthur defended himself by stressing that he had "lifted almost bodily" the regulations that had applied during World War II.[16]

The implementation of these regulations during the last two and a half years of the Korean War helped to hide some of the bitterest fighting from the home front.[17] Yet, crucially, the US military decided not to follow this precedent in its next war in Asia. When President Lyndon B. Johnson moved to escalate American involvement in Vietnam, senior PROs repeatedly discussed the feasibility of a censorship regime, only to decide against it on the grounds of an insufficient number of trained personnel and the media's preference for a looser set of guidelines. These officials also believed that they lacked legal jurisdiction to impose press controls inside South Vietnam, where the US military was acting as a guest of the Saigon government. Besides, they fretted, reporters would "get around the rules by filing from Hong Kong or Tokyo, and many of the leaks were likely to come from Washington rather than Saigon."[18]

Once again, senior generals were left ruing this decision as an increasingly unruly set of correspondents sent home a stream of negative news stories that undermined public support for the stalemated war. This, at least, was the conventional wisdom that emerged during the 1970s and 1980s, when the military, determined not to make the same mistake, launched a major inquest into the balance between freedom and control in the war zone. Convinced that the Vietnam defeat could be blamed in part on the reckless and biased media, PROs changed tack, instituting a total blackout during the Grenada invasion in 1983. They made another change twenty years later, embedding reporters within military units during the Iraq War with the intention of returning to the system of the World War II era, when both sides had worked together as a team.[19]

By this time, not all scholars agreed that this teamwork had been healthy for American democracy. Some lamented the war correspondent's "incorporation into the military machine" during World War II, claiming that the resulting deference resulted in too much being covered up.[20] Others argued the opposite point, focusing on the moments when the censors, working in tandem with the civilian propagandists, purposefully relaxed restrictions to let the public see a much gorier side of the war. Sometimes, as George Roeder pointed out, this was done by the use of graphic pictures to undermine the public's complacent sense that the war would soon be won. More broadly, according to John McCallum, it stemmed from a desire to cultivate "an emotional toughness indispensable to a democracy in a total war," creating a political culture that was prepared to accept the repeated conflicts America waged after 1945.[21]

War News versus Propaganda

War reporting had certainly mattered during World War II, often to a greater extent than the propaganda campaigns that dominate so much of the literature on selling war, but there was rarely a neat synergy between the government's efforts to explain why and how America was fighting.

For one thing, covering the battlefield encompassed much more than either censorship deletions or image manipulation. Each day during the conflict, the media published and broadcasted countless war stories. Some described the fighting, including the heroes, the victims, and the conditions. Others crunched the numbers, from the size of the forces involved to the losses in men and machines. And many more sought to sum up the current state of progress, not just in the most recent battles but also on the longer road to victory. Crucially, these reports—rather than the output of the propagandists—frequently dominated what the home front read and saw about the war, in part because the civilian propagandists' power waned so rapidly.[22]

Roosevelt created the OWI in 1942, tasking it with using the "press, radio, motion pictures and other facilities," including pamphlets and posters, information bulletins and fact sheets, town hall meetings and speakers' tours, to define "Why America Fights."[23] Yet Congress slashed the OWI's domestic budget in the summer of 1943. By this stage, the media had also become impatient with the deluge of material it received from the alphabet agencies that proliferated across Roosevelt's Washington. "As for press releases," remarked one editor toward the end of 1943 in a typically scathing comment, "I suppose it is impossible to persuade all the various agencies that they must be short and to the point, [and] send out *nothing* unless they have something real to say. But it is a fact that too much of it goes into waste baskets . . . because editors get so sick of seeing the stuff."[24]

By contrast, editors rarely trashed the dispatches they received from their own war correspondents. In a big war, where almost everyone had a family member or friend at the front, the demand for battlefield news was simply too great.[25] Even before Pearl Harbor, combat reports had provided a welcome boost to circulation in a newspaper industry that had suffered greatly during the depression.[26] After Pearl Harbor, the public's clamor for news about the latest battles reached fever pitch. According to one survey of radio-listening habits, no less than 64 percent of respondents tuned in primarily for "straight news broadcasts," compared with 49 percent who favored comedy shows, 42 percent popular music, 25 percent sports commentaries, and 24 percent soap operas.[27]

With the demand for the latest war news so high, many editors decided to invest large sums of money sending their own correspondents to far-flung battlefields—which helped to explain the increasing number of those reporting on the Pacific War. True, these same editors also gave priority to dispatches from the European theater from early 1942 to the spring of 1945, even when major battles were unfolding on islands like Saipan and Okinawa. But, overall, war reporting from both Europe and the Pacific invariably drowned out other types of news right up until the moment when the Japanese surrender became "the most thoroughly covered" story of all.

* * *

Although news from the battlefield was a crucial component of how the home front thought about the war, the military was never able to exert complete control over the media.[28] Both Roosevelt and the Navy Department clamped down hard on the Pearl Harbor story in December 1941, fearful of divulging any information to the enemy that would further threaten the already weakened Pacific fleet. This knee-jerk reaction then morphed into a broader emphasis on secrecy during the months of setback and defeat, which helped to throw a veil over the Pacific War for much of 1942 and 1943. Yet, although this outcome fitted with Roosevelt's desire to convince the public that America's war effort should focus on Germany, there was never a neat correlation between the president's wishes and the press's response. In fact, the shroud that covered much of the fighting in this period was the product of a range of factors, from the decision by MacArthur and King to play down humiliating defeats, to inexperienced censors erring on the side of caution and exhausted journalists struggling to cover and communicate stories from distant jungle locations.

Distance remained a key variable throughout this war, although it had two very different consequences. On the one hand, as historian Mary Dudziak points out, geographic remoteness meant that American civilians were "insulated from seeing and sensing the violence of their wars," which in turn magnified the importance of war reporting, for the correspondents bridged the gap between the fighting front and the home front.[29] On the other hand, the farther journalists traveled from the center of power, the more difficult it became for senior officials to exert control. To be sure, many reporters never got beyond the theater headquarters in Brisbane or Honolulu, where they remained reliant on communiqués and press briefings. But as MacArthur demonstrated, this command-level narrative often clashed with the line that the White House and Pentagon wanted the media to take, for the simple reason that the general felt Washington was denying him sufficient resources. Drumming up publicity in the press, MacArthur calculated, presented the best chance of rectifying this neglect—although it also caused a reaction from the US Navy, which gathered pace from 1944 when Forrestal decided that the public needed to appreciate the central role the fleet was playing in the defeat of Japan.

Often, therefore, the services used publicity for their own purposes, with little attention paid to how the resulting narratives chimed with the government's overall propaganda message, but this was not the only problem. Eyewitness battlefield accounts also tended to undercut official statements whenever the fighting was going badly. Sometimes, it was only at the conclusion of a battle that the media reported on how ugly the situation had really been, as with Nat Floyd's account of illness and hunger on Bataan that appeared after he had left the Philippines in late April 1942. Increasingly, though, some battle-hardened reporters managed to paint a darker picture, even if they were reporting on campaigns run by the most publicity-conscious of commanders. On Leyte, for example, Bigart vividly described the "slow, brutal slogging" at the front, even as Frank Kelley, his colleague on the *New York Herald Tribune*, regurgitated the optimistic claims of MacArthur's HQ.[30]

Although eyewitness accounts sometimes emphasized a grimmer, gorier reality, this was not the only complicating factor. The correspondents who made it to the battlefield had to write their stories after hours, sometimes days, without any proper sleep, having been exposed to constant danger and unimaginably macabre sights. Even after the guns fell silent, they faced numerous headaches unrelated to censorship. As the distinguished BBC correspondent John Simpson has noted, in any war, reporters "are simply doing their best to puzzle out what on earth is going on, then trying to fit their interpretation of it all into an unrealistically small number of words, before spending a disproportionate amount of time working on the technicalities of getting their material transmitted back home."[31] In World War II, such conditions were hardly conducive to the creation of predictable prose that conformed neatly to the PROs' preferences. On occasion, dazed correspondents found it difficult to produce anything intelligent at all; more often than not, they stuck to trying to make sense of their own constricted field of vision—as Robert Sherrod did immediately after Tarawa.

In such a traumatic environment, the underlying clashes between the two sides were always likely to bubble to the surface. Correspondents who had just risked their necks rarely had any patience for the communications glitches that, however commonplace on the battlefield, prevented them from getting a story back to an editor. Officers who had spent stressful hours sending men to fight, and perhaps die, seldom took kindly to having their actions second-guessed by reporters who had little military training. Small wonder that, even in this war, the media sometimes faced the charge that it needed to join the national team—or as one officer told a *Time* reporter, it "ought to get into uniform—and do it quickly and voluntarily; war permits no holdouts."[32]

Conflict existed within the press pack as well. As Peter Braestrup pointed out in his classic book on war reporting in Vietnam, "the major media do not constitute an organized, unified information conglomerate, but an array of relatively small, disparate, rival commercial organizations engaged in hurriedly assembling, variously processing, and distributing 'news.'"[33] In World War II, there were numerous cleavages that ensured that the close-knit gang emerging in Port Moresby in 1942 was an exception rather than the rule. Often, these were simply the professional rivalries and personal enmities common to all press packs, although another factor had also emerged by 1944: the disdain many veteran reporters felt toward those they considered dilettante interlopers seeking a brief moment of battlefield glory—those who Sherrod dubbed the "$40-a-week police reporters and $50-a-week sports writers . . . who systematically overwrite."[34]

Nor was partisan skirmishing entirely absent. Although frontline reporters faced too many existential threats to spend much time arguing about politics, the same could not be said of their stateside bosses. Here the *Chicago Tribune* led the way, its outspoken opposition to the government stemming not only from a deep-seated aversion to Roosevelt's foreign policy, including his Germany-first strategy, but also a circulation clash with Secretary of Navy Frank Knox's *Chicago Daily News*. The *Tribune's* opposition took numerous forms, from lavishing attention on MacArthur's campaign in an attempt to drum up support for a Pacific-first strategy, to buying the rights to the Dyess story, and then pushing hard for the release of news on the Bataan death march. But by far the most controversial moment came with the *Tribune's* publication of Stanley Johnston's stories on the Midway and Coral Sea battles in 1942.

What helped to make the Johnston controversy possible was the complexity of the censorship structure created at the start of the war. Stories written inside the United States were subject only to the voluntary regime overseen by the Office of Censorship, while the correspondents who traveled to the combat zone had to agree to submit anything written there to the censors of the relevant military service.[35] When reporters returned home with juicy scoops on subjects ranging from Stilwell's recall to the Smith versus Smith controversy, their editors often decided to publish. This was also the course taken by the *Chicago Tribune* in the summer of 1942, when it used information Johnston had acquired in the Pacific to disclose that the navy had prior knowledge of the Midway attack. In response, the government attempted to prosecute the newspaper under the Espionage Act. But the most striking thing about this episode was the government's failure to obtain an indictment, even though the offending story represented potentially the most dangerous security breach by any American reporter in any war.[36]

* * *

Unlike the military, the US media did not demobilize in 1945. Although there were retirements and redeployments, most news organizations entered the postwar world in a confident mood, determined to exploit the advances they had made in recent years. The AP provided the most conspicuous example of this trend. Before Pearl Harbor, America's preeminent wire service had been overly reliant on handouts from foreign news agencies like Reuters. By the end of 1945, it not only had broken this dependence, but had also established its own foreign news distribution service, which served 519 foreign newspapers and radio stations, a figure that shot up to 1,200 over the next five years. By that time, many of the AP's American newspaper clients were also investing heavily in their foreign news coverage—so much so that within a month of the outbreak of the Korean War, they had sent more than 200 reporters to cover the fighting.[37]

Change came gradually during the 1950s and 1960s. The advent of television, together with a series of labor strikes, precipitated the closure of some of the most prestigious newspapers, including the *Chicago Daily News* and the *New York Herald Tribune*. Alongside this market consolidation came a growing corporatization. Long before the advent of the internet, foreign reporters no longer found the profession so glamorous, as improvements in communications meant that, even without military intrusion, they came under ever closer supervision from their stateside editors. The foreign correspondent, concluded one study in 1967, was "unlike his dashing predecessors 'in at least one significant respect: he is not a loner but an organization man.'"[38]

By this stage, many old timers were already mourning the passing of the World War II era, viewing it as a period when newspapers had been so vibrant and the censor, rather than a manager, had been their main overseer. Yet the more self-critical veterans could still look back at their own record with a jaundiced eye, detecting a superficiality about war reporting—a tendency to focus on "magic-weapon stories, . . . hero stories, . . . sex-and-war stories," to the detriment of more serious news angles—that, they believed, continued into the Cold War period, and beyond.[39]

Certainly, a lot had remained hidden from view during World War II, not just the details of defeat in 1942, but also the role of black troops, the part played by America's allies, and the extent of civilian casualties from massive bombing raids. Even so, what stands out as the old world of print and broadcasting shifts so rapidly into a new world of the internet and social media are the strengths, rather than the weaknesses, of war reporting in the World War II era. The media discourse, although often divided by professional, political, and personal rivalries, was nowhere near as fractured as it has become in the twenty-first century. There were still unifying voices during the 1940s, among them the war correspondents working for big news organizations whose stories reached a massive national audience through syndication. These voices rarely had to worry about having their motives, or even their basic facts, challenged by partisan opponents. Yes, they sometimes pulled their punches or swallowed their disgust, especially when faced with some of MacArthur's more grandiose efforts to spin his battles. Yes, they often got too close to the men they had spent so long with in battle, and their empathy could cloud their judgment. And yes, they occasionally complained that their editors had not given their stories the treatment they were expecting, either by placing them under overoptimistic headlines or by burying them on the inside pages.

Overall, however, these war correspondents did a tremendous job of bridging the huge gap between the battlefield and the home front. To do so, they had to survive hair-raising journeys, fight debilitating illnesses, and brave bitter battles. Those who never made it home were honored during a moving ceremony in the Pentagon press room in 1948, with Forrestal leading the tributes to reporters like Asahel Bush, William Chickering, Byron Darnton, Melville Jacoby, and Ernie Pyle, who had died in distant lands, the victims of snipers, kamikazes, and accidents. Yet their most enduring monument remains the stories, broadcasts, and images that they produced between Pearl Harbor and the surrender ceremony on board the USS *Missouri*. We are unlikely to see reporting of this type ever again.[40]

Notes

Introduction

1. Casey, *War Beat, Europe*, 54–61, 80–81, 178–87, 201–204, 266–68, 283.
2. Pyle, Letter to wife, February 2, 1945, Mss., II, Pyle Papers.
3. Baldwin, Memo to James, October 12, 1942, Censorship Folder, box 125, New York Times Company Records: Arthur Hays Sulzberger Papers; "Staffs in Pacific Worry but Not Over Bullets," *Editor & Publisher*, May 29, 1943.
4. Hamilton, *Journalism's Roving Eye*, 70, 437–38.
5. White, *Green Armour*, 183.
6. Noderer, New Guinea Notebook, November 13–14, 1942, 2–5, XI-231, box 2, Noderer Papers. For a good summary of battlefield conditions, see Ellis, *Sharp End*, 29–35; Bergerud, *Touched with Fire*, 62–104.
7. Davis, "War Information and Military Security," November 19, 1942, Subject File: Office of War Information (OWI), box 10, Davis Papers; Baldwin, Memo to James, October 12, 1942, Censorship Folder, box 125, New York Times Company Records: Arthur Hays Sulzberger Papers. Journalists critical of censorship in 1942 and 1943 tended to focus on the Pacific and exonerate Eisenhower; see, for instance, Mowrer, "Bungling the News," 120–22.
8. Casey to Binder, May 23, 1942, Correspondence Series, box 3, Casey Papers; Brandenburg, "Casey Not Cynical After 30 Years of Newspapering," *Editor & Publisher*, January 23, 1943.
9. Of the sixteen killed in the Mediterranean and Western Europe, two were victims of plane crashes in Portugal. The remainder died in Yugoslavia, Iran, India, and the United States. See Chenoweth, "54 War Correspondents K.I.A."
10. Dower, *War Without Mercy*, 10.
11. The literature on this aspect of the war is vast. See, for example, Dower, "Race, Language, and War," 169–70; Dower, *War Without Mercy*, 81, 36–37, 78–79; Klein, *Cold War Orientalism*, 4; Thorne, *Issue of War*, 60; Thorne, "Racial Aspects," 348–54; Cameron, *American Samurai*, 89–93; Chappell, *Before the Bomb*, 23–38.
12. OWI, "Intelligence Report," No. 17, April 1, 1942, and OWI, "American Estimates of the Enemy," September 2, 1942, both in PSF-OWI, Survey of Intelligence, Roosevelt Papers; State Department, "Public Attitudes on Foreign Policy," Report No. 3, November 1, 1943, Foster Files, Entry 568J, box 1, RG59.
13. Lascher, *Eve*, 63; Lee, *They Call It Pacific*, 162–69; Steele, *Shanghai and Manchuria*, 7–9; Dower, *War Without Mercy*, ix, 36.
14. Minutes of Meeting of New York AP Members, November 16, 1942, City File: NY: AP, box 183, Howard Papers.

15. Tregaskis, Log, June 6, 1942, 11:32, Battle of Midway Folder 2, box 24, Tregaskis Papers.

16. Weller, *Weller's War*, 507.

17. The War Department prohibited all press interviews with prisoners of war. Dupuy to Chief of Branches, News Division, "Prisoner of War Policy," June 4, 1943, BPR File, 000.7, Entry 499, box 14, RG165. The navy allowed correspondents "to comment on prisoners to the extent of reporting any actual observations which they make by sight but [it] did not permit any quotes or other material which was obtained by conversation or hearsay." Ward to Jones, March 30, 1944, SOPAC Official and Semi-Official Letters, Entry 86, box 4, RG313.

18. Huebner, *Warrior Image*, 11,

19. The quote is the subtitle of Moseley, *Reporting the War*.

20. Pedelty, *War Stories*, 6-8, 29, 72-76; Carruthers, *Media at War*, 15.

21. *Gallup Poll*, 131. See also Borg, *United States and the Far Eastern Crisis*, 88-92; May, "US Press Coverage of Japan," 511-32.

22. "Wheeler Says Saipan Battle Under-played," *Editor & Publisher*, July 29, 1944.

23. Baldwin, "Japan's Hold on West Pacific Not Broken in Almost a Year," *New York Times*, October 23, 1942.

24. Fitch, "Special Press Facilities for M-1 Operation," November 30, 1944, Adjutant General: General Correspondence, 000.73, box 860, RG496; Dickinson, "Ideal Press Setup for Luzon," *Editor & Publisher*, January 27, 1945.

25. Price, "Navy Plans Help Cameramen in Speedy Coverage on Iwo," *Editor & Publisher*, February 24, 1945; Luter to Chapman, "News from Iwo Jima," February 23, 1945, Folder 253, Time Dispatches; editorial, "Picture Miracle," *New York Times*, February 21, 1945.

26. Heinrichs and Gallicchio, *Implacable Foes*, 79. See also Linderman, *World Within War*, 143-84.

27. Durdin, "Buna Battle Reflect Grim War" and Durdin "Buna Area Wind-Up and American Saga," *New York Times*, December 24, 1942, and January 8, 1943.

28. If, as Dudziak argues, "American civilian isolation from the war experience" is one of the most significant developments of recent US history, this isolation was particularly pronounced during the early period of the Pacific War. Dudziak, " 'You didn't see him lying,' " 2-3.

Chapter 1

1. Hightower, "AP—War Reporting," 1-12; Barbour and Gallagher, "While the Smoke," 245-47; Barth to Kuhn, "No 'Appeasement,' " December 5, 1941, PSF (Departmental): Treasury: Morgenthau: Editorial Opinion, Roosevelt Papers.

2. Associated Press, "Pearl Harbor Remembered 75 Years Later," December 5, 2016; Schneider, "Newsmen in Race to Call War Fronts as Dozens More Wait Call," *Editor & Publisher*, December 20, 1941; Hightower, "AP—War Reporting," 13-15; Richstad, "Press Under Martial Law," 3. A few hours later, the army told the press that there

would be "no news carrying description, composition, movement, or designation of troops outside the United States, and no information concerning movements of transports inside United States waters as well as outside." "Synopsis Press Conference of Brig. General Alexander Surles," December 7, 1941, A7-1 File, Office of the Secretary: General Correspondence, Entry 12, box 76, RG80.

3. "Radio Flashes News of Attack During Quiet Sunday Afternoon," *New York Herald Tribune*, December 8, 1941; Witmer to Mullen, "News in Commercial Programs," January 15, 1942, File 641: World War II, NBC History Files.

4. Roosevelt, *Public Papers*, December 8, 1941.

5. Halifax to Churchill, October 11, 1941, document 4.11, Halifax Papers.

6. "Entire City Put on War Footing," *New York Times*, December 8, 1941; "City Springs to Attention," *Los Angeles Times*, December 8, 1941. On the roundups, which were a prelude to the internment of Japanese Americans, see Robinson, *By Order of the President*, 75.

7. Kennett, *For the Duration*, 15; Barth to Kuhn, "The Nation Rallies," December 12, 1941, PSF (Departmental): Treasury: Morgenthau: Editorial Opinion, Roosevelt Papers.

8. Casey, *Cautious Crusade*, 12–13, 83–84.

9. Barth to MacLeish, "The Indivisible War," and Barth to MacLeish, "Response to Candor," January 23 and 30, 1942, both in PSF: Treasury, Editorial Opinion, Roosevelt Papers.

10. Office of Facts and Figures (OFF), "Intelligence Report" No. 21, April 29, 1942, PSF-OWI, Survey of Intelligence, Roosevelt Papers. For an analysis of the polls on this subject, see Casey, *Cautious Crusade*, 49–50.

11. SECNAV to ALLNAV, December 7, 1941, A7-2 File, Office of the Secretary: General Correspondence, Entry 12, box 80, RG80.

12. Schneider, "Newsmen in Race to Call War Fronts as Dozens More Wait Call," *Editor & Publisher*, December 20, 1941; Winfield, *FDR and the News Media*, 172, 191–93.

13. Buell, *Master of Sea Power*, 152.

14. Toll, *Pacific Crucible*, 159. See also Mueller, "Pearl Harbor," 173–86.

15. Krock, Private Memo, December 11, 1943, World War II Folder, box 274, New York Times Company Records: Arthur Hays Sulzberger Papers.

16. Hamilton, *Journalism's Roving Eye*, 181–85; Lobdell, "Knox," 2:678–81; Schneider, *Should America Go to War?*, 37–64; Edwards, *Foreign Policy of Col. McCormick's Tribune*, 150–71.

17. Toll, *Pacific Crucible*, 45.

18. Smith, "Navy's One Man Censorship Hit by Sen. Wheeler," *Chicago Tribune*, January 15, 1942.

19. Drummond, "Knox Is at Pearl Harbor for Facts," *Christian Science Monitor*, December 12, 1941.

20. Knox to Mowrer, December 18, 1941, General Correspondence, box 4, Knox Papers.

21. "2,897 Dead in Hawaii Raid," *Chicago Tribune*, December 16, 1941; "Heroism of Men Under Fire in Hawaii Related by Sec. Knox," *Boston Globe*, December 16, 1941.

22. Barth to Kuhn, "Meeting the Issue," December 19, 1941, PSF: Treasury, Editorial Opinion, Roosevelt Papers.

23. Editorial, "Censorship of War News Starts Off Hopefully," *Baltimore Sun*, December 18, 1941; Lippmann, "Some Measures Are Necessary Since We Are at War," *Boston Globe*, December 13, 1941.

24. Knox, Memo to all Chiefs of Bureaus and Offices, December 17, 1941, A7-1 File, Office of the Secretary: General Correspondence, Entry 12, box 75, RG80.

25. Sweeney, *Secrets of Victory*, 36–42; Sweeney, *The Military and the Press*, 65–71; Smith, *War and Press Freedom*, 149–51, 156–57; Carlson, *Johnston's Blunder*, 10–11; US War Department, *Regulations*.

26. Harsch, "Men at Pearl Harbor Rose Nobly to Emergency," *Christian Science Monitor*, December 23, 1941.

27. "Large US Losses Claimed by Japan," *New York Times*, December 9, 1941.

28. War Department, Bureau of Public Relations, "Whispering Campaign in Brooklyn, New York, Causes War Department to Issue Complete Denial," 16 January 1942, Legislative and Policy Precedent Files, Death-Notification Folder, Entry 390, box 1, RG407. On rumormongering after Pearl Harbor, see Sparrow, *Warfare State*, 80–81.

29. OFF, "Intelligence Report" No. 11, February 23, 1942, PSF-OWI, Survey of Intelligence, Roosevelt Papers.

30. Tupper and McReynolds, *Japan in American Public Opinion*, 319–26, 421–24. This survey points out that media opinion became "almost completely hostile to Japan" at the start of 1932, after a Sino-Japanese clash in Shanghai. See also *Gallup Poll*, 159, 168, 177, 208, 246, 296.

31. *Gallup Poll*, 131. See also Borg, *United States and the Far Eastern Crisis*, 88–92, and May, "US Press Coverage of Japan," 511–32, which argues that "American reportage on Japan was superficial, fragmentary, insensitive." When the news agencies were asked to rank their top stories for 1938, they all placed Munich first; the AP listed the fall of Hankow and Canton fifth, "but the other two agencies [made] no reference to the war in China." "1938 'the Biggest News Year Since the War,'" *Newspaper World*, December 24, 1938.

32. Barth to Kuhn, "East and West," July 18, 1941, PSF (Departmental): Treasury: Morgenthau: Editorial Opinion, Roosevelt Papers; "America Faces the War: Clusters and Determinants of Opinion," January 28, 1941, Table 9, OF 857, Roosevelt Papers.

33. Hamilton, *Journalism's Roving Eye*, 70, 437; Leff, *Buried*, 64–65; "Associated Press Foreign Service, List revised as of December 30, 1941," Newspapers, Series 3: Subject Files, AP 02A.3, box 51, AP Corporate Archives.

34. "AP Foreign Correspondents," June 22, 1942, AP War Correspondents and Bureaus, 1941–42, Series 3: Subject Files, AP 02A.3, box 51, AP Corporate Archives.

35. Stowe to Binder, December 1, 1941, General Correspondence Folder, box 4, Stowe Papers; Stowe, *They Shall Not Sleep*, 57–58, 132; Woods, *Reporting the Retreat*, 39.

36. Durdin to Chennault, October 19, 1941, Public Relations Folder, box 7, Chennault Papers; Pace, "Tillman Durdin, 91, Reporter in China during World War II," *New York Times*, July 9, 1998.

37. Noderer, New Zealand to Singapore Notebook, December 7 and 10, 1942, 13, XI-231, box 2, Noderer Papers.

38. Fisher to Hulbard, March 20, 1941, Far East Misc. Folder, box 414, Time Inc. Records.

39. Fisher to Luce, September 11, 1941, and Grover to Luce, September 23, 1941, Far East Misc. Folder, box 414, Time Inc. Records; Fisher to Hulbard, January 20, 1941, Far East Jacoby's Cables Folder, box 415, Time Inc. Records; Lascher, *Eve*, 7, 67–74, 100–101, 150–51, 200–22.

40. Lee, *They Call It Pacific*, 7–8, 19–24; Brines to John [Hightower], August 2, 1974, WWII Book Project: AP Correspondents: Lee Folder, AP28, Writings About the AP, Series II, box 14, AP Corporate Archives.

41. Fisher to Hulbard, March 20, 1941, Far East Misc. Folder, box 414, Time Inc. Records.

42. USAFFE Diary, December 5, 1941, box 3, RG2, MacArthur Papers.

Chapter 2

1. These paragraphs are based on Lee, *They Call It Pacific*, 27–29, 34–37; Quigg, "Pearl Harbor—40 Years After," *Los Angeles Times*, December 6, 1981; Hewlett, "UP's Hewlett Writes of a New December 7th," *Editor & Publisher*, December 23, 1944; Rogers, *The Good Years*, 248; Press Conference, December 9, 1941, Press Releases Folder, box 3, RG2, MacArthur Papers; Jacoby to Hulbard, December 8, 1941, Far East Jacoby's Cables Folder, box 415, Time Inc. Records.

2. On MacArthur's efforts to justify what happened, see MacArthur to Arnold, December 10, 1941, Personal Files, box 2, RG2, MacArthur Papers. For an assessment of who was to blame, see Bartsch, *MacArthur's Pearl Harbor*, 410–24.

3. Lee, *They Call It Pacific*, 29.

4. Hersey, *Men on Bataan*, 15; MacArthur to Marshall, December 13, 1941, Personal Files, box 2, RG2, MacArthur Papers; MacArthur, *Reminiscences*, 122; Morton, *Fall of the Philippines*, 150–52.

5. James, *Years of MacArthur*, 1:130–32, 573; Schneider, "Newsmen in Race to War Fronts," *Editor & Publisher*, December 20, 1941.

6. Rogers, *The Good Years*, 263.

7. "Invasion from North Stemmed," *New York Herald Tribune*, December 12, 1941; AP, "Japs Lose Luzon Toe Holds," *Los Angeles Times*, December 14, 1941. For more detail, see McManus, *Fire and Fortitude*, 73–74.

8. Lee, *They Call It Pacific*, 40–41; Hewlett, "Aerial Battle at Manila—Witness Story," *Chicago Daily News*, December 10, 1941.

9. Brines, "Witness Tells of Raid on US Manila Base," *Chicago Tribune*, December 11, 1941.

10. AP, "Jap Fleet Flees US Navy in First Encounter," *Chicago Daily News*, December 12, 1941; AP, "Bombs Wreck Area on Edge of Nichols Field," *New York Herald Tribune*, December 14, 1941.

11. Lee, *They Call It Pacific*, 46–47; USAFFE Diary, December 9, 1941, box 3, RG2, MacArthur Papers. On the dangers of driving around Manila, see Brines to John

[Hightower], August 2, 1974, WWII Book Project: AP Correspondents: Lee Folder, AP28, Writings About the AP, Series II, box 14, AP Corporate Archives; Van Landingham, "I Saw Manila Die," *Saturday Evening Post*, September 26, 1942.

12. Jacoby to Hulbard, December 10, 1941, Far East Jacoby's Cables Folder, box 415, Time Inc. Records.

13. Press Release of the CINC's Daily Communiqué, December 22, 1941, box 3, RG2, MacArthur Papers; Lee, *They Call It Pacific*, 52; "Major Attack in Philippines Seen on Way," *New York Herald Tribune*, December 22, 1941.

14. Lee, *They Call It Pacific*, 52–74; Schneider, "US Newsmen See Action on World's War Fronts," *Editor & Publisher*, December 27, 1941.

15. Brines, "A Bearded Scribe Gets Lots of Close Shaves," *Chicago Tribune*, December 27, 1941; Lee, *They Call It Pacific*, 74–75; Jacoby to Hulbard, December 25, 1941, Far East Jacoby's Cables Folder, box 415, Time Inc. Records.

16. Lee, "Jap Troops Near Manila Mere Boys," *Los Angeles Times*, December 26, 1941.

17. Diller received detailed accounts of the damage done in these attacks; see Ince to Diller, December 27, 1941, Personal Files, box 2, RG2, MacArthur Papers.

18. Prochnau, *Once Upon a Distant War*, 52; Smith, "Frank Hewlett, Reporter for Utah Newspaper," *New York Times*, July 9, 1983; "Soldiers of the Press," YouTube video; Morris, *Deadline*, 247–48; Fisher to Hulbard, March 20, 1941, Far East Misc. Folder, box 414, Time Inc. Records.

19. Lee, "Invaders on Luzon Held Back," *Baltimore Sun*, December 29, 1941; Schneider, "US War Coverage Pepped Up by Flood of Colorful Dispatches," *Editor & Publisher*, January 3, 1942.

20. Hewlett, "Great Manila Fires Raze Historic Sights," *Los Angeles Times*, December 28, 1941.

21. Lee, *They Call It Pacific*, 83–84.

22. "Franz Weissblatt Is Dead at 62" and Weisblatt, "Americans and Filipinos Show Mettle Combating Japanese on Lingayen Front," *New York Times*, December 24, 1941, and September 13, 1961.

23. Lee, *They Call It Pacific*, 91.

24. USAFFE Diary, December 24, 1941, box 3, RG2, MacArthur Papers.

25. Lee, *They Call It Pacific*, 93; AP, "Japanese Dive Bombers Control Roads as Tanks Smash Closer to Capital," *Baltimore Sun*, December 31, 1941.

26. Jacoby, "Dinner Meeting, River Club, New York City," July 13, 1942, 66, Far East Jacoby Dinner Folder, box 415, Time Inc. Records.

27. Jacoby, "Dinner Meeting, River Club, New York City," July 13, 1942, 1–3, 20–21, Far East Jacoby Dinner Folder, box 415, Time Inc. Records; Lee, *They Call It Pacific*, 94–96; Lascher, *Eve*, 7, 240–50.

28. Jacoby, "Dinner Meeting, River Club, New York City," July 13, 1942, 22–23, Far East Jacoby Dinner Folder, box 415, Time Inc. Records; Lee, *They Call It Pacific*, 96–99; Lascher, *Eve*, 7, 250–51. On the explosions in Manila, see Van Landingham, "I Saw Manila Die," *Saturday Evening Post*, September 26, 1942.

29. Romulo, *I Saw the Fall of the Philippines*, 59; Lee, *They Call It Pacific*, 99; Morton, *Fall of the Philippines*, 474–75; James, *Years of MacArthur*, 2:68–69.

30. Lee, *They Call It Pacific*, 99–100; Lascher, *Eve*, 257–61.

31. On overstretched communications on Corregidor, see MacArthur to Chief Signal Officer, December 23, 1941, Personal Files, box 2, RG2, MacArthur Papers. News organizations also stopped sending cables the other way; see Memo, January 15, 1942, Secretarial File: January 1942, box 260, Clare Boothe Luce Papers.

32. Morton, *Fall of the Philippines*, 224–31, 265–90; Lee, *They Call It Pacific*, 109.

33. Lee, *They Call It Pacific*, 106–107, 109–10; AP, "Lull Is Giving US Defenders Needed Rest," *Boston Globe*, January 10, 1942.

34. Morton, *Fall of the Philippines*, 290–95.

35. SecNav to Com 16, January 19, 1942, A7-1 File, Office of the Secretary: General Correspondence, Entry 12, box 75, RG80; Surles to CG USAFFE, January 20, 1942, Personal Files, box 2, RG2, MacArthur Papers; PRO to Surles, January 19, Chief of Staff: Radios and Letters Dealing with Plans and Policies, box 3, RG2, MacArthur Papers; Lee, *They Call It Pacific*, 127.

36. Floyd, "Writer Says Plea on Bataan Was for 'Chow' and Planes"; "Franz Weissblatt Is Dead at 62," *New York Times*, April 22, 1942, and September 13, 1961; Hersey, *Men on Bataan*, 237.

37. Lee, *They Call It Pacific*, 127.

38. "Dispersal as of April 1, 1943," AP War Correspondents and Bureaus Folder, Series 3: Subject Files, AP 02A.3, box 51, AP Corporate Archives; "Six Newsmen Assigned to Atlantic Fleet," *Editor & Publisher*, April 25, 1942; Lee, *They Call It Pacific*, 127.

39. Jacoby, "Bataan Writers Allowed to File 500 Words Daily," *Editor & Publisher*, February 7, 1942.

40. Jacoby, "Bataan Writers Allowed to File 500 Words Daily," *Editor & Publisher*, February 7, 1942.

41. Wainwright, *Wainwright's Story*, 58, 60, 107; Hewlett, "Bataan Guerrilla's Dig In," *Washington Post*, February 1, 1942; Hewlett, "Bataan Troops Eager to Attack," *Los Angeles Times*, February 14, 1942.

42. Lee, "Bataan Defenders Now Masters at Camouflage" and Lee, "Perilous Island Trip Completed," *Los Angeles Times*, January 21 and 30, 1942.

43. Hewlett, "Another Father Duffy Cheers Yanks," *Washington Post*, February 7, 1942; Hewlett, "Cook Forsakes Pots for Gun" and Hewlett, "Officer Hero of Artillery Shot Three Times at Bataan," *Los Angeles Times*, February 24, and March 31, 1942; Lee, "Difficulties in Bataan Travel," *New York Times*, February 9, 1942.

44. Hewlett, "26th Cavalry Plays Heroic Role in Defense of Philippines," *Washington Post*, January 24, 1942.

45. Lee, "Difficulties in Bataan Travel," *New York Times*, February 9, 1942; Lee, "Here and There in Bataan with a War Reporter," *Chicago Tribune*, February 10, 1942.

46. Lee, "Difficulties in Bataan Travel," *New York Times*, February 9, 1942; Lee, "Bataan Writer Asserts a Few Planes Could Swing Battle," *Los Angeles Times*, February 11, 1942; Hewlett, "Batan [*sic*] Army Surgeons Work Day and Night" and Hewlett, "MacArthur's Engineers Hailed for 'Dirty Work,'" *Los Angeles Times*, February 6, 1942.

47. Lee, *They Call It Pacific*, 114.

48. Marshall to MacArthur, January 31, 1942, Personal Files; MacArthur to AGWAR, January 2, 1942, Operations Radios to War Department, both in box 2, RG2, MacArthur Papers.

49. Lee, "Here and There in Bataan with a War Reporter," *Chicago Tribune*, February 10, 1942.

50. On the tension between the front and the rear, see Miller, *Bataan Uncensored*, 193–94; Morton, *Fall of the Philippines*, 375–76; Borneman, *MacArthur at War*, 115–23. On the ditties, see Kolakowski, *Last Stand on Bataan*, 142.

51. PRO to Surles, January 19, 1942, Press Releases Folder, box 3, RG2, MacArthur Papers; Miller, *Bataan Uncensored*, 190.

52. Manchester, *American Caesar*, 232–33; Rogers, *The Good Years*, 264; James, *Years of MacArthur*, 2:89.

53. Hewlett, "MacArthur's Engineers Hailed for 'Dirty Work,'" *Los Angeles Times*, February 12, 1942; Jacoby, "Dinner Meeting, River Club, New York City," July 13, 1942, 27, Far East Jacoby Dinner Folder, box 415, Time Inc. Records.

54. Lascher, *Eve*, 273.

55. USAFFE Diary, February 23, 1942, and Lee to Kenper, March 5, 1942, Press Releases Folder, both in box 3, RG2, MacArthur Papers; Jacoby, "Dinner Meeting, River Club, New York City," July 13, 1942, 29–30, Far East Jacoby Dinner Folder, box 415, Time Inc. Records; Hersey, *Men on Bataan*, 241–42; Lascher, *Eve*, 279–89.

56. Morton, *Fall of the Philippines*, 367–84; McManus, *Fire and Fortitude*, 120–24; Floyd, "Writer Says Plea on Bataan Was for 'Chow' and Planes," *New York Times*, April 22, 1942.

57. Morton, *Fall of the Philippines*, 352, 418–20; Morris to MacArthur, March 7, 1942, Press Releases Folder, box 3, RG2, MacArthur Papers.

58. Morton, *Fall of the Philippines*, 356–59; James, *Years of MacArthur*, 2:98–103; Borneman, *MacArthur at War*, 138–46; Masuda, *MacArthur in Asia*, 93–119.

59. Hewlett, "Bataan's 98 Days a Terrible Ordeal," *New York Times*, April 12, 1942.

60. "Bombers Fly Far" and Floyd, "Writer Tells of Philippine Escape," *New York Times*, April 16 and 18, 1942; Hutton, "World News Men Gather in Australia," *Australasian*, May 2, 1942, clipping in Folder 7, Kunz Papers; Adams, *Fightin' Texas Aggie Defenders*, 249–50n.46.

61. Ferrell, ed., *Eisenhower Diaries*, 51.

62. Hersey, *Men on Bataan*, 36–37.

63. Chamberlin, "Special Arrangements for General MacArthur's Arrival," March 20, 1942, Official and Personal Correspondence, box 1, RG36, Chamberlin Papers; Borneman, *MacArthur at War*, 158–61.

64. Lee, *They Call It Pacific*, 170–71; Knickerbocker, "How Gen. MacArthur Got to Australia," *Boston Globe*, March 19, 1942; Norris, "His Dramatic Shift at President's Order," *Washington Post*, March 18, 1942.

65. Cocheu to MacArthur, May 24, 1942, and MacArthur to Cocheu, June 2, 1943, Official Correspondence, box 1, RG3, MacArthur Papers.

66. Knickerbocker, "How Gen. MacArthur Got to Australia," *Boston Globe*, March 19, 1942.

67. "Godspeed of M'Arthur Given Writers on Dash from Bataan," *Baltimore Sun*, April 9, 1942; "Escape from Bataan," *Time*, April 13, 1942; Lascher, *Eve*, 328–29.

68. Hicks to Andrew, January 28, 1942, Life: Wartime Picture Pool Folder, box 433, Time Inc. Records; Brinkley, *Luce*, 282–83.

69. Jacoby, "The Battle of Bataan" and "MacArthur's Men," *Life*, February 9 and March 16, 1942.

70. "Philippine Epic," *Life*, April 13, 1942.

71. "Bombers Fly Far" and Floyd, "Writer Tells of Philippine Escape," *New York Times*, April 16 and 18, 1942.

72. Floyd, "Writer Says Plea on Bataan Was for 'Chow' and Planes," *New York Times*, April 22, 1942.

73. Schedler, "Wainwright Stays to End by Choice," *New York Times*, May 7, 1942.

74. OFF, "Intelligence Report" No. 19, April 15, 1942, PSF-OWI, Survey of Intelligence, Roosevelt Papers.

75. Editorial, "Bataan Was No Picnic," *New York Times*, April 23, 1942.

76. OFF, Survey No. 10, 16 February 1942, PSF-OFF, Roosevelt Papers.

77. OFF, "Intelligence Report" Nos. 20 and 23, April 22 and May 13, 1942, PSF-OWI, Survey of Intelligence, Roosevelt Papers.

78. OFF, "Intelligence Report" No. 23, May 13, 1942, PSF-OWI, Survey of Intelligence, Roosevelt Papers; OFF, Bureau of Information, "Weekly Media Report," No. 16, May 23, 1942, Entry 151, box 1720, RG44.

79. "To American Editors," *Time*, June 1, 1942.

80. Diller, GHQ Communiqués 19, 20, and 21, May 8 and 9, 1942, Series 5: Communiqués and Press Releases, box 47, RG4, MacArthur Papers; Marshall to MacArthur, and MacArthur to Marshall, May 10, 1942, War Department File, box 15, RG3, MacArthur Papers; Borneman, *MacArthur at War*, 203–204.

Chapter 3

1. Casey, *Torpedo Junction*, 19–33; Hailey, *Pacific Battle Line*, 41–44; COM 14 to COM 12, 11, 3, January 7, 1942, CINCPAC, Chronological File, Entry 125, reel 1, RG313; Letter to Herter, January 16, 1942, A7-1 File, Office of the Secretary: General Correspondence, Entry 12, box 75, RG80.

2. O'Donnell, "Honolulu," March 4, 1942, Publishing Enterprises: NY Daily News, 1939–42 File, box 30, Patterson Papers.

3. Hepburn to Commandant Twelfth Naval District, December 18, 1941; Hepburn to Com 14 CINCPAC, December 20, 1941, A7-1 File, Office of the Secretary: General Correspondence, Entry 12, box 75, RG80.

4. Surles to O'Donnell, March 4, 1942, Publishing Enterprises: NY Daily News, 1939–42, box 30, Patterson Papers. For another attempt to piece together what had happened, see Sherrod to Hulbard, January 23, 1942, Far East Folder, box 415, Time Inc. Records.

5. *Robert J. Casey*, 3–9; "R. J. Casey Dies," *Hartford Courant*, December 5, 1962; Stowe, *No Other Road*, 1–4, 13; Brandenburg, "Bob Casey Back After 7 Months in Pacific"

and "Casey Not Cynical After 30 Years of Newspapering," *Editor & Publisher*, July 11, 1942, and January 23, 1943. For his own account of his pre–Pearl Harbor experiences, see Casey, *I Can't Forget* and *This Is Where I Came In.*

6. Casey, *Torpedo Junction*, 11–13.

7. Borneman, *The Admirals*, 220–21, 228–29.

8. Casey to Mowrer, March 17, 1942, Correspondence Series, box 3, Casey Papers.

9. SECNAV to CINCPAC, January 7, 1942, A7-2 File, Office of the Secretary: General Correspondence, Entry 12, box 80, RG80. According to his biographer, Nimitz found "this patronizing message not a little irritating." See Potter, *Nimitz*, 36.

10. Casey to Mowrer, March 17, 1942, Correspondence Series, box 3, Casey Papers; Drake, January 30, 1942, Drake Correspondence Folder, Entry 86, box 4, RG313; "115 Accredited by War Dept. as Correspondents," *Editor & Publisher*, January 10, 1942.

11. Casey, *Torpedo Junction*, 52–53, 56–57; Toll, *Pacific Crucible*, 199–201.

12. Casey, *Torpedo Junction*, 57, 59, 66, 96.

13. "Reporter Tells How He Covered Midway Battle," *Editor & Publisher*, July 11, 1942.

14. Casey, *Torpedo Junction*, 64, 89–90.

15. SecNav to CINCPAC, February 3, 1942, A7-1 File, Office of the Secretary: General Correspondence, Entry 12, box 79, RG80; Drake to Kitte, February 20, 1942, Drake Correspondence Folder, Entry 86, box 4, RG313.

16. Casey, "Story of Navy's Attack on Jap Isles in Pacific," *Chicago Daily News*, February 13, 1942.

17. Casey to Mowrer, March 17, 1942, Correspondence Series, box 3, Casey Papers.

18. Fields to Hodgins, "Censorship in Hawaii," May 20, 1942, Censorship Folder, box 415, Time Inc. Records; Sweeney, *Secrets of Victory*, 51; Smith, *War and Press Freedom*, 149–52. For the complex series of censorship guidelines that the navy issued in the first months of the war, see "Censorship, 1942," Censorship Folder, Entry 3, box 19, RG428. For the position of local Hawaii papers, see Richstad, "Press Under Martial Law," 7–12.

19. Casey to Mowrer, March 17, 1942, Correspondence Series, box 3, Casey Papers.

20. Knox, Memo for Hepburn, February 5, 1942, A7-1 File, Office of the Secretary: General Correspondence, Entry 12, box 75, RG80; Casey to Mowrer, March 17, 1942, Correspondence Series, box 3, Casey Papers.

21. "Additional Press and Photographic Representatives in Hawaii," December 31, 1941, A7-1 File, Office of the Secretary: General Correspondence, Entry 12, box 79, RG80; Preston, *We Saw Spain Die*, 38.

22. Casey to Binder, May 23, 1942, Correspondence Series, box 3, Casey Papers.

23. Casey to Binder, May 23, 1942, Correspondence Series, box 3, Casey Papers.

24. Solbert to Macy, March 5, 1942, A7-1 File, Office of the Secretary: General Correspondence, Entry 12, box 80, RG80; Knox to Sulzberger, March 26, 1942, Sulzberger to Hailey, March 27 and 31, 1942, Hailey to Sulzberger, April 18, 1942, Sulzberger to Knox, May 4, 1942, Hailey Folder, box 30, New York Times Company Records: Arthur Hays Sulzberger Papers; Berry to Drake, March 26, 1942, Drake Correspondence Folder, Entry 86, box 4, RG313; Fenn to Censor, Honolulu, March 26, 1942, Violations and Suppressions Folder, Entry 1A, box 145, RG216; Hailey,

Pacific Battle Line, 141–42. The censor did allow the *Times* to carry Hailey's stories, but only if they deleted his byline.

25. OGR, "Weekly Analysis of Press Reaction," April 16, 1942, OF788, Roosevelt Papers; "Fortune Survey," [undated, but marked release on July 31, 1942] copy in PPF5437, Roosevelt Papers.

26. King, "Press Release," March 2, 1942, Press and Press Releases Folder, box 23, King Papers.

27. Casey to Mowrer, March 17, 1942, Correspondence Series, box 3, Casey Papers.

28. Casey, *Torpedo Junction*, 172.

29. Maloney to McCormick, undated, and May 31, 1941, Johnston Folder, McCormick: Foreign Correspondents, I-62, box 6, Chicago Tribune Company Archives; "Johnston, Tribune War Writer, Dies," *Chicago Tribune*, September 14, 1962; Carlson, *Johnston's Blunder*, 12–16.

30. Murchie to McCormick, November 4, 1940, Murchie Folder, McCormick: Foreign Correspondents, I-62, box 6, Chicago Tribune Company Archives.

31. Maloney to McCormick, undated, and May 31, 1941, Johnston Folder, McCormick: Foreign Correspondents, I-62, box 6, Chicago Tribune Company Archives.

32. Maloney to McCormick, undated and May 31, 1941, Johnston Folder, McCormick: Foreign Correspondents, I-62, box 6, Chicago Tribune Company Archives; "Johnston, Tribune War Writer, Dies," *Chicago Tribune*, September 14, 1962; Carlson, *Johnston's Blunder*, 19–21.

33. Sweeney and Washburn, "'Aint Justice Wonderful,'" 20–21.

34. Schneider, *Should America*, 7–8; Norton-Smith, *The Colonel*, 251–53, 300–301, 375–78; Hamilton, *Journalism's Roving Eye*, 156–91; "Evidence Shows Tribune's Link with Crackpots," *Chicago Daily News*, May 18, 1942. On the rivalry between the *Daily News* and *Tribune*, see "Chicago Newspapers Compete in Field of Foreign News," *Editor & Publisher*, June 12, 1943.

35. Johnston, Note, April 2, 1942, and Johnston to Maloney, undated [April 1942], Johnston Folder, McCormick: Foreign Correspondents, I-62, box 6, Chicago Tribune Company Archives

36. Johnston, "How Lexington Crew Trained to Battle Japs," *Chicago Tribune*, June 14, 1942; Johnston, *Queen of the Flat-Tops*, 18, 130, 158; Keith, *Stay the Rising Sun*, xvii; Carlson, *Johnston's Blunder*, 25.

37. Johnston, *Queen of the Flat-Tops*, 110–11.

38. Potter, *Nimitz*, 67; Toll, *Pacific Crucible*, 314–19; Johnston, *Queen of the Flat-Tops*, 125–26.

39. Johnston, "First Story of Coral Sea Battle Told by Eyewitness," *Chicago Tribune*, June 13, 1942; Morison, *History of United States Naval Operations*, 4:41–42; Symonds, *Battle of Midway*, 163–64.

40. Johnston, *Queen of the Flat-Tops*, 180, 186, 190; Morison, *History of United States Naval Operations*, 4:57–60.

41. Seligman, "Action in Coral Sea," May 14, 1942; Johnston, "Lexington's End! A Story of Valor" and "Lexington Crew Gives a Cheer on the Voyage Home, *Chicago Tribune*,

June 18 and 21, 1942; Johnston, *Queen of the Flat-Tops*, 211–24; "Johnston Hailed for Heroism as Lexington Sank," *Chicago Tribune*, July 12, 1942.

42. Carlson, *Johnston's Blunder*, 42–48.

43. Johnston, Memo, June 9, 1942, Johnston Folder, McCormick: Foreign Correspondents, I-62, box 6, Chicago Tribune Company Archives.

44. Johnston, Memo, June 9, 1942, Johnston Folder, McCormick: Foreign Correspondents, I-62, box 6, Chicago Tribune Company Archives.

45. Symonds, *Battle of Midway*, 132–51; Prados, *Combined Fleet Decoded*, 341.

46. Johnston, Memo, June 9, 1942, Johnston Folder, McCormick: Foreign Correspondents, I-62, box 6, Chicago Tribune Company Archives; Mason," Eyewitness," 42; Blair, *Silent Victory*, 257; Carlson, *Johnston's Blunder*, 51–55.

47. Maloney to McCormick, June 12, 1942, and attached statement; Johnston, Memo, June 9, 1942, both in Johnston Folder, McCormick: Foreign Correspondents, I-62, box 6, Chicago Tribune Company Archives; Norton-Smith, *The Colonel*, 429–30; "J. Loy Maloney Dies," *Chicago Tribune*, November 29, 1976.

48. Johnston, Memo, June 9, 1942, Johnston Folder, McCormick: Foreign Correspondents, I-62, box 6, Chicago Tribune Company Archives; Carlson, *Johnston's Blunder*, 10–11, 62–70, 89, 198; Sweeney and Washburn, "'Aint Justice Wonderful,'" 27–28; "Navy Had Word of Jap Plan to Strike at Sea," *Chicago Tribune*, June 7, 1942.

49. Buell, *Master of Sea Power*, 202–203.

50. Larrabee, *Commander in Chief*, 155, 186–87; Winkler, *Politics of Propaganda*, 49.

51. Prados, *Combined Fleet Decoded*, 341; Carlson, *Johnston's Blunder*, 3–4, 77–80, 84–85.

52. "Report of a Press Conference Held at 1700 June 7, 1942, in Admiral King's Office," Press and Press Releases Folder, box 23, King Papers.

53. Trohan, "Confidential for Patterson," undated, McCormick Papers File, box 54, Patterson Papers. On the background to this memo, see Washburn, "'Aint Justice Wonderful,'" 88n129.

54. Sweeney and Washburn, "'Aint Justice Wonderful,'" 38–41, 49–51; Carlson, *Johnston's Blunder*, 71–72, 104–105, 114–15.

55. Maloney to McCormick, June 12, 1942, and attached statement, Johnston Folder, McCormick: Foreign Correspondents, I-62, box 6, Chicago Tribune Company Archives. On the legal aspects of the case, see Sweeney and Washburn, "'Aint Justice Wonderful,'" 56–64.

56. GLB to McCormick, August 27, 1942, McCormick Papers File, box 54, Patterson Papers; Dupuy to Director, Bureau of Public Relations, "Letter from the Secretary of the Navy," June 30, 1942, BPR File, 000.77, Entry 499, box 7, RG165; Mayfield to Fleet Intelligence Officer, July 19, 1942, Johnston Folder, Entry 86, box 25, RG313; Stimson Diary, June 17, 1942, 39:94, Stimson Papers.

57. Maloney to McCormick, June 10, 1942, Johnston Folder, McCormick: Foreign Correspondents, I-62, box 6, Chicago Tribune Company Archives; Berry to Drake, July 7, 1942, Drake Correspondence Folder, Entry 86, box 4, RG313. Hoover included a lot of this nasty material in a memo for Roosevelt; see Carlson, *Johnston's Blunder*, 142–43.

58. King to Ament, June 7, 1942, Press and Press Releases Folder, box 23, King Papers; Beale to Smith, June 12, 1942, A7-1 File, Office of the Secretary: General Correspondence, Entry 12, box 75, RG80.

59. "Johnston Hailed for Heroism as Lexington Sank," *Chicago Tribune*, July 12, 1942.

60. Maloney to McCormick, June 13, 1942, and AP, Press Release, June 13, 1942, both in Johnston Folder, McCormick: Foreign Correspondents, I-62, box 6, Chicago Tribune Company Archives; editorial, "The Coral Sea Story," and "Johnston Only Correspondent to See Battle," *Chicago Tribune*, June 13, 1942. In a rare moment of interservice cooperation, the army, recognizing that the *Tribune* was trying to turn Johnston into a "hero," ordered that all of its personnel "take no part in any of the public appearances which would indicate official or semi-official approval of Mr. Johnston." Dupuy to PRO, Sixth Corps Area, July 7, 1942, BPR File, 000.7, Entry 499, box 4, RG165.

61. Johnston, "Blast Jap Fleet Off Alaska!" and "One Day's Score in Sea Battle: 63 Jap Planes," *Chicago Tribune*, June 16 and 19, 1942.

62. Johnston, "Lexington's End! A Story of Valor," *Chicago Tribune*, June 18, 1942.

63. Johnston, "Tells How Lexington Flyers Sank 14 Ships," *Chicago Tribune*, June 15, 1942. For the actual damage and Nimitz's conclusion, see Morison, *History of United States Naval Operations*, 4:26–28.

64. Johnston, "Lexington Crew Gives a Cheer on Voyage Home" and Johnston, "First Story of Coral Sea Battle Told by Eyewitness," *Chicago Tribune*, June 21 and 13, 1942.

65. Trohan, "Confidential for Patterson," undated, McCormick Papers File, box 54, Patterson Papers; Maloney to Manly, August 1, 1942, AP to McCormick, June 17, 1942, and Maloney to McCormick, July 27, 1942, Johnston Folder, McCormick: Foreign Correspondents, I-62, box 6, Chicago Tribune Company Archives.

66. Symonds, *Battle of Midway*, 288–308.

67. Casey, *Torpedo Junction*, 232–34, 242.

68. Casey, "Casey Tells of Midway Battle," *Chicago Daily News*, June 22, 1942.

69. See, for instance, Morison, *History of United States Naval Operations*, 4:151–52; Symonds, *Battle of Midway*, 5; Borneman, *The Admirals*, 254–55.

70. Casey, "Casey Reveals Navy's Experts Missed No Bets," *Chicago Daily News*, June 23, 1942.

71. Casey, "Casey's Story—How Japs Met Woe at Midway," Casey, "Casey Reveals Navy's Experts Missed No Bets," and Casey, "Massed Fleets Greatest Ever, Casey Reveals," *Chicago Daily News*, June 16, 23, and 24, 1942.

72. The titles that subscribed to the *Chicago Daily News* Foreign Service did, as a matter of course, receive Casey's dispatch for publication, a fact that the newspaper used in its marketing material. See "Bob Casey's Midway Battle World Beat," August 11, 1942, Foreign Correspondents Book, No. 16, box 10, Weller Papers.

73. Casey to Binder, May 23, 1942, Correspondence Series, box 3, Casey Papers; Berry to Drake, July 23, 1942, Drake Correspondence Folder, Entry 86, box 4, RG313; Brandenburg, "Bob Casey Back After 7 Months in Pacific" and "Casey Not Cynical After 30 Years of Newspapering," *Editor & Publisher*, July 11, 1942, and January 23,

1943. For his attitude toward British censors, see Casey, *Such Interesting People*, 308–11.

74. Maloney to McCormick, July 7, 1942, Johnston Folder, McCormick: Foreign Correspondents, I-62, box 6, Chicago Tribune Company Archives.

75. Casey to Knox, April 2, 1942, and McCloy to Knox, August 9, 1942, A7-1 File, Office of the Secretary: General Correspondence, Entry 13, box 14, RG80.

76. Maloney to McCormick, July 7, 1942, Johnston Folder, McCormick: Foreign Correspondents, I-62, box 6, Chicago Tribune Company Archives.

77. Mason, "Eyewitness," 40–45; Sweeney and Washburn, "It Ain't Over 'til It's Over," 365–69.

78. Carlson, *Johnston's Blunder*, 132–39, 200–208; Sweeney and Washburn, "It Ain't Over 'til It's Over," 363–64.

79. "Navy Announcement Says It Asked Quiz on Midway Article" and Manly, "'Smear Tribune' Attack to Bring Senate Debate," *Chicago Daily News*, August 8 and 9, 1942; Goren, "Communication Intelligence," 684. Representative Clare E. Hoffman also introduced H.RES.534 on August 13, accusing Knox of using "his official position for the advantage of his own newspaper." Memo to Capt. Beatty, August 15, 1942, File 12-1-37, Knox Office File, Entry 23, box 5, RG80.

80. "'Chicago Tribune' Exonerated by US Inquiry on Naval Story," *New York Herald Tribune*, August 20, 1942; "US Jury Clears Tribune," *Chicago Tribune*, August 20, 1942; Carlson, *Johnston's Blunder*, 122–25, 211–12; Sweeney and Washburn, "'Aint Justice Wonderful,'" 65–67. In private, senior Justice Department officials decried "the idiocy of the Navy" during this sorry saga; see Memo to the Attorney General, August 29, 1942, Attorney General Scrapbooks, box 16, Biddle Papers.

81. "US Jury Clears Tribune," *Chicago Tribune*, August 20, 1942; Carlson, *Johnston's Blunder*, 213; OWI, "Weekly Media Report," No. 31, September 5, 1942, box 1721, Entry 151, RG44.

82. Noderer, Chicago Notebook, February 4, 1943, XI-231, box 2, Noderer Papers. Johnston did submit the proofs of this book to the naval censors; see Hill to Howard, September 11, 1942, Censorship Folder, Entry 3, box 19, RG428.

83. Sweeney and Washburn, "'Aint Justice Wonderful,'" 35; Carlson, *Johnston's Blunder*, 150–51, 225–26. The *Tribune's* bosses had initially hoped to send Johnston back to Pearl Harbor; see Maloney to McCormick, June 25, 1942, Correspondents Folder (2), McCormick: Foreign Correspondents, I-62, box 2, Chicago Tribune Company Archives. On Johnston's plans after "the little bother that shook the country," see Johnston to Drake, September 14, 1942, War Correspondents Letters Folder, Entry 86, box 13, RG313.

84. "Knickerbocker Sees Better Copy in Europe," *Editor & Publisher*, July 4, 1942; Casey to Binder, May 23, 1942, Correspondence Series, box 3, Casey Papers.

85. Drake to Markey, July 16, 1942, Drake Correspondence Folder, Entry 86, box 4, RG313. In the wake of the Johnston affair, Roosevelt suggested "excluding all newspaper correspondents from expeditions of the army and navy except members of the AP, UP, and INS," although this idea went nowhere. See Stimson Diary, June 17, 1942, 39:94, Stimson Papers.

Chapter 4

1. Lee and Henschel, *MacArthur*, 161; Borneman, *MacArthur at War*, 158; Manchester, *American Caesar*, 282–83; James, *Years of MacArthur*, 2:109, 172–73; Masuda, *MacArthur in Asia*, 149–52; Sherrod, "At the Brink," 6, 8; Lee, *They Call It Pacific*, 170–71; Jacoby, "Dinner Meeting, River Club, New York City," July 13, 1942, 36–39, Far East Jacoby Dinner Folder, box 415, Time Inc. Records.

2. Rogers, *The Good Years*, 248.

3. Sebring to parents, March 4, 1942, Wartime Correspondence File, Sebring Papers; AP, "US Correspondents Arrive in Australia," Lardner, "Reporters Daunt Army in Australia," and "Robert Sherrod," *New York Times*, March 16 and 27, 1942, and February 15, 1994; Lardner, *Southwest Passage*, 23–32; Boomhower, *Dispatches*, 34–38; Kent, Oral History, December 21, 1970, Truman Library; "Last Appraisal," *Time*, November 2, 1942; Weller, *Weller's War*, 343.

4. Lardner, "Reporters Daunt Army in Australia," *New York Times*, March 27, 1942.

5. James, *Years of MacArthur*, 2:120–25.

6. MacArthur to Marshall, April 4, 1942, Adjutant General: General Correspondence, 000.73, box 863, RG496; MacArthur to Marshall, May 1, 1942, War Department File, box 15, RG3, MacArthur Papers.

7. Marshall to MacArthur, No. 1005, April 1, 1942, BPR File, 000.73, Entry 499, box 5, RG165; Marshall to MacArthur, undated [but discusses April 27, 1942, dispatch], and May 10, 1942, War Department File, box 15, RG3, MacArthur Papers.

8. MacArthur to Marshall, May 15, 1942, War Department File, box 15, RG3, MacArthur Papers; Commonwealth of Australia, "Release of Military Information," May 1, 1942, and War Cabinet Minute, "Censorship of Information Regarding Operations," May 7, 1942, both in Adjutant General: General Correspondence, 000.73, box 863, RG496. For the broader impact of MacArthur on command and strategic matters, see Bell, *Unequal Allies*, 103; Horner, *High Command*, 178–92; Dean, *MacArthur's Coalition*, 48–53. For the importance of the communiqué, see Dunn, *Pacific Microphone*, 161.

9. Durdin, "Singapore Press Relations," undated, and Durdin to Sulzberger, April 1, 1942, Durdin Folder, box 21, New York Times Company Records: Arthur Hays Sulzberger Papers.

10. DeLuce, Cable, undated, Censorship 1941 Folder, Series 3: Subject Files, AP 02A.3, box 39, AP Corporate Archives; Noderer, Singapore-Malaya Notebook, January 4, 1942, 13, XI-231, box 2, Noderer Papers; editorial, "British Brass Hats and American Reporters," *Chicago Tribune*, January 13, 1942; Carlson, *Cairo to Damascus*, 264; Weller, *Weller's War*, 195.

11. Tribune to Noderer, March 19, 1942, Noderer Folder, McCormick: Foreign Correspondents, I-62, box 6, Chicago Tribune Company Archives; "Press Wireless May Speed Up Australian News," *Editor & Publisher*, April 4, 1942.

12. Noderer to Maloney, June 6, 1942, XI-231, box 1, Noderer Papers.

13. Weller, "A Memorandum on Censorship and Press Relations in the SWPA," July 19, 1942, A7-1 File, Office of the Secretary: General Correspondence, Entry 13, box 13, RG80.

14. White, *Green Armour*, 55. Even after arriving in Australia, MacArthur retained the power to control "all press releases from the Philippines." See Marshall to MacArthur, No. 1434, April 22, 1942, BPR File, 000.7, Entry 499, box 4, RG165.

15. GHQ SWPA Communiqué, May 7 and 28, 1942, Series 5: Communiqués and Press Releases, box 47, RG4, MacArthur Papers.

16. Sebring to parents, April 7, 1942, Wartime Correspondence File, Sebring Papers.

17. Evans and Donegan, "Battle of Brisbane"; James, *Years of MacArthur*, 2:253–55.

18. Boni, *Want to Be a War Correspondent?*, 8.

19. James, *Years of MacArthur*, 2:245; MacArthur to AGWAR, July 16, 1942, BPR File, 000.77, Entry 499, box 6, RG165; Fitch to the Commander-in-Chief, December 14, 1942, BPR File, 000.7, Entry 499, box 13, RG165; Kunz, "Decisions That Counted," 24–25, box 59, Kunz Papers; Robinson, *Fight for New Guinea*, 15, 23; Lardner, *Southwest Passage*, 51.

20. Catledge to Surles, November 2, 1942, BPR File, 000.77, Entry 499, box 7, RG165. Catledge, the editor of the *Chicago Sun*, launched "an investigation to find out why we have not been getting more from our correspondent, Edward Angly," who had been based in Australia for months.

21. JE to LPY, September 17, 1942, AP War Correspondents and Bureaus Folder, Series 3: Subject Files, AP 02A.3, box 51, AP Corporate Archives; emphasis in the original. The consensus among executives was that costs had risen 15 percent since Pearl Harbor. See Schneider, "US War Staffs on All Fronts Face Toughest Job in 4th Year," *Editor & Publisher*, September 12, 1942.

22. MacGregor, *Integration*, 17–18, 24–25; Ralph, *They Passed This Way*, 243–49; McManus, *Fire and Fortitude*, 221–22; Boomhower, *Dispatches*, 61–63.

23. Hall, ed., *Love, War, and the 96th Engineers*, 47, 77; "Sherrod-LBJ Report: Australia," April 1942.

24. "Sherrod-LBJ Report: Australia," April 1942; Anderson, "Memo for the Files: Processing Note," November 18, 1991; Schaller, *MacArthur*, 65. On Johnson in the theater, see Caro, *Means of Ascent*, 35–44.

25. Manthorp to Hicks, June 18, 1942, Life: Wartime Picture Pool Folder, box 417, Time Inc. Records.

26. Milner, *Victory in Papua*, 8, 10, 54; "Sherrod-LBJ Report: Australia," April 1942; Noderer to Maloney, August 26, 1942, XI-231, box 1, Noderer Papers.

27. Woods to Pacini, July 4, 1942, Adjutant General: General Correspondence, 000.71, box 863, RG496; "Sherrod-LBJ Report: Australia," April 1942; Guard, *Pacific War Uncensored*, 198.

28. Darnton, "US Fliers Averaging 22 Years in Age Score in First Test by Effective Raid on Rabaul," "Young, Strong, Fearless," and "This War Dispatch Is for Home Folks," *New York Times*, April 12, May 10 and 18, 1942.

29. Kenney, Diary, July 28, 29 and August 3, 1942, box 1, Kenney Papers; Kenney, *Kenney Reports*, 33–61; Griffith, *MacArthur's Airman*, 46–47, 57–66, 81–89.

30. Kenney, Diary, August 3, 1942, box 1, Kenney Papers; Van Atta, "US Force in Australia Small," *Washington Post*, August 7, 1942; Marshall to MacArthur, August 10, 1942, War Department File, box 15, RG3, MacArthur Papers.

31. Noderer, "Hit with a Brick in Each Hand, Is Kenney's Motto," *Chicago Tribune*, September 17, 1942; Johnston, *New Guinea Diary*, 153–55.

32. McDaniel to Haugland, July 23, 1942, General Correspondence, box 1, Haugland Papers.

33. Sebring, "Allied Plight in New Guinea Due to Underestimating Japs' Ability," *Boston Globe*, September 13, 1942; White, *Green Armour*, 10–11, 150; Fitzsimmons, *Kokoda*, 353–54, 358–59; Dean, *MacArthur's Coalition*, 114.

34. "Death in Line of Duty Comes to *Life* Correspondent Jacoby," *Life*, May 11, 1942; Lascher, *Eve*, 344–48.

35. Lascher, *Eve*, 346–48; White, *Green Armour*, 183.

36. "AP Foreign Correspondents," June 22, 1942, AP War Correspondents and Bureaus Folder, Series 3: Subject Files, AP 02A.3, box 51, AP Corporate Archives; Thompson to Gould, January 22, 1942, General Correspondence, box 1, Haugland Papers; Bell to Berry, January 23, 1942, A7-1 File, Office of the Secretary: General Correspondence, Entry 12, box 79, RG80.

37. McDaniel to Haugland, July 23, 1942, General Correspondence, box 1, Haugland Papers; Haugland, *Letter from New Guinea*, 6–7.

38. Haugland, *43 Days*; Haugland, *Letter from New Guinea*, 3–5, 8–41, 46–69, 86–87, 110–12, 123–28; Schedler, Telegram, September 19 and 23, 1942, Telegrams from New Guinea Folder, box 23, Haugland Papers.

39. Schneider, "Haugland Diary Reveals Fight to Survive Jungle," *Editor & Publisher*, October 3, 1942; Middleton et al to Haugland, October 2, 1942, and McDaniel to Haugland, undated, General Correspondence, box 1, Haugland Papers.

40. Sebring, "Allied Plight in New Guinea Due to Underestimating Japs' Ability," *Boston Globe*, September 13, 1942; Sebring to parents, October 4, 1942, Wartime Correspondence File, Sebring Papers.

41. Noderer, "Reporter's Life in Guinea," *Chicago Tribune*, October 14, 1942; Sebring, "Reporter Tours War-Battered Port Moresby," *New York Herald Tribune*, October 11, 1942; Sebring to parents, October 4, 1942, Wartime Correspondence File, Sebring Papers; Robinson, *Fight for New Guinea*, 68–70; Lardner, *Southwest Passage*, 170–71, 175–76.

42. Sebring, "Seeds of Defeat for Japan Seen in New Guinea," *New York Herald Tribune*, December 11, 1942; Robinson, *Fight for New Guinea*, 68–70, 124–25; Marshall to MacArthur, "Censorship Personnel," September 7, 1942, Adjutant General: General Correspondence, 000.73, box 863, RG496.

43. Haugland, *Letter from New Guinea*, 128.

44. Milner, *Victory in Papua*, 103–119.

45. Milner, *Victory in Papua*, 108n19.

46. Milner, *Victory in Papua*, 108, 375–76; Robinson, *Fight for New Guinea*, 150.

47. MacArthur to James, October 20, 1942, Darnton Folder, box 15, New York Times Company Records: Arthur Hays Sulzberger Papers; Milner, *Victory in Papua*, 108n19.

48. UP, "Darnton Buried at Port Moresby," *New York Herald Tribune*, October 23, 1942; Sebring to parents, October 26, 1942, Wartime Correspondence File, Sebring Papers; Weller to Mrs. Darnton, October 22, 1942, WWII: New Guinea Dispatches

Folder, box 27, Weller Papers; Weller, *Weller's War*, 343; Haugland, *Letter from New Guinea*, 138.

49. Noderer, New Guinea Notebook, November 13, 1942, 1–2, XI-231, box 2, Noderer Papers.

50. Noderer, New Guinea Notebook, November 13–14, 1942, 2–5, XI-231, box 2, Noderer Papers.

51. Milner, *Victory in Papua*, 168–69; Noderer, New Guinea Notebook, November 17 and 18, 1942, 8–9, XI-231, box 2, Noderer Papers.

52. "Report of the Commanding General Buna Forces on the Buna Campaign," undated, 100–103, Folder 17, box 13, White Papers; "Noderer Sees Biggest Stories Yet from Pacific," *Editor & Publisher*, February 20, 1943; Noderer, New Guinea Notebook, November 16, 1942, 7–8, XI-231, box 2, Noderer Papers.

53. Noderer, New Guinea Notebook, November 18, 24, and 25, 1942, 9–10, 19, 20, XI-231, box 2, Noderer Papers; "This Story Came to Chicago by Runner, Canoe, Ship, Radio," *Chicago Tribune*, December 1, 1942.

54. Noderer, New Guinea Notebook, November 22, 1942, 15–16, XI-231, box 2, Noderer Papers.

55. "Dispersal, April 1/43," AP War Correspondents and Bureaus Folder, Series 3: Subject Files, AP 02A.3, box 51, AP Corporate Archives.

56. Harding Diary, November 29, 1942, Entry 53, box 3, RG319; Milner, *Victory in Papua*, 201; Noderer, New Guinea Notebook, November 23, 24, 26, and 29, 1942, 17–20, 29–30, XI-231, box 2, Noderer Papers.

57. Sutherland, Memo, November 29, 1942, Letters (Official) Folder, box 1, Eichelberger Papers; Eichelberger and MacKaye, *Jungle Road*, 21; Luvaas, ed., *Dear Miss Em*, 62; Borneman, *MacArthur at War*, 245–47.

58. Noderer, New Guinea Notebook, December 1, 1942, 33, XI-231, box 2, Noderer Papers. On Eichelberger and the press, see White, "Press Conference Remarks," September 2, 1942, Folder 17, box 13, White Papers.

59. Noderer, New Guinea Notebook, December 1, 1942, 33, 34–36, XI-231, box 2, Noderer Papers.

60. Durdin, "'Little Skunk Face' Flies to Buna Line," *New York Times*, December 6, 1942.

61. Noderer, New Guinea Notebook, December 3 and 5, 1942, 41, 43–45, XI-231, box 2, Noderer Papers.

62. Noderer, New Guinea Notebook, December 5, 1942, 45–47, XI-231, box 2, Noderer Papers.

63. Eichelberger to Sutherland, December 5, 1942, Letters (Official) Folder, box 1, Eichelberger Papers; Noderer, New Guinea Notebook, December 5, 1942, 47–51, XI-231, box 2, Noderer Papers; Milner, *Victory in Papua*, 241–45; McManus, *Fire and Fortitude*, 321–25.

64. Durdin was particularly delighted, and relieved, to discover that his editors had increased his life insurance policy to $25,000. Durdin to Sulzberger, December 11, 1942, Durdin Folder, box 21, New York Times Company Records: Arthur Hays Sulzberger Papers.

65. Noderer, "Tribune Writer in Front Lines of Buna Battle," *Chicago Tribune*, December 9, 1942; Durdin, "The Battle of Buna," *New York Times*, December 9, 1942.

66. "Noderer Sees Biggest Stories Yet from Pacific," *Editor & Publisher*, February 20, 1943; Noderer, "Allies Battle Hand to Hand in Buna Area," *Chicago Tribune*, December 11, 1942; Durdin, "Buna Beach Fight Led by Sergeant," *New York Times*, December 11, 1942.

67. "Col. M'Cormick Hails Tribune's Men at Fronts," *Chicago Tribune*, December 11, 1942; Maloney to Noderer, December 4, 1942, XI-231, box 1, Noderer Papers; Noderer to McCormick, December 15, 1942, Noderer Folder, McCormick: Foreign Correspondents, I-62, box 6, Chicago Tribune Company Archives; Johnston, *New Guinea Diary*, 242–43.

68. Weller, *Weller's War*, 382–83; Durdin, "Buna Battle Reflects Grim War" and Durdin, "Buna Area Wind-Up and American Saga," *New York Times*, December 24, 1942, and January 8, 1943.

69. AP, "Allies Rout Foe's Convoy Off Buna" and "US Bombers Rout Flotilla Off Buna," *New York Times*, December 3 and 9, 1942.

70. See, for example, UP, Allies Ring Buna in Stiff Fighting," AP, "Buna Reinforced Despite Sinkings," UP, "MacArthur's Forces Squeeze Foe Hard," AP, "Buna-Gona Fighting Is Close, AP, "Japanese Repulsed at Buna," UP, "Allies Send Tanks into Buna Attack," and AP, "Japanese Plight 'Desperate' at Buna, MacArthur Reports," *New York Times*, November 22 and 27, 1942, and December 2, 4, 11, 21, and 24, 1942.

71. Milner, *Victory in Papua*, 322.

72. "Africa Invasion Ranks First in Best Story Lists," *Editor & Publisher*, December 5, 1942.

73. Binder to Weller, February 19, 1943, WWII: New Guinea Dispatches Folder, box 27, Weller Papers.

74. Prentice to Luce, May 16, 1945, Far East Misc. Folder, box 417, Time Inc. Records.

75. Based on a content analysis of *New York Times* published stories, December 1942. On the process by which stories were placed on the front page, see Leff, *Buried*, 167–69.

76. Rogers, *The Good Years*, 265–66.

77. "Noderer Sees Biggest Stories Yet from Pacific," *Editor & Publisher*, February 20, 1943; Eichelberger and MacKaye, *Jungle Road*, 76–77; Eichelberger to Milner, January 6, 1951, Eichelberger Letter Folder, Entry 53, box 3, RG319; Borneman, *MacArthur at War*, 258; Noderer, Australia Notebook, January 4, 1943, 4, XI-231, box 2, Noderer Papers.

78. Noderer, Australia Notebook, January 9 and 10, 1943, 8–10, XI-231, box 2, Noderer Papers.

79. MacArthur, Order of the Day, January 1943, Official Correspondence, box 1, RG3, MacArthur Papers.

80. Copies of dispatches by Robertson of the INS, Haugland of the AP, McCullough of the *Philadelphia Inquirer*, in Letters (Official) Folder, box 1, Eichelberger Papers.

81. Noderer, Australia Notebook, January 12, 1943, 11, XI-231, box 2, Noderer Papers; "Noderer Sees Biggest Stories Yet from Pacific," *Editor & Publisher*, February 20, 1943;

Noderer, "Yanks' Leader in Guinea Fights Like a Private," *Chicago Tribune*, January 10, 1943.

82. Eichelberger himself bought into this idea; see Luvaas, ed., *Dear Miss Em*, 64.

83. UP, "M'Arthur Inspires New Guinea Front," *New York Times*, December 5, 1942.

84. Luvaas, ed., *Dear Miss Em*, 65; James, *Years of MacArthur*, 2:271–77; Borneman, *MacArthur at War*, 263–65.

85. Gottfried to Luce, June 6, 1943, Censorship Folder, box 416, Time Inc. Records; "Kenney: Air Commander of the Southwest Pacific," *Time*, January 18, 1943.

86. For the strategic reasons behind MacArthur's demand for a swift end to this campaign, see Dean, *MacArthur's Coalition*, 129, 142–44, 187–88.

Chapter 5

1. Jacobs to Lovette, "Change of Duty," Knox Office File: General Records, 57-2-17, Entry 23, box 3, RG80; Manning, "Lovette Says Navy Press Releases Must Be Factual" and "Navy News Not for Psychological Effect," *Editor & Publisher*, August 1 and October 24, 1942.

2. King to Edson, September 29, 1949, Correspondence: Edson Folder, box 17, King Papers; Morison, *History of United States Naval Operations*, 4:245–63; Millett, *Semper Fidelis*, 362–65; Frank, *Guadalcanal*, 16, 33–36, 46–53, 57.

3. Frank, *Guadalcanal*, 59–64, 72–79, 83–123; Merillat, *Guadalcanal Remembered*, 60.

4. Buell, *Master of Sea Power*, 221–22.

5. AP, "Navy Opens Pacific Offensive," *Los Angeles Times*, August 8, 1942; AP, "US Navy Still Attacking," *Chicago Tribune*, August 10, 1942.

6. "Press Release by COMINCH," August 10, 1942, Press and Press Releases Folder, box 23, King Papers.

7. AP, "Navy Opens Pacific Offensive," *Los Angeles Times*, August 8, 1942; AP, "Continuing Assault on Solomons," *Atlanta Constitution*, August 10, 1942.

8. AP, "Cautious Communiqué Gives No Hint of Losses," *Boston Globe*, August 15, 1942.

9. Borneman, *MacArthur at War*, 217–18; Frank, *Guadalcanal*, 90.

10. Marshall to MacArthur, August 14 and 15, 1942, War Department File, box 15, RG3, MacArthur Papers. For an earlier breach from MacArthur's HQ, see Heslep to Ryan, "Censors in Australia Apparently Remiss," August 12, 1942, Press Dispatches Misc. Folder, Entry 1A, box 145, RG216.

11. Marshall to MacArthur, August 14, 1942, and MacArthur to Marshall, August 15, 1942, War Department File, box 15, RG3, MacArthur Papers.

12. MacArthur to Marshall, August 19, 1942, War Department File, box 15, RG3, MacArthur Papers.

13. Price to James, August 19, 1942, A7- File, Office of the Secretary: General Correspondence, Entry 13, box 13, RG80; Clauson to Drake, August 14, 1942, War Correspondents Letters Folder, Entry 86, box 13, RG313.

14. Denig, Oral History (henceforth OH), 7, 24–25, box 2, Denig Papers; "First Conference of the Navy PROs," July 28–31, 1941, 17–18, PI Conference Folder, Entry 3, box 122, RG428; Ulbrich, *Preparing for Victory*, 89–90.

15. Denig, OH, 8, 16–17, 22–23, 27–28 box 2, Denig Papers; Ulbrich, *Preparing for Victory*, 90–91, 114–15, 160; Merillat, *Guadalcanal Remembered*, 18; Stavisky, *Marine Combat Correspondent*, 4, 6–8.

16. Denig, OH, 28–30, box 2, Denig Papers; Merillat to parents, April 26, 1942, Correspondence to Parents: WW2 Folder, box 1, Merillat Papers; Merillat, *Guadalcanal Remembered*, 8–21; "Marine Correspondent Back from Pacific," *Editor & Publisher*, March 13, 1943.

17. Merillat to parents, July 20, 1942, Correspondence Files: Specialist Commission in USMCR, box 2, Merillat Papers.

18. "Robert C. Miller—UPI War Correspondent," UPI website, July 29, 2004; "Richard Tregaskis, Author, Dead at 56," *New York Times*, August 17, 1973.

19. Miller to Drake, August 6, 1942, War Correspondents Letters Folder, Entry 86, box 13, RG313; Tregaskis, *Guadalcanal Diary*, 9, 23; Commanding Officer Combat Group "A," "The Coming Offensive Action in Guadalcanal Area," August 3, 1942, Folder 34: Correspondence 1941–44, box 26, Tregaskis Papers.

20. Merillat, "Press on Guadalcanal," undated, Press and Censorship Folder, box 1, Merillat Papers; Drake to Miller, August 29, 1942, Drake Correspondence Folder, Entry 86, box 4, RG313.

21. Merillat, "Press on Guadalcanal," undated, Press and Censorship Folder, box 1, Merillat Papers.

22. Montrose to Drake, August 13, 1942, War Correspondents Letters Folder, Entry 86, box 13, RG313.

23. Frank, *Guadalcanal*, 256–59.

24. Merillat, "Here's a Tip to War Reporters: Keep Shoes on!" *Chicago Tribune*, September 2, 1942; Tregaskis, *Guadalcanal Diary*, 67–83.

25. Tregaskis, *Guadalcanal Diary*, 83–85.

26. Miller to Drake, August 14, 1942, War Correspondents Letters Folder, Entry 86, box 13, RG313; Merillat, *Guadalcanal Remembered*, 76, 119; Baldwin, Memo to James, October 12, 1942, Censorship Folder, box 125, New York Times Company Records: Arthur Hays Sulzberger Papers.

27. Frank, *Guadalcanal*, 139–40, 156–57, 192–93; Toll, *Conquering Tide*, 69–75, 99.

28. Miller, "Eyewitness Tells Raid on Solomon Islands," *Los Angeles Times*, August 29, 1942; Tregaskis, "Marines Literally Blasted Japs Loose from Solomon Islands," *Washington Post*, August 29, 1942.

29. Merillat, *Guadalcanal Remembered*, 18–19; Merillat, "Eyewitness with Marines Tells of Storming Solomons," *Boston Globe*, August 30, 1942; Hurlbut, "Sergeant Tells Marines' Story of Guadalcanal," *New York Herald Tribune*, September 1, 1942.

30. Prochnau, *Once Upon a Distant War*, 264. Toll, *Conquering Tide*, 97, likewise claims that "[t]he campaign received fulsome press coverage," while Cameron, *American Samurai*, 99, argues that until the November invasion of North Africa, the Marines "held center stage in the public eye. The exotic setting of the campaign and the heavy press coverage guaranteed a large and receptive audience."

31. Pace, "Tillman Durdin, 91, Reporter in China during World War II," *New York Times*, July 9, 1998; Noderer, New Guinea Notebook, December 3, 1942, 41; James

to Sulzberger, May 13, 1946, Durdin Folder, box 21, New York Times Company Records: Arthur Hays Sulzberger Papers.

32. *AP Inter-Office*, April 16, 1941, General Information Folder, WWII Book Project Folder, AP28, Writings About the AP, Series II, box 14, AP Corporate Archives.

33. Merillat, *Guadalcanal Remembered*, 119; Tregaskis, *Guadalcanal Diary*, 163–64.

34. "Tough as Marines," *Time*, November 16, 1942; Schneider, "Stowe at Front with Red Army, Sets Precedent," *Editor & Publisher*, October 17, 1942; Merillat, *Guadalcanal Remembered*, 127–29; Tregaskis, *Guadalcanal Diary*, 193.

35. Tregaskis, *Guadalcanal Diary*, 209; Merillat, *Guadalcanal Remembered*, 137; Merillat to Markey, "Correspondents who have visited Guadalcanal," November 11, 1942, Press and Censorship Folder, box 1, Merillat Papers.

36. Merillat, *Guadalcanal Remembered*, 143–48.

37. Tregaskis, *Guadalcanal Diary*, 218, 224–25.

38. Cates to family, October 28, 1942, Correspondence: General Folder, box 2, Cates Papers; Durdin, "It's Never Dull on Guadalcanal," *New York Times*, September 18, 1942; Merillat, *Guadalcanal Remembered*, 149.

39. Frank, *Guadalcanal*, 252, 316–20; Merillat, *Guadalcanal Remembered*, 177; Vandegrift and Asprey, *Once a Marine*, 184.

40. Frank, *Guadalcanal*, 330–31.

41. AP, "Yanks in Grave Peril on Guadalcanal," *Boston* Globe, October 17, 1942; Minifie, "Japanese Fleet Massing North of Guadalcanal," *New York Herald Tribune*, October 17, 1942.

42. Baldwin, "Japan's Hold on West Pacific Not Broken in Almost a Year," *New York Times*, October 23, 1942.

43. Drake to Beecher, October 24, 1942, Drake Correspondence Folder, Entry 86, box 4, RG313; Tremaine to Drake, October 7 and 16, 1942, War Correspondents Letters Folder, Entry 86, box 13, RG313.

44. Hurd, "Sea Battle in Dark," *New York Times*, October 13, 1942, and "Rip Jap Fleet, Sink 6 Ships," *Chicago Tribune*, October 14, 1942.

45. Lovette to editor, *Detroit News*, October 22, 1942, Lovette to editor, *Chicago Times*, November 3, 1942, Lovette to Finnegan, November 3, 1942, and Lovette to Monroe, October 26, 1942, all in A7-1 File, Office of the Secretary: General Correspondence, Entry 13, box 12, RG80.

46. Miller to Sorrells, November 2, 1942, AP Folder, Entry 1A, box 145, RG216, Walsh to Knox, November 10, 1942, and Knox to Walsh, November 17, 1942, all in A7-1 File, Office of the Secretary: General Correspondence, Entry 13, box 12, RG80; King to Knox, November 22, 1942, Memo to Secretary of Navy Folder, box 22, King Papers.

47. McCoskrie, Special G-2 Report, November 28, 1942, BPR File, 000.77, Entry 499, box 6, RG165. On the creation of the *Chicago Sun*, see Edwards, *Foreign Policy of Col. McCormick's Tribune*, 194–205. Editorial writers at the *Sun* privately provided Roosevelt with stinging criticisms of MacArthur's censorship in the SWPA; see Brant to Roosevelt, August 26, 1942, PPF7859, Roosevelt Papers.

48. OWI, Bureau of Intelligence, "Military Information," November 14, 1942, Entry 171, box 1843, RG44; Maas, "Still No Unified Command in the Pacific, November 16,

1942, Maas Folder, box 15, Halsey Papers; Stimson Diary, October 29, 1942, 40:182, Stimson Papers.

49. Knox to Sulzberger, November 3, 1942, World War II Folder, box 274, New York Times Company Records: Arthur Hays Sulzberger Papers; Burlingame, *Don't Let Them Scare You*, 201–203. Davis, the head of the OWI, had been pushing for the prompt release of naval sinkings for months. See Hepburn, Memo for Commander-in-Chief, US Fleet, August 4, 1942, Censorship Folder, Entry 3, box 19, RG428.

50. CINCPAC to COMINCH, 2115, November 1, 1942, and COMINCH to CINCPAC, 1618, November 2, 1942, *Nimitz "Gray Book"*; Lawrence, "Damaged Ship Lost" and "Admiral Stresses Unity of Command," *New York Times*, November 1 and 16, 1942.

51. Merillat to Markey, "Correspondents who have visited Guadalcanal," November 11, 1942, Press and Censorship Folder, box 1, Merillat Papers; Merillat to parents, November 12, 1942, Correspondence Files: Specialist Commission in USMCR, box 2, Merillat Papers; "Tough as Marines," *Time*, November 16, 1942; Merillat, *Guadalcanal Remembered*, 152, 168.

52. "Carleton Kent Returns from South Pacific," *Editor & Publisher*, January 30, 1943.

53. "Carleton Kent Returns from South Pacific," *Editor & Publisher*, January 30, 1943; Merillat, *Guadalcanal Remembered*, 175–76, 179.

54. Kent to Drake, October 17, 1942, War Correspondents Letters Folder, Entry 86, box 13, RG313.

55. Berry to Drake, November 6, 1942, A7-2 File, Office of the Secretary: General Correspondence, Entry 13, box 15, RG80.

56. "Dowling Reports on Life on Guadalcanal," *Editor & Publisher*, November 7, 1942.

57. Drake to Markey, September 11, 1942, Drake Correspondence Folder, Entry 86, box 4, RG313; Bassett to Port Director, US Navy, Fiji, November 27, 1942, General Plans and Directives Concerning Civilian Correspondents Folder, Entry 86, box 13, RG313.

58. Cates to family, October 28, 1942, Correspondence: General Folder, box 2, Cates Papers.

59. McFadden, "Hanson Baldwin, Military Writer, Dies," and "Report on the Pacific," *New York Times*, November 4, 1991, and October 31, 1942; Baldwin to Sulzberger, May 1, 1942, Baldwin Folder, box 4, New York Times Company Records: Arthur Hays Sulzberger Papers.

60. Vandegrift and Asprey, *Once a Marine*, 163–64.

61. Vandegrift and Asprey, *Once a Marine*, 164.

62. Drake to Lovette, September 17, 1942, Drake Correspondence Folder, Entry 86, box 4, RG313; "Excerpt from letter from Secretary of Navy," October 24, 1942, Nimitz PR Letters Folder, Entry 86, box 4, RG313; Baldwin, Memo to James, October 12, 1942, Censorship Folder, box 125, New York Times Company Records: Arthur Hays Sulzberger Papers; Durdin to Sulzberger, November 27, 1942, Durdin Folder, box 21, New York Times Company Records: Arthur Hays Sulzberger Papers; Davies, *Baldwin of the Times*, 136–38.

63. Baldwin, "Three Islands Devastated Before Landing by US Marines" and "Solomons Operations a Magnet for Navies," *New York Times*, September 28 and October 25, 1942.

64. Hersey to Drake, September 18, 1942, War Correspondents Letters Folder, Entry 86, box 13, RG313; Toll, *Conquering Tide*, 108–109.

65. Hersey, "The Marines on Guadalcanal," *Life*, November 9, 1942. On Hersey's time on the island, see Merillat, *Guadalcanal Remembered*, 156, 169; Merillat, "Press on Guadalcanal," undated, Press and Censorship Folder, box 1, Merillat Papers; Hersey, *Into the Valley*.

66. Hicks to Andrew, January 28, 1942, Life: Wartime Picture Pool Folder, box 433, Time Inc. Records; Brinkley, *Luce*, 229.

67. Thompson to Hicks, January 19, 1942, Hicks to Lovette, February 23, 1942, and Sheridan, "Still Picture Pool," June 29, 1943, all in Life: Wartime Picture Pool Folder, box 433, Time Inc. Records.

68. "Gripes about the Pool," September 1942, Life: Wartime Picture Pool Folder, box 433, Time Inc. Records.

69. Montrose to Drake, August 13, 1942, War Correspondents Letters Folder, Entry 86, box 13, RG313; Drake to Berry, August 29, 1942, Drake Correspondence Folder, Entry 86, box 4, RG313; Assistant Picture Editor to Smith, February 22, 1944, Life: Wartime Picture Pool Folder, box 433, Time Inc. Records.

70. Greeley, *Two Thousand Yard Stare*, 1–2, 39, 62, 69; "Background Report: Editorial Review," March 16, 1943, Life, 1943 Folder, box 433, Time Inc. Records.

71. "Sinking of Wasp," *Life*, April 5, 1943.

72. Drake to Merillat, October 30, 1942, Drake Correspondence Folder, Entry 86, box 4, RG313; "US Fights for the Solomons," *Life*, November 9, 1942.

73. Cates to family, December 29, 1942, Correspondence: General Folder, box 2, Cates Papers.

74. Hurd, "Joy at Sea Victory" and Hurd, "750 Die on Island," *New York Times*, November 18 and 21, 1942.

75. Wolfert, "First Eyewitness Account of Greatest US Naval Victory," *Boston Globe*, November 27, 1942.

76. Merillat, "The Wolfert Story," undated, Press and Censorship Folder, box 1, Merillat Papers; Merillat, *Guadalcanal Remembered*, 214–15. Wolfert, like his colleagues, left the island because, as he put it, the "whole communications situation has me feeling full of SNAFU out here." Wolfert to Drake, October 30, 1942, War Correspondents Letters Folder, Entry 86, box 13, RG313.

77. Merillat to parents, November 2, 1942, Correspondence Files: Specialist Commission in USMCR, box 2, Merillat Papers; Merillat, *Guadalcanal Remembered*, 182–83

78. Division of Public Relations, US Marine Corps, "Progress Report," December 8, 1942, Entry 1005, box 1, RG127; Division of Public Relations, US Marine Corps, "Security Guide, undated, Entry 1008, box 3, RG127; Stavisky, *Marine Combat Correspondent*, 26–27.

79. "Marine Private Tells of Tenaru River Battle," Hurlbut, "'Missing in Action,' Six Guadalcanal Fighters Reach Safety after Jungle Ordeal," and Hurlbut, "Marine Patrol Wipes Out Jap Unit at Malaita," November 10 and 20, and December 12, 1942, Entry 1005, box 1, RG127.

80. Tregaskis, "Ideas for Stories," undated, Folder 3: Notes, box 25, Tregaskis Papers; Prochnau, *Once Upon a Distant War*, 264–65.

81. Vandegrift to Holcomb, September 10, 1942, box 2, Vandegrift Papers. See also Morriss, *South Pacific Diary*, 87.

82. Schneider, "Stowe at Front with Red Army, Sets Precedent," *Editor & Publisher*, October 17, 1942.

83. Tregaskis to parents, November 7, 1942, Folder 35: Correspondence 1941–44; "Notes Re: Guadalcanal Diary," November 14, 1965, Folder 12: 15th Anniversary Article, both in box 26, Tregaskis Papers.

84. "Runyon Lauds 'Guadalcanal Diary,'" *Atlanta Constitution*, January 31, 1943; Tregaskis, *Guadalcanal Diary*, 232–33.

85. "Defense of Diaries," *Washington Post*, January 31, 1943.

86. Tregaskis, *Guadalcanal Diary*, 130.

87. Editorial clipping, "That Man Halsey," *Seattle Journal*, January 5, 1943; Halsey to Haire, January 18, 1943, General Correspondence Folder, box 3, Halsey Papers. On Halsey and the press, see Hughes, *Halsey*, 225–28; Toll, *Conquering Tide*, 195–97.

88. Tregaskis to parents, January 23, 1943, Folder 35: Correspondence 1941–44, box 26, Tregaskis Papers; Tregaskis, "Halsey Sees 'Absolute Defeat' for Axis Forces This Year," *Washington Post*, January 3, 1943; McManus, *Fire and Fortitude*, 364–65.

89. "Army Takes over Guadalcanal Job," *New York Times*, January 22, 1943; Frank, *Guadalcanal*, 521–22, 593–97; Toll, *Conquering Tide*, 185.

90. Miller, "End of the Battle in Americans' Favor on Guadalcanal Related," *Los Angeles Times*, February 12, 1943; Miller, "Reunion in a South Seas Jungle," *New York Herald Tribune*, Februay 14, 1943.

91. Editorial, "Guadalcanal," *New York Times*, February 10, 1942.

Chapter 6

1. McCombs to Hulbard, "Rio Cable," August 14, 1942, Folder 45, Time Dispatches; "1,451 in Today from Far East on Gripsholm," *New York Herald Tribune*, August 25, 1942.

2. Daniell, "Eden Asserts Foe Murdered Britons," *New York Times*, March 11, 1942.

3. Minutes, CWI Meeting, May 12, 1942, and attached memorandum, "Pros and Cons on Hate Atrocities," Entry 6E, box 11, RG208.

4. McConaughy to Ragadale, "Japanese Atrocities," May 7, 1942, Folder 32, Time Dispatches. In late January, the Japanese had informed the Allies that "they would apply the Geneva Convention, even though they had not ratified it." See Tanaka, *Hidden Horrors*, 24, 76.

5. Heinrichs, *American Ambassador*, 361–62.

6. "Gripsholm at Rio," *New York Times*, August 11, 1942; McCombs to Hulbard, "Rio Cable," August 14, 1942, Folder 45, Time Dispatches.

7. "Gripsholm Brings 1,500 from Orient," *New York Times*, August 26, 1942.

8. AP, "Gripsholm Refugees Bare Japs' Tortures," *Atlanta Constitution*, August 27, 1942; "Gripsholm Brings 1,500 from Orient," *New York Times*, August 26, 1942; McConaughy to Ragadale, "Japanese Atrocities," May 7, 1942, Folder 32, Time Dispatches.

9. Arnold to Roosevelt, "Raid on Tokyo," May 3, 1942, PSF (Safe): Japan, Roosevelt Papers.

10. "Tokyo Raid Was First Long-Range Censorship Test," *Editor & Publisher*, May 1, 1943.

11. Arnold to Roosevelt, "Raid on Tokyo," May 3, 1942, PSF (Safe): Japan, Roosevelt Papers; "No Confirmation in Washington" and "Tokyo Adds Detail," *New York Times*, April 18 and 19, 1942; Roosevelt, *Press Conferences*, April 21, 1942, No. 820, 6–7.

12. Arnold to Roosevelt, "Raid on Tokyo," May 3, 1942, PSF (Safe): Japan, Roosevelt Papers; "Tokyo Raid Was First Long-Range Censorship Test," *Editor & Publisher*, May 1, 1943; Berry to Mylander, September 8, 1942, Censorship Folder, Entry 3, box 19, RG428.

13. Dower, *War Without Mercy*, 48–49; AP, "Japs Threaten to Kill Captive US Fliers," *New York Herald Tribune*, October 20, 1942. On the government's claim that it did not learn of the executions until the following March, see UP, "Japanese Executes Flyers in the Tokyo Raid," *Los Angeles Times*, April 22, 1943.

14. "Tokyo Raid Was First Long-Range Censorship Test," *Editor & Publisher*, May 1, 1943. In late 1942, Drew Pearson had tried to reveal that the planes had taken off from a carrier. The Office of Censorship had asked his syndicate to delete this information, which it did, although not before a few small newspapers carried the story. See Sweeney, *Secrets of Victory*, 148–50; Pearson, Memo to the Radio Censor, October 25, 1942, Columnists: Pearson Folder, Entry 1A, box 558, RG216.

15. BPR to New Delhi, April 4, 1943, Surles to Deputy Chief of Staff, April 10, 1943, and Warner to Fitzgerald, April 13, 1943, all in BPR File, 000.7, Entry 499, box 13, RG165.

16. Algiers to War, 5373, April 19, 1943, BPR File, 000.7, Entry 499, box 13, RG165; "Tokyo Raid Was First Long-Range Censorship Test," *Editor & Publisher*, May 1, 1943.

17. BPR to Commanding General, Allied Forces in North Africa, 6432, April 21, 1943, BPR File, 000.7, Entry 499, box 13, RG165.

18. Schaffer, "American Military Ethics," 321; Schaffer, *Wings of Judgment*, 61; Crane, *Bombs, Cities, Civilians*, 28, 33, 40.

19. UP, "Japanese Executes Flyers in the Tokyo Raid," *Los Angeles Times*, April 22, 1943.

20. Shalett, "Only Military Targets Hit, Tokyo Raid Fliers Declare," *New York Times*, April 23, 1943; UP, "Flyers Demand Revenge," *New York Herald Tribune*, April 24, 1943.

21. Director, Domestic Branch, OWI to Domestic Branch, "Policy Directive: Interpretation of Enemy Atrocities," February 18, 1943, box 11, Nash Papers.

22. On the government's handling of news about the Holocaust, see, for instance, Lipstadt, *Beyond Belief*, 180–83, 192–93; Wyman, *Abandonment*, 312–15; Leff, *Buried*, 242–43.

23. BPR to Commanding General, US Forces in Chungking, May 1, 1943, BPR File, 000.7, Entry 499, box 13, RG165.

24. Editorial, "The Tokio Raid," *New York Herald Tribune*, April 22, 1943.

25. Fisher, "Hit Japs, Senators Demand," *Chicago Tribune*, April 23, 1943. On Vandenberg and MacArthur, see Borneman, *MacArthur at War*, 383–87.

26. MacArthur to Marshall, July 28, 1943, War Department File, box 16, RG3, MacArthur Papers; Corbett, *Quiet Passages*, 48. For all MacArthur's lobbying for additional resources, it was "not until October 1943 [that] there were more [US] divisions in the European Theater than the Pacific." See Heinrichs and Gallicchio, *Implacable Foes*, 16.

27. "For the Men of Bataan," *Christian Science Monitor*, August 13, 1942.

28. Dyess and Leavelle, *The Dyess Story*, 134–36, 167. Only these three officers managed to make it by boat to Australia; the other seven escapees remained at large in the Philippines. Westlake to Surles, "Major W. E. Dyess," August 24, 1943, BPR File, 000.7, Entry 499, box 15, RG165.

29. Dyess and Leavelle, *The Dyess Story*, 8, 53–55, 59–63, 79, 99, 101–102.

30. James, *Years of MacArthur*, 2:512; MacArthur to Marshall, July 28, 1943, War Department File, box 16, RG3, MacArthur Papers; Dyess and Leavelle, "Dyess' Own Story!" *Chicago Tribune*, January 30, 1944; Dyess and Leavelle, *The Dyess Story*, 105, 111.

31. Wharton to BPR, "Publication of Soldier's Diary by the *Baltimore News Post*," June 14, 1943, BPR File, 000.7, Entry 499, box 15, RG165.

32. Westlake to Surles, "Major W. E. Dyess," August 24, 1943, and Surles to Strong, "Major Edward Dyess' Story," September 10, 1943, both in BPR File, 000.7, Entry 499, box 15, RG165. On Creel during World War I, see Vaughn, *Holding Fast*, 27, 30–31, 117–23, 194, 203–205.

33. Kelley to Mason, August 25, 1943, and "Agenda for Meeting with Mr. W. L. White, *Readers' Digest*," September 7, 1943, both in Correspondence Folder, box 3, Mason Papers; Surles to Strong, "Major Edward Dyess' Story," September 10, 1943, BPR File, 000.7, Entry 499, box 15, RG165; Vogel, *Pentagon*, 312–13.

34. "How Chicago Tribune Obtained Dyess Story," *Editor & Publisher*, February 5, 1944; Surles to Strong, "Major Edward Dyess' Story," September 10, 1943, BPR File, 000.7, Entry 499, box 15, RG165; "Transcript of McCoy-Mellnik Conversation," September 13, 1943, Correspondence Folder, box 3, Mason Papers; Maxwell to Surles, September 17, 1943, Dyess Series Folder, Chicago Tribune Company Records, XI-179, box 2, Chicago Tribune Company Archives; Dyess and Leavelle, *The Dyess Story*, 8.

35. Kelley to Mason, September 15, 1943, Correspondence Folder, box 3, Mason Papers.

36. Maxwell to Surles, September 17, 1943, Dyess Series Folder, Chicago Tribune Company Records, XI-179, box 2, Chicago Tribune Company Archives; "Comments following Captain Lovette's Talk with General Surles," September 13, 1943, Correspondence Folder, box 3, Mason Papers; "How Chicago Tribune Obtained Dyess Story," *Editor & Publisher*, February 5, 1944; Leavelle, "Unbelievable Story," *Chicago Tribune*, December 23, 1943; Dyess and Leavelle, *The Dyess Story*, 7.

37. Corbett, *Quiet Passages*, 169; on tortuous negotiations for the second exchange, see 72–95.

38. Roosevelt to the Secretary of War and the Secretary of the Navy, "Japanese Atrocities—Reports of by Escaped Prisoners," September 9, 1943, and Stimson, Memo to the President, September 17, 1943, both in BPR File, 000.7, Entry 499, box 15, RG165.

39. "Lovette's Side of the Conversation with Surles," September 13, 1943, and "Comments following Captain Lovette's Talk with General Surles," September 13, 1943, both in Correspondence Folder, box 3, Mason Papers.

40. Maxwell to Trohan, September 17, 1943, Dyess Series Folder, Chicago Tribune Company Records, XI-179, box 2, Chicago Tribune Company Archives; "Lovette's Side of the Conversation with Surles," September 13, 1943, Correspondence Folder, box 3, Mason Papers.

41. Mason, Daily Log, November 30, 1943, Telephone Logs Folder, box 3, Mason Papers; "Gripsholm Docks with 1,494 from Japanese Captivity," *New York Herald Tribune*, December 2, 1943; "1,440 on Gripsholm Wildly Happy Here," *New York Times*, December 2, 1943.

42. Brines, "Two Years of Refrigeration!," December 1943, WWII Supplemental, WWII Book Project Folder, AP28, Writings About the AP, Series II, box 14, AP Corporate Archives; Brines, "Japanese Prison Camps Under Threat of Famine," *Christian Science Monitor*, November 4, 1943; Cronin, "Filipinos Slew Many Pro-Japs at Manila after Islands Fell," *Washington Post*, November 4, 1943.

43. Maxwell to Trohan, September 17, 1943, Dyess Series Folder, Chicago Tribune Company Records, XI-179, box 2, Chicago Tribune Company Archives.

44. Simmons, "Where the Jap Has Been Is a Torture Trail!" and "How Barbaric Japs Bayoneted Wounded Yanks," *Chicago Tribune*, October 21 and 22, 1943.

45. "Let US Know Truth on Japs, Green Urges," *Chicago Tribune*, December 7, 1943. On Green's relationship with the *Tribune*, see Norton-Smith, *The Colonel*, 299.

46. AP, "Flying Hero of Bataan Killed in California Crash," *Chicago Tribune*, December 23, 1943.

47. Leavelle, "Unbelievable Story," *Chicago Tribune*, December 23, 1943.

48. Trohan to Maxwell, December 23, 1943, Dyess Series Folder, Chicago Tribune Company Records, XI-179, box 2, Chicago Tribune Company Archives.

49. Leavelle, "Bury Dyess," *Chicago Tribune*, December 28, 1943.

50. Trohan to Maxwell, December 23 and 24, 1943, Dyess Series Folder, Chicago Tribune Company Records, XI-179, box 2, Chicago Tribune Company Archives; Lockhart to Fitzgerald, November 19, 1943, BPR File, 000.73, Entry 499, box 17, RG165; Chappell, *Before the Bomb*, 30; "Smoking Out Jap Atrocities," *Hartford Courant*, January 30, 1944; Lindley, "The Jap Atrocities," *Washington Post*, January 31, 1944. King agreed with Davis on this issue; see Crane, *Bombs, Cities, Civilians*, 122.

51. Fleisher to Johnson, "Dyess Story," February 4, 1944, Folder 128, Time Dispatches. The magazine obtained this account from George Taylor, chief of the OWI's Far Eastern division, on a "not for attribution" basis. Taylor had attended many of the relevant meetings.

52. "US Cry: Annihilate Japs" and "Dyess' Own Story," *Chicago Tribune*, January 29 and 30, 1944; AP, "Japs Starved, Buried Internees Alive in Philippines," *Atlanta Constitution*, January 28, 1944.

53. Dyess and Leavelle, "Jap Barbarity Opens Bataan 'Death March'" and "Murder Stalks Battered Yanks on Bataan Road," *Chicago Tribune*, February 4 and 5, 1944; McCoy, Mellnik, and Kelley, "'Death Was Part of Our Life,'" *Life*, February 7, 1944. On the

reception to the *Life* story, see Heiskell to All *Life* Staff Members, January 9, 1945, Life Misc. File, box 433, Time Inc. Records.

54. "For the Attention of Editors," February 7, 1944, Murphy to Lavel, February 12, and NBC, "Words at War: The New Sun," February 15, 1944, all in Dyess Series Folder, Chicago Tribune Company Records, XI-179, box 2, Chicago Tribune Company Archives. For the impact of Dyess's account on the historiography of the death march, see Murphy, " 'Raw Individualists,' " 43–46.

55. OWI, "What the Civilian Thinks," Memo No. 82, July 18, 1944, box 1800, Entry 164, RG44; 8th Service Command, Dallas Texas to CGASF, No. 671, February 1, 1944, BPR File, 000.7, Entry 499, box 13, RG165; Andrews, "Nation Demands Vengeance upon Japan for Fiendish Crimes against Prisoners," *New York Herald Tribune*, January 29, 1944.

56. Taaffe, *MacArthur's Jungle War*, 15–20; MacArthur to Marshall, CA-138, December 30, 1943, BPR File, 000.7, Entry 499, box 15, RG165.

57. Gowran, "Pushes Demand M'Arthur Lead War in Pacific," *Chicago Tribune*, September 20, 1943; Heroux, INS Dispatch, January 29, 1944, and INS, Chicago, January 29, 1944, both in Atrocity Stories Folder, Chicago Tribune Company Records, XI-179, box 2, Chicago Tribune Company Archives

58. Sainsbury, *Turning Point*, 256.

Chapter 7

1. James, *Years of MacArthur*, 2:292–94; Griffith, *MacArthur's Airman*, 105–108; Borneman, *MacArthur at War*, 273–75; Pike, *Hirohito's War*, 597–99.

2. Kenney Diary, March 4, 1943, box 1, Kenney Papers.

3. GHQ SWPA Communiqué, March 4, 1943, Series 5: Communiqués and Press Releases, box 47, RG4, MacArthur Papers.

4. James, *Years of MacArthur*, 2:295; AP, "Jap Naval Disaster," *Chicago Tribune*, March 4, 1943.

5. Schneider, "War Staffs Abroad at New Peak for 2nd Year of US Offensive," *Editor & Publisher*, April 17, 1943.

6. Purcell Cable No. 4, March 17, 1943, Folder 58, Time Dispatches.

7. Editorial, "General MacArthur," *New York Times*, March 18, 1943; Nover, "MacArthur's Victory," *Washington Post*, March 6, 1943.

8. Kenney Diary, March 17, 1943, box 1, Kenney Papers.

9. Andrews, "Tug-o'-War on Plane Allotment May Yield More for MacArthur," *New York Herald Tribune*, March 18, 1943; James, "Will Washington Give MacArthur More Planes?," *New York Times*, March 14, 1943. The censors in Washington clamped down hard on another claim—that MacArthur and Kenney had been "neglected to the point where it is difficult for them to carry out their assignment"—on the basis "that it told the enemy that we couldn't hold our Pacific positions without reinforcements." See Mylander to Howard, March 18, 1943, Columnists: Clapper Folder, Entry 1A, box 555, RG216.

10. James, *Years of MacArthur*, 2:297–303; Rogers, *The Bitter Years*, 50–51; Borneman, *MacArthur at War*, 277–78; Secretary, General Staff to MacArthur, No. 7679, September 6, 1943, BPR File, 000.7, Entry 499, box 15, RG165; Marshall to MacArthur, September 7, 1943, and MacArthur to Marshall, September 7, 1943, War Department File, box 16, RG4, MacArthur Papers.

11. Weller, "Yanks Describe Final, Deadly Blow at Japs," *Boston Globe*, March 5, 1943.

12. Kenney, Diary, February 6, 1943, box 1, Kenney Papers; GHQ SWPA Communiqué, March 4, 1943, Series 5: Communiqués and Press Releases, box 47, RG4, MacArthur Papers.

13. Schneider, "3 US Writers Expelled from Papua by Army," *Editor & Publisher*, March 20, 1943. On Diller's policy, see Diller to Weller, June 14, 1943, WWII: New Guinea Dispatches Folder, box 27, Weller Papers.

14. Noderer, Australia Notebook, January 9 and 10, 1943, 8–10, XI-231, box 2, Noderer Papers; Weller, Press Collect, March 24, [1943,] WWII: New Guinea Dispatches Folder, box 27, Weller Papers.

15. "More US Writers Due in Australia, Says Col. Lehrbas," *Editor & Publisher*, March 20, 1943; Johnston, *New Guinea Diary*, 152–53. Monks was married to Mary Welch, a correspondent who worked for *Time* magazine's London bureau. See Hemingway, *How It Was*, 42–43.

16. Toll, *Conquering Tide*, 222.

17. Weller to Binder, April 3 and 23, 1943, and July 4, 1943, WWII: New Guinea Dispatches Folder, box 27, Weller Papers.

18. Taaffe, *MacArthur's Jungle War*, 3.

19. Miller, *Cartwheel*, 26.

20. Diller, Memo, August 31 and September 1, 1943, SOWESPAC Official and Semi-Official Letters Folder, Entry 86, box 4, RG313.

21. Schneider, "3 US Writers Expelled from Papua by Army" and "More US Writers Due in Australia, Says Col. Lehrbas," *Editor & Publisher*, March 20, 1943.

22. Schneider, "3 US Writers Expelled from Papua by Army" and "More US Writers Due in Australia, Says Col. Lehrbas," *Editor & Publisher*, March 20, 1943. Guard was not quite so trusted. A security check had revealed that as a UP correspondent in Hong Kong in 1935, he had been "classified as doubtful by Hong Kong police because under Japanese influence." Another check in late 1942 had not unearthed anything to corroborate this allegation. See War to Brisbane, C-704, October 14, 1942, BPR File, 000.77, Entry 499, box 6, RG165.

23. O'Flaherty, "Written not for publication," undated [June 1943], Knox Office File 98-2-23, Entry 23, box 59, RG80. On O'Flaherty, see Hemingway, *How It Was*, 30, 34.

24. Holzimmer, *Krueger*, 102; Taaffe, *MacArthur's Jungle War*, 36–37, 83.

25. Miller, *Cartwheel*, 26; Baulch, "Pacific Coverage Pattern Set in Capture of Japanese Islands," *Editor & Publisher*, July 24, 1943.

26. Cromie, "Tribune Writer Tells How US Men Took Isle," *Chicago Tribune*, July 5, 1943; Baulch, "Pacific Coverage Pattern Set in Capture of Japanese Islands," *Editor & Publisher*, July 24, 1943.

27. Baulch, "Pacific Coverage Pattern Set in Capture of Japanese Islands," *Editor & Publisher*, July 24, 1943.

28. Baulch, "Pacific Coverage Pattern Set in Capture of Japanese Islands," *Editor & Publisher*, July 24, 1943; Kunz, "Decisions That Counted," 30, box 59, Kunz Papers.

29. Gailey, *MacArthur's Victory*, 49, 106–7; Dean, *MacArthur's Coalition*, 74, 85, 135, 197, 211–13, 253, 287; Duffy, *War at the End of the World*, 209; Clements, "'Digger' Troops Assault Vital Japanese Bases from Two Sides," and Runser, "How MacArthur Saved Australia," *Washington Post*, October 3 and August 8, 1943.

30. Nimitz to Halsey, April 3, 1943, and Halsey to Nimitz, April 12, 1943, both in Special Correspondence: Nimitz Folder, box 15, Halsey Papers; Bassett, Memo to All War Correspondents: Air Transportation, April 13, 1945, Civilian Correspondents, General Policies and Directives Folder, Entry 86, box 11, RG313; Sherman to Harmon, "Publicity," April 15, 1943, BPR File, 000.7, Entry 499, box 14, RG165; Nimitz to Knox, May 13, 1945, Nimitz PR Letters Folder, Entry 86, box 1, RG313.

31. Hughes, *Halsey*, 254–57; James, *Years of MacArthur*, 2:315; Miller, *Cartwheel*, 13.

32. Hughes, *Halsey*, 259, 263–64; MacArthur, *Reminiscences*, 173.

33. Halsey to Nimitz, June 29, 1943, Special Correspondence: Nimitz Folder, box 15, Halsey Papers.

34. Bassett to Drake, September 29, 1943, and Drake to Bassett, October 9, 1943, SOPAC Official and Semi-Official Letters, Entry 86, box 4, RG313; Hughes, *Halsey*, 277–78.

35. Keys, "First Eyewitness Story of Rendova," *Boston Globe*, July, 2, 1943. See also Walker, "New Georgia Eyewitness Tells of Allied Invasion," *Christian Science Monitor*, July 3, 1943; Jones, "Thousands of Infantry, Marines, and Sailors Landed on Rendova," *New York Herald Tribune*, July 3, 1943.

36. Hulbard to Ingraham, "Communiques (Naval Angles)," March 26, 1943, Folder 59, Time Dispatches.

37. Davies, "'Real Offensive' Now on in Pacific, Knox Says," *New York Times*, July 3, 1943.

38. Turcott, "M'Arthur Drive Called Periled by Knox 'Scoops,'" *Chicago Tribune*, July 4, 1943; Marshall to MacArthur, No. 5531, July 9, 1943, Adjutant General: General Correspondence, 000.73, box 863, RG496.

39. Clayton to Hulburd, "Honolulu Cable," November 21, 1943, Folder 107, Time Dispatches.

40. Hughes, *Halsey*, 282–88; Bergerud, *Touched with Fire*, 226–31.

41. AP, "Fight at Munda Settles Down to Slow Advance," *New York Herald Tribune*, July 15, 1943; Durdin, "Americans Are Closing in on Munda," *New York Times*, July 18, 1943.

42. Editorial, "Well Done!," *New York Times*, July 9, 1943.

43. Drake to Bassett, November 1, 1943, SOPAC Official and Semi-Official Letters, Entry 86, box 4, RG313; Sebring, "Bougainville Landing Made by US Troops," *New York Herald Tribune*, November 2, 1943; MacArthur to AGWAR, C-7885, November 16, 1943, BPR File, 000.7, Entry 499, box 15, RG165.

44. Miller, *Cartwheel*, 244–46; Bassett to Drake, November 12, 1943, SOPAC Official and Semi-Official Letters, Entry 86, box 4, RG313; Walker, "Bougainville Landing,"

Christian Science Monitor, November 4, 1943; Jones, "8 Pillboxes Key to Bougainville Victory," *New York Herald Tribune*, November 5, 1943.

45. Bassett to Carney et al., November 26, 1943, SOPAC Official and Semi-Official Letters, Entry 86, box 4, RG313; Miller, *Cartwheel*, 267–69.

46. Memo, April 3, 1945, Far East Misc. Folder, box 417, Time Inc. Records.

47. Peters to Director, Division of PR, July 28, 1943, Correspondents—Policy Folder, Entry 86, box 11, RG313; Millett, *Semper Fidelis*, 382; M'Gurn, "Bougainville: Bombs, Films, Nudes," *Baltimore Sun*, April 2, 1944.

48. Burma, "Analysis of the Present Negro Press," 172, 174; Washburn, "Black Press," 359.

49. Bissell, Memo for the Chief, BPR, May 18, 1942, and Bissell, Memo for BPR, December 19, 1942, both in BPR File, 000.77, box 7, RG165; Casey, *War Beat, Europe*, 312–16.

50. Washburn, *Question of Sedition*, 99, 113–14; Dower, *War Without Mercy*, 175. Black stewards could, and did, engage in combat when their ships were under attack; see Alkebulan, *African-American Press*, 68–70.

51. Beecher to Bassett, October 22, 1943, SOPAC Official and Semi-Official Letters, Entry 86, box 4, RG313.

52. MacGregor, *Integration*, 40–44; Miller, *Cartwheel*, 378. At the start of this election year, the White House also allowed a member of the Negro Newspaper Publishers Association to attend the president's press conferences. See Scott to Early, February 9, 1944, OF36, Roosevelt Papers. The navy also began to reconsider its policy of discrimination. See Buell, *Master of Sea Power*, 343–44.

53. Martin, "24th Infantry Attacks on Bougainville," *Atlanta Daily World*, March 18, 1944; Martin, "24th Infantry Finds Bougainville Isle of Rain, Mud, Decaying Bodies," *Chicago Defender*, April 22, 1944.

54. Dean, "MacArthur's War," 52–53.

55. Cromie, "Just a Line in a Communiqué, Here You Live the Thrill of It," *Chicago Tribune*, May 30, 1943.

56. For the exploits of war reporters jumping into battle in the European theater, see Casey, *War Beat, Europe*, 139–45.

57. Weller to Diller, June 7, 1943, and Diller to Weller, June 14, 1943, WWII: New Guinea Dispatches Folder, box 27, Weller Papers. For Weller's description of a jump, see Weller, *Weller's War*, 442–45.

58. Miller, *Cartwheel*, 207–9; Manchester, *American Caesar*, 319–20; Kenney, *Kenney Reports*, 163–64; Weston to Hulburd, "New Guinea Cable," September 7, 1943, Folder 90, Time Dispatches.

59. Griffith, *MacArthur's Airman*, 135–36.

60. James, *Years of MacArthur*, 2:325–27; Weston to Hulburd, "New Guinea Cable," September 7, 1943, Folder 90, Time Dispatches; AP, "M'Arthur in Plane Directs Paratroop Blow," *Chicago Tribune*, September 7, 1943.

61. Monchak, "11 US, Aussie Newsmen Covered Big Rabaul Raid," *Editor & Publisher*, October 16, 1943.

62. Monchak, "War Writers Active in Pacific Theater," *Editor & Publisher*, November 6, 1943.

63. Bassett to Drake, December 6, 1943, SOPAC Official and Semi-Official Letters, Entry 86, box 4, RG313; Miller, *Cartwheel*, 273–79.

64. Jones, "Covering New Guinea Is Strictly GI, Jones Says," *Editor & Publisher*, January 22, 1944; Diller to Surles, CA91, December 18, 1943, BPR File, 000.7, Entry 499, box 15, RG165.

65. "Interview with Bob Eunson," June 1974, 10, 14, WWII Book Project Folder, AP28, Writings About the AP, Series II, box 14, APCA; Eunson, "Dramatic Story of Commando Ambush Told," *Los Angeles Times*, December 17, 1943. On the battle, see Miller, *Cartwheel*, 284–85; Gailey, *MacArthur's Victory*, 111–13.

66. Monchak, "Two US Newsmen on Admiralty Raid," *Editor & Publisher*, March 4, 1944; Taaffe, *MacArthur's Jungle War*, 62–64; Duffy, *War at the End of the World*, 287–88.

67. Shaplen, "H-Hour," *Newsweek*, March 13, 1944; Dickinson, "MacArthur Visits Scene," *New York Herald Tribune*, March 1, 1944; GHQ SWPA Press Release, March 1, 1944, box 48, RG4, MacArthur Papers; James, *Years of MacArthur*, 2:382–86.

68. Taaffe, *MacArthur's Jungle War*, 3, 15–21, 28, 57; Gailey, *MacArthur's Victory*, 148–51; James, *Years of MacArthur*, 2:379–81.

69. AP, "Invasion by MacArthur," *Chicago Tribune*, March 1, 1944; editorial, "Road to the Philippines," *Christian Science Monitor*, March 1, 1944.

70. Taaffe, *MacArthur's Jungle War*, 78–82; Holzimmer, *Krueger*, 142–45; Gailey, *MacArthur's Victory*, 167–71; James, *Years of MacArthur*, 2:444–49.

71. "Wire Staffers Land at Hollandia," *Editor & Publisher*, April 28, 1944.

72. Eunson letter, March 11, 1975, WWII Book Project Folder, AP28, Writings About the AP, Series II, box 14, APCA; Barbour and Gallagher, "While the Smoke," 265.

73. AP, "M'Arthur Leaps Ahead 500 Miles," *Boston Globe*, April 24, 1944; Murlin, "Not a Jap Shot Fired as Yanks Hit the Beach," *Chicago Tribune*, April 24, 1944.

74. McDaniel, "AP 'Getting Thar Fustest with Mostest," *AP Inter-Office*, June–July 1944.

75. Taaffe, *MacArthur's Jungle War*, 146–47, 157–75; James, *Years of MacArthur*, 2:458–60; Smith, *Approach to the Philippines*, 392–96; AP, "US Invades Biak Island, 900 Miles Off Philippines," May 28, 1944; AP, "MacArthur's Men Gain in Bitter Fighting on Biak," *Boston Globe*, May 30, 1944. MacArthur also made sure that the press could not mention what units were involved in the battle, because he wanted to deny the enemy this information. See HQ, SWPA to War Department, No. c13215, June 3, 1944, BPR File, 000.7, Entry 499, box 36, RG165.

76. GHQ SWPA, Press Release, June 4, 1944, Whitney's Copy, box 49 and "Data on Malaria Incidence in US Army Forces in SWPA," June 1, 1944, War Department File, box 17, both in RG4, MacArthur Papers; Taaffe, *MacArthur's Jungle War*, 117, 174. On the changes that led to this happy outcome, see Heinrichs and Gallicchio, *Implacable Foes*, 57–58.

77. Gottfried to Luce, June 6, 1943, Censorship Folder, box 416, Time Inc. Records.

78. Brandenburg, "Press Lifts Morale at Front, Says Reporter," *Editor & Publisher*, June 24, 1944.

79. Schaller, *MacArthur*, 77–84.

80. Sulzberger to James, April 5, 1943, Kluckhohn Folder, box 37, New York Times Company Records: Arthur Hays Sulzberger Papers; Schneider, "Press Misses Historic Juncture in Tunisia," *Editor & Publisher*, April 10, 1943.

81. Kluckhohn, "New Britain Landing Made in Eerie, Thunderous Dawn," *New York Times*, December 17, 1943; Kluckhohn to Sulzberger, April 15, 1944, New York Times Company Records: Arthur Hays Sulzberger Papers; editorial, "General MacArthur's Letters," *New York Times*, April 14, 1944.

82. GHQ SWPA, Press Release, April 30, 1944, Whitney's Copy, box 49, RG4, MacArthur Papers; Borneman, *MacArthur at War*, 392–93.

83. Yarbrough to Nimitz, July 27, 1943, Nimitz PR Letters Folder, Entry 86, box 1, RG313.

84. Bassett to Drake, Octobe 27, 1943, SOPAC Official and Semi-Official Letters, Entry 86, box 4, RG313.

Chapter 8

1. On Drake, see Drake, Oral History (henceforth, OH), 2–5; Healy, *A Lifetime on Deadline*, 141–43; Hotchkiss to O'Flaherty, June 16, 1941, A7-1 File, Office of the Secretary: General Correspondence, Entry 12, box 756, RG80; Clayton to Hulburd, "Honolulu Cable," November 21, 1943, Folder 107, Time Dispatches; Drake, "Memo for 6," June 3, 1944, Data Concerning Correspondents Folder, Entry 86, box 11, RG313. On his relations with Casey, see O'Keefe to Nimitz, July 10, 1943, Nimitz's PR Letters Folder, Entry 86, box 1, RG313. Drake was a big critic of Casey's "highly-vituperative" attitude toward naval censorship; see Drake to Lovette, April 1, 1942, Drake Correspondence Folder, Entry 86, box 4, RG313. On his relations with Hailey, see Sulzberger to Knox, April 28, 1943, World War II Folder, box 274, New York Times Company Records: Arthur Hays Sulzberger Papers. The *Times*' bosses came to believe that this "personal" clash was the reason Nimitz opposed Hailey's return to the Pacific in March 1944; see James to Sulzberger, March 10, 1944, Hailey Folder, box 30, New York Times Company Records: Arthur Hays Sulzberger Papers.

2. Healy, *A Lifetime on Deadline*, 141–43; Drake, OH, 10, 13, 24, Clayton to Hulburd, "Honolulu Cable," November 21, 1943, Folder 107, Time Dispatches.

3. Perry, "*Dear Bart*," 79–85, 106–109; Graybar, "King's Toughest Battle," 42–45; Buell, *Master of Sea Power*, 259–62.

4. "'Cards-on-Table' Parley to Air Naval Censorship" and Schneider, "Better War Coverage May Result from Meeting of Navy PR Staff," *Editor & Publisher*, April 24 and May 1, 1943.

5. Schneider, "Better War Coverage May Result from Meeting of Navy PR Staff," *Editor & Publisher*, May 1, 1943; Nimitz to Halsey, April 3, 1943, and Halsey to Nimitz, April 12, 1943, both in Special Correspondence: Nimitz Folder, box 15, Halsey Papers; Bassett, Memo to All War Correspondents: Air Transportation, April 13, 1945, Civilian Correspondents, General Policies and Directives Folder, Entry 86, box 11, RG313; Commander in Chief, US Pacific Fleet to Commanders, South and North Pacific Force, "Press Correspondents—Increased Facilities For," April 26, 1943, Correspondents—Policy Folder, Entry 86, box 11, RG313; Lovette to Knox, "OPR, Annual Report of," July 31, 1943, File 67-2-36, Knox Office File, Entry 23, box 51, RG80.

6. Boomhower, *Dispatches*, 29–38; Pace, "Robert Sherrod, 85, a Journalist and Author of 'Tarawa' Is Dead," *New York Times*, February 15, 1994.

7. Sherrod, *Tarawa*, 1–2; Boomhower, *Dispatches*, 17, 51, 67–68, 76–88; "Sherrod-LBJ Report: Australia," April 1942; Pace, "Robert Sherrod, 85, a Journalist and Author of 'Tarawa' Is Dead," *New York Times*, February 15, 1994; Luce to Larsen et al., January 31, 1944, Time-Life-Fortune Papers, box 1, Billings Papers; Spector, *Eagle Against the Sun*, 257.

8. Clayton to Hulburd, "Honolulu Cable," November 21, 1943, Folder 107, Time Dispatches. Sherrod reached a similar conclusion; see Sherrod to Meek, "Navy Public Relations," February 10, 1944, Censorship Folder, box 416, Time Inc. Records. As well as Sherrod, there were nineteen writers, four photographers, two artists, and one newsreel cameraman.

9. Clayton to Hulburd, "Honolulu Cable," November 21, 1943, Folder 107, Time Dispatches; Green, "27 Newsmen Covered Central Pacific Drive," *Editor & Publisher*, December 12, 1943.

10. The Marines' target was actually the island of Betio, which formed the southern part of the Tarawa atoll, but because the press invariably referred to this battle as Tarawa, the name of the atoll, not the island, is used throughout.

11. Sherrod, *Tarawa*, 4.

12. Sherrod, *Tarawa*, 5–6, 11–21; Crowl and Love, *Seizure of the Gilberts and Marshalls*, 31–33; Sherrod to Hulbard, "Central Pacific Dispatch No. 5," November 3, 1943, Folder 102, Time Dispatches.

13. Sherrod, *Tarawa*, 21–24, 41–43.

14. Sherrod, *Tarawa*, 49–52.

15. Sherrod, *Tarawa*, 52–67; Alexander, *Across the Reef*, 10–22; Alexander, *Utmost Savagery*, 98–105; Crowl and Love, *Seizure of the Gilberts and Marshalls*, 127–39.

16. Sherrod, *Tarawa*, 67–74; Burgess, "The Story of the AP's Coverage of the Gilberts Offensive in Pacific," undated, WWII Book Project Folder, AP28, Writings About the AP, Series II, box 14, AP Corporate Archives.

17. Monchak, "US Newsmen in Thick of Battles at Tarawa, Makin," *Editor & Publisher*, December 4, 1943; Sherrod, *Tarawa*, 100.

18. Sherrod to Hulbard, "Central Pacific Dispatch No. 7" and "No. 7 Second Take," November 22 and 23, 1943, both in Folder 107, Time Dispatches.

19. Sherrod, *Tarawa*, 138.

20. "Lifts Picture Ban on War's Realism," *New York Times*, September 5, 1943; Casey, *War Beat, Europe*, 163–65.

21. Mendelson and Smith, "Part of the Team," 286; Roeder, *Censored War*, 14.

22. Drake, OH, 52.

23. Horne, "Beachheads Won," *New York Times*, November 22, 1943.

24. Knox, Press Conference, November 26, 1943, box 6, Mason Papers; "Tarawa Life Loss Heavy, Knox Warns," *New York Times*, November 27, 1943.

25. "Marines' Toughest Battle!," *Chicago Tribune*, November 27, 1943; Johnston, "Tarawa Won in 'Toughest' Marine Fight," *Christian Science Monitor*, November 27, 1943; Hipple, "AP Writer Tells of Tarawa," *Hartford Courant*, November 28, 1943; Henry,

"Writer Tells of Bodies Draping Broken Landing Craft," *Washington Post*, November 29, 1943.

26. Sherrod to Hulbard, "Central Pacific Dispatch No. 7," "No. 7 Second Take" and "No. 8," November 22, 23, and 24, 1943, all in Folder 107, Time Dispatches; "Report on Tarawa: Marines' Show," *Time*, December 6, 1943.

27. Hipple, "Nimitz Visits Death-Laden Tarawa Atoll," *Washington Post*, December 1, 1943; "Navy Reveals 1,092 Yanks Die in Gilberts," *Chicago Tribune*, December 2, 1943.

28. Lucas, "Combat Writer Describes Marines' Conquest of Tarawa," *Baltimore Sun*, December 4, 1943; AP, "Costly Lesson of Tarawa," *Christian Science Monitor*, November 30, 1943; McManus, *Fire and Fortitude*, 514

29. Mason, Daily Log, December 6 and 10, 1943, Telephone Logs, box 4, Mason Papers.

30. "Knox Attempts to Defend Navy Battle Tactics" and editorial, "Losses at Tarawa," *Chicago Tribune*, December 4, 1943.

31. "Knox Justifies Tarawa," *Boston Globe*, December 4, 1943; AP, "Vandegrift Defends Tarawa Toll," *New York Herald Tribune*, December 18, 1943.

32. Sherrod to Meek, "Navy Public Relations," February 10, 1944, Censorship Folder, box 416, Time Inc. Records.

33. Boomhower, *Dispatches*, 138–39; Sherrod, *Tarawa*, 129.

34. Sherrod, *Tarawa*, 129.

35. Marine Newsmen Made History at Tarawa," *Editor & Publisher*, December 11, 1943; Neushul and Neushul, "With the Marines," 74–80; Jones, *War Shots*, 8–9, 91–92.

36. "Young Men as Photographers," undated, Life: Edit Misc. Folder, box 417, Time Inc. Records.

37. "Meeting of *Life* Photographers, Hotel Dorset, NYC," December 7, 1943, Life: Edit Folder, box 417, Time Inc. Records; "The Fight at Tarawa," *Life*, December 13, 1943; Moeller, *Shooting War*, 238.

38. "Marine Newsmen Made History at Tarawa," *Editor & Publisher*, December 11, 1943; Jones, *War Shots*, 8, 96, 123–25, 132–35; Neushul and Neushul, "With the Marines," 74–80; Pearlman, *Warmaking*, 250; Maslowski, *Armed with Cameras*, 259–60; Boomhower, *Dispatches*, 9, 135–36. Roosevelt had already agreed to release color pictures of the battle "to give the public a real comprehension of what war is like and the sacrifices that must be made." See Knox to Holcomb, December 23, 1943, File 98-2-45, Knox Office File, Entry 23, box 59, RG80.

39. OWI, "The Effect of Realistic War Pictures," Special Memo No. 112, March 13, 1944, box 1803, and OWI, "Public Appraisal of War Information," Memo No. 77, May 12, 1944, box 1800, both in Entry 164, RG44.

40. Crowl and Love, *Seizure of the Gilberts and Marshalls*, 137–39; Alexander, *Utmost Savagery*, 232–37.

41. Morison, *History of United States Naval Operations*, 7:207.

42. Frank, *Guadalcanal*, 16–17; Lacey, *Pacific Blitzkrieg*, 10, 52, 80; Potter, *Nimitz*, 238, 270; Millett, *Semper Fidelis*, 400; Toll, *Conquering Tide*, 20–21, 317–19.

43. Marshall, *Bringing Up the Rear*, 77–78; Gailey, *Howlin' Mad*, 27, 31–32, 59–60, 87–88; Lacey, *Pacific Blitzkrieg*, 80, 96–97, 101.

44. On Wheeler's background, see "A Reunion on the Gangland Beat," *Life*, April 21, 1967; Wheeler, *Pacific Is My Beat*; Sherrod Cable, February 24, 1945, Folder 254, Time Dispatches. On his Midway experience, see Wheeler to Drake, June 18, 1942, and Drake to Wheeler, July 19, 1942, War Correspondents Letters Folder, box 13, and Berry to Drake, July 7, 1942, Drake's Correspondence Folder, box 4, all in Entry 86, RG313.

45. Drake to McArdle, February 2, 1944, and Drake to Binder, August 22, 1944, both in Semi-Official PR Matter Folder, Entry 86, box 5, RG313; Crowl and Love, *Seizure of the Gilberts and Marshalls*, 170, 172; Sherrod, *On to Westward*, 250, 255; Turner, "Press Correspondents, Facilities For," January 7, 1944, Letters to and from Forward Area Folder, Entry 86, box 4, RG313.

46. Drake to McArdle, February 2, 1944, Semi-Official PR Matter Folder, Entry 86, box 5, RG313; Worden, "Witness Describes Invasion," *Baltimore Sun*, February 2, 1944; Reed, "Yanks Got Good Breaks in Island Push," *Washington Post*, February 3, 1944; Dopking, "Warship Fire Tore to Pieces Big Namur-Roi Blockhouses," *New York Times*, February 4, 1944; Johnston, "40 Japs Slain for 1 Yank," *Chicago Sun*, February 7, 1944.

47. Drake to McArdle, January 26, 1944, Semi-Official PR Matter Folder, Entry 86, box 5, RG313.

48. Drake, OH, 19; Drake to McArdle, February 2, 1944, Semi-Official PR Matter Folder, Entry 86, box 5, RG313.

49. Drake to McArdle, February 19, 1944, and Drake, "To Whom It May Concern," March 7, 1944, both in Semi-Official PR Matter Folder, Entry 86, box 5, RG313; Smith, "Tribune Writer Tells 'Rat Hunt' on Eniwetok" and "Tribune Writer Tells Lessons of Pacific War," *Chicago Tribune*, February 28 and December 8, 1944; Monchak, "Two US Newsmen on Admiralty Raid," *Editor & Publisher*, March 4, 1944.

50. UP, "Yanks Slay 8122 Marshalls Japs" and "How We Shall Get Revenge," *Los Angeles Times*, February 8 and 1, 1944.

51. "Seize 10 Marshall Beachheads" and "Wheeler Blunders into Jap Hot Box, *Chicago Sun*, February 2 and 8, 1944; "Hal O'Flaherty's Marshalls Story," *Chicago Daily News*, February 8, 1944.

52. King to Knox, February 13, 1944, Correspondents—Policy Folder, Entry 86, box 11, RG313; Bassett to Drake, February 4, 1944, SOPAC Official and Semi-Official Letters, Entry 86, box 4, RG313. Harold Smith refused to accept the Purple Heart for the wound he suffered on Eniwetok; see "Tribune Writer Tells Lessons of Pacific War," *Chicago Tribune*, December 8, 1944.

53. Monchak, "Largest Press Corps Covers Marshall Blow," *Editor & Publisher*, February 5, 1944.

54. Folliard, "Reporter's Zest for Truth Leads to Fatal Mission," *Washington Post*, February 4, 1944; "Clapper Killed in Air Crash off Marshalls," *Editor & Publisher*, February 5, 1944; "Average Man Lost His Columnist When Raymond Clapper was Killed," *Newsweek*, February 14, 1944.

55. Beal to Johnson, "Combat Correspondents," March 31, 1944, Folder 146, Time Dispatches.

56. Toll, *Conquering Tide*, 389–96; Lacey, *Pacific Blitzkrieg*, 119.

57. Drake to McArdle, February 2, 1944, Semi-Official PR Matter Folder, Entry 86, box 5, RG313.

58. Chickering, "Cable 57," February 17, 1944, Folder 132, Time Dispatches; Marshall, *Bringing Up the Rear*, 78; Lacey, *Pacific Blitzkrieg*, 120, 124.

59. Sherrod to Meek, "Navy Public Relations," February 10, 1944, Censorship Folder, box 416, Time Inc. Records.

60. Drake to Binder, August 22, 1944, Semi-Official PR Matter Folder, box 5, and Drake to Turner and Horne, June 14, 1944, and Drake to McArdle, July 4, 1944, Letters to and from Forward Area, box 4, all in Entry 86, RG313.

61. Sherrod, *On to Westward*, 52–53. On editorial calculations about D-Day, see Casey, *War Beat, Europe*, 223–24, 232.

62. "From My Notebooks: May–December 1944 Notes Pertinent to the Army-Marine Controversy on Saipan," November 1, 1948, Notes: Saipan Controversy Folder, box 36, Sherrod Papers; Sherrod, *On to Westward*, 37–39.

63. Crowl, *Campaign in the Marianas*, 78–79; Sherrod, *On yo Westward*, 44–63.

64. Johnston, "Claw Way to Shore," *Chicago Tribune*, June 17, 1944; Bassett to McArdle, June 17, 1944, SECNAV PR Material Folder, Entry 86, box 4, RG313.

65. Morison, *History of United States Naval Operations*, 8:255–56, 306–16; Crowl, *Campaign in the Marianas*, 119–22.

66. Sherrod, *On to Westward*, 124; AP, "Nippon Fleet Flees after Fight in Which 14 Ships Are Sunk or Damaged," *Los Angeles Times*, June 23, 1944. On Spruance, see Potter, *Nimitz*, 175; Larrabee, *Commander in Chief*, 156, 391–92.

67. Morison, *History of United States Naval Operations*, 8:210, 242–43; Crowl, *Campaign in the Marianas*, 98–99; Alexander, *Storm Landings*, 72.

68. Drake to Turner, "Press Facilities on Saipan," June 26, 1944, Letters to and from Forward Area, Entry 86, box 4, RG313; Worden, "Terrific Pacific," *AP Inter-Office*, November 1944; Levin, *From the Battlefield*, 12; Norton, "Norton Depicts Biggest, Toughest Pacific Battle," *Baltimore Sun*, June 25, 1944.

69. Sherrod to Hulbard, "Western Pacific Cable 3," June 17, 1944, and "Cable 5," June 24, 1944, both in Folder 172, Time Dispatches.

70. McArdle to Drake, June 25, 1944, Letters to and from Forward Area, Entry 86, box 4, RG313.

71. Levin, *From the Battlefield*, 19.

72. Hulbard to Matthews, Grover, Alexander, and Kay, "Sherrod's Letter," July 18, 1944, Saipan Story Folder, box 448, Time Inc. Records.

73. Hulbard to Matthews, Grover, Alexander, and Kay, "Wheeler's Letter," July 18, 1944, Saipan Story Folder, box 448, Time Inc. Records; "Wheeler Says Saipan Battle Underplayed," *Editor & Publisher*, July 29, 1944; "The Press: I Accuse," *Time*, August 7, 1944; Sherrod, *On to Westward*, 175–76.

74. AP, "Carriers Smash Attack," *Chicago Tribune*, June 20, 1944.

75. Chapin, *Breaching the Marianas*, 14; Heinrichs and Gallicchio, *Implacable Foes*, 116; Handleman, "Japs on Saipan Take Stand for Final Battle," *Los Angeles Times*, June 28, 1944.

76. Gailey, *Howlin' Mad*, 4–6; Lacey, *Pacific Blitzkrieg*, 157–61; Boomhower, *Dispatches*, 157–58; Price to Vandegrift, July 11, 1944, box 2, Vandegrift Papers.

77. "From My Notebooks: May–December 1944 Notes Pertinent to the Army-Marine Controversy on Saipan," November 1, 1948, Notes: Saipan Controversy Folder, box 36, Sherrod Papers.

78. Gailey, *Howlin' Mad*, 1–2; "Some Reports on the 27th Division at Saipan, 1944," undated, and "From My Notebooks: May–December 1944 Notes Pertinent to the Army-Marine Controversy on Saipan," November 1, 1948, both in Notes: Saipan Controversy Folder, box 36, Sherrod Papers; Sherrod, *On to Westward*, 89–90; Boomhower, *Dispatches*, 166–67.

79. "The Generals Smith," *Time*, September 18, 1944; Gailey, *Howlin' Mad*, 9.

80. Boomhower, *Dispatches*, 167; Sherrod to Hodgins, November 6, 1944, Nast to Forrestal, copy to Luce, September 29, 1944, Hal [Horan], Memo to Elson, January 22, 1945, and Luce to Nast, November 30, 1944, all in Saipan Story Folder, box 448, Time Inc. Records.

81. Marshall to King, November 27, 1944, and Surles to Marshall, "Robert Sherrod Articles," November 28, 1944, both in BPR File, 000.7, Entry 499, box 35, RG165; "From My Notebooks: May–December 1944 Notes Pertinent to the Army-Marine Controversy on Saipan," November 1, 1948, Notes: Saipan Controversy Folder, box 36, Sherrod Papers; Boomhower, *Dispatches*, 165, 168; Gailey, *Howlin' Mad*, 10–11.

82. McArdle to Drake, August 4 and 12, 1944, Letters to and from Forward Area, Entry 86, box 4, RG313; Sherrod, *On to Westward*, 133–37; Hoffman, *Saipan*, 222–30; Dower, *War Without Mercy*, 45.

83. McArdle to Drake, August 4 and 12, 1944; Drake to McArdle, August 25, 1944, Letters to and from Forward Area, Entry 86, box 4, RG313.

84. "The Nature of the Enemy," *Time*, August 7, 1944; Wheeler, "80 Million Japs Held Ready to Die Rather than Quit," *Boston Globe*, November 12, 1944.

85. Wheeler, "Yanks Face Fierce Fight," "A Foxhole View of Saipan Battle," and "Plane Deaths Stir Saipan's Marines," *Chicago Times*, June 23 and 25 and July 11, 1944.

86. "Wheeler Says Saipan Battle Under-played," *Editor & Publisher*, July 29, 1944.

87. Sherrod to Meek, "Navy Public Relations," February 10, 1944, Censorship Folder, box 416, Time Inc. Records.

88. "Wheeler Says Saipan Battle Under-played," *Editor & Publisher*, July 29, 1944.

Chapter 9

1. On Surles's background, see McCloy to Stimson, August 1, 1941, BPR Folder, Stimson "Safe File," Entry 99, box 11, RG 107; "War Orders," *Time*, December 15, 1941; "Heads Army Press Bureau" and "Maj. Gen. Surles Dies in Capital, 61," *New York Times*, August 6, 1941, and December 7, 1947. On Surles's conception of his job, see "Statement of Governmental Wartime Information Policy," [undated], OFF Folder, Stimson: "Official File," Entry 100, box 3, RG 107; Shepley to McConaughy, "Communiqués (Army Angles)," March 26, 1943, folder 59, Times Dispatches; Surles

to Marshall, "US Correspondents Abroad," September 11, 1942, BPR File, 000.77, Entry 499, box 6, RG165.

2. Surles to CG ETO USFOR, May 30, 1943, BPR File, 000.7, Entry 499, box 13, RG165.

3. Stilwell's lowly position in the pecking order of resource allocation had recently been underlined at the Anglo-American Trident Conference. See Tuchman, *Stilwell*, 371–72.

4. Romanus and Sunderland, *Stilwell's Mission to China*, 78–79.

5. Stowe to Binder, December 1 and 5, 1941, General Correspondence Folder, box 4, Stowe Papers; Stowe, *They Shall Not Sleep*, 57–58, 132; Woods, *Reporting the Retreat*, 4, 37–39.

6. Brinkley, *Luce*, 276–77.

7. White, ed., *Stilwell Papers*, 60, 69; Tuchman, *Stilwell*, 246, 254; Woods, *Reporting the Retreat*, 104–5; Hamilton, *Journalism's Roving Eye*, 318–20.

8. Luce, "Burma Mission," *Life*, June 15, 1942; Reminder to IH, May 30, 1942, Secretarial File, 1942, box 260, Clare Boothe Luce Papers.

9. De Luce, "Allied Forces Cut Way Out of Jap Traps," *Boston Globe*, April 2, 1942; AP, "Chinese Attack in Burma," *New York Herald Tribune*, May 10, 1942; AP, "Japs Routed on Burma Road," *Chicago Tribune*, May 11, 1942; Allen, *Burma*, 59–63; Woods, *Reporting the Retreat*, 57; White, ed., *Stilwell Papers*, 94; Tuchman, *Stilwell*, 299–300.

10. Not until May 2 did Marshall tell reporters that "playing down the prominence of General Stilwell [was] no longer in force." See O'Donnell to Patterson, May 12, 1942, Publishing Enterprises: NY Daily News, 1939–42 File, box 30, Patterson Papers.

11. Belden, "How British in Burma Escaped a Jap Trap," *Life*, May 18, 1942.

12. Belden, *Retreat with Stilwell*, 250–51; Dorn, *Walkout*, 98–99.

13. Belden, *Retreat with Stilwell*, 260–61; Belden to Hulbard, "Burma Cable," May 2, 4, and 6, 1942, Folders 31 and 32, Time Dispatches.

14. "March of the 400," *Time*, June 1, 1942; "Uncle Joe Turns Up," *Time*, June 1, 1942.

15. Romanus and Sunderland, *Stilwell's Mission to China*, 191–221.

16. Fitzgerald, Memo for Chief PRO, "Negro Correspondents for Attachment to Units on Far Shore," Correspondents-Military, box 6, Redding Papers; Stevens, "Black Correspondents of World War II," 398; MacGregor, *Integration*, 17–18, 24–25; Dower, *War Without Mercy*, 175; Alkebulan, *African-American Press*, 53, 64–65.

17. "Archibald T. Steele; Journalist Reported from China in the 30s," *Los Angeles Times*, March 13, 1992; Stowe, *They Shall Not Sleep*, 8; Steele, "Find Heroes among Soldiers in India Jungle," *Atlanta Daily World*, February 25, 1944; Steele, "Burma Jungles Teem with Japs and Death but Vets Laugh It Off," *Chicago Defender*, March 11, 1944.

18. Chennault to Stowe, January 25, 1944, Public Relations Folder, box 7, Chennault Papers.

19. Woods, *Reporting the Retreat*, 65; Chennault, *Way of a Fighter*, 179–84; Romanus and Sunderland, *Stilwell's Mission to China*, 199, 251–54; Ford, *Flying Tigers*, 320–21; "End of the AVG," *Time*, July 24, 1942; Wiant, *Between the Bylines*, 115.

20. "End of the AVG," "Into the Stolen Empire," and "Chennault on the Japs," *Time*, July 13, 1942, November 9, 1942, and May 3, 1943; Belden, "Chennault Fights to Hold the China Front," *Life*, August 10, 1942.

21. Surles to Chungking, No. 1219, August 20, 1942, and Stilwell to AGWAR, No. 1093, August 30, 1942, both in BPR File, 000.77, Entry 499, box 6, RG165. Belden told his bosses that all of his stories from US air bases in China had been submitted to Chinese authorities for censorship. See Belden Cable, August 24, 1942, Far East Folder, box 415, Time Inc. Records. This was not the last time the Chennault-Luce alliance caused consternation. *Time* also published a "very vicious article" in early 1943 that revealed Chennault's hostility toward a number of Stilwell's actions. See ACQUILA to AMMISCA, February 26, 1943, in Romanus and Sunderland, eds., *Stilwell's Personal File*, 2:590.

22. Alexander to Smith, "Publicity Policy," March 20, 1943, and Military Intelligence Division to Commanding General New Delhi, October 4, 1943, both in BPR File, 000.7, Entry 499, boxes 13 and 15, RG165. On the ATC, see Tuchman, *Stilwell*, 302, 309, 352; Romanus and Sunderland, *Stilwell's Mission to China*, 163–67.

23. Wiant, *Between the Bylines*, 96, 109; Noderer, Chicago Home on Leave Notebook, March 5, 1943, 44, XI-231, box 2, Noderer Papers.

24. Sevareid to Francis, July 31, 1942, and Murrow to Sevareid, January 25, 1943, both in Personal Correspondence, box A1, Sevareid Papers; Sevareid, *Not to So Wild*, 225.

25. Chungking to AGWAR, No. 633, July 9, 1943, Wood to Warner, "Proposed Publicity for CBI Theater," July 19, 1943, and AGWAR to Chungking, No. 663, July 22, 1943, all in BPR File, 000.7, Entry 499, box 13, RG165; Sevareid, *Not So Wild*, 228–29.

26. Sevareid, Broadcasts and Notes from India, undated, box D3, Sevareid Papers; Sevareid, *Not So Wild*, 250–55.

27. New Delhi to AGWAR, August 6, 1943, Chabua to War, August 13, 1943, and New Delhi to Chungking, August 25 and 27, 1943, all in BPR File, 000.7, Entry 499, box 15, RG165; AP, "19 Bail Out in Burma Jungle," *New York Herald Tribune*, August 9, 1943; Sevareid, *Not So Wild*, 294.

28. Sevareid, Broadcasts and Notes from India, undated, box D3, Sevareid Papers; Smith to Westlake, "Publicity Policy—India-China," September 21, 1943, and Fitzgerald to Smith, "Publicity Policy on the China-Burma Wing of the ATC," September 22, 1943, both in BPR File, 000.7, Entry 499, box 15, RG165; Sevareid, "Tells on Hand Radio of Trek by 18 in Crash," *Chicago Tribune*, August 28, 1943.

29. White, "Background: China," February 3, 1940, Far East Folder, box 414, Time Inc. Records; Stowe, *They Shall Not Sleep*, 62–85; McLynn, *The Burma Campaign*, 53, 121.

30. Sevareid, Chungking Notes, September 1943, Scripts: Broadcasts from China Folder, box D3, Sevareid Papers.

31. Sevareid, Chungking Notes, September 13 and 16, 1943, and Sevareid "Press," 1, Scripts: Broadcasts from China Folder, box D3, Sevareid Papers.

32. Howard to Tong, August 18, 1939, Foreign File: China, box 157, Howard Papers; Morin, "The Sinister Censor," February 28, 1941, Censorship Folder, AP02A.3, Subject Files, Series III, box 39, AP Corporate Archive; Woods, *Reporting the Retreat*, 38. On the transformation of White's thinking, see Hoffmann, *White*, 49–50.

33. Sevareid, *Not So Wild*, 311; Sevareid, "Press," 1, 2, and 3, and Sevareid, Chungking Broadcast, September 11, 17, and 26, 1943, all in Scripts: Broadcasts from China Folder, box D3, Sevareid Papers. Emphasis in original.

34. Sevareid, "Press," 5, Scripts: Broadcasts from China Folder, box D3, Sevareid Papers.

35. Sevareid, *Not So Wild*, 229, 351; Davies, *Baldwin*, 156–57; Baldwin, "Too Much Wishful Thinking About China," *Reader's Digest*, August 1943, 63–67.

36. McDermott to Davidson, "Articles by Sevareid, Snow, and White," April 10, 1944, BPR File, 000.7, Entry 499, box 34, RG165; Sevareid, *Not So Wild*, 229, 351.

37. McDermott to Davidson, "Articles by Sevareid, Snow, and White," April 10, 1944, BPR File, 000.7, Entry 499, box 34, RG165; White, "'Life' Looks at China," *Life*, May 1, 1944, and Luce to White, April 3, 1944, both in Time-Life-Fortune Papers, box 1, Billings Papers. While White's central thesis was that Chiang's "Nationalist Party is dominated by a corrupt political clique that combines some of the worst features of Tammany Hall and the Spanish Inquisition," Luce remained convinced that the war-time conditions were the main reasons for China's problems. Edgar Snow was another reporter to write in this way; see Hamilton, *Snow*, 164–65, 170.

38. Sevareid, "Press," 5, Scripts: Broadcasts from China Folder, box D3, Sevareid Papers.

39. New Delhi to AGWAR, October 11, 1943, Smith to George, "Publicity on India-China Operations of This Command," November 20, 1943, and Surles to Stilwell, No. 4118, December 21, 1943, all in BPR File, 000.7, Entry 499, box 15, RG165.

40. Shepley to Hulburd, November 21, 1943, Folder 107, Time Dispatches.

41. Surles to Stilwell, No. 3382, October 5, 1943, BPR File, 000.7, Entry 499, box 16, RG165.

42. Grover, "US Is Training Mighty Chinese Army in India," *New York Herald Tribune*, September 18, 1943.

43. Van De Ven, "Stilwell in the Stocks," 243–45.

44. White and Jacoby, *Thunder*, 147; Sevareid, Broadcast, October 12, 1943, Scripts: Broadcasts from China Folder, box D3, Sevareid Papers.

45. Chennault to Stilwell, February 12, April 8, and May 29, 1944, all in Subject File: China: Stilwell-Chennault Record, box 149, Alsop Papers.

46. White, ed., *Stilwell Papers*, 249; Van de Ven, *War and Nationalism*, 37–38; Mitter, *China's War*, 302.

47. Ritter, *Stilwell and Mountbatten*, 55; Thorne, *Allies of a Kind*, 299–300; Sbrega, "Anglo-American Relations," 139–44.

48. Ritter, *Stilwell and Mountbatten*, 42, 90–92; White, ed., *Stilwell Papers*, 258–59; Ziegler, *Mountbatten*, 247, 278.

49. MacKenzie, "Vox Populi," 677; Ziegler, *Mountbatten*, 255–57; McLynn, *The Burma Campaign*, 238; Wood, "Allies of a Kind," 3–4.

50. Governor General Delhi to Secretary of State for India, No. 6532, November 15, 1943, Organization of Press and Publicity in SEAC, WO203/5160, NA-UK. Whether this reliance meant there was formally a joint censorship arrangement became a matter of heated debate between SEAC and India Command. See Rowlands, "Report by Adviser to the Viceroy on War Administration on Responsibility for Press Censorship in India," May 31, 1944, File 462/18K: SEAC Censorship—Stilwell-Mountbatten Dispute, British Library.

51. "Issue of Communiqués after Prelude," February 10, 1944, and Eade to SAC, CICA/603/10/PR2, March 31, 1944, both in Organization of Press and Publicity in SEAC, WO203/5159, NA-UK; Ziegler, ed., *Personal Diary*, 50.

52. "Battle of Asia: Difference of Opinion," *Time*, February 14, 1944; Eldridge, *Wrath in Burma*, 234–35; MacCormac, "A Rift Over Burma Put to Roosevelt," *New York Times*, March 3, 1944; Monteath to Bridges and Bridges to Monteath, March 8 and 9, 1944, File 462/18K: SEAC Censorship—Stilwell-Mountbatten Dispute, British Library. For more on who might have leaked, see Van de Ven, *War and Nationalism*, 49.

53. Stilwell feared that Mountbatten had no desire to launch a Burma campaign. See Stimson Diary, February 17, 1944, 46:56–57, Stimson Papers.

54. "James Shepley Cable," February 21, 1944, Folder 133, Time Dispatches.

55. Wiant, *Between the Bylines*, 120, 123, 164, 171.

56. Shepley to Hulbard, "Stilwell's Chinese and American Forces in Northern Burma: Via London Cable," March 6 and 10, 1944, Folders 137 and 138, both in Time Dispatches; Durdin, "Ability of Chinese Is Shown in Burma," *New York Times*, March 16, 1944.

57. Ogburn, *Marauders*, 9; Mortimer, *Merrill's Marauders*, 38–39; Prefer, *Vinegar Joe's War*, 43; Baker, *Merrill's Marauders*, 27–28; Tuchman, *Stilwell*, 433, 441.

58. Romanus and Sunderland, *Stilwell's Command Problems*, 32, 34–36; AP, "Merrill Tried Six Times Before He Got into West Point," *Boston Globe*, March 7, 1944; Shepley to Hulbard, "Stilwell's Chinese and American Forces in Northern Burma: New Delhi Cable," March 6, 1944, Folder 137, Time Dispatches.

59. Durdin, "US Unit in Burma a Dashing Outfit," *New York Times*, March 8, 1944; Plotkin, "Gen. Merrill's Wife, Children Thrilled," *Boston Globe*, March 12, 1944; Shepley to Hulbard, "With Stilwell's Chinese and American Forces in Northern Burma: New Delhi Cable," March 6, 1944, Folder 137, Time Dispatches; Tuchman, *Stilwell*, 432; Ogburn, *Marauders*, 70.

60. Ogburn, *Marauders*, 106–19; Prefer, *Vinegar Joe's War*, 60–74; Morris, "Two US War Writers Look at CBI Front," *Editor & Publisher*, April 22, 1944; Hewlett, "Americans Mow Japanese Down in Burma Trap," *New York Herald Tribune*, March 10, 1944.

61. Shepley to Hulbard, "With Stilwell's Chinese and American Forces in Northern Burma: New Delhi Cable," March 12, 1944, Folder 139, Time Dispatches; Durdin, "Ability of Chinese Shown in Burma," *New York Times*, March 16, 1944.

62. Morris, "Two US War Writers Look at CBI Front," *Editor & Publisher*, April 22, 1944; Durdin, " 'Uncle Joe' Footslogs with His Soldiers," *New York Times*, April 30, 1944.

63. McLynn, *The Burma Campaign*, 35.

64. Wiant, *Between the Bylines*, 186–87; Eldridge, *Wrath in Burma*, 206; AP, "Americans Seize Vital Jap Airdrome in Burma," *Los Angeles Times*, May 19, 1944.

65. Romanus and Sunderland, *Stilwell's Command Problems*, 204–205, 230; Ogburn, *Marauders*, 1–6, 143.

66. White, ed., *Stilwell Papers*, 275; Tuchman, *Stilwell*, 449; AP, "Americans Seize Jap Airdrome in Burma," *Los Angeles Times*, May 19, 1944; Romanus and Sunderland, *Stilwell's Command Problems*, 230–38.

67. Durdin, "C-47 Relic Shields Myitkyina Press," *New York Times*, May 27, 1944; Ogburn, *Marauders*, 249–50, 252.

68. White, ed., *Stilwell Papers*, 279; Romanus and Sunderland, *Stilwell's Command Problems*, 239–40; Ogburn, *Marauders*, 196–200, 227, 256, 279; Baker, *Merrill's Marauders*, 120–30.

69. Wiant, *Between the Bylines*, 186, 192–93.

70. "Jack Bell Joins Chicago News Foreign Service," *Editor & Publisher*, January 13, 1945.

71. Bell, "Myitkyina—Killed, Not for Publication," undated, BPR File, 000.7, Entry 499, box 38, RG165.

72. Bell, "Myitkyina—Killed, Not for Publication," undated, and Thompson to Surles, "War Correspondent's Story Stopped in CBI," September 27, 1944, both in BPR File, 000.7, Entry 499, box 38, RG165.

73. Hunter, *Galahad*, 130, 192–94; Mortimer, *Merrill's Marauders*, 189–90; Durdin, "Stilwell in Strong Position," *New York Times*, August 7, 1944.

74. AP, "Merrill Marauders Break in Morale," *New York Times*, August 6, 1944.

75. Mortimer, *Merrill's Marauders*, 195, 197.

76. Editorial, "The Story of Myitkyina," *New York Daily News*, August 8, 1944.

77. Thompson to Surles, "War Correspondent's Story Stopped in CBI," September 27, 1944, BPR File, 000.7, Entry 499, box 38, RG165.

78. The chilling effect of censorship might explain why even in his 1948 account Bell claimed, "This was one phase of the action I dared not write." See Bell, *Line of Fire*, 15.

79. Durdin, "Myitkyina Siege Difficult," *New York Times*, August 6, 1944.

80. "The Bitter Tea of General Joe," *Time*, August 14, 1944; AP, "Merrill Says Mistake on Order Sent Ill Marauders to the War Front," *New York Times*, August 26, 1944; Tuchman, *Stilwell*, 475.

81. Mitter, *China's War*, 321–22.

82. Chennault, *Way of a Fighter*, 228; Wiant, *Between the Bylines*, 114; Tomana, "Gen. Chennault's Men in China," *New York Herald Tribune*, August 18, 1943.

83. Milner to Commanding General, Army Air Forces, "Release of 14th Air Force News to US Newspapers," January 25, 1944, Adjutant General, Correspondence, DF 000.71, Entry 36, box 36, RG493.

84. HQs 14th Air Force, "Modification of Stop," October 5, 1944, Adjutant General, Correspondence, DF 000.71, Entry 36, box 36, RG493; Rundle to Bloom, August 13, 1944, and Surles to Stilwell, September 2, 1944, both in BPR File, 000.7, Entry 499, box 37, RG165. On Hlavacek in China, see Hlavacek, *United Press Invades India*, 1.

85. Fenby, *Generalissimo*, 425–26; McLynn, *The Burma Campaign*, 116.

86. Secretary of State for India to Government of India, April 17, 1944, Secretary of State to Viceroy, April 18, 1944, and War Office to SAC, May 10, 1944, all in File 462/18K: SEAC Censorship—Stilwell-Mountbatten Dispute, British Library; "Charles Eade Reviews Press and Censorship in India," *World Press News*, June 1, 1944.

87. Wiant to Eldridge, undated, "SEAC Newspaper Clippings and Correspondence on American Press Reactions," WO203/5080, UK-NA.

88. Joyce, May 23, 1944, File 462/18K: SEAC Censorship—Stilwell-Mountbatten Dispute, British Library; "Burma Censorship: SEAC's Reply to Protest," *Newspaper World*, April 29, 1944.

89. Mountbatten to Ismay, April 22, 1944, SEAC Newspaper Clippings and Correspondence on American Press Reactions," WO203/5080, UK-NA.

90. Eldridge to Grogman, March 1, 1844, in Romanus and Sunderland, eds., *Stilwell's Personal File*, 4:1438–39; "Notes on Issuance of Communiques and Press Notes," June 29, 1944, Folder 10, box 23, Stilwell Papers; Eldridge, *Wrath in Burma*, 236–37.

91. White, ed., *Stilwell Papers*, 275; Eldridge, *Wrath in Burma*, 264.

92. McLynn, *The Burma Campaign*, 331, 345, 351–53; Bidwell, *The Chindit War*, 266–73; Ziegler, ed., *Personal Diary*, 114; Stilwell to Ferris, June 2, 1944, in Romanus and Sunderland, eds., *Stilwell's Personal File*, 4:1752.

93. "Interview of General Stilwell by the Press at Kandy, Ceylon," August 5, 1944, Folder 9, box 33, Stilwell Papers.

94. Ziegler, *Mountbatten*, 284; McLynn, *The Burma Campaign*, 352, 361; Ritter, *Stilwell and Mountbatten*, 134–36; Wood, "Allies of a Kind," 7–8.

95. "Copy of letter from Mr. Morgan of the British Information Service to Mr. Cruickshank of the Ministry of Information," August 1, 1944, BPR File, 000.7, Entry 499, box 39, RG165.

96. The literature on the protracted process leading to the recall is huge; see, for example, Feis, *China Tangle*, 194–99; Romanus and Sunderland, *Stilwell's Command Problems*, 379–87, 413–30, 443–72; Tuchman, *Stilwell*, 465–71, 483–502; Larrabee, *Commander in Chief*, 571–78; Mitter, *China's War*, 338–50.

97. "Special Guidance on General Stilwell," October 30, 1944, Adjutant General, Correspondence, DF 000.71, Entry 36, box 36, RG493; Jones to Surles, No. 18252, October 29, 1944, BPR File, 000.7, Entry 499, box 37, RG165.

98. Hoffmann, *White*, 55; AP, "War Reporters Hit Heavy Censorship of Communist Area," *Christian Science Monitor*, October 12, 1944.

99. White, *In Search of History*, 176; White, ed., *Stilwell Papers*, 314–16; Bentel, "China Wall of Censorship Smashed by Stilwell Story," *Editor & Publisher*, November 4, 1944.

100. "Confidential Note to Members," November 1, 1944, China Folder, box 133, New York Times Company Records: Arthur Hays Sulzberger Papers; White, *In Search of History*, 178.

101. Tuchman, *Stilwell*, 505; US Congress, Senate Foreign Relations Committee, *State Department Loyalty Investigation*, 1753.

102. Atkinson, "Long Schism Seen," *New York Times*, October 31, 1944.

103. Wiant, *Between the Bylines*, 213, 229; Wiant, "Chiang Declared Husbanding Resources against Civil War," *Baltimore Sun*, November 1, 1944.

104. Stimson Diary, November 3, 1944, 49:12, Stimson Papers; Press Release, October 28, 1944, OF48-k, Roosevelt Papers; Hulen, "Stilwell Moved from Orient at Request Laid to Chiang," *New York Times*, October 29, 1944.

105. Tuchman, *Stilwell*, 507; Surles to Marshall, October 27, 1944, BPR File, 000.7, Entry 499, box 39, RG165.

106. Stilwell to Surles, November 9, 1944, BPR File, 000.7, Entry 499, box 37, RG165; White, ed., *Stilwell Papers*, 321–22.

Chapter 10

1. Chickering, "Cable 14," October 20, 1944, Folder 217, Time Dispatches; James, *Years of MacArthur*, 2:537, 545–48.

2. Morison, *History of United States Naval Operations*, 12:55–58.

3. Nimitz to MacArthur, "Press Material—Policy Concerning," September 3, 1944, Adjutant General: General Correspondence, 000.73, box 860, RG496.

4. Kluckhohn to James, October 30, 1944, World War II Folder, box 274, New York Times Company Records: Arthur Hays Sulzberger Papers; Kunz, Oral History (henceforth, OH), 49.

5. Surles to Sulzberger and Sulzberger to Surles, May 4 and 6, 1944, both in Parrott Folder, box 56, New York Times Company Records: Arthur Hays Sulzberger Papers.

6. Chickering, "Cable 14," October 20, 1944, Folder 217, Time Dispatches.

7. Kluckhohn to James, October 30, 1944, World War II Folder, box 274, New York Times Company Records: Arthur Hays Sulzberger Papers.

8. James, Years of MacArthur, 2:553–57; Dunn, OH, 2–5.

9. Cannon, Leyte, 68.

10. Kunz, "Decisions That Counted," 44–46, box 59, Kunz Papers; Kunz, OH, 44–51.

11. "When the Lights Go on Again in New Guinea," AP Inter-Office, January–February 1945; Dunn, OH, 2–6. The first pictures of the invasion were published three days later. See "First Pictures of American Invasion of the Philippine Islands," New York Herald Tribune, October 24, 1944.

12. Kluckhohn to James, October 30, 1944, World War II Folder, box 274, New York Times Company Records: Arthur Hays Sulzberger Papers; Dickinson, "Bataan Torturers Trapped on Leyte," New York Times, October 21, 1944; Dickinson, "Yanks Find Japs Who Did Dirty Work at Bataan," Los Angeles Times, October 21, 1944.

13. "45 US Writers See Philippine Landing," New York Times, October 21, 1944.

14. "When the Lights Go on Again in New Guinea," AP Inter-Office, January–February 1945; Kluckhohn to James, October 30, 1944, World War II Folder, box 274, New York Times Company Records: Arthur Hays Sulzberger Papers; MacArthur to AGWAR, October 21, 1944, Adjutant General: General Correspondence, 000.73, box 860, RG496.

15. Dowling, "Tanks, Guns, and Chickens Mingle on Roads in Leyte," Chicago Sun, October 31, 1944.

16. Kluckhohn to James, October 30, 1944, World War II Folder, box 274, New York Times Company Records: Arthur Hays Sulzberger Papers.

17. Bigart, "GIs Existence Is Dreary on Leyte," New York Herald Tribune, December 19, 1944; James, Years of MacArthur, 2:561, 568, 583–85; Cannon, Leyte, 92–94.

18. "Two Newsmen Added to Leyte Death Toll" and Dickinson, "Leyte Perils Described," Editor & Publisher, November 18 and 25, 1944; "Asahel Bush Is Killed on Leyte," AP Inter-Office, November 1944; Dowling, "New Hate for Japs Born in Shambled of Bombed Hut," Chicago Sun, November 3, 1944.

19. Bigart, "GIs Existence Is Dreary on Leyte," New York Herald Tribune, December 19, 1944; Veysey, "Tribune Men Swap Packard for a Ford," Chicago Tribune, November 14, 1944; Mydans, More than Meets the Eye, 180–81.

20. Kluckhohn, " 'Philippine Invasion Opens New Phase of Pacific War" and "MacArthur Chiefs Veteran Fighters," New York Times, October 22, 1944.

21. Diller, GHQ SWPA Communiqué, October 25, 1944; Dowling, "Leyte Is Heavy with Battle as Americans Drive Inland," and Dickinson, "Most of Leyte in Yank Hands,

Chicago Sun, October 24 and 30, 1944; UP, "Americans Make Big Leyte Jumps," and UP, "M'Arthur Sweeps 15 Towns," *New York Times*, October 26 and 27, 1944; "'A Place to Run To,'" *Time*, November 6, 1944.

22. Early to Hopkins, October 27, 1944, Map Room: Presidential Trips File, box 20, Roosevelt Papers; Roosevelt, *Public Papers*, October 27, 1944; Rosenman, *Working with Roosevelt*, 480; AP, "FDR Elated Over Return to Islands," *Hartford Courant*, October 21, 1944.

23. Lee and Henschel, *MacArthur*, 172; James, *Years of MacArthur*, 2: 533–34, 587.

24. Morison, *History of United States Naval Operations*, 12:159–300; Cutler, *Battle of Leyte Gulf*, 69, 91–93, 162–65.

25. Cant, "Bull's Run," *Life*, November 24, 1947; Morison to Halsey, January 29, 1951, Special Correspondence: Morison Folder, box 15, Halsey Papers; Pfitzer, *Morison's Historical Mind*, 244–45.

26. Rachlis, "Force Routed in Philippines, *Chicago Sun*, October 26, 1944; Wood, "President Elated," *New York Times*, October 26, 1944.

27. Dunn, "On Leyte During Battle," *New York Times*, October 26, 1944.

28. Teatsworth, "'17 Hours of Hell 'Raised in Sea Battle Off Leyte," and Jones, "4 Carriers Claimed by Halsey's Force," *New York Times*, October 26 and 29, 1944; INS, "Play by Play: Reporters Describe Sea Battle," *Atlanta Constitution*, October 27, 1944.

29. AP, "Sea Showdown On," *Boston Globe*, October 25, 1944; O'Flaherty to Miller, November 13, 1944, Hipple to Miller, November 30, 1944, Eldred, "News story written by Mr. William Hipple of Newsweek—circumstances surrounding," December 1, 1944, and Memo, "Handling of Hipple and Warner Copy at Saipan," December 11, 1944, all in A7-1 Miller PR Letters Folder, Entry 86, box 3, RG313.

30. McCall to Brooks, "Pacific War Coverage," November 2, 1944, World War II Folder, box 1, McCormick Papers.

31. McCall to Brooks, "Pacific War Coverage," November 2, 1944, World War II Folder, box 1, McCormick Papers; Potter, *Nimitz*, 176, 343–44; Hughes, *Halsey*, 372–75.

32. Crozier, "Japan's Loss in Battle: 27 Ships Sunk or Hit," *New York Herald Tribune*, October 27, 1944.

33. McCall to Brooks, "Pacific War Coverage," November 2, 1944, World War II Folder, box 1, McCormick Papers; Horne, "Main Fleet Broken," *New York Times*, October 27, 1944.

34. NBC, "1346 Days," File 644: World War II—Publications, NBC History Files.

35. Cannon, *Leyte*, 221; James, *Years of MacArthur*, 2:575–76; Holzimmer, *Krueger*, 195–99; Dickinson, "Leyte Perils Described," *Editor & Publisher*, November 25, 1944.

36. Bigart, "Reporter at Leyte After Europe Finds It's Different Kind of War," *New York Herald Tribune*, November 15, 1944; Wade, ed., *Forward Positions*, 55–56. On Bigart's European experiences, see Casey, *War Beat, Europe*, 96–104, 192–98, 270–71.

37. "Two Newsmen Added to Leyte Death Toll," *Editor & Publisher*, November 18, 1944.

38. "Parrott Evacuated from Leyte by Plane," *New York Times*, November 27, 1944; Kluckhohn to Sulzberger, undated, Parrott Folder, box 56, New York Times Company Records: Arthur Hays Sulzberger Papers.

39. "Rain and the Enemy," *Time*, November 27, 1944; Dowling, "Tiny, Desolate Limon Scene of Bitter Battles," *Chicago Sun*, November 21, 1944.

40. Bigart, "Story of Leyte," *New York Herald Tribune*, December 2, 1944.

41. Kelley, "Leyte Troops Tighten Grip on Trapped Foe," "Foe on Leyte Press Back Near Ormoc," and "77th Drives North out of Ormoc," *New York Herald Tribune*, November 17 and 18, and December 12, 1944.

42. James, *Years of MacArthur*, 2:602–3; Cannon, *Leyte*, 361–65; Eichelberger and MacKaye, *Jungle Road*, 187.

43. Hulbard to Luce, March 28, 1945, Far East: Misc. Folder, box 417, Time Inc. Records.

44. "D-Day Heads UP List of Biggest Stories," *Editor & Publisher*, December 16, 1944.

45. Dowling, "How It Feels to Wait for an Invasion to Start," *Chicago Sun*, January 16, 1945; Kluckhohn, "Lead Ship's Voyage to Luzon a Grim Saga Written in Fire," *New York Times*, January 13, 1945.

46. Morison, *History of United States Naval Operations*, 12:345; Stenbuck, *Typewriter Battalion*, 257.

47. "Excerpt from *Time* issue of November 6, 1944," World War II Folder, box 274, New York Times Company Records: Arthur Hays Sulzberger Papers. This sentence appeared in "Battle of the Pacific," *Time*, November 6, 1944. The UP also put a dispatch on the wires recounting Tokyo's boast that the US fleet had been attacked "by a new suicide bomber—'A V-1 with a pilot.'" See "'Suicide' Planes Attack Leyte Fleet, Japs Report," *Chicago Sun*, November 3, 1944.

48. Kluckhohn, "Lead Ship's Voyage a Grim Saga Written in Fire," *New York Times*, January 13, 1945.

49. Arnold to King, "Public Release of Statement on Reported Suicide Attack," December 2, 1944, 000.7 File, Entry 57, box 1, RG18; Lockhart, Memo, December 12, 1944, Columnists: Lawrence Folder, Entry 1A, box 555, RG216; Potter, *Nimitz*, 371.

50. James to Sulzberger, January 4, 1945, and Sulzberger to Kluckhohn, January 5, 1945, both in World War II Folder, box 274, New York Times Company Records: Arthur Hays Sulzberger Papers; Kluckhohn, "Lead Ship's Voyage a Grim Saga Written in Fire," *New York Times*, January 13, 1945.

51. Elson, *Time Inc.*, 54; "Bill Chickering Dies in Action," *Life*, January 22, 1945; Gottfried to Luce, June 6, 1943, Censorship Folder, box 416, Time Inc. Records; Surles to MacArthur, Nos W-90854, January 15, 1945, Official Correspondence, box 2, RG3, MacArthur Papers; Mydans, OH, 18.

52. Fitch, "Special Press Facilities for M-1 Operation," November 30, 1944, Adjutant General: General Correspondence, 000.73, box 860, RG496; Dickinson, "Ideal Press Setup for Luzon," *Editor & Publisher*, January 27, 1945.

53. Richardson to Nimitz, "Radio Broadcast Facilities for Forward Area," November 30, 1944, A7-1 Miller PR Letters Folder, Entry 86, box 2, RG313.

54. James, *Years of MacArthur*, 2:621; McDaniel, "General at Rail of Warship as Bomb Drops Near-by," *Chicago Tribune*, January 10, 1945; NBC, "1346 Days," File 644: World War II—Publications, NBC History Files.

55. Dickinson, "On Fifteen-Mile Beachhead" and Jones, "Only Feeble Defenses Found on Lingayen's Beachheads," *New York Times*, January 10 and 11, 1945; Kelley, "Lingayen

Gulf Landings Set a Pacific Record," *New York Herald Tribune*, January 13, 1945. On the battle, see Smith, *Triumph in the Philippines*, 73, 77–83. Krueger, by contrast, was worried that the weather and the surf were hampering the unloading of supplies. See Holzimmer, *Krueger*, 214–15.

56. Jones, "Big Japanese Guns Harass Lingayen," *New York Times*, January 16, 1945.

57. Dowling, "Garbage Pit Happy Refuge When Japs Start Shelling," *Chicago Sun*, January 18, 1945.

58. Kelley, "Luzon Foe Crumbles on Flank," *New York Herald Tribune*, January 21, 1945; Wolters, "Door to Manila Virtually in Sight: M'Arthur," *Chicago Tribune*, January 16, 1945.

59. Kelley, "1st Cavalry Won Neck and Neck Race for Manila," *New York Herald Tribune*, February 6, 1945; Connaughton, Pimlott, and Anderson, *Battle for Manila*, 83, 209–14; James, *Years of MacArthur*, 2:637, 640; Smith, *Triumph in the Philippines*, 249; Holzimmer, *Krueger*, 219–23.

60. Connaughton, Pimlott, and Anderson, *Battle for Manila*, 107–38; Smith, *Triumph in the Philippines*, 246, 255, 306–307; James, *Years of MacArthur*, 2:642.

61. "D Plus Four" and "Picture of the Week," *Life*, May 22, 1944. The skull picture, the magazine confessed, had "stirred up quite a rumpus among the church and lady club set." See "Skull Scandal," Life Editorial News, May 29, 1944, Wartime Picture Pool Folder, box 433, Time Inc. Records.

62. AP, "Yank Survivor of Death March Joins US Lines," *Chicago Tribune*, January 22, 1945.

63. Surles to MacArthur and Diller, Nos. WX-87968 and XW-21094, January 8 and 17, 1945, both in 000.73, box 860, RG496, NARA.

64. Bigart, "Luzon Prison Camp Falls," *New York Herald Tribune*, January 24, 1945; AP, "Graves Tell Horror of Camp O'Donnell," *New York Times*, January 24, 1945; Veysey, "Japanese Cross Mocks Survivor of Death March," *Chicago Tribune*, January 26, 1945.

65. Bigart, "Tales of Rescued Americans," *New York Herald Tribune*, February 3, 1945; AP, "Bataan Men Sight Flag with Mad Joy," *New York Times*, February 2, 1945.

66. Hewlett, "Hewlett Writes of a New December 7th," *Editor & Publisher*, December 23, 1944; UP, "Correspondent Gets Praise from General," *New York Times*, February 18, 1945; Mydans, *More than Meets the Eye*, 116; Veysey, "Invasion Bound Writer Slowed by Navy Detour," *Chicago Tribune*, January 21, 1945.

67. Hewlett, "Hewlett Writes of a New December 7th," *Editor & Publisher*, December 23, 1944; UP, "Correspondent Gets Praise from General," *New York Times*, February 18, 1945; Morris, *Deadline*, 282; Mydans, *More than Meets the Eye*, 116, 186–88.

68. James, *Years of MacArthur*, 2:632–33; Hewlett, "Finds Wife Safe After 3 Years at Santo Tomas," *New York Herald Tribune*, February 6, 1945; Schedler and Hampson, "GIs Empty Own Packs to Half-Starved Internees," *Atlanta Constitution*, February 6, 1945.

69. Marshall to MacArthur, WAR35116, February 8, 1945, and War Department BPR to Assistant Director for Army Air Forces, February 15, 1945, both in BPR File, 000.7, Entry 499, box 57, RG165. Surles also arranged for twelve of the rangers who had liberated prisoners from Cabanatuanto to visit the White House. See Daniels, Memo, March 8, 1945, OF25-kk, Roosevelt Papers.

70. AP, "Army Nurses in Philippines All Found Safe," *New York Herald Tribune*, February 6, 1945; Morris, *Deadline*, 283.

71. Hewlett, "Hewlett Writes of a New December 7th," *Editor & Publisher*, December 23, 1944; UP, "Correspondent Gets Praise from General," and Weissblatt, "6,000 Americans Listed Dead by Former Prisoner on Luzon," *New York Times*, February 18 and 19, 1945.

72. Smith, *Triumph in the Philippines*, 309; Weissblatt, "MacArthur Sees Bataan Again," *New York Herald Tribune*, February 19, 1945. This trip must have been a major ordeal for Weissblatt, whose wound had received minimal medical attention during his time in captivity—just a dressing consisting of "mosquito netting soaked in picric acid." With one leg three inches shorter than the other and "twisted 90 degrees out of position," he still had to hobble around on crutches. See "Weissblatt's Leg," *Time*, July 2, 1945.

73. Weissblatt, "MacArthur Sees Bataan Again," *New York Herald Tribune*, February 19, 1945.

74. Kelley, "Civilians Being Killed Wantonly by Manila Foe," "Luzon Civilians Wantonly Slain by Vengeful Foe," and "Manila Battle Over as Infantry Kills Last of Foe in Intramuros," *New York Herald Tribune*, February 17, 23, and 25, 1945.

75. Dowling, "New Hate for Japs Born in Shambles of Bombed Hut," *Chicago Sun*, November 3, 1944.

76. Editorial, "Thus to Revisit," *Washington Post*, January 13, 1945; editorial, "Geography and MacArthur," *New York Herald Tribune*, January 13, 1945.

77. Gallup, "Sterner Treatment of Japan Favored than for Germany," *Washington Post*, December 20, 1944 (ellipses in original); "Japs Will Always Want War Say Americans," *New Journal and Guide*, February 17, 1945.

Chapter 11

1. Crozier, Diary, August 2, 1944, and Summary 1944, both in War Correspondent File, box 2, Crozier Papers. For the military's impact on the islands, see Allen, *Hawaii's War Years*, 219–21, 246–48, 281–84, 349–57.

2. Miller, Oral History (henceforth, OH), 143–44; Harris, *Nimitz*, 146.

3. "Toughest Yet," *Time*, October 16, 1944.

4. "For Your Information" and Hipple, "Manila Way Station," *Newsweek*, July 17 and September 25, 1944; Folkart, "Bill Hipple, 74; Press Agent with a Flair," *Los Angeles Times*, October 18, 1988.

5. Lambert, "Harold Miller, 89, Navy Publicist," *New York Times*, May 18, 1992; McCall to Brooks, "Pacific War Coverage," November 2, 1944, World War II Folder, box 1, McCormick Papers.

6. Harris, *Nimitz*, 144–47; "Biographical Information of Guests," undated, Iwo Jima Folder, box 22, Sherrod Papers; Lambert, "Harold Miller, 89, Navy Publicist," *New York Times*, May 18, 1992; Miller, "Censorship of Press Copy," September 25, 1944, A7-1 Miller PR Letters Folder, Entry 86, box 3, RG313.

7. Miller to Radford, December 15, 1944, A7-1 Miller PR Letters Folder, Entry 86, box 3, RG313.

8. Miller to CO, "CINCPAC-CINCPOA PR Personnel Requirements," December 20, 1944, A3-1 Organization (PR) Folder, Entry 86, box 1, RG313.

9. Merillat to parents, May 21, 1945, Merillat, Correspondence to Parents: WW2 Folder, box 1, Merillat Papers.

10. Scheetz to All Hands, "Correspondence—Handling of Expeditiously," December 29, 1944, A3-1 Organization (PR) Folder, Entry 86, box 1, RG313.

11. Lobdell, "Knox," 2:717, 720–21; Zikmund, "Forrestal," 730; Buell, *Master of Sea Power*, 253.

12. Harris, *Nimitz*, 144–45.

13. Miller, OH, 143–44, 162; Miller to Blakeslee, February 5, 1945, and Blakeslee to Miller, February 20, 1945, both in A7-1 Miller PR Letters Folder, Entry 86, box 2, RG313.

14. Levin, *From the Battlefield*, 12–13; Forrestal to Nimitz, November 2, 1944, A3-1 Organization (PR) Folder, Entry 86, box 1, RG313; Division of Public Relations, US Marine Corps, "Memo for Combat Correspondents," January 15, 1945, Entry 1008, box 3, RG127.

15. Miller, OH, 138; Nimitz to Halsey, April 18, 1945, Special Correspondence: Nimitz Folder, box 15, Halsey Papers. Forrestal was a bitter opponent of service unification at this stage; see Zikmund, "Forrestal," 736–37.

16. "Public Relations Organization," attached to Asst. Chief of Staff to G2, December 19, 1944, A3-1 Organization (PR) Folder, Entry 86, box 1, RG313.

17. Heinrichs and Gallicchio, *Implacable Foes*, 283.

18. Luter to Chapman, "News from Iwo Jima," February 23, 1945, Folder 253, Time Dispatches; Lovett to Miller, February 2, 1945, A7-1 Miller PR Letters Folder, Entry 86, box 2, RG313; Miller, OH, 145.

19. "Tarawa Island," *Life*, December 13, 1943; Jones, *War Shots*, 123; Moeller, *Shooting War*, 238.

20. AP to Dorman, Levy, and Hicks, February 10, March 3, and December 10, 1943, and August 3, 1944, all in Life: Wartime Picture Pool Folder, box 433, Time Inc. Records.

21. "Photo's Woes in Pacific," *Editor & Publisher*, August 14, 1943; Moeller, *Shooting War*, 195.

22. Drake to McArdle, June 27, 1944, Letters from Forward Area Folder, Entry 86, box 3, RG313.

23. Cooper to Miller, November 15, 1944, A7-5 Photos—Still, General Policy Folder, Entry 86, box 3, RG313.

24. Drake, "Photographic Activities, Pacific Ocean Areas—Administration of," August 6, 1944, and Sherman to Chief of Staff, August 13, 1944, both in A7-4 Motion Picture Photography Folder, Entry 86, box 10, RG313.

25. "Public Relations Organization," attached to Asst. Chief of Staff to G2, December 19, 1944, A3-1 Organization (PR) Folder, Entry 86, box 1, RG313.

26. Price, "Navy Plans Help Cameramen in Speedy Coverage on Iwo," *Editor & Publisher*, February 24, 1945; Luter to Chapman, "News from Iwo Jima," February 23, 1945, Folder 253, Time Dispatches; Miller, OH, 145–46.

27. "McDaniel Doesn't See Early End in Pacific," *Editor & Publisher*, May 12, 1945.

28. Sherrod, "Cable 24," February 19, 1945, Folder 252, Time Dispatches; Sherrod, *On to Westward*, 154, 156; Rosenthal and Heinz, "The Picture That Will Live Forever," *Collier's*, February 18, 1955; Marling and Wetenhall, *Iwo Jima*, 28; Bradley and Powers, *Flags of Our Fathers*, 198, 224–25.

29. Miller to Duffield, February 26, 1945, A7-1 Miller PR Letters Folder, Entry 86, box 2, RG313.

30. McCormick to Miller, March 13, 1945, McCormick Folder, Entry 86, box 28, RG313; "Landings of Troops on Iwo Provided Radio with Another 'Exclusive' Beat," *Broadcasting*, February 26, 1945; AP, "Battle for Iwo Is Hell Popping Seen from Air," *New York Herald Tribune*, February 20, 1945; "Eyewitness' Landing Story!," *Chicago Times*, February 19, 1945.

31. Sherrod, *On to Westward*, 172–74.

32. Lardner, "Deep Sand on Beaches," and Trumbull, "Marines Find Iwo a Hilly 'Tarawa,'" *New York Times*, February 20 and 22, 1945.

33. "The Battlefield of Iwo," *Life*, April 9, 1945.

34. Lardner, "Eyewitnesses Tell Iwo Fury," *Chicago Times*, February 20, 1944; Landsberg, "All Iwo Is No Man's Land," *New York Times*, February 22, 1945.

35. Dempsey, "Ghastly Ruin Lines Iwo Landing Beach," *New York Times*, February 23, 1945; Levin, *From the Battlefield*, 72–73.

36. "Tough Iwo to Fall, Says Marine Chief," *New York Times*, February 23, 1945.

37. "Iwo Invasion Held Vital Need in War," *New York Times*, February 24, 1945.

38. Sherrod, Cable 27, February 24, 1945, Folder 253, Time Dispatches; Sherrod, *On to Westward*, 177–81; Lindley, Dodging Sells on Iwo," *Los Angeles Times*, February 21, 1945.

39. Sherrod, *On to Westward*, 175–76.

40. Wheeler, *We Are the Wounded*, 26–31, 49; Sherrod Cable, February 24, 1945, Folder 254, Time Dispatches.

41. Wheeler to Miller, February 28, 1945, Wheeler Folder, box 35, and Stewart and Pflaum to Morrow, February 22, 1945, Morrow Folder, box 28, both in Entry 86, RG313; "Wheeler Wounded," *Chicago Times*, February 22, 1945.

42. AP, "Iwo Correspondent Hurt," *New York Times*, February 26, 1945; Allen to Lardner, March 10 1945, Lardner Folder, Entry 86, box 26, RG313; Division of Public Relations, US Marine Corps, "Memo for Combat Correspondents," March 20, 1945, Entry 1008, box 3, RG127.

43. Price, "Navy Plans Help Cameramen in Speedy Coverage on Iwo," *Editor & Publisher*, February 24, 1945; Rosenthal and Heinz, "The Picture That Will Live Forever," *Collier's*, February 18, 1955; Buell, *Uncommon Valor*, 50–53.

44. Rosenthal and Heinz, "The Picture That Will Live Forever," *Collier's*, February 18, 1955; Reed-Hill to Miller, February 22, 1945, A7-1 Miller PR Letters Folder, Entry 86, box 2, RG313; "Iwo Invasion Pictures Arrive," *New York Herald Tribune*, February 20, 1945.

45. "Marines Charge over a Crest on Iwo Island" and editorial, "Picture Miracle," *New York Times*, February 21, 1945.

46. Rosenthal and Heinz, "The Picture That Will Live Forever," *Collier's*, February 18, 1955; Buell, *Uncommon Valor*, 49, 74, 97–112; Bradley and Powers, *Flags of Our Fathers*, 315–23.

47. Buell, *Uncommon Valor*, 128–30; Renn, "'The Famous Flag-Raising,'" 254.

48. Turnblad to Rosenthal, February 23 and March 1, 1945, both in Rosenthal Folder, Entry 86, box 31, RG313; AP, "Rosenthal Gets Outstanding Photos on Iwo by Staying in Front Lines," *Hartford Courant*, February 24, 1945; AP, "Press Photo Proposed as Model for Monument," *New York Times*, March 2, 1945.

49. Vandegrift to Smith, March 6, 1945, box 2, Vandegrift Papers; "Navy Hails Joe Rosenthal," *New York Times*, March 9, 1945.

50. Henry, "Tanks Climb Grades," *New York Times*, February 20, 1945; Crozier, "Iwo Japanese Still Dug In on Volcano Slopes," *New York Herald Tribune*, February 21, 1945; Bradley and Powers, *Flags of Our Fathers*, 236.

51. Heinrichs and Gallicchio, *Implacable Foes*, 274; Alexander, *Storm Landings*, 143–44; Marling and Wetenhall, *Iwo Jima*, 73–75.

52. Rosenthal and Heinz, "The Picture That Will Live Forever," *Collier's*, February 18, 1955.

53. "The General Returns with His Armies to Luzon" and "Our Flag Goes Up over Corregidor—The Fighting Goes on at Iwo," *New York Times*, January 20 and March 8, 1945.

54. Sherrod, "Cable Unnumbered," March 13, 1945, Folder 261, Time Dispatches; Boomhower, *Dispatches*, 193.

55. Buell, *Uncommon Valor*, 182–84; Boomhower, *Dispatches*, 192–94; Renn, "'The Famous Flag-Raising,'" 256–57; "The Famous Iwo Flag Raising," *Life*, March 26, 1945.

56. Smith, "The Battlefield of Iwo," *Life*, April 9, 1945; Sherrod, "Cable 25," February 25, 1945, Folder 252, Time Dispatches; "It Was Sickening to Watch," *Time*, March 5, 1945; Renn, "'The Famous Flag-Raising,'" 256–59.

57. Sherrod, *On to Westward*, 216–17; Sherrod, "Cable Unnumbered," March 9, 1945, Folder 259, Time Dispatches; "Medicine: On Iwo Jima," *Time*, March 19, 1945.

58. Nimitz to Forrestal, "Accreditation of Woman Correspondents," November 30, 1944, General Policies and Directives Concerning Civilian Correspondents Folder, box 11; Miller to Blakeslee, February 5, 1945, A7-1 Miller PR Letters Folder, box 2; both in Entry 86, RG313. Women reporters "had filed Navy new from the Pacific as early as 1942." See Edy, *Woman War Correspondent*, 85, 96.

59. Campbell to Nimitz, "Public Relations, Various Matters Concerning," January 23, 1945, Chapelle Folder, Entry 86, box 20, RG313.

60. Miller to Daigh, June 26, 1945, Chapelle Folder, Entry 86, box 20, RG313.

61. Myers, "Lifesaving Blood Flows on Iwo, Thanks to Last Month's Donors," *New York Times*, March 2, 1945.

62. Sorel, *Women Who Wrote the War*, 306–8, 310–13; Ostroff, *Fire in the Wind*, 86–99.

63. Ostroff, *Fire in the Wind*, 100–104.

64. Sherrod, Cable 44, March 17, 1945, Folder 262, Time Dispatches. Sherrod meticulously recorded the various casualty figures on the island; see Iwo Jima Folder, box 22, Sherrod Papers.

65. Sherrod, Cable 38, March 13, 1945, Far East Misc. Folder, box 417, Time Inc. Records; Boomhower, *Dispatches*, 205.

66. Miller to Blakeslee, January 28 and 30, 1945, both in A7-1 Miller PR Letters Folder, Entry 86, box 2, RG313; Miller, OH, 148; Potter, *Nimitz*, 252–54.

67. Pyle to Stone, undated [c. 1944], and January 5, 1945, both in Pyle Correspondence Folder, box 10, Stone Papers; Pyle, Letter to his wife, February 2, 1945, Mss., II, Pyle Papers; Sherrod, "Cable No. 41," March 14, 1945, Folder 261, Time Dispatches; Sherrod, *On to Westward*, 196; Boomhower, *Dispatches*, 198.

68. Sherrod, "Cable 50," April 1, 1945, Far East Misc. Folder, box 417, Time Inc. Records

69. Pyle, "Okinawa 'Snake-Talk,'" *Washington Daily News*, April 3, 1945; Sherrod, "Cable 54," April 5, 1945, Folder 269, Time Dispatches; Sherrod, *On to Westward*, 268, 270.

70. Pyle, "On Okinawa Beaches," *Washington Daily News*, April 4, 1945; Belote and Belote, *Typhoon of Steel*, 55–65

71. Sherrod, "Cable 51," April 2, 1945, Folder 268, Time Dispatches.

72. Smith to Howard, April 18, 1945, Pyle Folder, Entry 86, box 31, RG313.

73. Sherrod, "Cables 51, 55, and 56," April 1, 5, and 6, Folders 268 and 269, Time Dispatches; Sarantakes, "Warriors of Word and Sword," 343.

74. Appleman, Burns, Gugeler, and Steven, *Okinawa*, 93–96, 249–53; Belote and Belote, *Typhoon of Steel*, 18–19, 21, 87; Leckie, *Okinawa*, 6–7; Frank, *Downfall*, 70.

75. Bigart, "Okinawa Foe Holds Ridge for Third Day," *New York Herald Tribune*, April 12, 1945.

76. Smith, "Yanks Smash Ahead on Okinawa," *Chicago Tribune*, April 25, 1945.

77. Beaufort, "Okinawa," *Christian Science Monitor*, May 15, 1945.

78. Miller to Smith, May 14, 1945, A7-1 Miller PR Letters Folder, Entry 86, box 2, RG313.

79. "Wonderful Smith," *Editorial News*, May 28, 1945, Life Edit: Misc. Folder, box 433, Time Inc. Records; "US Photographer Wounded on Okinawa," *New York Times*, May 25, 1945.

80. Chapelle to Miller, March 13, 1945, and Miller to Daigh, June 26, 1945, both in Chapelle Folder, Entry 86, box 20, RG313.

81. Ostroff, *Fire in the Wind*, 110–12; Smith to Turner, April 10, 1945, Chapelle Folder, Entry 86, box 20, RG313.

82. Smith to Turner, April 9 and 12, 1945, and Frederick to Say, April 26, 1945, all in Chapelle Folder, Entry 86, box 20, RG313; Ostroff, *Fire in the Wind*, 115–16.

83. For Frederick, April 19, 1945, Frederick to Say, April 26, 1945, and Miller to Daigh, June 26, 1945, all in Chapelle Folder, Entry 86, box 20, RG313; Ostroff, *Fire in the Wind*, 114–22.

84. Miller, *Story of Ernie Pyle*, 419–25; Tobin, *Pyle's War*, 240.

85. Tobin, *Pyle's War*, 1–3; Miller, "Ernie Wrote His Own Story—in Blood," *Washington Daily News*, April 21, 1945.

86. Smith to Scheetz, April 21, 1945, and Sutton to Scheetz, April 21, 1945, both in Pyle Folder, Entry 86, box 31, RG313.

87. During the first days of the battle, Sherrod cabled his editor that "the play given the Okinawa story is not known here." Sherrod, "Cable 55," April 5, 1945, Folder 269, Time Dispatches.

88. Leckie, *Okinawa*, 49.

89. Beaufort, "Okinawa Troops Honor Roosevelt," *Christian Science Monitor*, April 14, 1945.

90. Gratke to Beaufort, April 22, 1945, Beaufort Folder, Entry 86, box 18, RG313.

91. Tribune to Morrow, May 12, 1945, Morrow Folder, box 28, Shawn to Lardner, April 30, 1945, Lardner Folder, box 26, and, Beaufort to Gratke, undated, Beaufort Folder, box 18, all in Entry 86, RG313.

92. Casey, *War Beat, Europe*, 336–41.

93. Lee to Miller, May 22, 1945, and Miller to Lee, June 4, 1945, both in Miller Folder, Entry 86, box 2, RG313.

94. Luce, for instance, assigned his coeditor, Manfred Gottfried, to Guam to become *Time*'s chief Pacific correspondent because he thought "the Pacific is so very important that it rates the full-time service of a very important editor." Luce to Staffs of Time, Life, and Fortune, July 19, 1945, Far East Misc. Folder, box 417, Time Inc. Records.

Chapter 12

1. Merillat to parents, May 26, 1945, Merillat, Correspondence to Parents: WW2 Folder, box 1, Merillat Papers.

2. Barnes to Crozier, April 18, Crozier Folder, Entry 86, box 21, RG313; Crozier to Barnes, undated, box 2, Crozier Papers.

3. Newmyer to Director, "Fleet Hometown Distribution Center," May 24, 1945, Miller Folder, Entry 86, box 2, RG313. See also Sarantakes, "Warriors of Word and Sword," 345–46.

4. "US Attacks Fail on Okinawa," *New York Herald Tribune*; "Inch On in Bloody Okinawa," *Chicago Tribune*, May 19, 1945.

5. Bigart, "Offensive Gains Slowly," *New York Herald Tribune*, May 13, 1945.

6. Bigart, "Hill 196 Taken in Bitter 17-Day Okinawa Fight," *New York Herald Tribune*, May 8, 1945.

7. Bigart, "US Wins Okinawa Crest on Seventh Try" and "Marine Units Reinforced in Fight in Naha," *New York Herald Tribune*, May 20 and 25, 1945.

8. Bigart, "Tactics Called Conservative," *New York Herald Tribune*, May 29, 1945; Chappell, *Before the Bomb*, 77.

9. Lawrence, "Critics in Capital Hit Okinawa 'Mistakes'" and "Writer Calls for Truth on Okinawan Fiasco," *Washington Evening Star*, May 30 and June 4, 1945.

10. Lee to Miller, May 11, 1945, Miller Folder, Entry 86, box 2, RG313.

11. Shallett, "Forrestal Denies Okinawa Bungling," *New York Times*, June 6, 1945; Bigart, "Nimitz Upholds Army Tactics, Denies Okinawa Is a 'Fiasco,'" *New York Herald Tribune*, June 17, 1945.

12. Bigart, "What Okinawa Taught the Americans," *New York Herald Tribune*, June 22, 1945; Rae, "Okinawa Is a Lesson for Invasion of Japan," *New York Times*, May 27, 1945.

13. Editorial, "Japanese Hysteria," *New York Herald Tribune*, April 4, 1945.

14. AP, "Human Bombs Fail to Hold Up Okinawa Drive," *Chicago Tribune*, May 11, 1945.

15. AP, "15 Ships Lost in Fight for Okinawa," *Baltimore Sun*, April 21, 1945; AP, "US Naval Casualties at Okinawa Reach 5551," *Los Angeles Times*, May 4, 1945.

16. AP, "Okinawa Fleet Again Attacked by Foe's Flyers," *New York Herald Tribune*, April 13, 1945; Sherrod, *On to Westward*, 293–94.

17. Commanding General to Commandant of the Marine Corps, "Censorship Policy, Suicide Plans, Fire Bombs," April 27, 1945, 1365-25 File: Censorship Over-Censors, Entry 18-B, box 291, RG127.

18. "Captain Dixie and the Ti," *Time*, July 23, 1945; Lawrence to Sulzberger, September 16, 1945, Censorship Folder, New York Times Company Records: Arthur Hays Sulzberger Papers.

19. Lee, "Suicides Help End Jap Air Power," *Washington Post*, May 20, 1945.

20. Lawrence, "Enemy Suicide Pilot Dives Plane on US Hospital Ship Off Okinawa," *New York Times*, April 30, 1945.

21. In early June, an AP report disclosed that the Japanese had beheaded sixteen US citizens, including eleven Baptist missionaries, on the Philippines two years earlier. AP, "Japs Behead 16 From US," *Chicago Tribune*, June 6, 1945.

22. Walsh, Memo, May 4, 1945, Columnists: Wilson Folder, Entry 1A, box 556, RG216; Wilson, "Air War in the Pacific," May 4, 1945, *New York Herald Tribune*.

23. Lee to Miller, June 14, 1945, Miller Folder, Entry 86, box 2, RG313; Crozier, "Letter of a Japanese Admiral, About to Die, to US President," *New York Herald Tribune*, July 11, 1945.

24. Editorial, "Imperial Mumbo Jumbo," *New York Herald Tribune*, July 12, 1945.

25. "On to Tokyo and What?" *Life*, May 21, 1945; OWI, "Current Surveys," No. 7, February 23, 1945, Entry 149, box 1719, RG44.

26. Frank, *Downfall*, 30, 126–27; Heinrichs and Gallicchio, *Implacable Foes*, 427–30.

27. Editorial, " 'Kamikaze,' " *New York Times*, May 20, 1945.

28. UP, "US Suicide Crisis in Suicide Attacks," *Los Angeles Times*, June 3, 1945.

29. Moscow, "Isles Declared Won," and Lawrence, "General at Front," *New York Times*, June 22 and 19, 1945; Sarantakes, "Warriors of Word and Sword," 358–59.

30. Rae, "Okinawa Is a Lesson for Invasion of Japan," *New York Times*, May 27, 1945; Chappell, *Before the Bomb*, 41.

31. *Foreign Relations of the United States: Potsdam*, 1:903–10; Frank, *Downfall*, 132–48; Sarantakes, "Warriors of Word and Sword," 360–67; Heinrichs and Gallicchio, *Implacable Foes*, 476–79.

32. Hoffman, "American Wolf Packs," 132.

33. Casey, *War Beat, Europe*, 104–105.

34. Parker to Hodge, June 11, 1943, Tharp, "Safeguarding of Information on the B-29 and B-32 Airplanes," July 7, 1943, and Giles, "Security Affecting the B-29 Aircraft," October 16, 1943, BPR all in File 000.7, Entry 499, boxes 14, 18, and 16, RG165.

35. Wiant, *Between the Bylines*, 171, 197–98.

36. "We Are Only 10 Minutes from Japan," *AP World*, June–July 1944, WWII Book Project Folder: The War in Japan, AP28, Writings About the AP, Series II, box 14, AP

Corporate Archives; Wiant, *Between the Bylines*, 198–202; Durdin, "B-29 Bombing Trip to Japan Is Described by Eyewitness," *New York Times*, June 17, 1944.

37. Durdin, "B-29 Bombing Trip to Japan Is Described by Eyewitness," *New York Times*, June 17, 1944; Wiant, "Frequent B-29 Raids on Japan Out till Gas Supply Improves," *Atlanta Constitution*, June 17, 1944.

38. Watson to Lockhart, June 20, 1944, AP Folder, Entry 1A, box 145, RG216; Wiant, *Between the Bylines*, 201–203; Catledge to Lawrence, July 31, 1945, Lawrence Folder, Entry 86, box 26, RG313.

39. White to Chief of Staff, "Publicity on B-29 and Twentieth Air Force Activities," June 20, 1944, 000.7 File, Entry 57, box 1, RG18.

40. White to Chief of Staff, "Publicity on B-29 and Twentieth Air Force Activities," June 20, 1944, 000.7 File, Entry 57, box 1, RG18; Sherry, *Rise of American Air Power*, 184.

41. Norstad to LeMay, October 5, 1944, Special Official Correspondence with Norstad Folder, box B11, LeMay Papers; Norstad, Memo for the Commanding General, XXI Bomber Command, October 27, 1944, 000.7 File, Entry 57, box 1, RG18; Sherry, *Rise of American Air Power*, 182–83.

42. Haugland, "B-29s Complete Their Mission with Atomic Bombs!," *Reporting to Remember: Unforgettable Stories and Pictures of the War by AP Correspondents*, D811 A2 A8 (Oversize), AP Corporate Archives; McElway, "A Reporter with the B-29s: I-Possum, Rosy, and the Thousand Kids," *New Yorker*, June 9, 1945;

43. Johnson, "Eyewitness Describes B-29 Attack on Tokyo," *Los Angeles Times*, November 25, 1944.

44. Frank, *Downfall*, 53.

45. Hipple to Miller, November 30, 1944, Eldred, "News story written by Mr. William Hipple of Newsweek—circumstances surrounding," December 1, 1944, and Memo, "Handling of Hipple and Warner Copy at Saipan," December 11, 1944, all in A7-1 Miller PR Letters Folder, Entry 86, box 3, RG313. Hipple's editors compensated by rounding up three of his stories and publishing them together. See Hipple, "What B-29s Are Saying with Bombs," *Newsweek*, December 4, 1944.

46. Pyle, Letter to his wife, February 2, 1945, Pyle mss.; Pyle, "Heart of the Pacific War," *Washington Daily News*, February 22, 1945.

47. McElway, "A Reporter with the B-29s: II—The Doldrums, Guam, and Something Coming Up," *New Yorker*, June 16, 1945.

48. Norstad to Westlake, "Policy on War Correspondents Accompanying B-29 Missions," December 29, 1944, 000.74 File, Entry 57, box 1, RG18.

49. Norstad to LeMay, December 9 and October 5, 1944, Special Official Correspondence with Norstad Folder, box B11, LeMay Papers.

50. McElway, "A Reporter with the B-29s: II—The Doldrums, Guam, and Something Coming Up," *New Yorker*, June 16, 1945; Frank, *Downfall*, 53; Coffey, *Iron Eagle*, 131, 134.

51. McElway, "A Reporter with the B-29s: II—The Doldrums, Guam, and Something Coming Up," *New Yorker*, June 16, 1945; Coffey, *Iron Eagle*, 123, 133–34, 138, 144–45; Frank, *Downfall*, 58–59.

52. Coffey, *Iron Eagle*, 155–56, 160–61; Sherry, *Rise of American Air Power*, 272–73; Frank, *Downfall*, 62–64; Crane, *Bombs, Cities, Civilians*, 129–31.

53. Sevareid, "Press: McElway," undated, box D3, Sevareid Papers; Sevareid, *Not So Wild*, 265, 298, 307–308.

54. McElway, "A Reporter with the B-29s: III—The Cigar, Three Wings, and the Low-Level Attacks," *New Yorker*, June 23, 1945; Frank, *Downfall*, 66.

55. UP, "Tokyo's Heart Left Rubble by Vast Fires," and Sheridan, "Reporter Sees Tokyo Aflame, Smells Smoke," *New York Herald Tribune*, March 11, 1945.

56. "Tokyo Put in Panic by B-29 Fire Bombs," *New York Times*, March 16, 1945; UP, "Nip 'Thousands' Slain by Bombs," *Los Angeles Times*, March 16, 1945.

57. Sherry, *Rise of American Air Power*, 289–90; Press briefing, undated, Text Folder, Army Air Forces: Office of Information Services: General Subject File, Entry 55, box 30, RG18; UP, "Tokyo's Heart Left Rubble by Vast Fires," *New York Herald Tribune*, March 11, 1945; McElway, "A Reporter with the B-29s: III—The Cigar, Three Wings, and the Low-Level Attacks," *New Yorker*, June 23, 1945.

58. Frank, *Downfall*, 68–77.

59. AP, "Mikado's Three Palaces Struck in Raid on Tokyo," *Chicago Tribune*, April 15, 1945.

60. UP, "Tokyo No Longer Vital Target," *Los Angeles Times*, June 4, 1945; "LeMay Promises 'Ruin' for Japan," *New York Times*, June 20, 1945.

61. Dopking, "B-29s Will Be Lacking Targets by Christmas, Augurs Air Boss LeMay," *Washington Post*, July 22, 1945; AP, "Jap Civilians to Get More Warnings and Raids, Says LeMay," *Boston Globe*, July 30, 1945; "12 Nippon Targets Names," *Christian Science Monitor*, July 31, 1945.

62. Sherry, *Rise of American Air Power*, 289–90; McElway, "A Reporter with the B-29s: III—The Cigar, Three Wings, and the Low-Level Attacks," *New Yorker*, June 23, 1945

63. McElway, "A Reporter with the B-29s: III—The Cigar, Three Wings, and the Low-Level Attacks," *New Yorker*, June 23, 1945.

64. Sherry, *Rise of American Air Power*, 291, 185.

65. McElway, "A Reporter with the B-29s: I—Possum, Rosy, and the Thousand Kids," *New Yorker*, June 9, 1945.

66. Laurence, *Dawn Over Zero*, 165–67.

67. Washburn, "Office of Censorship's Attempt to Control Press Coverage," 4–19, 35.

68. Consodine to Groves, June 27, 1945, and Groves to Nichols, July 10, 1945, both in Records of Commanding General Manhattan Project, 000.71, box 31, RG77; "War Department Called Times Reporter to Explain Bomb's Intricacies to Public," *New York Times*, August 7, 1945; Laurence, *Dawn Over Zero*, xvi–xvii, 173–79; Keever, *News Zero*, 1–2; Keever, "Top Secret," 186–87.

69. Laurence, *Dawn Over Zero*, 177.

70. Laurence, *Dawn Over Zero*, 179–86, 190–203.

71. Laurence, *Dawn Over Zero*, 178, 199.

72. Robinson, June 6, 1945, Records of Commanding General Manhattan Project, 000.71, box 31, RG77; "War Department Called Times Reporter to Explain Bomb's Intricacies

to Public," *New York Times*, August 7, 1945; Laurence, *Dawn Over Zero*, 187; Keever, "Top Secret," 193–95. A few weeks later, the *Times* also published Laurence's ten-part series on the bomb's development, which it distributed to other newspapers free of charge. See Keever, *News Zero*, 18–19.

73. Henning, "Atomic Bomb Story!," *Chicago Tribune*, August 7, 1945; AP, "Atomic Bomb Hits Japan," *Los Angeles Times*, August 7, 1945.

74. James to Lawrence, August 7, 1945, Lawrence Folder, Entry 86, box 26, RG313.

75. Groves to Surles, August 7, 1945, Records of Commanding General Manhattan Project, 000.71, box 31, RG77; Howland, "Cable 5," August 8, 1945, Folder 298, Time Dispatches; Spaatz, "Air Force Press Release," August 8, 1945, Misc. Press Releases Folder, box B40, LeMay Papers; AP, "Col. Tibbets, Pilot of B-29, Tells of Raid," *New York Herald Tribune*, August 8, 1945.

76. UP, "Russia Attacks Japan, Second Atomic Bombing!," *Los Angeles Times*, August 9, 1945; AP, "Atom Bomb's 2d Target Is Kyushu Port," *New York Herald Tribune*, August 9, 1945.

77. AP, "Col. Tibbets, Pilot of B-29, Tells of Raid," *New York Herald Tribune*, August 8, 1945.

78. AP, "Atom Bomb's 2d Target Is Kyushu Port," *New York Herald Tribune*, August 9, 1945; Jacoby, "Chungking Cable 266," August 18, 1945, Folder 300, Time Dispatches.

79. "Pacific Veterans Hail Atomic Bomb on Return," *Los Angeles Times*, August 9, 1945; Henning, "Atomic Bomb Story!," *Chicago Tribune*, August 7, 1945.

80. Boyer, "Exotic Resonances," 145; Boyer, *By the Bomb's Early Light*, 183–84.

81. Luter, "Cable 36," August 19, 1945, and White, "Cable 19," August 25, both in Far East: Misc. Folder, box 417, Time Inc. Records.

82. To Commanding Generals, CM-OUT-5165, August 18, 1945, BPR File, 000.73, Entry 499, box 62, RG165; US Pacific Fleet, Press Release, No. 769 and No. 827, September 18 and October 16, 1945, Censorship Folder, Entry 3, box 18, RG428.

83. Trammel to Principal Members of Program, Sales, Station Relations, and News Departments of All Divisions, August 28, 1945, File 641: World War II, NBC History Files; "Clues Unearthed in 'Flash' Inquiry," *New York Times*, August 14, 1945.

84. Lawrence to Sulzberger, September 16, 1945, Censorship Folder, box 125, New York Times Company Records: Arthur Hays Sulzberger Papers.

85. "70-Year Effect of Bombs Denied," *New York Times*, August 9, 1945; Washburn, "Office of Censorship's Attempt to Control Press Coverage," 28–29; Boyer, *By the Bomb's Early Light*, 188. On the government's continued efforts to play down radioactivity in the weeks after the war, see Keever, *News Zero*, 52–62.

86. FCCP A71, August 22, 1945, Records of Commanding General Manhattan Project, 000.71, box 31, RG77; Laurence, "US Atom Bomb Site Belies Tokyo Tales," *New York Times*, September 12, 1945.

87. Weller to Russell, September 26, 1945, Letters to Russell Churchill Folder and Weller to Yolan, June 20, 1966, WWII: Japan Defeated Folder, both in box 38, Weller Papers; Weller, ed., *First into Nagasaki*, 3–12; Keever, *News Zero*, 76–78.

88. Weller, ed., *First into Nagasaki*, 18, 29–30.

89. Weller, ed., *First into Nagasaki*, 38–39.

90. Burchett, *Memoirs of a Rebel Journalist*, 229–51.

91. Weller, ed., *First into Nagasaki*, 301–306.

92. Kelly, *Tex McCrary*, 79.

93. Spaatz to MacArthur for Diller, August 13, 1945, Special Official Correspondence with Norstad Folder, box B11, LeMay Papers; Lawrence to Sulzberger, September 16, 1945, Censorship Folder, New York Times Company Records: Arthur Hays Sulzberger Papers; Kelly, *Tex McCrary*, 82.

94. Dowling, "I Saw Ruined Nagasaki," *Boston Globe*, August 28, 1945; Wade, ed., *Forward Positions*, 81–83.

95. Lawrence to Sulzberger, September 16, 1945, Censorship Folder, New York Times Company Records: Arthur Hays Sulzberger Papers. On McCrary, see Casey, *War Beat, Europe*, 112–13.

Conclusion

1. Spencer, "The 'Rising Sun' Sets on the 'Missouri,'" *Reporting to Remember*, D811 A2 A8 (Oversize), AP Corporate Archives; Potter, *Nimitz*, 393–94; James, *Years of MacArthur*, 2:788–89. Although many accounts state that the US Capitol flag was flown, Admiral Stuart S. Murray categorically refuted this claim; see Murray, "Oral History Re Surrender Table, September 2, 1945."

2. AP, "315 Correspondents Covered Surrender," *New York Times*, September 3, 1945.

3. Dower, *Embracing Defeat*, 42–43; Lee, *One Last Look Around*, 22.

4. Manchester, *American Caesar*, 450–52; James, *Years of MacArthur*, 2:788–89.

5. ISCOM Okinawa to CINCPOA, July 15, 1945, BPR File, 000.73, Entry 499, box 62, RG165; Hagenah to Vandegrift, August 6, 1945, box 3, Vandegrift Papers.

6. McCrary to LeMay, "USATAF PRO Plans for Coverage Inside Japan," undated, Special Official Correspondence with Norstad Folder, box B11, LeMay Papers; McDaniel, "Tokyo—End of the Line," AP World, September–October 1945, WWII Book Project Folder: The War in Japan, AP28, Writings About the AP, Series II, box 14, AP Corporate Archives.

7. James, *Years of MacArthur*, 2:788–91.

8. Miller to Lee, June 4, 1945, A7-1 Miller PR Letters Folder, Entry 86, box 2, RG313.

9. James, *Years of MacArthur*, 2:790.

10. Dower, *Embracing Defeat*, 42–43, 46.

11. Schaller, *American Occupation*, 46; Dower, *Embracing Defeat*, 74–75, 406–7; Braw, *Atomic Bomb Suppressed*, 27.

12. Coughlin, *Conquered Press*, 111–19; Elliott, *American Press*, 37–38; Inoshita, "The Occupation and the Korean War Years," 13–14; James, *Years of MacArthur*, 3:304–6; Schaller, *MacArthur*, 128.

13. Roth, *Historical Dictionary*, 92; Smith, "Frank Hewlett, Reporter for Utah Paper," *Washington Post*, July 9, 1983; Boomhower, *Dispatches*, 213–15; Moseley, *Reporting the War*, 360.

14. Carroll to Beheller, October 10, 1950, Bigart Folder, box III:5, Reid Family Papers; Bigart to Bigart, September 10, 1950, Correspondence Folder, box 1, Bigart Papers; Higgins and Bigart, "On the Battlefront in Korea," *New York Herald Tribune*, December 6, 1950.

15. On MacArthur's Korean War press system and the reasoning behind it, see Echols to Correspondents, July 2, 1950, RG 6, box 4, MacArthur Papers; Echols to Dabney, July 31, 1950, Official Correspondence Folder, box 2, Echols Papers; Erwin, "Voluntary Censorship Asked in Korean War," *Editor & Publisher*, July 8, 1950; Echols, "Information in the Combat Zone," 61–64.

16. MacArthur to Brown, January 18, 1951, General Correspondence, box 1, RG 6, MacArthur Papers; Casey, *Selling the Korean War*, 154–65.

17. Casey, *Selling the Korean War*, 306–11.

18. Hammond, *Public Affairs*, 1:138–39, 143–45, 159–61, 193–95; Hallin, "*Uncensored War*," 127.

19. Braestrup, *Battle Lines*, 88–104; Seib, *Beyond the Front Lines*, 51–64; Casey, *When Soldiers Fall*, 215; Brewer, *Why America Fights*, 252–53.

20. Knightley, *First Casualty*, 274–76, 330. See also Pratt, "How the Censors Rigged the News," 100, 101–2; Matthews, *Reporting*, 175–78.

21. Roeder, *Censored War*, 11–15; McCallum, "US Censorship," 565; Huebner, *Warrior Image*, 29–36.

22. Leff, *Buried*, 341–42, makes the same point in the context of news about the Holocaust.

23. Winkler, *Politics of Propaganda*, 22–31.

24. Correspondence Panels Section to Rodgers, "Information Services and Newspapers—Some Criticisms," December 9, 1943, Entry 149, box 1710, RG44.

25. Only a few polls conducted during the war differentiated between those with and without family in service, but the ones that did revealed that "those with immediate relatives in the armed service offer more support for realism in the news than those with no close relatives in the war." See OWI, "Public Appraisal of the War News," Memo No. 67, October 29, 1943, Entry 164, box 1799, RG44.

26. Long, "Possible Effect of War on Price of Paper Considered" and "Dailies Circulation Up 3.24%," *Editor & Publisher*, October 28 and December 9, 1939.

27. OWI, "Surfeit with the Government's War Messages," Memo No. 71, December 6, 1943, Entry 164, box 1799, RG44.

28. For an excellent discussion of the public's response to the war from a political science perspective, see Berinsky, *In Time of War*, 36–57, 87–100.

29. Dudziak, "'You didn't see him lying,'" 16.

30. Bigart, "Story of Leyte," *New York Herald Tribune*, December 2, 1944.

31. Cited in Woods, *Reporting the Retreat*, xix.

32. Jackson and Stillman to Luce, October 28, 1942, Edit Misc. Folder, box 416, Time Inc. Records.

33. Braestrup, *Big Story*, 528.

34. Sherrod to Meek, "Navy Public Relations," February 10, 1944, Censorship Folder, box 416, Time Inc. Records.

35. Sweeney, *Secrets of Victory*, 5–11, 36–42; Sweeney, *The Military and the Press*, 65–71; Smith, *War and Press Freedom*, 149–51, 156–57.
36. Whether the story had any impact on Japan has long been hotly debated. For a recent assessment, see Carlson, *Johnston's Blunder*, 231–42.
37. Hightower, "AP—World Services," 6–7; Allen, "Catching up with the Competition," 758–59; Casey, *Selling the Korean War*, 45; Hammond, *Reporting Vietnam*, 63.
38. Hamilton, *Journalism's Roving Eye*, 189–91, 214; Kluger, *The Paper*, 709–41.
39. Weller, ed., *First into Nagasaki*, 249.
40. Chenoweth, "54 War Correspondents K.I.A."; "Reporters Killed in War Honored," *New York Times*, September 21, 1948.

Bibliography

Primary Sources

British Library, Asian and African Studies, London
File 462/18K. SEAC Censorship—Stilwell, Mountbatten Dispute

Manuscript Collections: Media
Agronsky, Martin. Library of Congress, Washington, DC
Alsop, Joseph and Stewart [Alsop]. Library of Congress, Washington, DC
Associated Corporate Archives. New York, NY
Bigart, Homer. Wisconsin Historical Society, Madison
Billings, John Shaw: Time-Life Fortune Papers. South Caroliniana Library, Columbia, SC
Binder, Carroll. Newberry Library, Chicago
Casey, Robert J. Newberry Library, Chicago
Chicago Tribune Company Records. Cantigny, IL
Clapper, Raymond. Library of Congress, Washington, DC
Crozier, Emmett. Wisconsin Historical Society, Madison
Haugland, Vern. Mansfield Library, University of Montana, Missoula
Howard, Roy W. Library of Congress, Washington, DC
Krock, Arthur. Princeton University, Princeton, NJ
Luce, Clare Boothe. Library of Congress, Washington, DC
Luce, Henry. Library of Congress, Washington, DC
McClean, Robert. Associated Press Corporate Archives, New York, NY
McCormick, Robert. Wisconsin Historical Society, Madison
NBC History Files. Library of Congress, Washington, DC
NBC Radio Collection. Library of Congress, Washington, DC
New York Times Company Records: Arthur H. Sulzberger Papers. New York Public
    Library
Noderer, E. R. Chicago Tribune Company Records. Cantigny, IL
Patterson, Joseph Medill. Lake Forest College, Lake Forest, IL
Pyle, Ernie. Lilly Library, Indiana University, Bloomington
Reid Family. Library of Congress, Washington, DC
Sebring, Lewis B. Wisconsin Historical Society, Madison
Sevareid, A. Eric. Library of Congress, Washington, DC
Sherrod, Robert L. Syracuse University Library, Syracuse, NY
Stone, Walker. Wisconsin Historical Society, Madison
Stowe, Leland. Wisconsin Historical Society, Madison
Strout, Richard L. Library of Congress, Washington, DC
Time, Inc. Records. New York Historical Society, New York, NY
Time Magazine Dispatches. Houghton Library, Harvard University, Cambridge, MA

Tregaskis, Richard. Howard Gotlieb Archival Research Center, Boston University, Boston
Weller, George. Houghton Library, Harvard University, Cambridge, MA

Manuscript Collections: Military and Government

Arnold, Charles J. MacArthur Memorial, Norfolk, VA
Arnold, Henry H. Library of Congress, Washington, DC
Biddle, Francis. Roosevelt Presidential Library, Hyde Park, NY
Cates, Clifton B. Marine Corps Archives, Quantico, VA
Chamberlin, Stephen J. MacArthur Memorial, Norfolk, VA
Chennault, Claire. Hoover Institution Archives, Stanford, CA
Davis, Elmer. Library of Congress, Washington, DC
Denig, Robert. Marine Corps Archives, Quantico, VA
Doolittle, James H. Library of Congress, Washington, DC
Early, Stephen. Roosevelt Presidential Library, Hyde Park, NY
Echols, Marion P. Military History Institute, Carlisle, PA
Eichelberger, Robert L. MacArthur Memorial, Norfolk, VA
Forrestal, James V. Princeton University, Princeton, NJ
Halifax, Lord. Churchill College, Cambridge, UK
Halsey, William F. Library of Congress, Washington, DC
Hopkins, Harry, L. Roosevelt Presidential Library, Hyde Park, NY
Kenney, George C. MacArthur Memorial, Norfolk, VA
King, Ernest J. Library of Congress, Washington, DC
Knox, Frank. Library of Congress, Washington, DC
Kunz, Frank. MacArthur Memorial, Norfolk, VA
LeMay, Curtis. Library of Congress, Washington, DC
MacArthur, Douglas. MacArthur Memorial, Norfolk, VA
   RG-2, United States Army Forces in the Far East
   RG-3, GHQ Southwest Pacific Area
   RG-4, US Army Forces, Pacific
MacLeish, Archibald. Library of Congress, Washington, DC
Marshall, George C. Marshall Library, Lexington, VA
Merillat, Herbert C. Howard Gotlieb Archival Research Center, Boston University, Boston
Nash, Phileo. Truman Presidential Library, Independence, MO
Redding, John M. Truman Presidential Library, Independence, MO
Roosevelt, Franklin D. Roosevelt Presidential Library, Hyde Park, NY
Stilwell, Joseph W. Hoover Institution Archives, Stanford, CA
Stimson, Henry. Yale University, New Haven, CT
Vandegrift, A. Archer. Marine Corps Archives, Quantico, VA
White, Robert M. MacArthur Memorial, Norfolk, VA

National Archives, College Park, MD

RG18. Army Air Forces
RG44. Office of Government Reports
RG59. State Department
RG77. Office of Chief of Engineers
RG80. Office of the Secretary of the Navy
RG107. Office of the Secretary of War
RG127. Marine Corps

RG165. War Department
RG208. Office of War Information
RG216. Office of Censorship
RG218. Joint Chiefs of Staff
RG313. Naval Operating Forces
RG319. Army Chief of Staff
RG407. Adjutant General's Office
RG428. Navy Department
RG493. US Forces in the CBI Theater of Operations
RG494. US Army Forces in the Middle Pacific
RG496. General HQ Southwest Pacific Area

National Archives: UK, Kew Gardens, London

ADM. Records of the Admiralty
PREM. Records of the Prime Minister
WO. Records of the War Office

Newspapers and Magazines

AP Inter-Office
Atlanta Constitution
Atlanta Daily World
Boston Globe
Broadcasting
Chicago Daily News
Chicago Defender
Chicago Sun
Chicago Tribune
Christian Science Monitor
Collier's
Editor & Publisher
Hartford Courant
Life
Los Angeles Times
New Journal and Guide
New York Herald Tribune
New York Times
Newspaper World
Newsweek
Reader's Digest
Saturday Evening Post
Time
Washington Daily News
Washington Post
World Press News

Oral Histories

Denig, Robert. Marine Corps Archives, Quantico, VA
Diller, LeGrande A. MacArthur Memorial, Norfolk, VA

Drake, Waldo. US Naval Institute, Annapolis, MD
Dunn, William. MacArthur Memorial, Norfolk, VA
Kent, Carleton. Truman Presidential Library, Independence, MO
Kunz, Frank. MacArthur Memorial, Norfolk, VA
Miller, Harold B. US Naval Institute, Annapolis, MD
Mydans, Carl. MacArthur Memorial, Norfolk, VA
Romulo, Carlos P. MacArthur Memorial, Norfolk, VA
Sherrod, Robert. MacArthur Memorial, Norfolk, VA
White, Robert M. MacArthur Memorial, Norfolk, VA

Secondary Sources

Books

Adams, John A. *Fightin' Texas Aggie Defenders of Bataan and Corregidor*. College Station: Texas A&M University Press, 2016.
Adams, Michael C. C. *The Best War Ever: America and the Second World War*. 2nd ed. Baltimore: Johns Hopkins University Press, 2015.
Alexander, Joseph H. *Across the Reef: The Marine Assault on Tarawa*. Washington, DC: Marine Corps Historical Center, 1993.
———. *Storm Landings: Epic Amphibious Battles in the Central Pacific*. Annapolis, MD: Naval Institute Press, 2012.
———. *Utmost Savagery: Three Days on Tarawa*. Annapolis, MD: Naval Institute Press,1995.
Alkebulan, Paul. *The African-American Press in World War II: Toward Victory at Home and Abroad*. Lanham, MD: Lexington Books, 2014.
Allen, Gwenfread. *Hawaii's War Years, 1941–1945*. Honolulu: University of Hawaii Press, 1950.
Allen, Louis. *Burma: The Longest War, 1941–1945*. London: Phoenix Press, 1984.
Appleman, Roy E., James M. Burns, Russell A. Gugeler, and John Stevens. *Okinawa: The Last Battle*. Washington, DC: Center of Military History, 1993.
Arnold, Henry H. *Global Mission*. New York: Harper, 1949.
Ault, Phil. *News Around the Clock: Press Associations in Action*. New York: Dodd, Mead, 1960.
Baker, Alan D. *Merrill's Marauders*. New York: Ballantine Books, 1972.
Barnow, Erik. *The Golden Web: A History of Broadcasting in the United States*. Vol. 2, *1933 to 1953*. New York: Oxford University Press, 1968.
Bartsch, William H. *December 8, 1941: MacArthur's Pearl Harbor*. College Station: Texas A&M University Press, 2003.
Belden, Jack. *Retreat with Stilwell*. New York: Alfred Knopf, 1943.
Bell, Jack. *Line of Fire*. Coral Gables, FL: Glade House, 1948.
Bell, Roger J. *Unequal Allies: Australian-American Relations and the Pacific War*. Melbourne: Melbourne University Press, 1977.
Belote, James and William Belote. *Typhoon of Steel: The Battle for Okinawa*. London: Bantam Books, 1984.
Berger, Meyer. *The Story of the New York Times, 1941–1951*. New York: Simon and Schuster, 1951.

Bergerud, Eric. *Touched with Fire: The Land War in the South Pacific*. New York: Penguin, 1997.

Berinsky, Adam J. *In Time of War: Understanding Public Opinion from World War II to Iraq*. Chicago: University of Chicago Press, 2009.

Bidwell, Shelford. *The Chindit War: Stilwell, Wingate, and the Campaign in Burma, 1944*. New York: Macmillan, 1979.

Bilek, Tony. *No Uncle Sam: The Forgotten of Bataan*. Kent, OH: Kent State University Press, 2003.

Blair, Clay. *Silent Victory: The US Submarine War against Japan*. Annapolis, MD: Naval Institute Press, 1975.

Bodnar, John. *The "Good War" in American Memory*. Baltimore: Johns Hopkins University Press, 2010.

Boni, William F. *Want to Be a War Correspondent?* Highland City, FL: Rainbow Books, 1995.

Boomhower, Ray E. *Dispatches from the Pacific: The World War II Reporting of Robert L. Sherrod*. Bloomington: Indiana University Press, 2017.

Borg, Dorothy. *The United States and the Far Eastern Crisis of 1933–1938*. Cambridge, MA: Harvard University Press, 1964.

Borneman, Walter R. *MacArthur at War: World War II in the Pacific*. New York: Little, Brown, 2016.

———. *The Admirals: Nimitz, Leahy, and King—The Five-Star Admirals Who Won the War at Sea*. New York: Little, Brown, 2012.

Boyer, Paul S. *By the Bomb's Early Light: American Thought and Culture at the Dawn of the Nuclear Age*. Chapel Hill: University of North Carolina Press, 1994.

Bradley, James with Ron Powers. *Flags of Our Fathers*. New York: Bantam Books, 2000.

Braestrup, Peter. *Battle Lines*. New York: Priority Press, 1985.

———. *Big Story*. New York: Anchor Press, 1978.

Braw, Monica. *Atomic Bomb Suppressed: American Censorship in Occupied Japan*. Armonk, NY: M. E. Sharpe, 1991.

Brewer, Susan A. *Why America Fights: Patriotism and War Propaganda from the Philippines to Iraq*. New York: Oxford University Press, 2009.

Brinkley, Alan. *The Publisher: Henry Luce and the American Century*. New York: Alfred Knopf, 2010.

Buell, Hal. *Uncommon Valor, Common Virtue: Iwo Jima and the Photograph That Captured America*. New York: Penguin, 2006.

Buell, Thomas B. *Master of Sea Power: A Biography of Fleet Admiral Ernest J. King*. Annapolis, MD: Naval Institute Press, 1980.

Burchett, Wilfred. *Memoirs of a Rebel Journalist: The Autobiography of Wilfred Burchett*. Sydney: University of New South Wales Press, 2005.

Burlingame, Roger. *Don't Let Them Scare You: The Life and Times of Elmer Davis*. Philadelphia: Lippincott, 1961.

Cameron, Craig M. *American Samurai: Myth, Imagination, and the Conduct of Battle in the First Marine Division, 1941–1951*. Cambridge: Cambridge University Press, 1994.

Cannon, M. Hamlin. *Leyte: The Return to the Philippines*. Washington, DC: Center of Military History, 1993.

Carlson, Elliot. *Stanley Johnston's Blunder: The Reporter Who Spilled the Secret behind the US Navy's Victory at Midway*. Annapolis, MD: Naval Institute Press, 2017.

Carlson, John Roy. *Cairo to Damascus*. New York: Alfred Knopf, 1951.

Caro, Robert A. *Means of Ascent: The Years of Lyndon Johnson*. New York: Vintage, 1990.

Carpenter, Iris. *No Woman's World*. Boston: Houghton Mifflin, 1946.

Carruthers, Susan L. *The Media at War: Communication and Conflict in the Twentieth Century*. Palgrave: Basingstoke, 2000.

Casey, Robert J. *I Can't Forget: Personal Experiences of a War Correspondent in France, Luxembourg, Germany, Belgium, Spain, and England*. New York: Bobbs-Merrill, 1941.

———. *Such Interesting People*. New York: Bobbs-Merrill, 1943.

———. *This Is Where I Came In*. New York: Bobbs-Merrill, 1945.

———. *Torpedo Junction: With the Pacific Fleet from Pearl Harbor to Midway*. London: Jarrold's, 1943.

Casey, Steven. *Cautious Crusade: Franklin D. Roosevelt, American Public Opinion, and the War against Nazi Germany*. New York: Oxford University Press, 2001.

———. *Selling the Korean War: Propaganda, Politics, and Public Opinion, 1950–53*. New York: Oxford University Press, 2008.

———. *The War Beat, Europe: The American Media at War against Nazi Germany*. New York: Oxford University Press, 2017.

———. *When Soldiers Fall: How Americans Have Confronted Combat Casualties, from World War I to Afghanistan*. New York: Oxford University Press, 2014.

Chapin, John C. *Breaching the Marianas: The Battle for Saipan*. Washington, DC: Marine Corps Historical Center, 1994.

Chappell, John D. *Before the Bomb: How America Approached the End of the Pacific War*. Lexington: University Press of Kentucky, 1997.

Chennault, Claire Lee. *Way of a Fighter: The Memoirs of Claire Lee Chennault*. New York: G. P. Putnam's Sons, 1949.

Coffey, Thomas M. *Iron Eagle: The Turbulent Life of General Curtis LeMay*. New York: Crown, 1986.

Collier, Richard. *The Warcos: The War Correspondents of World War II*. London: Weidenfeld and Nicolson, 1969.

Colman, Penny. *Where the Action Was: Women War Correspondents in World War II*. New York: Crown, 2002.

Connaughton, Richard, John Pimlott, and Duncan Anderson. *The Battle for Manila*. London: Bloomsbury, 1995.

Cook, Jeffrey B. *American World War II Correspondents*. Farmington Hills, MI: Gale, 2012.

Cooper, Kent. *Barriers Down: The Story of the News Agency Epoch*. New York: Farrar and Rinehart, 1942.

———. *Kent Cooper and the Associated Press: An Autobiography*. New York: Random House, 1959.

Corbett, P. Scott. *Quiet Passages: The Exchange of Civilians between the United States and Japan During the Second World War*. Kent, OH: Kent State University Press, 1987.

Coughlin, William J. *Conquered Press: The MacArthur Era in Japanese Journalism*. Palo Alto, CA: Pacific Books, 1952.

Crane, Conrad C. *Bombs, Cities, Civilians: American Airpower Strategy in World War II*. Lawrence: University Press of Kansas, 1993.

Craven, Wesley Frank and James Lea Cate. *The Army Air Forces in World War II*. Washington, DC: Office of Air Force History, 1983.

Crowl, Philip A. *Campaign in the Marianas*. Washington, DC: Center of Military History, 1993.

Crowl, Philip A. and Edmund G. Love. *Seizure of the Gilberts and Marshalls*. Washington, DC: Center of Military History, 1993.

Cutler, Thomas J. *The Battle of Leyte Gulf, 23–26 October 1944*. Annapolis, MD: Naval Institute Press, 1994.

Davies, Robert B. *Baldwin of the* Times: *Hanson W. Baldwin, A Military Journalist's Life, 1903–1991*. Annapolis, MD: Naval Institute Press, 2011.

Dean, Peter J. *MacArthur's Coalition: US and Australian Operations in the Southwest Pacific Area, 1942–1945*. Lawrence: University Press of Kansas, 2018.

Dell'Orto, Giovanna. *AP Foreign Correspondents in Action: World War II to Present*. Cambridge: Cambridge University Press, 2015.

Desmond, Robert W. *Tides of War: World News Reporting, 1931–1945*. Iowa City: University of Iowa Press, 1984.

Dorn, Frank. *Walkout with Stilwell in Burma*. New York: Thomas Crowell, 1971.

Dower, John W. *Embracing Defeat: Japan in the Wake of World War II*. New York: W. W. Norton, 1999.

———. *War Without Mercy: Race and Power in the Pacific War*. London: Faber and Faber, 1986.

Duffy, James P. *War at the End of the World: Douglas MacArthur and the Forgotten Fight for New Guinea, 1942–1945*. New York: NAL Caliber, 2016.

Dunn, William J. *Pacific Microphone*. College Station: Texas A&M University Press, 1988.

Dyess, William E. and Charles Leavelle. *The Dyess Story: The Eyewitness Account of the Death March from Bataan, Japanese Prison Camps, and Escape*. New York: G. P. Putnam's Sons, 1944.

Edwards, Jerome E. *The Foreign Policy of Col. McCormick's* Tribune. Reno: University of Nevada Press, 1971.

Edy, Caroline M. *The Woman War Correspondent, the US Military, and the Press, 1846–1847*. Lanham, MD: Lexington Books, 2017.

Eichelberger, Robert L. and Milton MacKaye. *Jungle Road to Tokyo*. New York: Viking Press, 1951.

Eldridge, Fred. *Wrath in Burma: The Uncensored Story of General Stilwell in the Far East*. Garden City, NY: Doubleday, 1946.

Elliott, Oliver. *The American Press and the Cold War: The Rise of Authoritarianism in South Korea, 1945–1954*. Basingstoke: Palgrave, 2018.

Ellis, John. *The Sharp End: The Fighting Man in World War II*. London: Aurum, 2009.

Elson, Robert T. *Time Inc.: The Intimate History of a Publishing Enterprise*. Vol. 2, *1941–1960*. New York: Athenaeum, 1968.

Feis, Herbert. *The China Tangle: The American Effort in China from Pearl Harbor to the Marshall Mission*. Princeton, NJ: Princeton University Press, 1953.

Fenby, Jonathan. *Generalissimo: Chiang Kai-shek and the China He Lost*. London: Free Press, 2003.

Ferrell, Robert H., ed. *The Eisenhower Diaries*. New York: W. W. Norton, 1981.

Fitzsimmons, Peter. *Kokoda*. Sydney: Hachette, 2004.

Ford, Daniel. *Flying Tigers: Claire Chennault and His American Volunteers, 1941–42*. Washington, DC: Smithsonian Books, 2007.

Frank, Richard B. *Downfall: The End of the Imperial Japanese Empire*. New York: Penguin, 1999.

———. *Guadalcanal*. New York: Penguin, 1990.

Gailey, Harry A. *Howlin' Mad vs the Army: Conflict in Command, Saipan, 1944.* Novato, CA: Presidio, 1986.

———. *MacArthur's Victory: The War in New Guinea, 1943–1944.* New York: Ballantine Books, 2004.

Gallup, George H. *The Gallup Poll: Public Opinion, 1935–1971.* 3 vols. New York: Random House, 1972.

Gay, Timothy M. *Assignment to Hell: The War against Nazi Germany with Correspondents Walter Cronkite, Andy Rooney, A. J. Liebling, Homer Bigart, and Hal Boyle.* New York: NAL Caliber, 2012.

Ginneken, Jaap van. *Understanding Global News: A Critical Introduction.* London: Sage, 1998.

Gramling, Oliver. *AP: The Story of News.* London: Kennikat Press, 1969.

Greeley, Brendan M., ed. *The Two Thousand Yard Stare: Tom Lea's World War II.* College Station: Texas A&M University Press, 2008.

Griffith, Thomas E. *MacArthur's Airman: General George C. Kenney and the War in the Southwest Pacific.* Lawrence: University Press of Kansas, 1998.

Guard, Harold with John Tring. *The Pacific War Uncensored: A War Correspondent's Unvarnished Account of the War against Japan.* Philadelphia: Casemate, 2011.

Hailey, Foster. *Pacific Battle Line.* New York: Macmillan, 1944.

Hall, Gwendolyn Midlo, ed. *Love, War, and the 96th Engineers (Colored).* Urbana: University of Illinois Press, 1995.

Hallin, Daniel C. *The "Uncensored War": The Media and Vietnam.* Berkeley: University of California Press, 1986.

Hamilton, John Maxwell. *Edgar Snow: A Biography.* Baton Rouge: Louisiana State University Press, 1988.

———. *Journalism's Roving Eye: A History of American Foreign Reporting.* Baton Rouge: Louisiana State University Press, 2009.

Hammond, William M. *Public Affairs: The Military and Media, 1962–1973.* 2 vols. Washington, DC: Center of Military History, 1990–96.

———. *Reporting Vietnam: The Media and Military at War.* Lawrence: University Press of Kansas, 1998.

Harris, Brayton. *Admiral Nimitz: The Commander of the Pacific Ocean Theater.* Basingstoke: Palgrave, 2012.

Haugland, Vern. *43 Days: An Epic of Journalistic Devotion.* Missoula: Montana State University, 1942.

———. *Letter from New Guinea.* New York: Farrar and Rinehart, 1943.

Healy, George W. *A Lifetime on Deadline.* Gretna, LA: Pelican, 1976.

Heinrichs, Waldo H. *American Ambassador: Joseph C. Grew and the Development of the United States Diplomatic Tradition.* New York: Oxford University Press, 1966.

Heinrichs, Waldo H. and Marc Gallicchio. *Implacable Foes: War in the Pacific, 1944–1945.* New York: Oxford University Press, 2017.

Hemingway, Mary Welsh. *How It Was.* New York: Knopf, 1976.

Hersey, John. *Into the Valley: Marines at Guadalcanal.* Lincoln: University of Nebraska Press, 2002.

———. *Men on Bataan.* New York: Alfred Knopf, 1942.

Hlavacek, John. *United Press Invades India: Memoirs of a Foreign Correspondent, 1944–1952.* Omaha, NE: Hlucky Books, 2006.

Hoffman, Carl W. *Saipan: The Beginning of the End.* Washington, DC: Marine Corps Historical Division, 1950.

Hoffmann, Joyce. *Theodore White and Journalism as Illusion.* Columbia: University of Missouri Press, 1995.

Hohenberg, John. *Foreign Correspondence: The Great Reporters and Their Times.* New York: Columbia University Press, 1964.

Holzimmer, Kevin C. *General Walter Krueger: Unsung Hero of the Pacific War.* Lawrence: University Press of Kansas, 2007.

Horner, David M. *High Command: Australia and Allied Strategy, 1939–1945.* Canberra: Australian War Memorial, 1982.

Hosley, David H. *As Good as Any: Foreign Correspondence on American Radio, 1930–1940.* Westport, CT: Greenwood Press, 1984.

Huebner, Andrew J. *The Warrior Image: Soldiers in American Culture from the Second World War to the Vietnam Era.* Chapel Hill: University of North Carolina Press, 2008.

Hughes, Thomas Alexander. *Admiral Bill Halsey: A Naval Life.* Cambridge, MA: Harvard University Press, 2016.

Hunter, Charles N. *Galahad.* San Antonio, TX: Naylor, 1963.

James, Clayton D. *The Years of MacArthur.* 3 vols. Boston: Houghton Mifflin, 1970–85.

Johnston, George H. *New Guinea Diary.* Sydney: Angus and Robertson, 1943.

Johnston, Stanley. *Queen of the Flat-Tops.* London: Bantam Books, 1979.

Jones, Charles. *War Shots: Norm Hatch and the US Marine Corps Cameramen of World War II.* Mechanicsburg, PA: Stackpole, 2011.

Keever, Beverly Ann Deepe. *News Zero: The* New York Times *and the Bomb.* Monroe, ME: Common Courage Press, 2004.

Keith, Phil. *Stay the Rising Sun.* Minneapolis: Zenith Press, 2015.

Kelly, Charles J. *Tex McCrary: Wars, Women, Politics—An Adventurous Life Across the American Century.* Lanham, MD: Hamilton Books, 2009.

Kennett, Lee. *For the Duration: The United States Goes to War, Pearl Harbor—1942.* New York: Charles Scribner, 1985.

Kenney, George C. *Kenney Reports: A Personal History of the Pacific War.* N.p.: Progressive Management Publications, 2017.

King, Ernest J. and Walter Muir Whitehill. *Fleet Admiral King: A Naval Record.* London: Eyre and Spottiswoode, 1953.

Kirby, Edward M. and Jack W. Harris, *Star-Spangled Radio.* Chicago: Ziff-Davis, 1948.

Klein, Christina. *Cold War Orientalism: Asia in the Middlebrow Imagination, 1945–1961.* Berkeley: University of California Press, 2003.

Kluger, Richard. *The Paper: The Life and Death of the* New York Herald Tribune. New York: Vintage Books, 1989.

Knightley, Phillip. *The First Casualty: From the Crimea to the Falklands—The War Correspondent as Hero, Propagandist and Myth Maker.* Rev. ed. London: Pan Books, 1989.

Kolakowski, Christopher L. *Last Stand on Bataan: The Defense of the Philippines, December 1941-May 1942.* Jefferson, NC: McFarland, 2016.

Lacey, Sharon Tosi. *Pacific Blitzkrieg: World War II in the Central Pacific.* Denton: University of North Texas Press, 2013.

Lardner, John. *Southwest Passage: Yanks in the Pacific.* Lincoln: University of Nebraska Press, 2013.

Larrabee, Eric. *Commander in Chief: Franklin Delano Roosevelt, His Lieutenants, and Their War.* New York: Harper and Row, 1987.

Lascher, Bill. *Eve of a Hundred Midnights.* New York: HarperCollins, 2016.

Laurence, William L. *Dawn Over Zero: The Story of the Atomic Bomb.* London: Museum Press, 1947.

Leckie, Robert. *Okinawa: The Last Battle of World War II.* New York: Penguin, 1996.

Lee, Clark. *One Last Look Around.* New York: Duell, Sloan, and Pearce, 1947.

———. *They Call It Pacific: An Eyewitness Story of the War against Japan from Bataan to the Solomons.* London: John Long, 1943.

Lee, Clark and Richard Henschel. *Douglas MacArthur.* New York: Henry Holt, 1952.

Leff, Laurel. *Buried by the* Times: *The Holocaust and America's Most Important Newspaper.* New York: Cambridge University Press, 2005.

Levin, Dan. *From the Battlefield: Dispatches of a World War II Marine.* Annapolis, MD: Naval Institute Press, 1995.

Linderman, Gerald F. *The World Within War: America's Combat Experience in World War II.* Cambridge, MA: Harvard University Press, 1997.

Lipstadt, Deborah E. *Beyond Belief: The American Press and the Coming of the Holocaust, 1933–1945.* New York: Free Press, 1986.

Luvaas, Jay, ed. *Dear Miss Em: General Eichelberger's War in the Pacific, 1942–1945.* Westport, CT: Greenwood Press, 1972.

MacArthur, Douglas. *Reminiscences.* New York: McGraw-Hill, 1964.

MacGregor, Jr., Morris J. *Integration of the Armed Forces, 1940–1965.* Washington, DC: Center of Military History, 1981.

Manchester, William. *American Caesar: Douglas MacArthur, 1880–1964.* Boston: Little, Brown, 1978.

Mander, Mary S. *Pen and Sword: American War Correspondents, 1898–1975.* Urbana: University of Illinois Press, 2010.

Marling, Karal Ann and John Wetenhall. *Iwo Jima: Monuments, Memories, and the American Hero.* Cambridge, MA: Harvard University Press, 1991.

Marshall, Samuel L. A. *Bringing Up the Rear: A Memoir.* San Rafael, CA: Presidio, 1979.

Maslowski, Peter. *Armed with Cameras: The American Military Photographers of World War II.* New York: Free Press, 1993.

Masuda, Hiroshi. *MacArthur in Asia: The General and His Staff in the Philippines, Japan, and Korea.* Ithaca, NY: Cornell University Press, 2013.

Matloff, Maurice. *Strategic Planning for Coalition Warfare, 1943–1944.* Washington, DC: Center of Military History, U.S. Army, 1959.

Matloff, Maurice and Edwin M. Snell. *Strategic Planning for Coalition Warfare, 1941–1942.* Washington, DC: Department of the Army, Office of the Chief of Military History, 1953.

Matthews, Joseph J. *Reporting the Wars.* Minneapolis: University of Minnesota Press, 1957.

McLynn, Frank. *The Burma Campaign: Disaster into Triumph, 1942–45.* London: Vintage, 2011.

McManus, John C. *Fire and Fortitude: The US Army in the Pacific War, 1941–1943.* New York: Caliber, 2019.

Merillat, Herbert C. *Guadalcanal Remembered.* New York: Avon Books, 1990.

Miller, Ernest B. *Bataan Uncensored.* Long Prairie, MN: Hart Publications, 1949.

Miller, Lee G. *The Story of Ernie Pyle.* New York: Viking, 1950.

Miller, John. *Cartwheel: The Reduction of Rabaul.* Washington, DC: Center of Military History, 1990.

Millett, Allan R. *Semper Fidelis: The History of the United States Marine Corps.* New York: Macmillan, 1980.

Milner, Samuel. *Victory in Papua.* Washington, DC: Department of the Army, Office of the Chief of Military History, 1957.

Mitter, Rana. *China's War with Japan, 1937–1945: The Struggle for Survival.* London: Allen Lane, 2013.

Moeller, Susan D. *Shooting War: Photography and the American Experience of Combat.* New York: Basic Books, 1989.

Moïse, Edwin E. *Tonkin Gulf and the Escalation of the Vietnam War.* Chapel Hill: University of North Carolina Press, 1996.

Moore, William T. *Dateline Chicago: A Veteran Newsman Recalls Its Heyday.* New York, Taplinger, 1973.

Morison, Samuel Eliot. *History of United States Naval Operations in World War II.* 15 vols. Boston: Little, Brown, 1947–62.

Morris, Joe A. *Deadline Every Minute: The Story of the United Press.* Garden City, NY: Doubleday, 1957.

Morriss, Mack. *South Pacific Diary, 1942–1943.* Lexington: University Press of Kentucky, 1996.

Mortimer, Gavin. *Merrill's Marauders.* Minneapolis: Zenith Press, 2015.

Morton, Louis. *The Fall of the Philippines.* Washington, DC: Department of the Army, Office of the Chief of Military History, 1953.

Moseley, Ray. *Reporting the War: How Foreign Correspondents Risked Capture, Torture and Death to Cover World War II.* New Haven, CT: Yale University Press, 2017.

Mydans, Carl. *More than Meets the Eye.* London: Hutchinson, 1961.

Nichols, David, ed., *Ernie's War: The Best of Ernie Pyle's World War II Dispatches.* New York: Random House, 1986.

Norton-Smith, Richard. *The Colonel: The Life and Legend of Robert R. McCormick, 1880–1955.* Evanston, IL: Northwestern University Press, 1997.

Ogburn, Jr., Charlton. *The Marauders.* New York: Overlook Press, 2002.

Ostroff, Roberta. *Fire in the Wind: The Life of Dickey Chapelle.* Annapolis, MD: Naval Institute Press, 2001.

Paul, Christopher and James J. Kim. *Reporters on the Battlefield: The Embedded Press System in Historical Context.* Santa Monica, CA: Rand, 2004.

Pearlman, Michael D. *Warmaking and American Democracy: The Struggle over Military Strategy, 1700–Present.* Lawrence: University Press of Kansas, 1999.

Pedelty, Mark. *War Stories: The Culture of Foreign Correspondents.* New York: Routledge, 1995.

Perry, Glen C. H. *"Dear Bart": Washington Views of World War II.* Westport, CT: Greenwood Press, 1982.

Pfitzer, Gregory M. *Samuel Eliot Morison's Historical Mind.* Boston: Northeastern University Press, 1991.

Pike, Francis. *Hirohito's War: The Pacific War, 1941–1945.* London: Bloomsbury, 2015.

Pogue, Forrest C. *George C. Marshall: Ordeal and Hope, 1939–1942.* London: MacGibbon and Kee, 1965.

———. *George C. Marshall: Organizer of Victory, 1943–1945.* New York: Viking Press, 1973.

Pollock, James Crothers. *The Politics of Crisis Reporting: Learning to be a Foreign Correspondent*. New York: Praeger, 1981.

Potter, E. B. *Nimitz*. Annapolis, MD: Naval Institute Press, 1976.

Prados, John. *Combined Fleet Decoded: The Secret History of American Intelligence and the Japanese Navy*. New York: Random House, 1995.

Prange, Gordon. *Miracle at Midway*. Norwalk, CT: Eaton Press, 1982.

Prefer, Nathan N. *Vinegar Joe's War: Stilwell's Campaigns for Burma*. Novato, CA: Presidio, 2000.

Preston, Paul. *We Saw Spain Die: Foreign Correspondents in the Spanish Civil War*. London: Constable, 2008.

Prochnau, William. *Once Upon a Distant War: David Halberstam, Neil Sheehan, Peter Arnett—Young War Correspondents and Their Early Vietnam Battles*. New York: Vintage Books, 1995.

Ralph, Barry. *They Passed This Way: The United States of America, the States of Australia, and World War II*. Roseville, NSW: Kangaroo Press, 2000.

Reporting World War II. 2 vols. New York: Library of America, 1995.

Ritter, Jonathan Templin. *Stilwell and Mountbatten in Burma: Allies at War, 1943–1944*. Denton: University of Northern Texas Press, 2017.

Robert J. Casey: A Biographical Sketch and a Description of His Books. New York: Bobbs-Merrill, 1945.

Robinson, Greg. *By Order of the President: FDR and the Internment of Japanese Americans*. Cambridge, MA: Harvard University Press, 2001.

Robinson, Pat. *The Fight for New Guinea: General Douglas MacArthur's First Offensive*. New York: Random House, 1943.

Roeder, George H. *The Censored War: American Visual Experience During World War II*. New Haven, CT: Yale University Press, 1993.

Rogers, Paul P. *The Bitter Years: MacArthur and Sutherland*. Westport, CT: Greenwood Press, 1991.

———. *The Good Years: MacArthur and Sutherland*. Westport, CT: Greenwood Press, 1990.

Romanus, Charles F. and Riley Sunderland. *Stilwell's Command Problems*. Washington, DC: Center of Military History, 1987.

———. *Stilwell's Mission to China*. Washington, DC: Center of Military History, 1987.

———, eds. *Stilwell's Personal File: China, Burma, India, 1942–1944*. 5 vols. Wilmington, DE: Scholarly Resources, 1976.

Romulo, Carlos P. *I Saw the Fall of the Philippines*. London: George G. Harrap, 1943.

Roosevelt, Franklin D. *Complete Press Conferences of Franklin D. Roosevelt*. 25 vols. New York: Da Capo Press, 1972.

Rosenman, Samuel I. *Working with Roosevelt*. New York: Harper & Brothers, 1952.

Roth, Mitchel P. *Historical Dictionary of War Journalism*. Westport, CT: Greenwood Press, 1992.

Ruppenthal, Roland G. *Logistical Support of the Armies*. 2 vols. Washington, DC: Department of the Army, Office of the Chief of Military History, 1953.

Sainsbury, Keith. *The Turning Point: Roosevelt, Stalin, Churchill, and Chiang-Kai-shek, 1943—The Moscow, Cairo, and Teheran Conferences*. Oxford: Oxford University Press, 1986.

Schaffer, Ronald. *Wings of Judgment: American Bombing in World War II*. New York: Oxford University Press, 1985.

Schaller, Michael. *American Occupation of Japan: The Origins of the Cold War in Asia.* New York: Oxford University Press, 1985.

———. *Douglas MacArthur: Far Eastern General.* New York: Oxford University Press, 1989.

Schneider, James C. *Should America Go to War? The Debate over Foreign Policy in Chicago, 1939–1941.* Chapel Hill: University of North Carolina Press, 1989.

Seib, Philip. *Beyond the Front Lines: How the News Media Cover a World Shaped by War.* Basingstoke: Palgrave, 2004.

Sevareid, Eric. *Not So Wild a Dream: A Personal Story of Youth and War and the American Faith.* New York: Athenaeum, 1976.

Sherrod, Robert. *On to Westward: War in the Central Pacific.* New York: Duell, Sloan, and Pearce, 1945.

———. *Tarawa: The Story of a Battle.* New York: Duell, Sloan, and Pearce, 1944.

Sherry, Michael S. *The Rise of American Air Power: The Creation of Armageddon.* New Haven, CT: Yale University Press, 1987.

Sherwood, Robert E. *Roosevelt and Hopkins: An Intimate History.* Rev ed. New York: Harper and Row, 1950.

Smith, Jeffrey A. *War and Press Freedom: The Problem of Prerogative Power.* New York: Oxford University Press, 1999.

Smith, Robert Ross. *Approach to the Philippines.* Washington, DC: Center of Military History, 1996.

———. *Triumph in the Philippines.* Washington, DC: Center of Military History, 1993.

Sorel, Nancy Caldwell. *The Women Who Wrote the War: The Riveting Saga of World War II's Daredevil Women Correspondents.* New York: Arcade, 2011.

Soule, Thayer. *Shooting the Pacific War: Marine Corp Combat Photography in WWII.* Lexington: University Press of Kentucky, 2001.

Sparrow, James T. *Warfare State: World War II Americans and the Age of Big Government.* New York: Oxford University Press, 2011.

Spector, Ronald H. *Eagle against the Sun: The American War with Japan.* New York: Vintage, 1985.

Stavisky, Samuel E. *Marine Combat Correspondent: World War II in the Pacific.* New York: Ivy Books, 1999.

Steele, A. T. *Shanghai and Manchuria, 1932: Reflections of a War Correspondent.* Tempe: Arizona State University, 1977.

Stenbuck, Jack. *Typewriter Battalion: Dramatic Frontline Dispatches from World War II.* New York: William Morrow, 1995.

Sterne, Joseph R. L. *Combat Correspondents: The Baltimore Sun in World War II.* Baltimore: Maryland Historical Society, 2009.

Stowe, Leland. *No Other Road to Freedom.* New York: Alfred Knopf, 1941.

———. *They Shall Not Sleep.* New York: Alfred Knopf, 1944.

Sweeney, Michael S. *Secrets of Victory: The Office of Censorship and the American Press and Radio in World War II.* Chapel Hill: University of North Carolina Press, 2001.

———. *The Military and the Press: An Uneasy Truce.* Evanston, IL: Northwestern University Press, 2006.

Symonds, Craig L. *The Battle of Midway.* New York: Oxford University Press, 2011.

Taaffe, Stephen R. *MacArthur's Jungle War: The 1944 New Guinea Campaign.* Lawrence: University Press of Kansas, 1998.

Talese, Guy. *The Kingdom and the Power.* New York: World, 1969.

Tanaka, Yuki. *Hidden Horrors: Japanese War Crimes in World War II*. Lanham, MD: Rowman and Littlefield, 2018.

Thorne, Christopher. *Allies of a Kind: The United States, Britain and the War Against Japan, 1941–1945*. Oxford: Oxford University Press, 1978.

———. *The Issue of War: States, Societies and the Far Eastern Conflict of 1941–1945*. London: Hamish Hamilton, 1985.

Thussu, Daya Kishan and Des Freedman, eds. *War and the Media: Reporting Conflict 24/7*. London: Sage, 2003.

Tobin, James. *Ernie Pyle's War: Eyewitness to World War II*. New York: Free Press, 2006.

Toll, Ian W. *Pacific Crucible: War at Sea in the Pacific, 1941–1942*. New York: W. W. Norton, 2012.

———. *The Conquering Tide: War in the Pacific Islands, 1942–1944*. New York: W. W. Norton, 2015.

Tregaskis, Richard. *Guadalcanal Diary*. New York: Modern Library, 2000.

Trimble, Vance H., ed. *Scripps-Howard Handbook*. Cincinnati, OH: E. W. Scripps, 1981.

Tuchman, Barbara. *Stilwell and the American Experience in China*. London: Phoenix Press, 2001.

Tupper, Eleanor and George E. McReynolds, *Japan in American Public Opinion*. New York: Macmillan, 1937.

Ulbrich, David J. *Preparing for Victory: Thomas Holcomb and the Making of the Modern Marine Corps, 1936–1943*. Annapolis, MD: Naval Institute Press, 2011.

US Congress, Senate Foreign Relations Committee. *State Department Loyalty Investigation*. Washington, DC: US Government Printing Office, 1950.

US State Department. *Foreign Relations of the United States: Conference at Potsdam*. 2 vols. Washington, DC: US Government Printing Office, 1960.

US War Department. *Regulations for Correspondents Accompanying U.S. Army Forces in the Field*. Washington, DC, 1941.

Van de Ven, Hans J. *War and Nationalism in China, 1925–1945*. London: Routledge, 2003.

Vandegrift, Alexander A. and Robert B. Asprey. *Once a Marine: The Memoirs of General A. A. Vandegrift*. New York: W. W. Norton, 1964.

Vaughn, Stephen. *Holding Fast the Inner Lines: Democracy, Nationalism, and the Committee on Public Information*. Chapel Hill: University of North Carolina Press, 1980.

Vogel, Steve. *The Pentagon: A History*. New York: Random House, 2007.

Voss, Frederick S. *Reporting the War: The Journalistic Coverage of World War II*. Washington, DC: Smithsonian, 1994.

Wade, Betsy, ed. *Forward Positions: The War Correspondence of Homer Bigart*. Fayetteville: University of Arkansas Press, 1992.

Wainwright, Jonathan M. *General Wainwright's Story: The Account of Four Years of Humiliating Defeat, Surrender, and Captivity*. Garden City, NY: Doubleday, 1946.

Waldrop, Frank C. *MacArthur on War*. New York: Duell, Sloan, and Pearce, 1942.

Washburn, *A Question of Sedition: The Federal Government's Investigation of the Black Press During World War II*. New York: Oxford University Press, 1986.

Weller, Anthony, ed. *First into Nagasaki: The Censored Eyewitness Dispatches on Post-Atomic Japan and Its Prisoners of War*. New York: Crown, 2006.

———. *Weller's War*. New York: Crown, 2009.

Wheeler, Keith. *The Pacific Is My Beat*. New York: Dutton, 1943.

———. *We Are the Wounded*. New York: Dutton, 1943.

White, Graham J. *FDR and the Press*. Chicago: University of Chicago Press, 1979.

White, Osmar. *Green Armour*. London: Corgi Books, 1975.

White, Theodore H. *In Search of History: A Personal Adventure*. New York: Harper and Row, 1978.

————, ed. *The Stilwell Papers*. London: MacDonald, 1949.

White, Theodore H. and Annalee Jacoby. *Thunder Out of China*. New York: William Sloane, 1961.

Wiant, Susan E. *Between the Bylines: A Father's Legacy*. New York: Fordham University Press, 2011.

Winfield, Betty Houchin. *FDR and the News Media*. New York: Columbia University Press, 1994.

Winkler, Allan M. *The Politics of Propaganda: The Office of War Information*. New Haven, CT: Yale University Press, 1978.

Wolfert, Ira. *Battle for the Solomons*. London: Jarrolds, 1943.

Woods, Philip. *Reporting the Retreat: War Correspondents in Burma*. London: Hurst, 2016.

Wyman, David S. *The Abandonment of the Jews: America and the Holocaust, 1941–1945*. New York: Pantheon Books, 1985.

Ziegler, Philip. *Mountbatten: The Official Biography*. London: Collins, 1987.

————, ed. *Personal Diary of Admiral The Lord Louis Mountbatten, Supreme Allied Commander, South-East Asia, 1943–1946*. London: Collins, 1988.

Articles

Allen, Gene. "Catching up with the Competition: The International Expansion of the Associated Pressm 1920-1945." *Journalism Studies* 17 (2016): 747–62.

Beasley, Maurine H. "Women and Journalism in World War II: Discrimination and Progress." *American Journalism* 12 (2013): 321–33.

Boyer, Paul. "Exotic Resonances: Hiroshima in American Memory." In *Hiroshima in History and Memory*, edited by Michael J. Hogan, 143–67. Cambridge: Cambridge University Press, 1996.

Burma, John H. "An Analysis of the Present Negro Press." *Social Forces* 26 (1947–48): 172–80.

Casey, Steven. "Reporting from the Battlefield: Censorship and Journalism." In *The Cambridge History of the Second World War*, edited by Richard J. Bosworth and Joe Maiolo, 2:117–38. Cambridge: Cambridge University Press, 2015.

————. "Wilfred Burchett and the United Nations Command's Media Relations During the Korean War." *Journal of Military History* 74 (2010): 523–56.

Dean, Peter J. "MacArthur's War: Strategy, Command, and Plans for the 1943 Offensives. In *Australia 1943: The Liberation of New Guinea*, edited by Peter J. Dean, 45–67. Cambridge: Cambridge University Press, 2014.

Dower, John W. "Race, Language, and War in Two Cultures: World War II in Asia." In *The War in American Culture: Society and Consciousness During World War II*, edited by Lewis A. Erenberg and Susan E. Hirsch, 169–201. Chicago: University of Chicago Press, 1996.

Dudziak, Mary. "'You didn't see him lying . . . beside the gravel road in France': Death, Distance, and War in American Politics." *Diplomatic History* 42 (2018): 1–16.

Echols, Marion P. "Information in the Combat Zone." *Army Information Digest* 6 (1951): 60–64.

Goren, Dina. "Communication Intelligence and the Freedom of the Press: The *Chicago Tribune*'s Battle of Midway Dispatch and the Breaking of the Japanese Naval Code." *Journal of Contemporary History* 16 (1981): 663–90.

Graybar, Lloyd J. "Admiral King's Toughest Battle." *Naval War College Review* 32 (1979): 38–47.

Hoffman, F. G. "The American Wolf Packs: A Case Study in Wartime Adaption." *Joint Force Quarterly* 80 (2016): 131–39.

Inoshita, Day. "The Occupation and the Korean War Years, 1945–54." In *Foreign Correspondents in Japan: Reporting a Half Century of Upheavals—From 1945 to the Present*, edited by Charles Pomeroy, 2–149. Rutland, VT: Charles E. Tuttle, 1998.

Keever, Beverly Ann Deepe. "Top Secret: Censoring the First Rough Drafts of Atomic-Bomb History." *Media History* 14 (2008): 185–204.

Lobdell, George H. "Frank Knox." In *American Secretaries of the Navy*, edited by Paolo E. Coletta, 2:677–727. Annapolis, MD: Naval Institute Press, 1980.

MacKenzie, S.P. "Vox Populi: British Army Newspapers in the Second World War." *Journal of Contemporary History* 24 (1989): 665–81.

Mason, Robert. "Eyewitness." *Proceedings of the US Naval Institute* 108 (1982): 40–45.

May, Ernest. "US Press Coverage of Japan, 1931–1941." In *Pearl Harbor as History: Japanese-American Relations, 1931–1942*, edited by Dorothy Borg and Shumpai Okamoto, 511–32. New York: Columbia University Press, 1973.

McCallum, John. "US Censorship, Violence, and Moral Judgement in a Wartime Democracy." *Diplomatic History* 41 (2017): 543–66.

Mendelson, Andrew and C. Zoe Smith. "Part of the Team: LIFE Photographers and Their Symbiotic Relationship with the Military in World War II." *American Journalism* 12 (2013): 276–89.

Mowrer, Paul Scott. "Bungling the News." *Public Opinion Quarterly* 7 (1943): 116–24.

Mueller, John. "Pearl Harbor: Military Inconvenience, Political Disaster." *International Security* 15 (1991–92): 172–203.

Murphy, Kevin C. "'Raw Individualists': American Soldiers on the Bataan Death March Reconsidered." *War and Society* 31 (2012): 42–63.

Neushul, Peter and James D. Neushul. "With the Marines at Tarawa." *Proceedings* 125 (1999): 74–80.

Pratt, Fletcher. "How the Censors Rigged the News." *Harper's*, February 1946, 100, 101–102.

Renn, Melissa. "'The Famous Iwo Flag-Raising': Iwo Jima Revisited." *History of Photography* 39 (2015): 253–62.

Richstad, Jim A. "The Press Under Martial Law: The Hawaiian Experience." *Journalism Monographs* 17 (1970): 1–41.

Sarantakes, Nicholas Evan. "Warriors of Word and Sword: The Battle of Okinawa, Media Coverage, and Truman's Reevaluation of Strategy in the Pacific." *Journal of American-East Asian Relations* 22 (2016): 343–67.

Sbrega, John J. "Anglo-American Relations and the Selection of Mountbatten as Supreme Commander, South East Asia." *Military Affairs* 46 (1982): 139–45.

Schaffer, Ronald. "American Military Ethics in World War II: The Bombing of German Civilians." *Journal of American History* 67 (1980): 318–34.

Sherrod, Robert. "At the Brink: An American Journalist's Memoir." *Pacific Defence Reporter* 15 (February 1988): 6–8.

Stevens, John D. "Black Correspondents of World War II Cover the Supply Routes." *Journal of Negro History* 57 (1972): 396–406.

Stoler, Mark A. "Selling Different Kinds of War: Franklin D. Roosevelt and American Public Opinion During World War II." In *Selling War in a Media Age: The Presidency and Public Opinion in the American Century*, edited by Kenneth Osgood and Andrew K. Frank, 67–92. Gainesville: University Press of Florida, 2010.

Sweeney, Michael S. and Patrick S. Washburn. "'Aint Justice Wonderful': The *Chicago Tribune*'s Battle of Midway Story and the Government's Attempt at an Espionage Act Indictment in 1942." *Journalism and Communication Monographs* 16 (2014): 7–97.

———. "It Ain't Over 'til It's Over: Ending (?) the Narrative about the *Chicago Tribune* and the Battle of Midway." *American Journalism* 35 (2018): 357–69.

Thorne, Christopher. "Racial Aspects of the Far Eastern War of 1941–1945." *Proceedings of the British Academy* 66 (1980): 329–77.

Van De Ven, Hans. "Stilwell in the Stocks: The Chinese Nationalists and the Allied Powers in the Second World War." *Asian Affairs* 34 (2003): 243–59.

Washburn, Patrick S. "The Black Press: Homefront Clout Hits a Peak in World War II." *American Journalism* 12 (2013): 359–66.

———. "The Office of Censorship's Attempt to Control Press Coverage of the Atomic Bomb During World War II." *Journalism Monographs* 120 (1990): 1–43.

Williams, Greer. "I Worked for McCormick." *The Nation*, October 10, 1942, 348.

Zikmund, Joseph. "James V. Forrestal." In *American Secretaries of the Navy*, edited by Paolo E. Coletta, 2:729–44. Annapolis, MD: Naval Institute Press, 1980.

Internet Sources

Anderson, Claudia. "Memo for the Files: Processing Note," November 18, 1991. Accessed May 2019. https://www.discoverlbj.org/item/lbja-b74-f02-sherrodrpt.

Associated Press. "Pearl Harbor Remembered 75 Years Later," December 5, 2016. Accessed January 2017. https://apimagesblog.com/blog/2016/12/5/pearl-harbor-day-remembered-75-years-later.

Chenoweth, Doral. "54 War Correspondents K.I.A. WWII." Accessed January 2017. http://www.54warcorrespondents-kia-30-ww2.com.

Evans, Raymond and Donegan, Jacqui. "The Battle of Brisbane," *Politics and Culture*, Issue 4, 2004. Accessed June 2017. http://www.politicsandculture.org/2010/08/10/the-battle-of-brisbane-by-raymond-evans-and-jacqui-donegan-2/.

Murray, Stuart S. "Admiral Murray's Oral History Re Surrender Table, September 2, 1945." Accessed May 2018. https://web.archive.org/web/20070821191456/http://www.ussmissouri.org/coll_MurryHistory.htm.

Nimitz "Gray Book": War Plans and Files of the Commander-in-Chief, Pacific Fleet. American Naval Records Society. Accessed May 2017. http://www.ibiblio.org/anrs/graybook.html.

"Robert C. Miller—UPI War Correspondent," UPI website, July 29, 2004. Accessed January 2019. https://www.upi.com/Robert-C-Miller-UPI-war-correspondent/43611091106138/.

Roosevelt, Franklin D. *Public Papers of the Presidents*, The American Presidency Project. Accessed January 2017. https://www.presidency.ucsb.edu/people/president/franklin-d-roosevelt.

Seligman, Morton T. "Action in Coral Sea," May 14, 1942. Accessed May 2019. https://www.ibiblio.org/hyperwar/USN/ships/logs/CV/CV2-Coral.html.

"Sherrod-LBJ Report: Australia," April 1942. Accessed May 2019. https://www.discoverlbj. org/item/lbja-b74-f02-sherrodrpt.

"Soldiers of the Press." YouTube video. Accessed March 2019. https://www.youtube.com/ watch?v=naBhwzIdiKc&feature=share.

Unpublished Material

Barbour, John and Wes Gallagher. "While the Smoke Is Still Rising." AP28, Writings About the AP, Series I: Unpublished Writings, box 1, AP Corporate Archives.

Hightower, John. "AP: The Chief Source of the News—War Reporting." AP28, Writings About the AP, Series I: Unpublished Writings, box 3, AP Corporate Archives.

———. "AP: The Chief Source of the News—World Services." AP28, Writings About the AP, Series I: Unpublished Writings, box 3, AP Corporate Archives.

Index

For the benefit of digital users, indexed terms that span two pages (e.g., 52–53) may, on occasion, appear on only one of those pages.